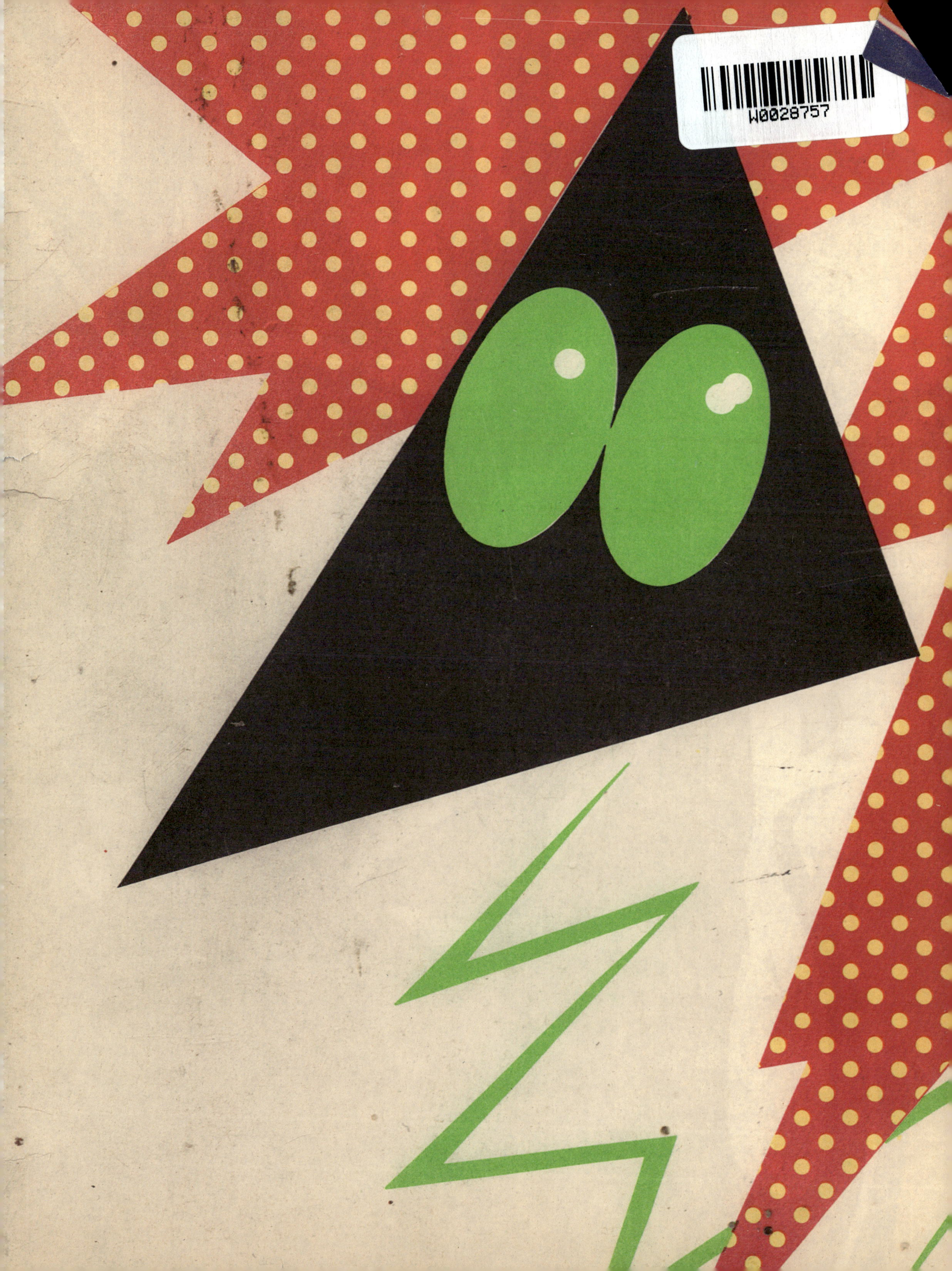

ENGLAND'S SCREAMING!

POP FRENZY!

RICHARD HEL[L]

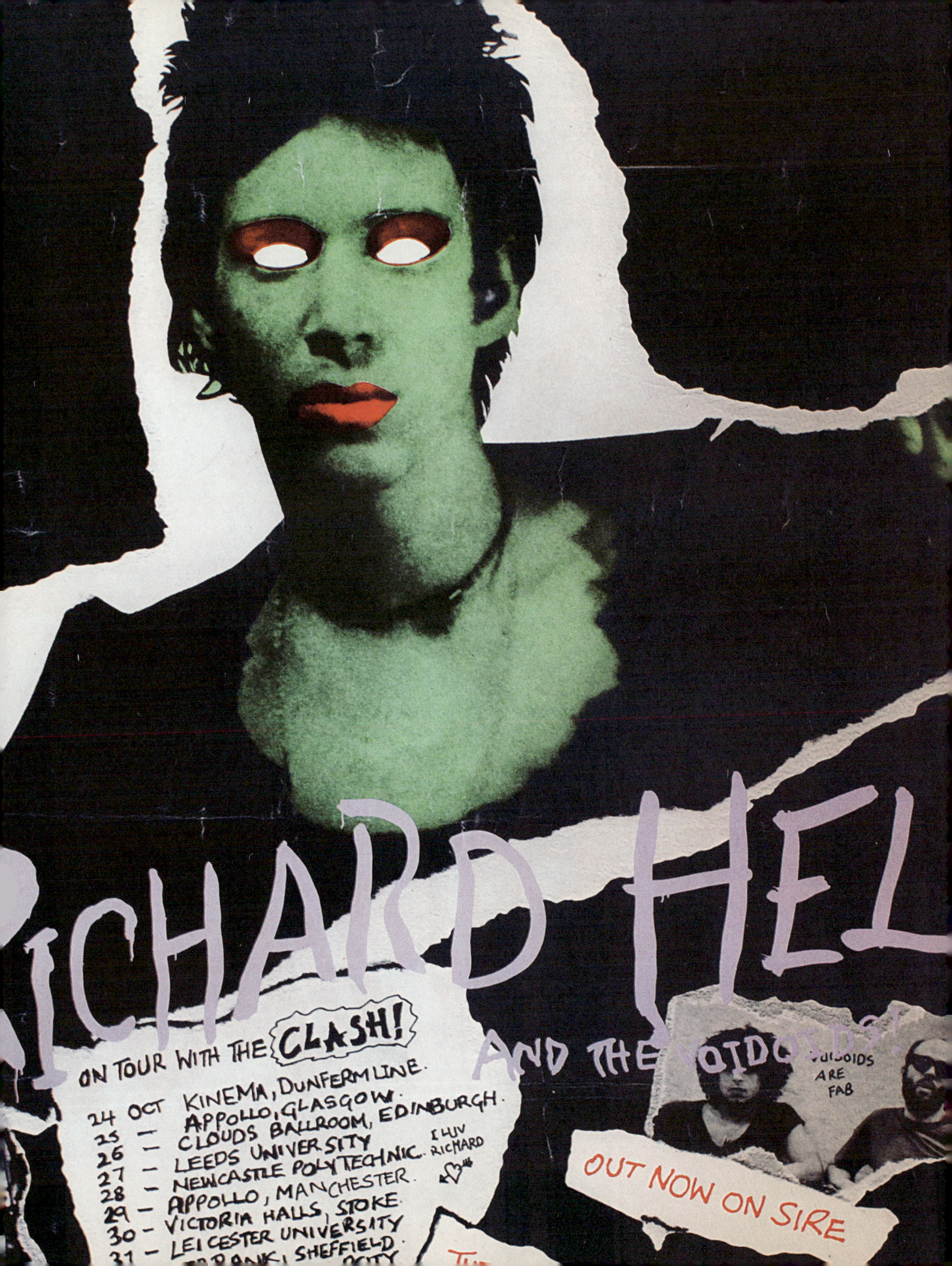

AND THE VOIDOIDS

ON TOUR WITH THE CLASH!

- 24 OCT — KINEMA, DUNFERMLINE.
- 25 — APPOLLO, GLASGOW.
- — CLOUDS BALLROOM, EDINBURGH.
- 26 — LEEDS UNIVERSITY
- 27 — NEWCASTLE POLYTECHNIC. I LUV RICHARD
- 28 — APPOLLO, MANCHESTER.
- 29 — VICTORIA HALLS, STOKE.
- 30 — LEICESTER UNIVERSITY
- 31 — TOP RANK, SHEFFIELD

VOIDOIDS ARE FAB

OUT NOW ON SIRE

he magic is you.Girl's voice well anyway
KNEW THEN WE HAD A WORKABLE BOMB
and 'WHY NOT' ends 'You,you,you.
-'The one they threw out of the aeroplane!
-'Yea,they threw his body out of the aeroplane,right,and then,so what did they do!
 'Thats where the Germans went and attacked
 them in Mogadishu or somewhere.'
 'Yea and this bloke right,he hadn't a bit
 of rope or anything so they murdered him!
-'Isn't that the three of them that were
 all....Do you mean the Baader-Meinhof
 people in Germany is this.There were
 three of them who were meant to have
 killed themselves,and then yesterday
 they discovered,one of the ones who was
 meant to have killed themselves had been
 shot through the back of the head'.
error ist ultimatum from Mogadishu.
odak representative 'At 18 frames a second.'
n injection of Methadine or similar drug.
ould not in fact object if Russia built
ver its limit of submarine launched ballist
c missiles.....And frankly I doubt it.
UICIDE bass line
PERATED ON THIS MORNING...He's said to
ave died from stomach cancer...DR.GROVES
LEASE.
RASS-'YOU find that it's not easy would you
       like to see me dead.'
uicide bass line
RASS-'You poke your knives into my brain
       You send me insane.'
ALKING HEADS-'PSYCHO KILLER qu'est ce que
             c'est.'
KNEW THEN WE HAD A WORKABLE BOMB
RASS-sections from four songs'Is it working
      do you really believe in-I am a subject
      of useless,futureless endless mindless

damned dead
damned dead
damned dead
damned dead
damned dead
damned dead
on tour

PL
MOU

49cc of trouble

HTON POLY   NUS 5

THE CLASH

Perfect Hits

ok! Soft-sprung

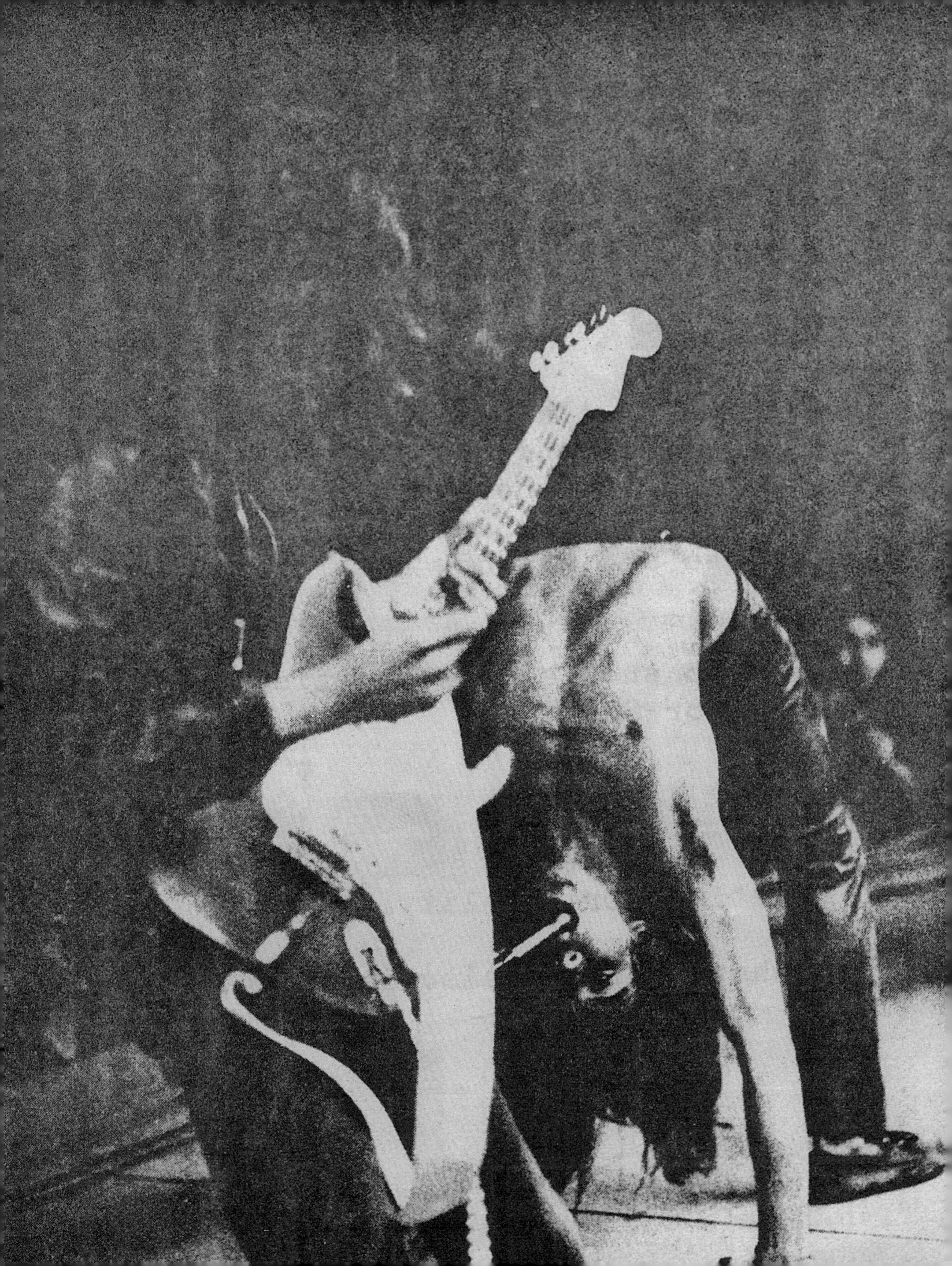

OH SO PRETTY
PUNK IN PRINT 1976–80

ESSAY BY RICK POYNOR

THE MOTT COLLECTION

ring:

...man spare
...letchford

...inn notes
...smith

...tes on
...e stones,
etc......
....

sep

A PUNK'S PROGRESS

TOBY MOTT
15

GRAPHIC ANARCHY IN THE UK

RICK POYNOR
19

1976–80

25

INDEX

508

...RY & THE BLOCKHEADS ON TOUR I A N D U...

NORMAN BLOCKHEAD

...RY & THE BLOCKHEADS ON TOUR I A N D U...

MICKY BLOCKHEAD

A PUNK'S PROGRESS

TOBY MOTT

**Album out now.
Play it at your sister.**

1977: a defining moment, not just for me but for Britain. It started for me in Pimlico, London, living just minutes from the Kings Road, Chelsea, the epicentre of punk. I had spiky soaped hair, charity-shop paint-splattered DIY punk clothes with Dr Martens boots (but no BOY or Seditionaries tartan bondage trousers or mohican hair – they were for poseurs, 'plastic' weekend punks). We didn't use the term 'punk' to describe ourselves: that was another label to reject. We were the 'new wave', preoccupied with music, drink, speed and sex. I had an identity away from dull pedestrian conformity – anti-establishment – and for us that meant anti-everything. Coming from a troubled, chaotic home life, here was a world for me: I was part of something else.

We called ourselves ASA, Anarchist Street Army ... a bunch of dispossessed glue- and solvent-sniffing kids from Pimlico Comprehensive. Our attempt at forming a band resulted in noise that even by punk standards was rubbish. Playing truant, half my days were spent at Recordsville on Wilton Road or Rough Trade and Jock McDonald's stall at Beaufort Market. Listening intently to new single releases, adding to my collection of picture-sleeve 45s at 90 pence each, with 'In the City', 'White Riot', 'Oh Bondage Up Yours' spinning endlessly on my Dansette record player. On those sleeves, record companies printed their addresses, where we would show up and receive badges, posters, anything given out for free: Step Forward, Stiff, Polydor ... most obliged. We marched to save the Roxy, running up the stairs of Capital Radio attempting to crash on air during the Nicky Horne show.

I scoured the gig pages of the *NME* (*New Musical Express*) and reviews in *Ripped & Torn*. Life revolved around seeing bands every night regardless of school – Menace, Chelsea, the Adverts, the Ants, 999, reggae bands like Steel Pulse or Aswad – my parents having essentially lost control of their teenage children. Bunking the tube to the Nashville in West Kensington, Electric Ballroom in Camden Town, Music Machine in Mornington Crescent, Greyhound in Croydon, various student-union gigs, often ending up at the all-night café on Whitehall, off Trafalgar Square – the city was ours.

This was vacant space, a free for all. Political leaflets from both the extreme left and right were circulated inside and outside gigs, vying for our attention: Socialist Workers Party, Anti-Nazi League, National Front, British Movement. I was taken with the utopian ideas of anarchy, often visiting the Freedom bookshop at Aldgate East to buy *Black Flag*.

We followed the Clash around the south of England on National Express coaches, manager Bernie Rhodes opening the back doors for us ticketless London punks. After the show, wet with cold sweat and stranded in a coastal town – it could've been Plymouth or Southampton – sleeping on a hard bench until the first coach back to London. Smashing fake bottles on each other as extras in *The Great Rock 'n' Roll Swindle*. I can be seen pogoing around as a jazz-funk band plays. But for me and the other London punk kids Adam and the Ants, often appearing with punk princess Jordan of Seditionaries fame, was the band to follow with a cult-like devotion. They combined dark eroticised violence with a fetishistic edge that drove us into a frenzied trance, sweating rhythmic dancing, lashing out at songs like 'Kick', or the hypnotic rising crescendo of 'Physical'. Adam had an intense stage presence, white face adorned with black eyeliner, topless in leather trousers with robotic dance moves. His falsetto voice sang 'Zerox' and 'Plastic Surgery', lyrics that voiced the preoccupations and repetition of daily life.

My bedroom was covered with posters and flyers, my shelves full of records and fanzines: all four walls were 'punked'. I collected the posters from the venues at the end of the gigs; we just took them down or 'liberated them'. As we left a show, flyers would be thrust into our hands telling us about the next gigs. If of merit, they too would go up on my bedroom walls, often on top of what was already there, thus creating a punk wallpaper engulfing me and fighting against the conformity of homework or even attending school.

My fanzine collection grew. Although they were not easy to come by, they were not considered 'rare' since they had no monetary value at the time. These were sold at London's many independent record stores – the Virgin Records megastore and Tower Records were yet to open. The big record-store chains at the time were Woolworths, HMV, Our Price and WHSmith's, and they didn't cater to us or stock the independent label 7" releases or the self-produced zines; this created a relationship with and loyalty to our local record store.

Before the modern boom, London had many vacant lots, undeveloped bomb sites from the war, where covered markets sprang up. One of these in the West End housed Soho Records, a punk hangout, like the first Rough Trade shop on Kensington Park Road. There were also second-hand record shops, which catered to the Teddy Boys of the 1970s' rock 'n' roll revival and stocked the recent picture-sleeve singles and coloured vinyl 45s – a novelty then. On the cramped counter space we could find flyers for shows and on the walls amongst the layered posters would be photocopied 'musician-wanted' band advertisements.

In addition to the records, clothes and haircut, punk found a prominent place on my school books in the way of stickers, stencils of the Crass logo and slogans, as well as badges on my school blazer. I read *Sniffin' Glue* in class and swapped it for other zines within my small circle of fellow delinquents. I visited record companies to cadge whatever was handed out – promo posters, PR photos and the like. When I left home these significant symbols of my past were stored away.

Twenty years later I moved back to London after living in America and began adding to my collection. I appreciated the visual immediacy of punk graphics, which never seemed tired or dated. The Mott Collection – a selection of which appears in the pages of this book – illustrates the energy, boredom, dynamism and diverse political social and class issues that were all part of punk. It includes iconic images created by now celebrated names, such as Peter Saville, Jamie Reid and Linder Sterling, but more important are the multitude of flyers and zines crudely cut and pasted by anonymous hands, whose raw, immediate aesthetic represents the urgency of this explosive DIY culture. The ideals of self-empowerment, motivation, action and common cause are evident throughout. To me, they are the spirit of punk.

THE CORTINAS

new single forward *independence*

GRAPHIC ANARCHY IN THE UK

RICK POYNOR

PRESS DARLINGS

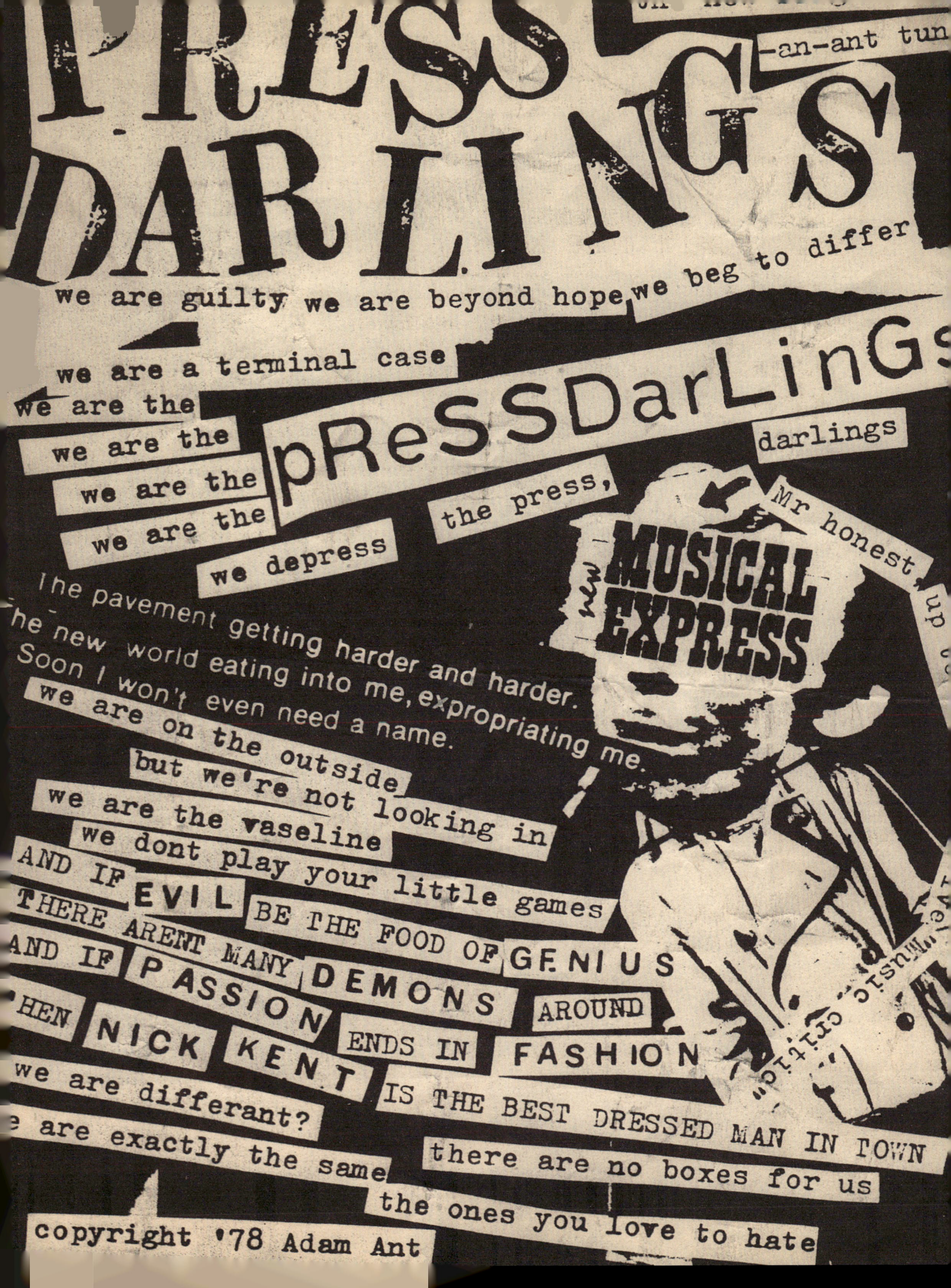

we are guilty we are beyond hope, we beg to differ

we are a terminal case

we are the
we are the pReSSDarLinGs
we are the   the press,   darlings
we are the
          we depress   Mr honest
                                  new MUSICAL EXPRESS

the pavement getting harder and harder.
the new world eating into me, expropriating me.
Soon I won't even need a name.
we are on the outside
but we're not looking in
we are the vaseline
we dont play your little games
AND IF EVIL BE THE FOOD OF GENIUS
THERE ARENT MANY DEMONS AROUND
AND IF PASSION ENDS IN FASHION
THEN NICK KENT IS THE BEST DRESSED MAN IN TOWN
we are differant?
we are exactly the same   there are no boxes for us
                the ones you love to hate

copyright '78 Adam Ant

GRAPHIC ANARCHY IN THE UK

THE SEX PISTOLS' ANARCHY IN THE UK ZINE #1
Jamie Reid
December 1976
45 x 31.7 cm, 17¾ x 12½ in

48 THRILLS #5
May 1977
29.8 x 20.9 cm, 11¾ x 8¼ in

Improbable as it might once have seemed, forty years after it snarled into public consciousness via the scandalised media, punk has become part of Britain's cultural heritage. It is as inseparable from our national identity as the long-serving Queen it once dared to skewer with a safety pin. That anti-establishment gesture looks almost lovably eccentric now, like a warped kind of affection.
In the story commonly told today, punk gave the UK a vigorous and necessary shaking. Its blast of DIY anarchy flushed out the pipes to allow a whoosh of creativity that spread from music (though punk was never only about the music) into the arts, fashion and media worlds of the 1980s and beyond. As I write, a year-long programme of events titled 'Punk London' – supported by the Mayor's office – is celebrating the supposedly catalytic influence of punk 'in all its ragged glory'. A house in Denmark Street where the Sex Pistols once lived has been awarded listed-building status on the advice of Historic England. Vivienne Westwood and Malcolm McLaren's son, Joe Corré, was in the news for threatening to burn his collection of punk memorabilia in protest against these signs that a movement that despised bloated convention had been stripped of its offensive barbs and repackaged as a cosy landmark moment in national pop culture.

Toby Mott's collection captures the life cycle of early British punk from its turbulent inception to its swift assimilation. The chronological sequencing of the pieces gives the narrative a welcome clarity. Any private collection is personal and contingent, especially when it comes to objects collected at the time through being a participant in some events but not others. No stockpile of ephemera could claim to be definitive, though it might be broadly representative. This is a record of British printed material, much of it from London, where Mott lived. American musicians such as Iggy Pop, Patti Smith, the Ramones, Suicide and Richard Hell feature when they visit the UK, but the graphic interpretations of these acts are done in local styles. Mott concentrates mainly on disposable items – concert and promotional posters, flyers, fanzines, music papers and pop magazines – rather than more lasting artefacts, such as record sleeves. Some sleeve graphics do resurface on the posters, although often in a modified form. He also salted away some pungent contextual evidence: Silver Jubilee souvenirs, National Front and Socialist Workers Party stickers, Anti-Nazi League and Rock Against Racism posters.

How should we assess this riotous assembly of pieces? Their documentary value as cultural and sociological evidence is obvious enough. For those who weren't there at the time, these relics give a vivid impression of punk's abrasive and uncompromising style. For those who were, they are charged with fond memories. Yet they are also graphic artefacts now deemed worthy of display in exhibitions and published collections like this one. Punk's telltale devices – rough photocopied images, hand-drawn letters, ransom-note lettering, crudely cut and torn edges – have become a category in the history of graphic style, where they are seen to represent a deliberate flouting of the rules of professional practice. For the punks who put together fanzines and flyers, this categorisation may be highly questionable. Some of these raucous 'sites of resistance' (as academics have dubbed them) may have looked as they did, not in order to make any particular point, but because that was all that could be achieved using limited reprographic resources. Their makers cared about the subject matter – the bands and the music – rather than the relatively arcane question of the meaning of graphic style.

Deciding what yardsticks to apply to this mass of print is complicated by the varying status of the items in the collection. Only a few designers are known by name, notably Jamie Reid, Barney Bubbles and Malcolm Garrett, all regarded as key figures. Another category is formed by pieces created for record companies by non-punk designers with professional experience of all kinds of music packaging. A poster based on Eckford and Stimpson's 'V sign' cover for *Pure Mania* by the Vibrators even has a tidied-up take on ransom-note lettering. Other industry designers are often uncredited.

WHITE STUFF #1
Sandy Robertson
February 1977
29.8 x 20.9 cm, 11¾ x 8¼ in

RIPPED & TORN #14
Tony Drayton
October 1978
29.8 x 20.9 cm, 11¾ x 8¼ in

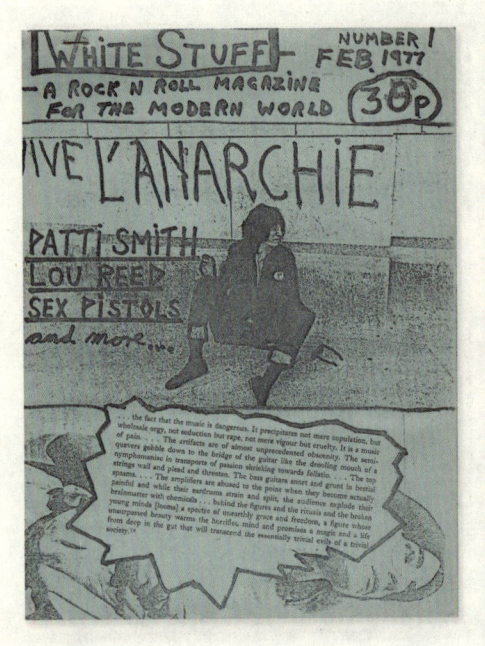

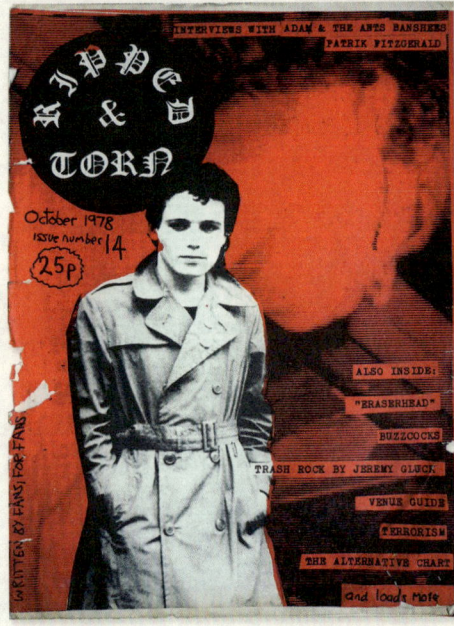

With audience-produced fanzines, the editor tended also to be the layout person – Sandy Robertson (*White Stuff*) and Adrian Thrills (*48 Thrills*) soon became music journalists – while flyers for gigs, now valuable mementoes, are often by unknown hands. A fourth category consists of pieces produced in the course of punk's commercialisation, which didn't take long, and these, too, are frequently unsigned.

In Mott's punk hoard, Jamie Reid stands out as a special case. Reid was the ultimate punk auteur and by far the most inventive British designer/artist working in the punk idiom. Although Bubbles is now regarded as one of the UK's most conceptually imaginative graphic designers – see the Philishave face masks he gives the Blockheads – he is more 'new wave' in manner than strictly punk, and the same is true of Garrett. Reid's thematically coherent body of work was carried out for the most notorious and publicly visible British punk band, the Sex Pistols, and by association, as well as by its tremendous rhetorical clout, it immediately defined the essence of punk's graphic style, as it is commonly understood. The roots of this graphic method lie in the countercultural publications and graphics of the 1960s and early 1970s, and for the Sex Pistols, Reid was able to draw on and refine techniques he had used as the designer of *Suburban Press*, a Situationist-like publication. His *Never Mind the Bans* poster, a collage of cancellation letters, is not only an incisively satirical idea but also a deftly crafted essay in graphic chaos. The cover of the *Anarchy in the UK* fanzine, with Reid's urgent red lettering and a photo of London punk Soo Catwoman by Ray Stevenson, remains one of the quintessential images of British punk.

One of the revelations of this collection is the unswerving focus on the bands. No matter how wild and thrashy the lettering and graphics may be, the pieces produced by fans mainly deliver pictures of the performers rather than other kinds of imagery. Punk was a highly sociable scene and it attracted people who loved to dress up and show off. They identified with the groups, and in fanzines like *Sniffin' Glue* and *Ripped & Torn* they celebrated them as makers of their own grassroots culture. This is an illuminating departure from the usual picture of punk as an essentially political act of rebellion and the scene's fixation on punk's stars hasn't been so obvious in previous surveys. Within only a few years, some post-punk groups would shun the spotlight and insist that the music was the essential thing, but the 1970s punks embraced the performer as an anti-glamorous star figure just as surely as earlier audiences embraced conventional versions of the pop star. The means of adulation were much the same. By 1977, *Punk* magazine was publishing a double-sided colour poster featuring all the favourite bands, the Clash were posing moodily for a pin-up in *Oh Boy!* magazine and punk was ripe for 'punxploitation' in a picture publication titled *Punk Rock Rules OK?*

Where visual punk becomes more challenging is when it starts to play dialectically with other kinds of imagery than singers and guitarists. An eye-watering example from 1978 is the flyer Adam Ant designed for a gig at the 100 Club, using drawings from a medical textbook demonstrating the insertion of a catheter to 'illustrate' a series of dance moves described in numbered captions. This gleefully sinister exercise in black humour foreshadows the extreme and abject imagery that would preoccupy participants in the industrial music scene that branched from punk. Even abrasive texture can work as a kind of imagery. On the cover of the second issue of *48 Thrills*, built around a photo of the Clash, Joe Strummer's face has been whited out and the photocopied layers of paper fuse in a spatial blur under a banner of scratchy lettering. It's both graphically exciting and slightly disturbing in a way that is hard to pin down. In the early 1980s, graphic design would go seriously murky and textural as designers at labels such as 4AD sought a new aesthetic for visualising the dark, immersive grain of post-punk music. Space itself is an integral component of the graphic image and there are also signs of design trends to come in the unusually emptied-out covers

THE SECRET PUBLIC (ORG 2)
1978
41.9 x 59 cm, 16½ x 23¼ in

of *The New Wave Magazine*. On issue eight, in a kind of exploded collage, the four musicians occupy separate zones of the layout, connected only by the visual tension between them. In new wave design, punk's boiling energy would be distilled into subtler kinds of graphic stimulant and we can see this emerging already.

From Dada and Surrealism to Pop Art and the 1960s' counterculture, collage and photomontage were the most potent tools for cutting up reality and constructing revelatory alternatives. *Photomontage* by Dawn Ades, art historian and expert on Surrealism, was published as a paperback in 1976, offering punk agitators a crash course in the history and practice of radical image making. Linder Sterling, already cutting up pictures when the book appeared, has spoken about the confidence it gave her to pursue this technique of visual engineering. An early outcome was the naked woman with mouths for nipples and an iron for a head used in 1977 in Malcolm Garrett's design for Buzzcocks' 'Orgasm Addict' single and poster, one of punk's most memorable images.

The following year Sterling and the music journalist Jon Savage joined forces on *The Secret Public*, a self-published magazine, both contributing several pages of photomontages. Sterling's images show women in the home, their bare bodies fractured by domestic objects that represent their socially assigned gender role and acquiescence. Savage's targets include the laddish 'masculine principle', which by the late 1970s had returned to punk with a vengeance, narrowing the freedom of sexual identity the scene initially offered. 'It was a deliberately hermetic document that forced you to enter on its own terms,' wrote Savage in 2006. 'There were few concessions to any ideas of marketing and accessibility.' This is the authentic spirit of punk, angry, questioning and critical of the milieu it comes from. *The Secret Public* is one of the highlights of an exceptional collection.

It has become routine to look back wistfully at punk from our increasingly monitored and corporate world and see it as a halcyon interlude when the audience took charge of its own culture. The familiarity of the sentiment doesn't make it any less pressing. Punk was a moment of social and cultural insubordination when the established ways of forming a band, writing a song, dressing in the street, or laying out a page or a flyer were thrown aside. The crucial thing was to participate, to make your own scene and not meekly accept what the market decided you should consume. Now that the X-Factorised music business is more controlling and deterministic than ever, punk's core message is even more urgent. An authentic living culture should have DIY entwined in its DNA. Toby Mott's collection is raw, messy and seething with life. It's both an arresting document of what happened and an incitement to seize the moment, reject the obvious choices, find some like-minded collaborators and construct something challenging and new.

TOM ROBINSON BAND

1976–80

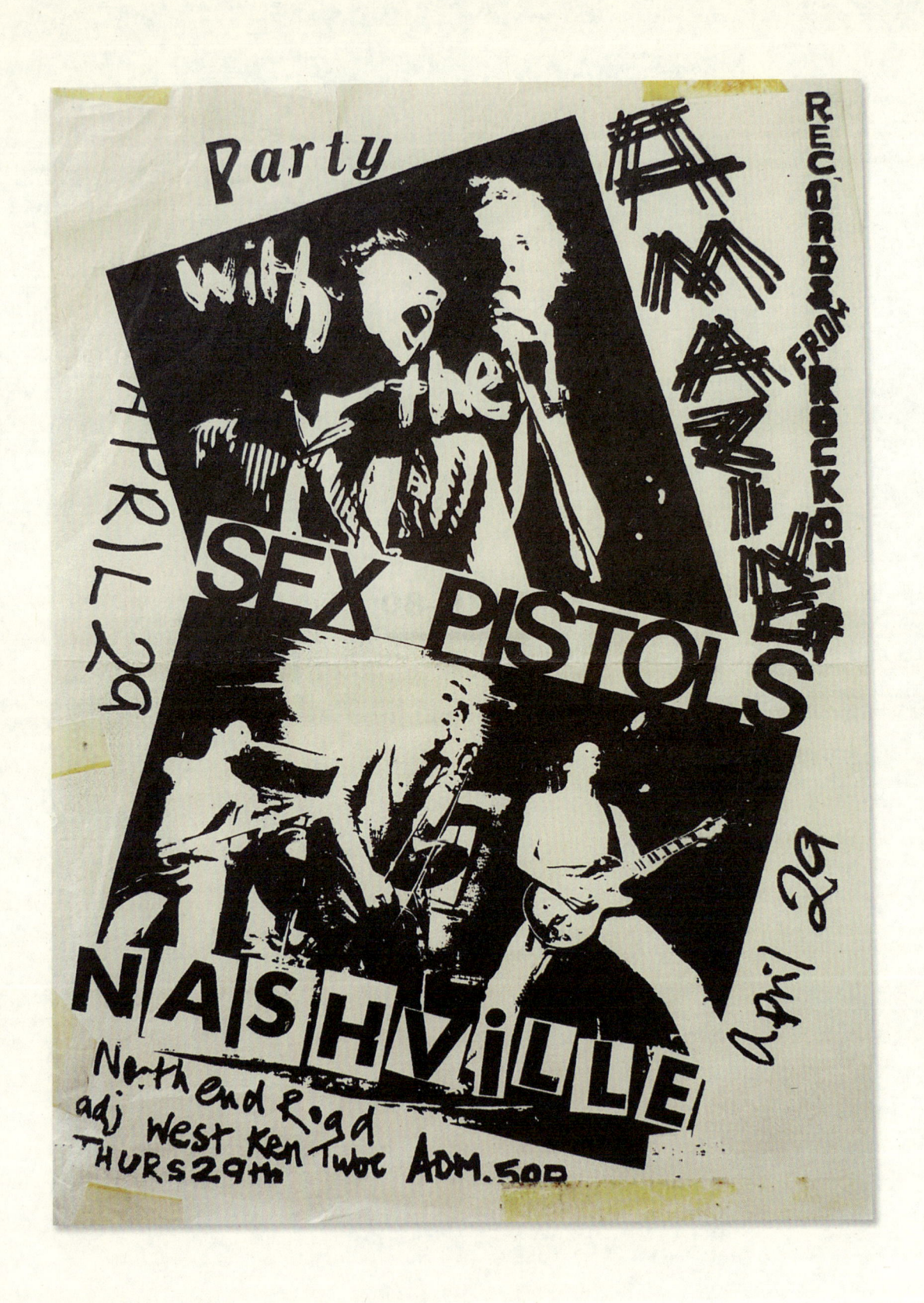

**FLYER FOR THE SEX PISTOLS
AT THE NASHVILLE, LONDON**
Nils Stevenson, Helen Wellington-Lloyd
29 April 1976
29.2 x 20.9 cm, 11½ x 8¼ in

The Sex Pistols' road manager, Nils Stevenson, designed much of the band's promotional material with Helen Wellington-Lloyd. A prominent, well-known fixture at the Sex Pistols' shows, Wellington-Lloyd was a longtime friend of the band's manager, Malcolm McLaren.

Wellington-Lloyd is also rumored to have created the first Sex Pistols 'blackmail letter' logo.

FLYER FOR THE SEX PISTOLS AT THE SCREEN ON ISLINGTON GREEN
17 May 1976
29.8 × 21.5 cm, 11¾ × 8½ in

Promoting the Screen on Islington Green at midnight. The flyer includes quotes about the band and Geoff Hutt's *New Musical Express* (*NME*) review of the Pistols' gig at the Nashville, in which he suggests that 'the Pistols are too good for anyone to really hate them'. The advertised concert was rescheduled for 29 August 1976, when the Sex Pistols were joined by the Clash and Buzzcocks.

**FLYER FOR THE SEX PISTOLS
AT THE 100 CLUB, LONDON**
11, 18 & 25 May 1976
29.2 x 20.3 cm, 11½ x 8 in

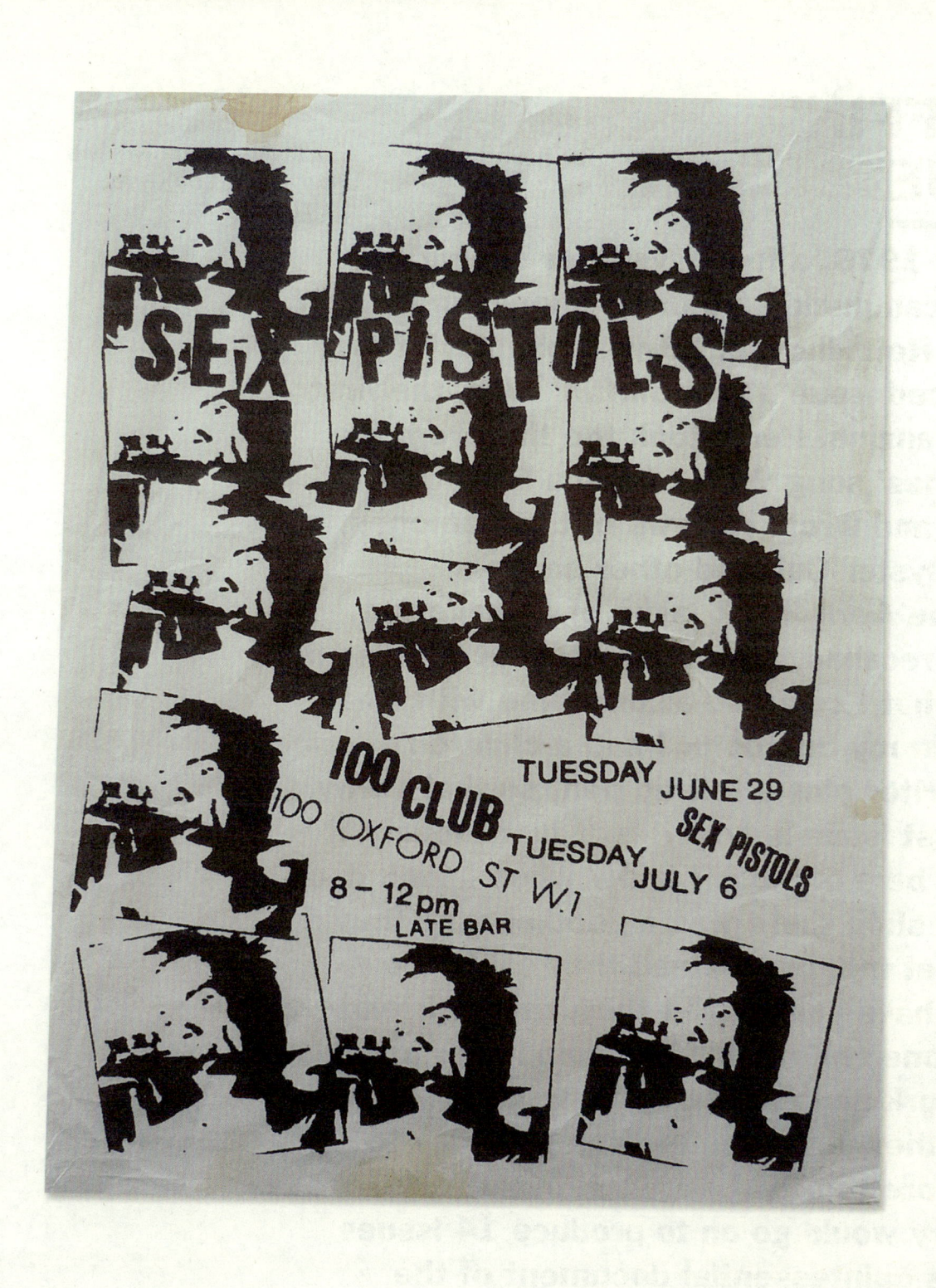

**FLYER FOR THE SEX PISTOLS
AT THE 100 CLUB, LONDON**
Nils Stevenson, Helen Wellington-Lloyd
29 June 1976
28.5 x 20.9 cm, 11¼ x 8¼ in

SNIFFIN' GLUE

In July 1976, a few days after seeing American punk band the Ramones in London at the Roundhouse, 19-year-old Mark Perry produced issue #1 of *Sniffin' Glue*, the first punk fanzine. Perry took the title from the Ramones' song 'Now I Wanna Sniff Some Glue', and wrote reviews of the Ramones, Blue Öyster Cult and other bands.

In the April 2002 issue of *Q* magazine, Perry recalled, 'The whole of that first issue was what I could do at that time with what I had in my bedroom. I had a children's typewriter plus a felt-tip pen, so that's why the first issue is how it is. I just thought it would be a one-off. I knew when I took it to the shop there was a good chance they'd laugh at me, but instead they said, "How many have you got?" I think my girlfriend had done twenty on the photocopier at her work and they bought the lot off me. Then they advanced me some money to get more printed.'

Perry would go on to produce 14 issues of this quintessential document of the punk movement.

SNIFFIN' GLUE...
+ OTHER ROCK'N'ROLL HABITS FOR PUNKS! NO.1 OF MANY, WE HOPE!

THIS THING IS NOT MEANT TO BE READ...IT'S FOR SOAKING IN GLUE AND SNIFFIN'.

IN THE FIRST ISSUE:

THE RAMONES
ALBUM & CONCERT REVIEWS!

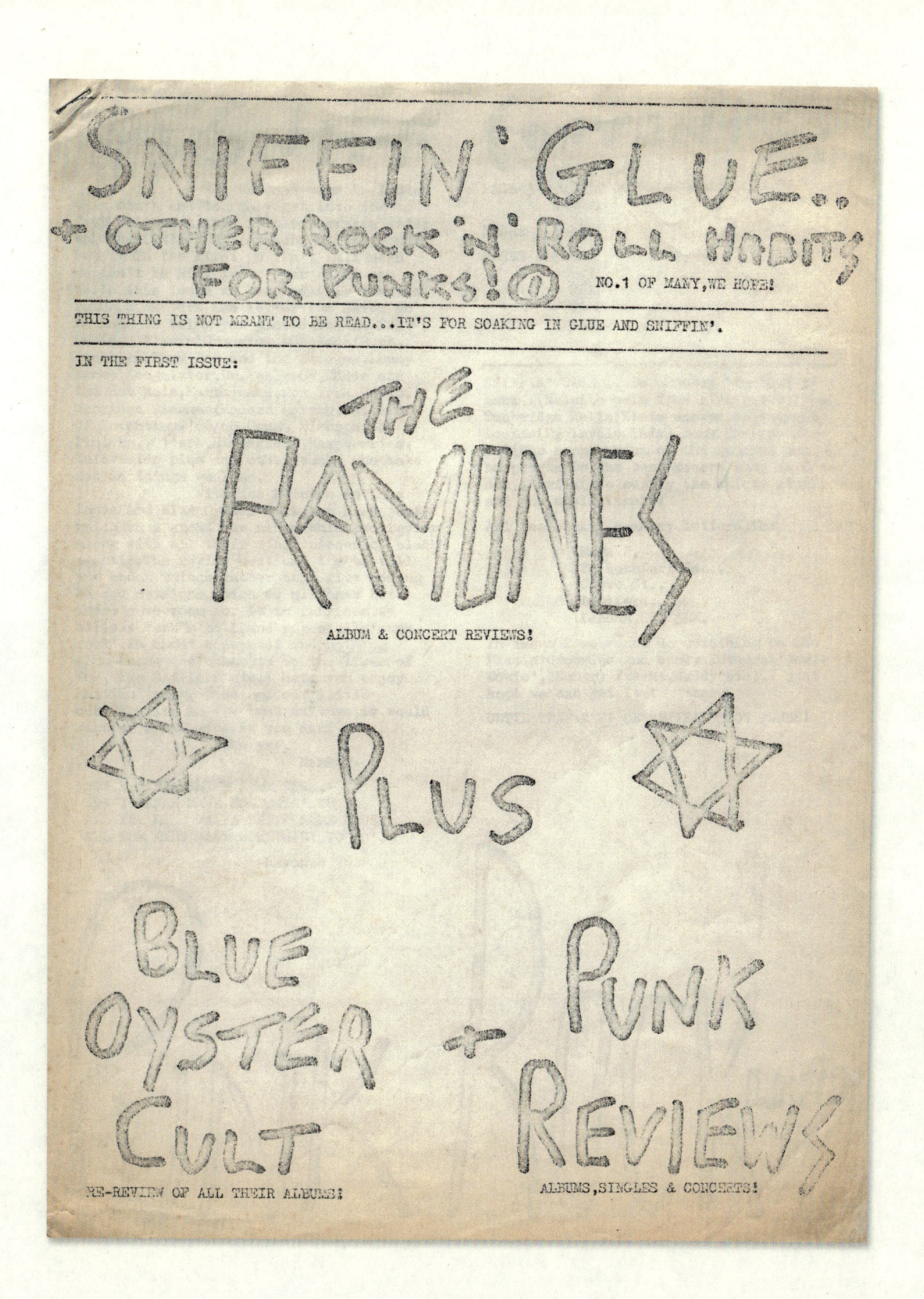

☆ **PLUS** ☆

BLUE OYSTER CULT + **PUNK REVIEWS**
RE-REVIEW OF ALL THEIR ALBUMS! ALBUMS, SINGLES & CONCERTS!

SNIFFIN' GLUE #1
Mark Perry
July 1976
29.8 x 20.9 cm, 11¾ x 8¼ in

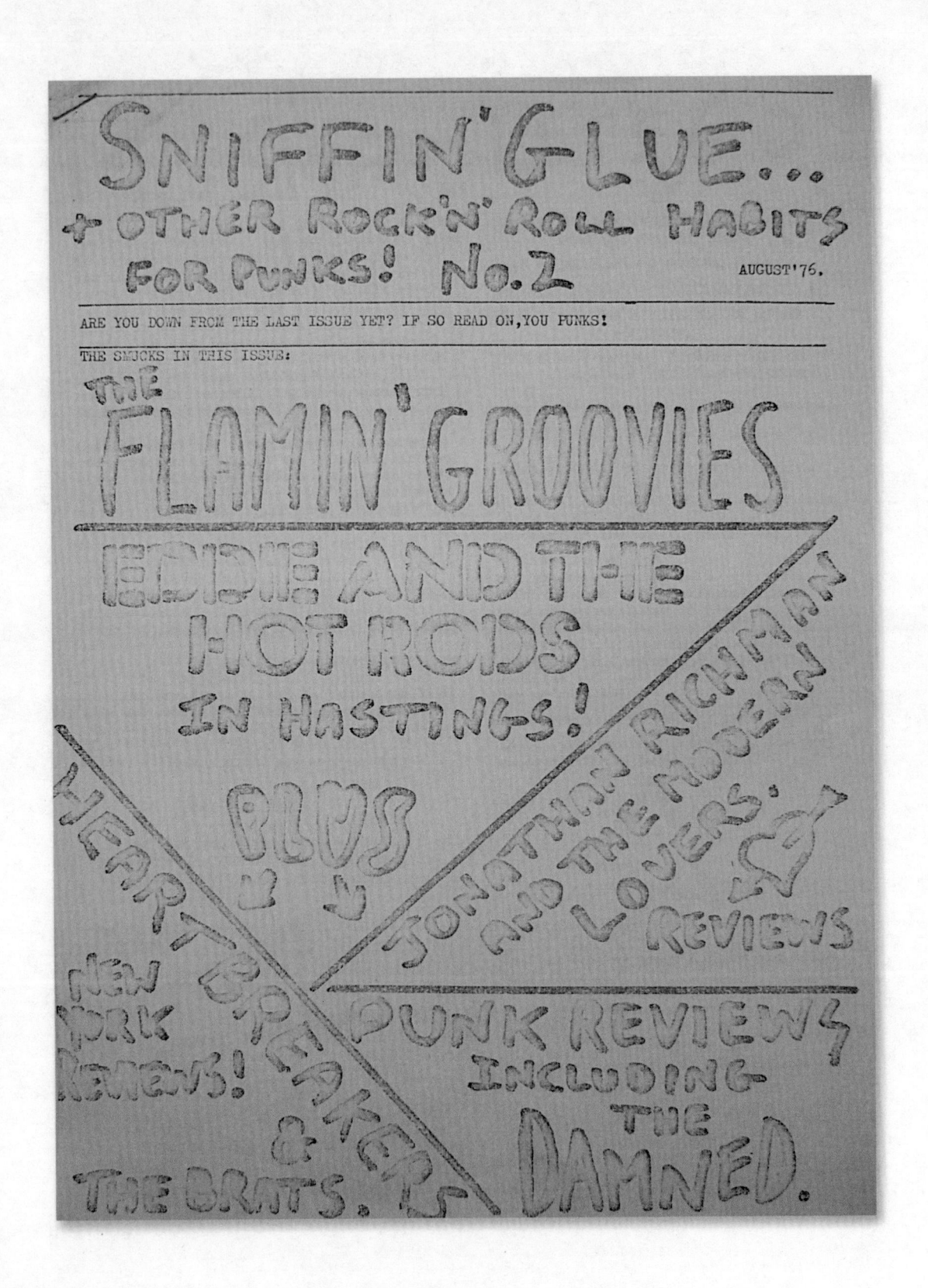

SNIFFIN' GLUE #2
Mark Perry
August 1976
29.8 x 20.9 cm, 11¾ x 8¼ in

**FLYER FOR THE SEX PISTOLS
AT THE 100 CLUB, LONDON**
Jamie Reid
31 August 1976
23.5 x 17.7 cm, 9¼ x 7 in

This flyer is Jamie Reid's first use of the Sex Pistols' logo in ransom-style lettering, with a similar typography for the song titles.

PiSToLs in PRiSON

Chelmsford maximum security prison isn't no council tenancy, but it is in the suburbs, right next to some office buildings and a service station on the corner (quick getaway). The prisoners are in for ~~serving~~ three years *and up*. ~~------~~ To while away the hours they can join inter-prison weightlifting, join the film society for 11p a week (mostly recent releases), rent a colour tv for 3p a week, and see rock bands once a month.

Any band that cares to can play, ~~------~~ except for Hawkwind. Everyone was on acid—

"Uh, you mean Hawkwind?"

No, I mean the prisoners. Anyway, Hawkwind (started yelling 'Kill! Kill!' *i.e., they won't be asked back* and there was a minor riot. So no encores for them. Tonight it's the Pistols. Most of the lads will be digging them behind a variety of chemicals. *the group came in the van*

It was Paul's last day at the brewery, so he came down separately, ~~------~~ *walking through* the front door, talk to the screw sitting behind an inch thick sheet of glass, walk through a noisy, dull grey sliding door into a small, dull grey room with a low ceiling, table with chair at each end, the door slides shut, instant claustrophobia, the metal grey door in front noisily slides open, walk into a puke green room and sit under the bulletin board—'Charlie Smith is having a leaving party (at his request) after 28 years of service. We are presenting him with a silver cup'—to wait for a screw to take you into the prison's innards. Upstairs in the mess, the band wait for Paul, sitting at a table devouring sandwiches and tea. John has dressed for the occasion: NO FUTURE FUTURE FUTURE down the front of his shirt, ANARCHY dripping across the back. Through the barred windows, across the courtyard, a cell block, the rows of windows criss-crossed with three sets of bars, turns golden in the afternoon sun. At a table at the other end of the room a group of screws have afternoon tea, all in blue uniforms with large, thick silver chains hanging from their belt, looping to their knee and ending in a fistful of keys. It really needs Godard, camera slowly tracking from one end of the room to the other, from Pistols to Police, to get the full effect.

Screw (incredulous): 'Is that the pop group?'

Other Screw (superior sneer): 'Well. They're supposed to be.'

The small theatre echoes a lot. There is a backdrop behind the equipment, a cityscape with lots of billboards, in between the Coke and Cinzano ads the simple messages POT and LSD. The band warm up with a diamond hard 'Wham Bam Thank You Maam', then a few of their own. When the sound check finishes everyone except sound wizards Dave and Kim have to go backstage, and the audience are let in.

They run. Long hair, short hair, young, middle aged, their clothes a jumble of jackets, sweaters, slippers, boots. Six blacks stroll in; five of them walk out after ten minutes. Some guys have sewn flares into their levis.

"God, there won't be any girls in the audience," says Steve.

"That's alright," jeers Nils, "You'll still be able to play."

They walk on one by one. Steve gets a few wolf whistles, John gets a lot. He welcomes them with a greeting from the Queen (cheers and whistles) and a message from the recently released Ron, who would have loved to come, but he's been banned. Dead silence.

John enunciates 'Anarchy' very clearly. There is wild applause. 'I Wanna Be Me' gets a little less approval, the third tune a little less, and so on. And they are playing great. In the short breaks between songs John taunts them. You're like a bunch of fucking statues! I bet you've all got a good case of piles! Move!

"We're not allowed to."

I don't care—tear the fucking place apart!

The audience loves it, yelling back with no hesitation. They even warm to *AND WHERE WAS MALCOLM?*

FLYER FOR THE SEX PISTOLS AT CHELMSFORD PRISON
19 September 1976
29.8 × 20.9 cm, 11¾ × 8¼ in

This double-sided flyer titled 'Pistols in Prison' reports on the Sex Pistols' gig on the 17 September in high-security Chelmsford Prison.

some of the songs; 'Sub Mission', 'No Fun', 'Stepping Stone', 'Problems', 'Liar', all get heavy cheers and whistles. Steve is exploring clean country, lots of clear, precise notes. Middles and ends have been altered, tidied up. John is enunciating what he considers the important lyrics very clealry. Paul and Glen hammer it all home mercilessly. A beat for the feet.

"We try to keep it down to five chords a song," Steve confesses afterwards.

In 'New York' he breaks two strings. While new ones are strung the audience want John to tell a joke. "No, you tell me one."

"Okay," replies the Captain. He sits in the Captain's Seat, front row centre. He is big, tanned, middle-aged. He always sits in the Captain's Seat. "There was this guy, see, and he didn't have a dick. So when he got home at night he gave his wife a good bollocking!" Laughs.

"Fuckin' 'ell! That's twenty years old!" John's choice of a first word cracks the place apart.

As the intro to 'Seventeen' winds up Paul leans back, both arms in the air. Only instead of crashing down into his skins he just keeps on going over backwards, stool and all. "Pissed!" yells John, pointing an accusing finger at the culprit lying on the floor helpless with laughter. "Sorry," he waves when he finally regains his seat.

The prison hippie—long hair, flares, beads, bare feet, ultra glazed eyes—throws his denim coat on stage. John stands on it, then ignores it. The owner asks for it back. With great effort John lands it three feet short. With a nervous look around the hippie gets up and grabs his jacket. During the last-song reprise of 'Anarchy' he leaps to his feet and starts dancing. Nobody stops him. Afterwards, two of the cons say that the first couple of times he did that he got beaten on. The pipes just bent on his head.

As they walk off there's dead silence. For five minutes it's quiet, then a sudden eruption of applause and yells for more. After the encore there is another eruption. The longer the band play, the longer they're out of their cells. "Go on," says a screw. "Give them another one." John refuses. "I'm selfish," he smiles. It is 7.45.

The cons leave, some wringing their ears. Three stack chairs while the band pack equipment. "Jesus," says one, surveying the stage. "We were going to try and scive some clothes off you lot, but you're all dressed in rags!" They help load the van; three guards stand and watch, the Alsatian at their feet periodically howling. One guy sits in the front of the van, talking to the band. A joke is made about hiding in the van on the way out.

"No thanks. I'm out in a month."

"Not if we can help it," a young guard says with a jokey smile.

The van crosses the courtyard to the exit gate. It opens noisily, the van rolls in, the gate closes behind it, then after a minute the front one rolls back. It's a few seconds before the shock sinks in: traffic, people walking about, lights, noise.

"That was really strange," says John, "Not having any girls in the audience."

Terry
19/9/76

SNIFFIN' GLUE #3
Mark Perry
September 1976
29.8 × 20.9 cm, 11¾ × 8¼ in

Features articles on the Damned, the Sex Pistols and Iggy Pop, amongst others.

POSTER FOR THE SEX PISTOLS, THE CLASH AND
SIOUXSIE AND THE BANSHEES AT THE 100 CLUB
20 September 1976
42.5 x 29.8 cm, 16¾ x 11¾ in

SNIFFIN' GLUE #3½
Mark Perry
28 September 1976
29.8 x 20.9 cm, 11¾ x 8¼ in

Stiff from... Stiff Records
"The World's Most Flexible Record Label"
32 Alexander Street, London W2

OCT 76

STIFF NEWSHEET

Here are the releases that are currently available.
Order now to ensure delay and avoid disappointment.

BUY 1   NICK LOWE   "HEART OF THE CITY"/"SO IT GOES" 70p
Single of the week in M.M. and Sounds.

BUY 2   PINK FAIRIES "BETWEEN THE LINES"/"SPOILING FOR A FIGHT" Picture sleeve. 70p

BUY 3   ROOGALATOR   "ALL ABOARD"/"CINCINATTI FATBACK"
$33\frac{1}{3}$ maxi single. Picture sleeve. £1

BUY 4   TYLA GANG   "STYRAFOAM"/"TEXAS CHAINSAW MASSACRE BOOGIE" Special Double B side release. 70p

BUY 5   LEW LEWIS   "BOOGIE ON THE STREET"/"CARAVAN MAN"
Ex Hot Rods, Harp player with Oil City Band.
MM. single of the week. Pic. sleeve. 70p

BUY 6   THE DAMNED   "NEW ROSE"/"HELP" Pic. sleeve.
"The first real punk single" Sniffin' Glue
Dynamite. 70p

BUY 7   RICHARD HELL "BLANK GENERATION"/"YOU GOTTA LOSE"/
"IN ANOTHER WORLD" E.P. by "Punk Superstar" (Erk!)
of New York. Pressing limited to 5,000 copies.
Order now. £1.50

More to follow: Free DAMNED poster with any DAMNED order!
Free post and packing in U.K. only: Overseas take care to
send enough. Too much welcome.

TODAY'S SOUND TODAY

STIFF RECORDS NEWS SHEET
October 1976
32.3 x 20.3 cm, 12¾ x 8 in

Describes the label's latest releases, including Nick Lowe, Pink Fairies, Roogalator, Tyla Gang, Lew Lewis, the Damned and Richard Hell.

POSTER FOR THE RUNAWAYS AND SUBURBAN STUDS AT THE ROUNDHOUSE, LONDON
1 October 1976
71.7 x 97.7 cm, 28¼ x 38½ in

Silkscreened concert poster for the American rock band the Runaways, fronted by Joan Jett, with guests Suburban Studs of Birmingham. This concert was documented by Andy Blade in his book *The Secret Life of a Teenage Punk Rocker*.

NEW MUSICAL EXPRESS
2 October 1976
42.5 × 30.4 cm, 16¾ × 12 in

Includes articles on the Sex Pistols, Dr Feelgood and the Runaways. *NME* has been in circulation in the UK since 1952.

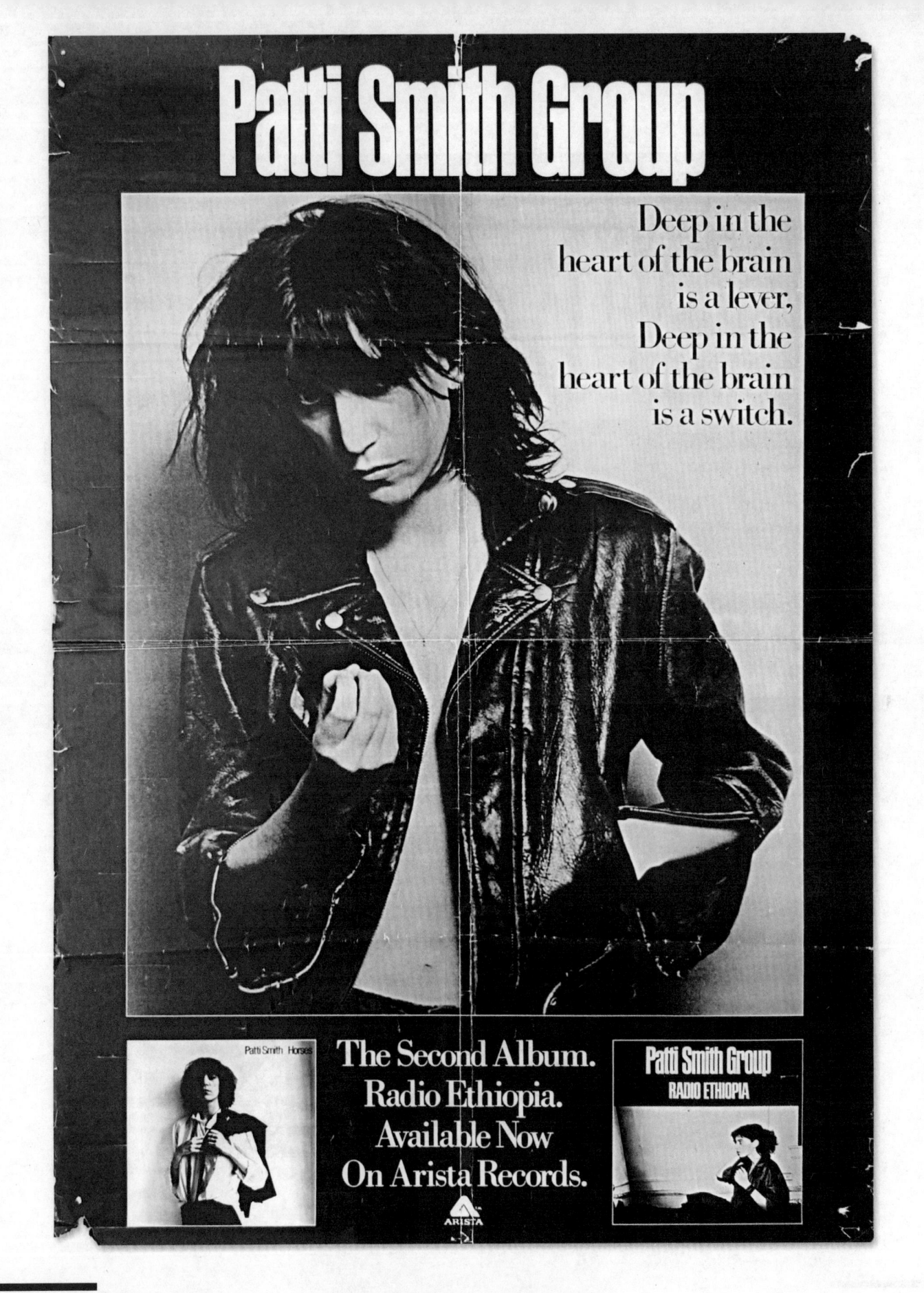

POSTER FOR PATTI SMITH'S ALBUM RADIO ETHIOPIA
October 1976
91.4 x 60.9 cm, 36 x 24 in

Patti Smith's second album, *Radio Ethiopia*, was issued by Arista Records. Lynn Goldsmith took the black-and-white photo of a nonchalant Smith in a black leather jacket.

SNIFFIN' GLUE #4
Mark Perry
October 1976
29.8 x 20.9 cm, 11¾ x 8¼ in

Mark Perry had a knack for predicting the influential acts of the era, a talent showcased in this 'New Wave' issue, featuring the Clash, who had formed in July and were gaining notoriety after appearing in August at the Screen on the Green in a triple bill with Buzzcocks and the Sex Pistols. This zine also features Patti Smith Group's new LP *Radio Ethiopia*.

POSTER FOR THE DAMNED'S SINGLE 'NEW ROSE'
October 1976
60.3 × 45 cm, 23¾ × 17¾ in

The Damned's song 'New Rose' was the UK's first punk rock single, and came in a black-and-white picture sleeve that set the tone for the subculture's monochromatic style. Posters proclaimed the song to be 'Young, hot, loud and stiff' (a reference, at least in part, to label Stiff Records) and 'available from even the dumbest dealer!' Signed on the back by guitarist and songwriter Brian James.

FLYER FOR AMOS POE'S THE BLANK GENERATION AT THE OTHER CINEMA
14–27 October 1976
29.8 × 20.9 cm, 11¾ × 8¼ in

Underground director Amos Poe collaborated with songwriter Ivan Král, who played guitar with the Patti Smith Group, to create a documentary about the genesis of the New York punk scene. *The Blank Generation* features Poe's cutting-edge visual style with pre-recorded performances of punk and new wave acts like Blondie, Richard Hell, Johnny Thunders & the Heartbreakers, the Ramones, the Patti Smith Group and Talking Heads.

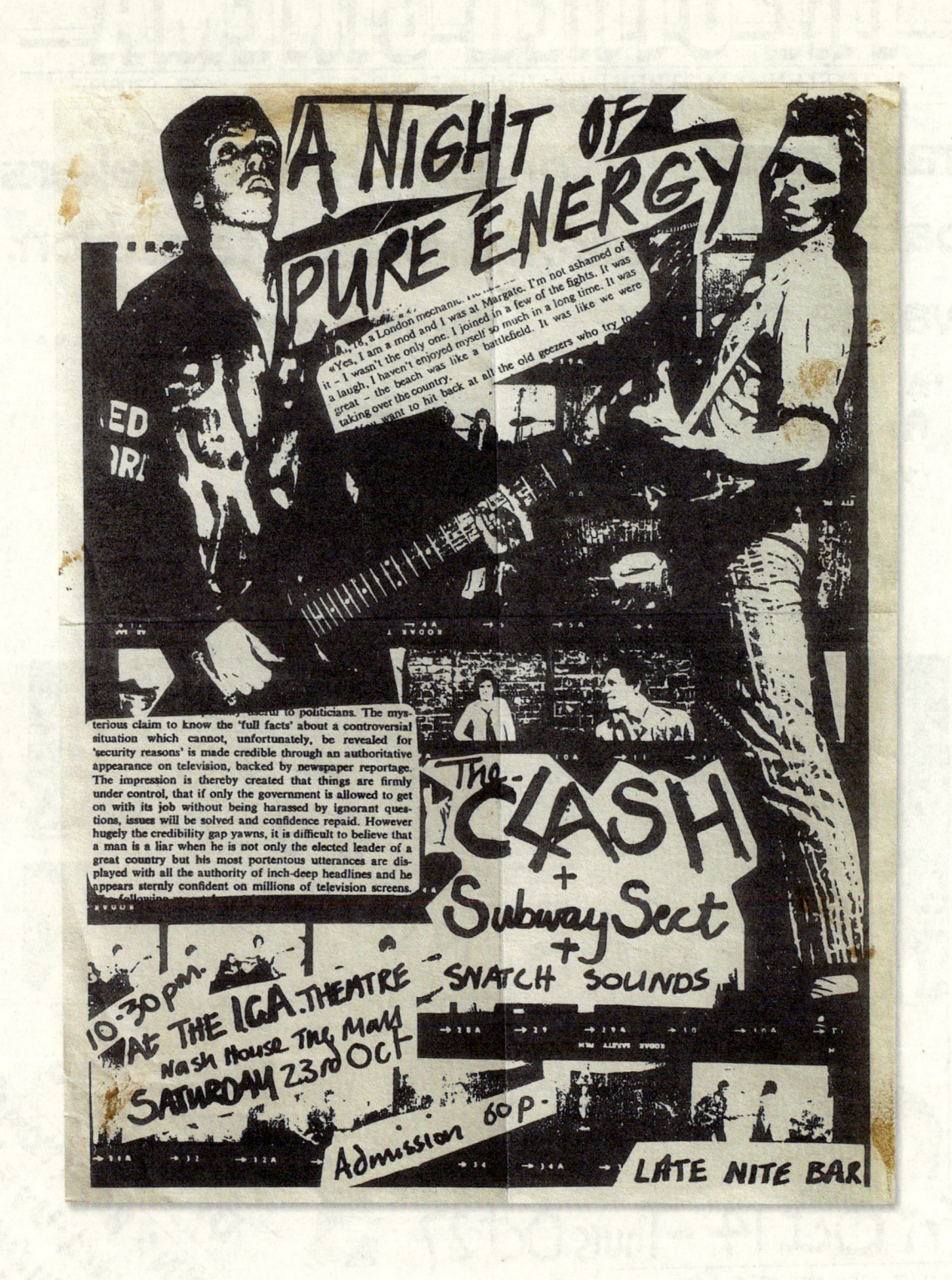

FLYER FOR THE CLASH, SUBWAY SECT AND SNATCH AT THE ICA THEATRE, LONDON
23 October 1976
27.3 × 20.3 cm, 10¾ × 8 in

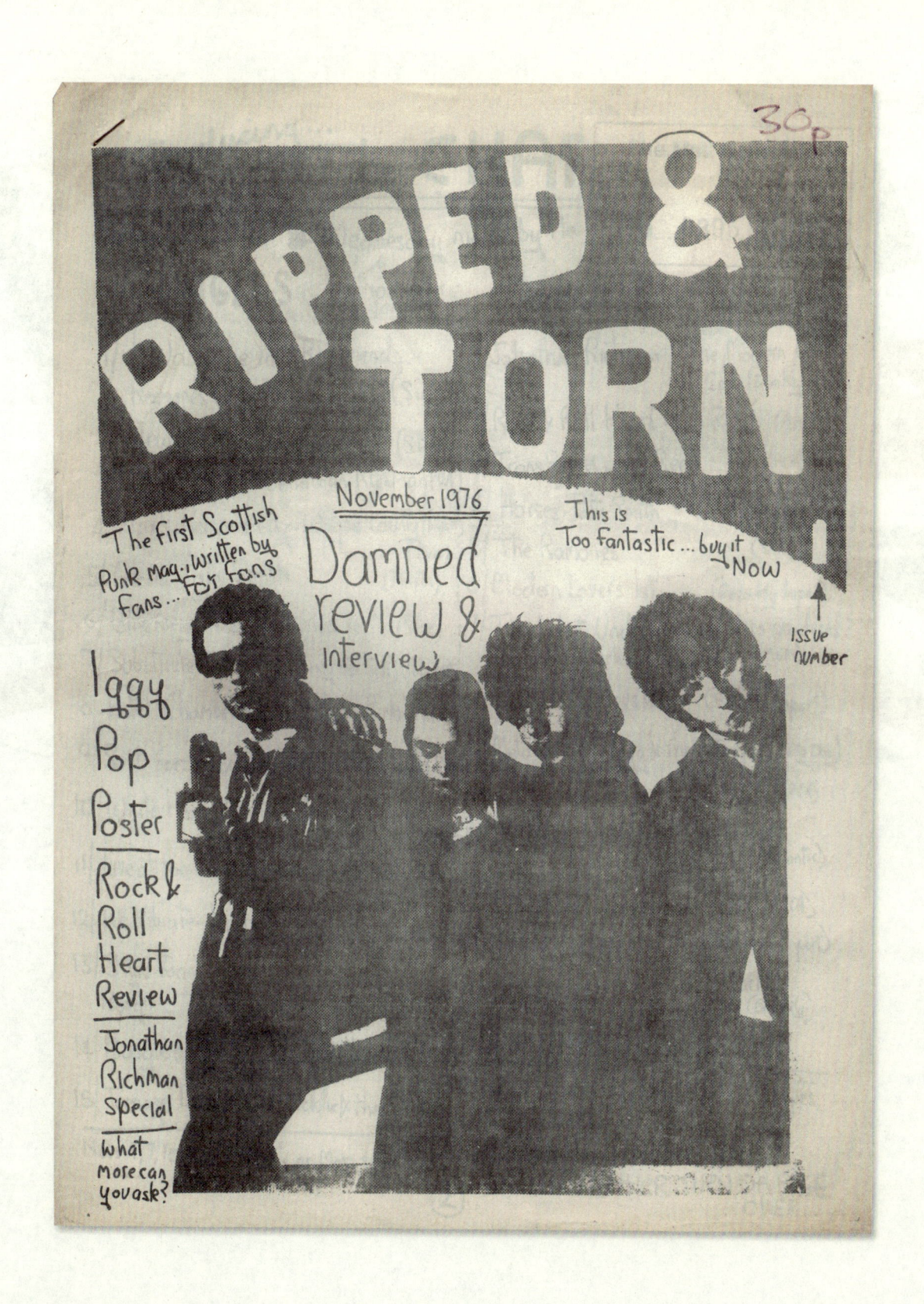

RIPPED & TORN #1
Tony Drayton
November 1976
29.8 × 20.9 cm, 11¾ × 8¼ in

Tony Drayton (aka Tony D) published the first issue of *Ripped & Torn* in Glasgow, Scotland, in November 1976. The third and subsequent issues were distributed from the Rough Trade shop in Notting Hill, London. After the fourth issue, Drayton also produced them in London.

**POSTER FOR THE SEX PISTOLS' SINGLE
'ANARCHY IN THE UK'**
Jamie Reid
26 November 1976
72.3 x 97.1 cm, 28½ x 38¼ in

In the iconic poster for the Sex Pistols' first single, Jamie Reid clipped 'blackmail' lettering to a shredded, pinned-together souvenir flag. Photographed by Ray Stevenson, the poster's symbolism suggests the political dimension of the burgeoning punk rock movement, and Reid's handmade graphic style contributed to the DIY ethos of punk subculture.

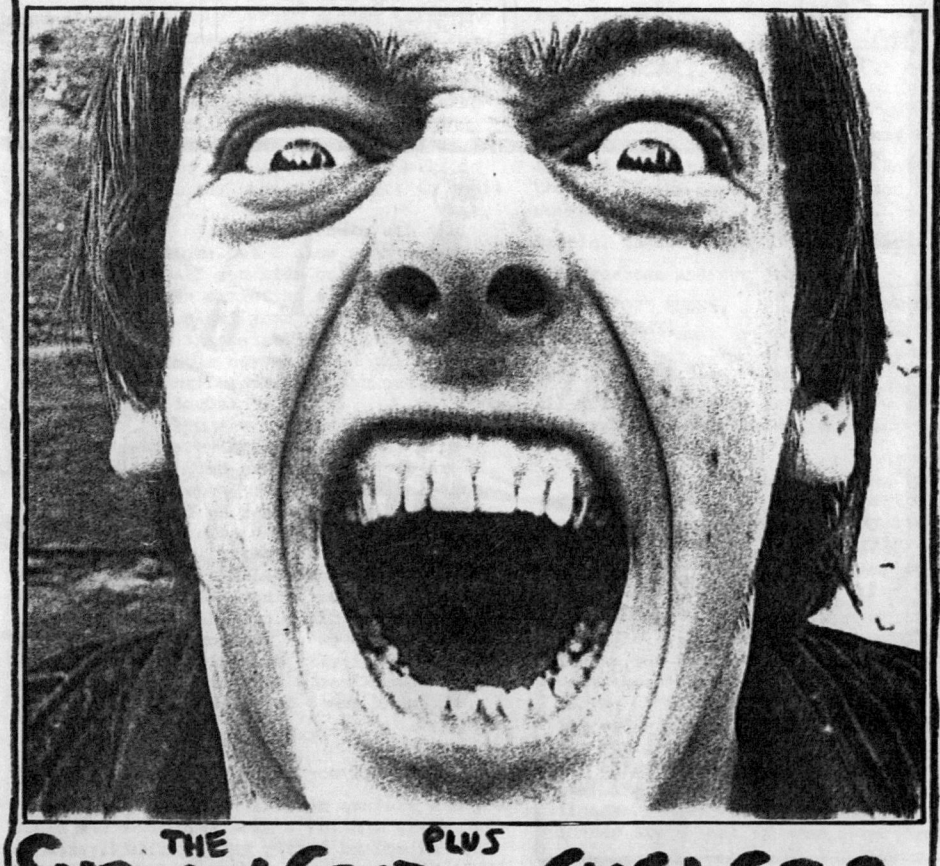

SNIFFIN' GLUE #5
Mark Perry
November 1976
29.8 x 20.9 cm, 11¾ x 8¼ in

Contains concert and album reviews of Eddie and the Hot Rods, Subway Sect and Chelsea; a review of the Sex Pistols' single 'Anarchy in the UK'; and a membership form for the Roxy.

FIRST DIVISION v DERBY COUNTY
SATURDAY DECEMBER 4th 1976
K.O. 3.00 pm

OFFICIAL PROGRAMME PATRONS
SUPPORT THE PATRONS WHO SUPPORT CITY!

The Royal Scot (Marjorie & Ian Niven)	Carlsberg	SMC Fashion Menswear
Robertshaw's Private Hire	Burrows (Grass Machinery) Ltd.	W. H. Holden (Builders) Ltd.
Halliday Transport Organisation	G. R. Entwistle & Son, Plumbers	Dee Dee Metals Ltd.
L. V. Lawlor—Printers	Harry Haworth (Glassware) Ltd.	Scottish and Newcastle Breweries Ltd.
F. H. Lee (Paper Convertors) Ltd.	Jacquard Design Services (Blackburn) Ltd.	COFFER SPORTS
Amusement Hire Service	Roberts Laboratories Ltd.	Northgate Joinery Co. Ltd.
Taylock Metals	Combined Carpets, Oldham Street, Manchester.	East Ridge Construction Ltd.
	Eastridge Construction, Roofing Contractors.	W. E. Cowden, Millers Cottage Holiday Camp Ltd., Towyn, Abergele, North Wales.

ANARCHY IN THE U.K.
Sex Pistols

FIRST SINGLE
EMI 2566

See them live at
SAT 4 DEC DERBY Kings Hall
MON 6 DEC LEEDS Polytechnic
THU 9 DEC MANCHESTER Electric Circus
FRI 10 DEC LANCASTER University
SAT 11 DEC LIVERPOOL Stadium
FRI 17 DEC SHEFFIELD City Hall

ten

SEX PISTOLS ADVERTISEMENT, MANCHESTER CITY VS. DERBY COUNTY MATCH PROGRAMME
4 December 1976
43.8 x 22.8 cm, 17¼ x 9 in

The Sex Pistols' first advertisement appeared in this 1976 Manchester City football programme, and promoted the group's single 'Anarchy in the UK', as well as the infamous 'Anarchy' tour.

SEX PISTOLS ADVERTISEMENT, IPSWICH TOWN VS. LIVERPOOL MATCH PROGRAMME
4 December 1976
19.6 x 20.3 cm, 7¾ x 8 in

An early, full-page ad for the 'Anarchy' tour and single. Six northern dates and four southern dates are listed, including the cancelled gig at the Roxy Theatre, Harlesden, on Boxing Day.

**THE SEX PISTOLS'
ANARCHY IN THE UK ZINE #1**
Jamie Reid
December 1976
45 x 31.7 cm, 17¾ x 12½ in

The Sex Pistols' manager Malcolm McLaren's company, Glitterbest, published this promotional zine *Anarchy in the UK* to sell on the 1976 'Anarchy' tour; copies were first sold on 20 December at the Cleethorpes concert. A collaboration by Pistols' graphic designer Jamie Reid, his partner Sophie Richmond, McLaren and designer Vivienne Westwood, the zine contains graphics and slogans Reid created while working with the radical political magazine *Suburban Press*. The front cover features Soo Catwoman, a London punk icon.

Published by Glitterbest Ltd. 40 Dryden Chambers, 119 Oxford St. London W.1.
Further copies from Glitterbest
Printed by:- zigzag (WE AIN'T PROUD) LTD. 0734-583958

FLYER FOR THE SEX PISTOLS' 'ANARCHY IN THE UK' TOUR AT THE ELECTRIC CIRCUS, MANCHESTER
Jamie Reid
9 December 1976
29.2 x 20.9 cm, 11½ x 8¼ in

Featuring guests the Damned, Johnny Thunders & the Heartbreakers and the Clash. Designer Jamie Reid said the design was meant to continue 'the deliberately rushed and jumbled "criminality" of the band's previous graphics and press releases – which looked as though they were communiqués from arch villains or freedom fighters'.

MORE ON #2
December 1976
[dims unknown]

Reviews the Roxy and Louise's on Poland Street, Soho.
Pages are fastened with a safety pin.

**POSTER FOR BLONDIE'S
DEBUT ALBUM BLONDIE**
c. December 1976
70.4 x 43.1 cm, 27¾ x 17 in

Issued by the band's first label, Private Stock Records, Blondie's eponymous debut album appeared in the United States in December 1976. The small independent company argued that the large colour photograph of singer Debbie Harry in a translucent blouse was necessary to market an unknown act, but the sexualised image met with an unfavourable reaction from the band. Disagreements over the publicity and weak album sales led Blondie to buy back their contract and sign with Chrysalis in 1977.

SNIFFIN' GLUE, CHRISTMAS ISSUE
Mark Perry
December 1976
29.8 x 20.9 cm, 11¾ x 8¼ in

The Christmas edition subtly altered the title to read 'Sniffin' Snow'. This was one of two special editions within the regular run of 12 issues.

BONDAGE #1
Shane MacGowan
1976
[dims unknown]

Shane MacGowan, who would later become the lead singer of the band the Pogues, produced this fanzine, which includes articles on the Jam, the Sex Pistols, Just Another Country and Eater; MacGowan sold them at punk shows.

LONDON'S BURNING #1
Jonh Ingham
1976
28.5 × 20.3 cm, 11¼ × 8 in

'The fanzine by a Clash fan for Clash fans', claims the copy for Jonh Ingham's stylish *London's Burning*. There was only one issue, notable for its collage work. Ingham was a staff writer for *Sounds*, which published his interview with the Sex Pistols in its 24 April 1976 issue. Ingham also wrote a newsletter for the label Rough Trade, and later became the manager of Generation X and the Go-Go's.

POSTER FOR NEW WAVE COMPILATION ALBUM (VERTIGO)
1977
71.7 x 49.5 x cm, 28¼ x 19½ in

The compilation includes the Ramones, Dead Boys, Patti Smith, New York Dolls, the Runaways, Skyhooks, the Voidoids, Little Bob Story, the Boomtown Rats, Talking Heads, the Damned and the Flamin' Groovies. The sleeve and poster both feature a photo of the Satellites' vocalist Derek Gibbs spitting beer with bass player John Johnson in a swimming cap in the background. The album helped establish the musical term 'new wave' and affirmed the importance of these participating bands in that movement.

POSTER FOR THE CLASH AND CHELSEA
AT THE ROXY, LONDON
January 1, 1977
[dims unknown]

PUNK
Julie Davis
Millington/Davison Publishing Ltd, 1977
27.9 x 20.9 cm, 11 x 8¼ in

Julie Davis's heavily illustrated book contains many candid photographs and first-hand accounts of the early punk scene.

THE PUNK
Gideon Sams
1977
17.7 x 11.4 cm, 7 x 4½ in

Written as a school project when Gideon Sams was only 14, this novel was published by Polytantric Press in an edition of less than 1,000 copies, each with a real safety pin in its cover. This later, mass-market paperback edition ran to approximately 50,000 copies. Sams died at age 26.

SIDEBURNS #1
Tony Moon
January 1977
[dims unknown]

Tony Moon's fanzine includes a five-page feature on the Stranglers with a Jet Black interview, live reviews of Eddie and the Hotrods at the Roundhouse, plus bits on Lew Lewis as well as the Darts. On page three, a short editorial vividly recounts the beginnings of the London punk scene. In order to fill a blank page two, Moon wrote and illustrated what turned out to be an iconic directive of the punk era: 'This is a chord. This is another. This is a third. Now form a band.' The stark simplicity of the instructions encapsulates punk's DIY ethos.

PLAY'IN IN THE BAND...FIRST AND LAST IN A SERIES..........

A

← THIS IS A CHORD

E

THIS IS ANOTHER

G

This is a THIRD

NOW FORM A BAND

SNIFFIN' GLUE #6
Mark Perry
January 1977
28.5 x 20.3 cm, 11¼ x 8 in

With the Clash on the cover, this issue, dedicated to John Collis, features articles on the Sex Pistols, Eater and Generation X, amongst others.

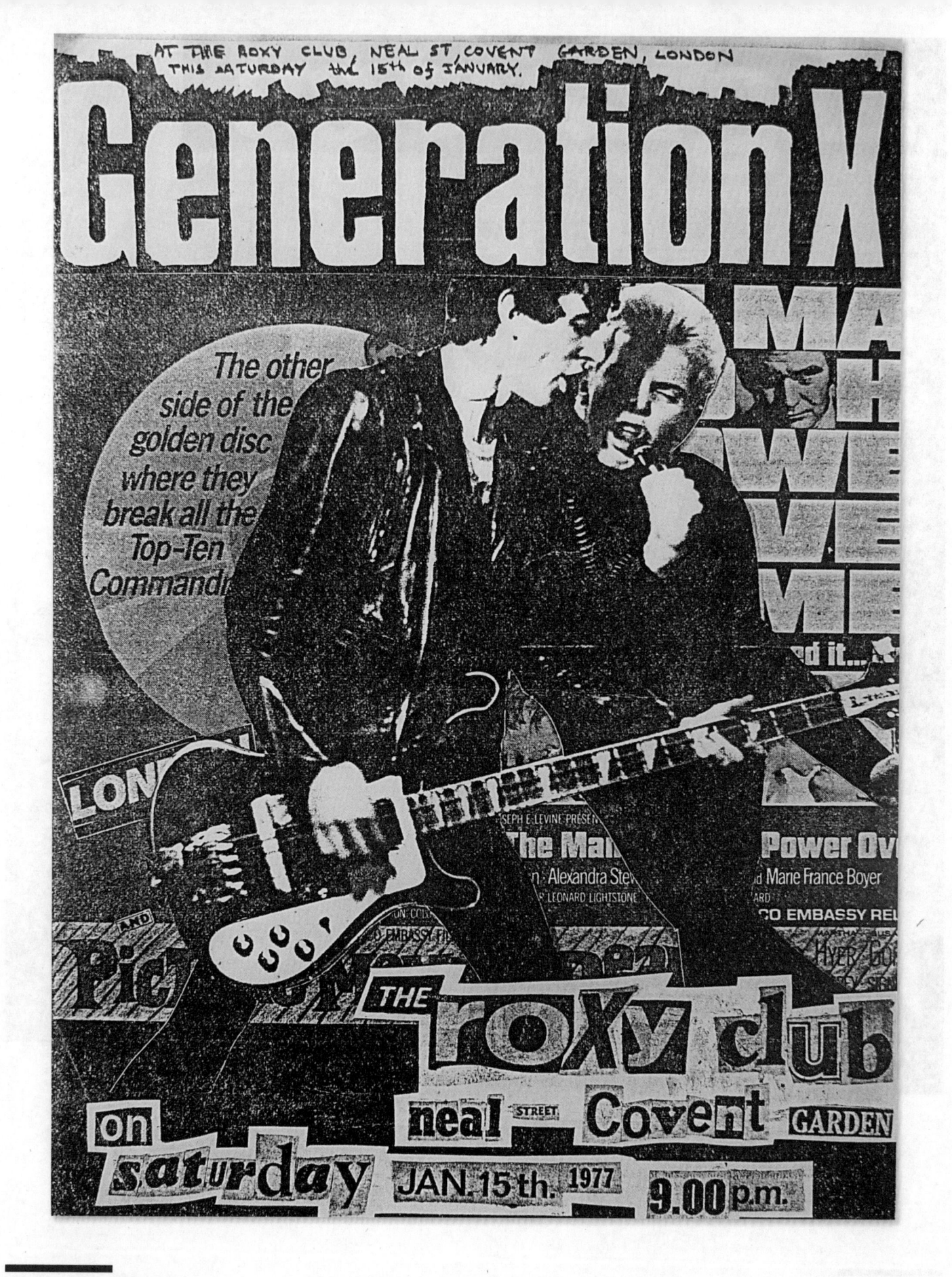

**POSTER FOR GENERATION X
AT THE ROXY, LONDON**
15 January 1977
[dims unknown]

'The other side of the golden disc where they break all the Top-Ten Commandments'. The Roxy nightclub, located at 41–43 Neal Street in London's Covent Garden, fostered the British punk music scene in its infancy. Three of the four original members of seminal London punk band Chelsea, amongst them Billy Idol, went on to form another influential band: Generation X.

zigzag 68

30 PENCE

JACKSON BROWNE
Graham Parker
Ian Matthews
Santana
& more

OVER THE TOP!
THE MAGAZINE WITHIN A MAGAZINE!

INSTRUCTIONS: Rip out this supplement and throw the rest away (or keep the rest and throw this away... it's up to you)

Picture by Geoffrey Tyrell

ZIGZAG #68
January 1977
[dims unknown]

Features Jackson Browne, Graham Parker and Santana. The Kris Needs supplement 'Over The Top!' focuses on punk – 'Instructions: Rip out this supplement and throw the rest away (or keep the rest and throw this away … it's up to you)' – with a photo of Needs eating the sleeve of the Eagles' *Hotel California*, alongside an article on Patti Smith in London, a John Otway interview, reviews and more.

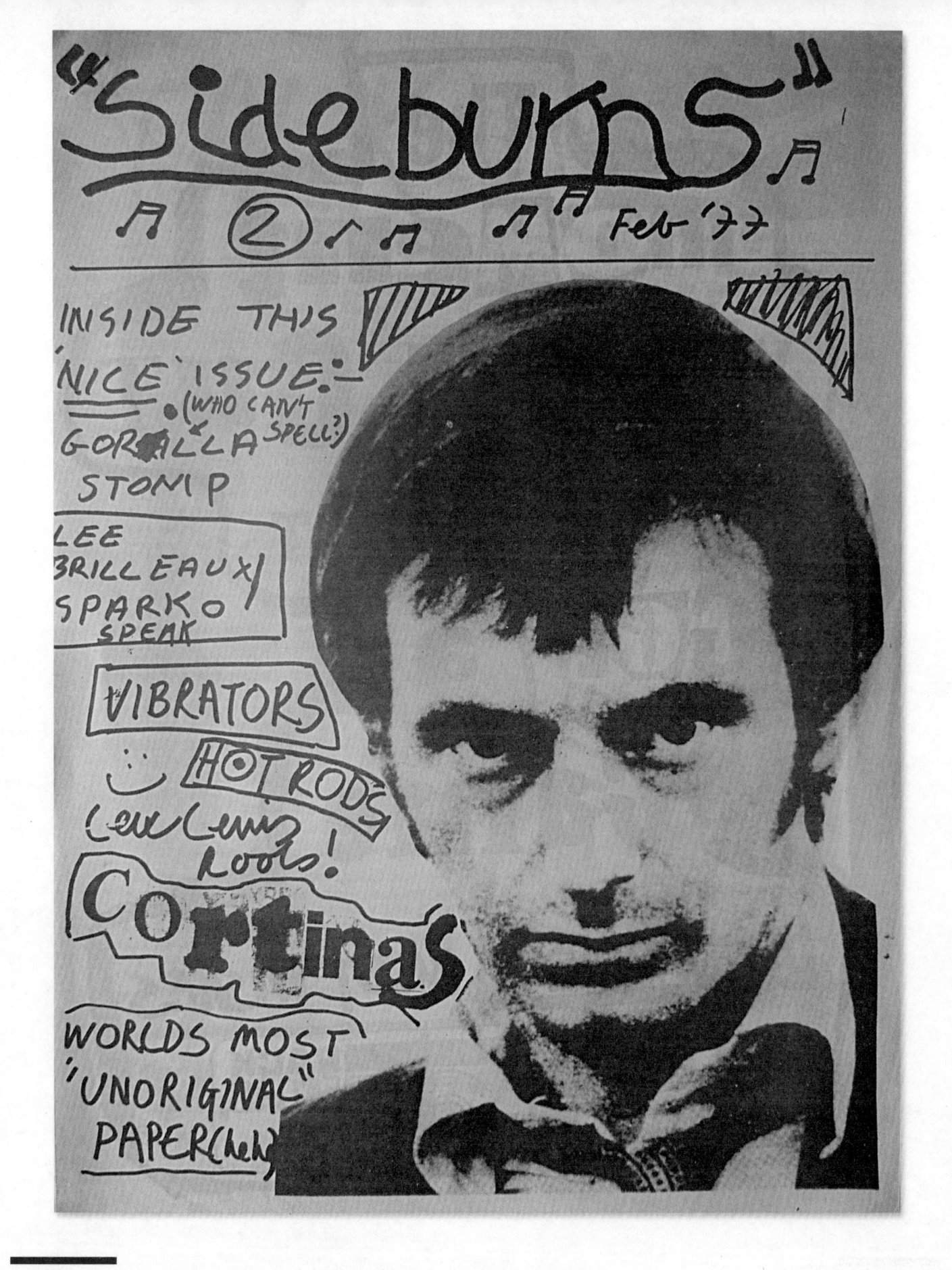

SIDEBURNS #2
February 1977
[dims unknown]

Includes articles on Lee Brilleaux, Dr Feelgood, the Vibrators, Eddie and the Hotrods and the Cortinas.

SNIFFIN' GLUE #7
Mark Perry
February 1977
29.2 x 20.9 cm, 11½ x 8¼ in

The Adverts, Don Letts and Jesse Hector of the Gorillas appear on the cover of this issue, which includes features on all three bands.

WHITE STUFF #1
Sandy Robertson
February 1977
29.8 x 20.9 cm, 11¾ x 8¼ in

This London-based zine was chiefly devoted to Patti Smith, billing itself as 'a rock n roll magazine for the modern world'; it has articles on Lou Reed and reviews of the Sex Pistols and the Ramones. Sandy Robertson took his title from Smith's song 'Ain't It Strange', which includes the lyrics, 'Down in vineland there's a clubhouse / Girl in white dress, boy shoot white stuff.' *White Stuff* attracted an artsy following and its publication coincided with the publication of Robertson's poetry books. Robertson later joined the British music magazine *Sounds*.

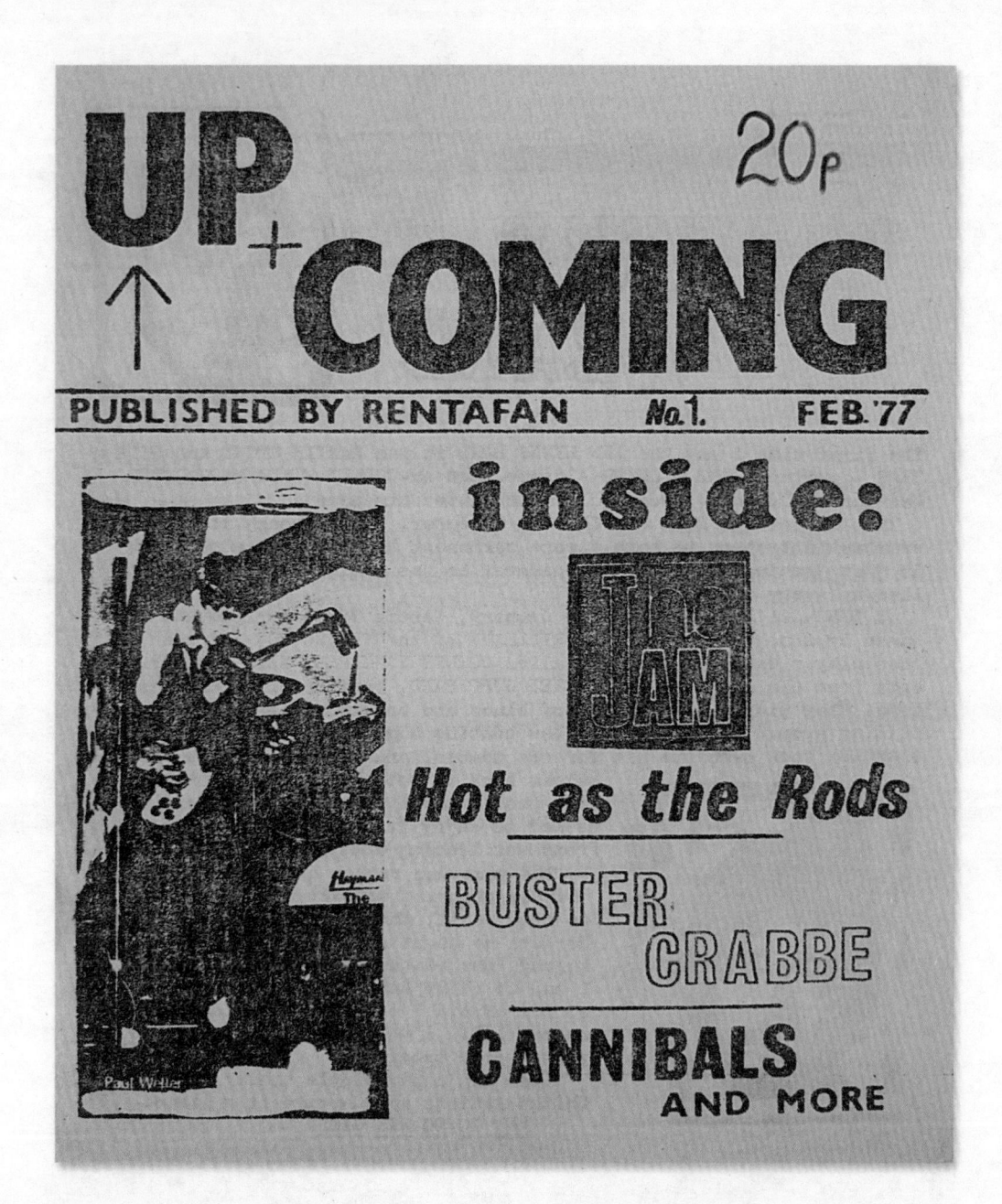

UP 'N' COMING #1
February 1977
20.3 x 16.5 cm, 8 x 6½ in

This zine features several punk bands, including the Jam, Hot as the Rods, Buster Crabbe and the Cannibals.

"sideburns" NO. 3

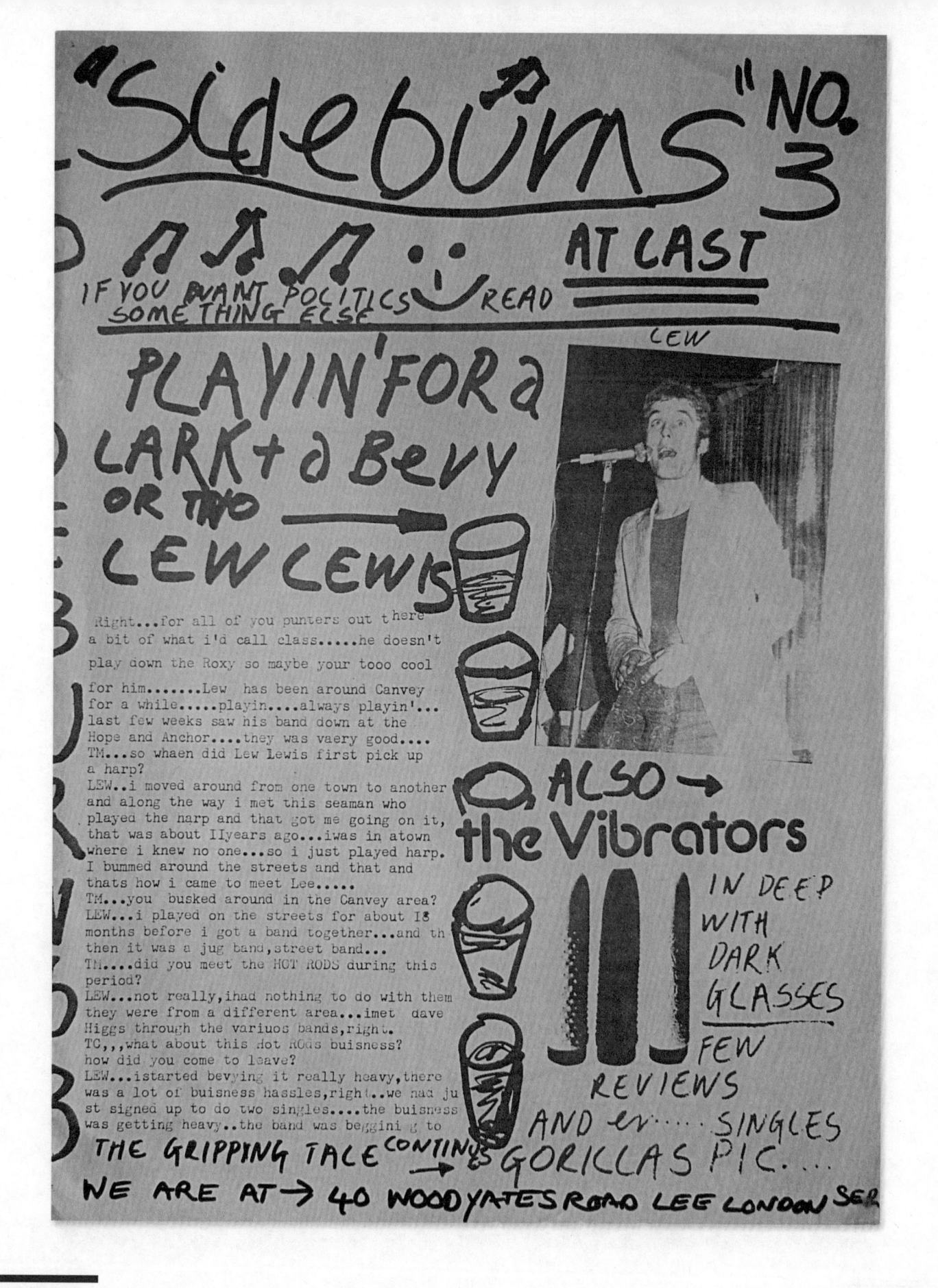

AT LAST
IF YOU WANT POLITICS READ SOMETHING ELSE

PLAYIN' FOR a LARK + a Bevy OR TWO → LEW LEWIS

LEW

Right...for all of you punters out there
a bit of what i'd call class.....he doesn't
play down the Roxy so maybe your tooo cool
for him.......Lew has been around Canvey
for a while.....playin....always playin'...
last few weeks saw his band down at the
Hope and Anchor....they was vaery good....
TM...so whaen did Lew Lewis first pick up
a harp?
LEW..i moved around from one town to another
and along the way i met this seaman who
played the harp and that got me going on it,
that was about 11years ago...iwas in atown
where i knew no one...so i just played harp.
I bummed around the streets and that and
thats how i came to meet Lee.....
TM...you busked around in the Canvey area?
LEW...i played on the streets for about 18
months before i got a band together...and th
then it was a jug band,street band...
TM....did you meet the HOT RODS during this
period?
LEW...not really,ihad nothing to do with them
they were from a different area...imet dave
Higgs through the variuos bands,right.
TC,,,what about this Hot Rods buisness?
how did you come to leave?
LEW...istarted bevying it really heavy,there
was a lot of buisness hassles,right..we had ju
st signed up to do two singles....the buisness
was getting heavy..the band was beggini g to

ALSO → the Vibrators

IN DEEP WITH DARK GLASSES
FEW REVIEWS
AND er.... SINGLES
GORILLAS PIC....

THE GRIPPING TALE CONTINS →

WE ARE AT → 40 WOODYATES ROAD LEE LONDON SE12

SIDEBURNS #3
[February] 1977
[dims unknown]

Features the Vibrators.

48 THRILLS #2
Adrian Thrills
February 1977
[dims unknown]

Features the Clash, Generation X, the Jam, Chelsea, Disease and more.

FLYER FOR CHELSEA AT THE ROXY
4 February 1977
20.9 × 29.8 cm, 8¼ × 11¾ in

**FLYER FOR SHAM 69
AT BROOKLANDS COLLEGE**
11 February 1977
29.8 x 20.9 cm, 11¾ x 8¼ in

This original five-member Sham 69 would undergo notable changes by the end of the year. Vocalist Jimmy Pursey would recruit new musicians, amongst them Dave Parsons, prior to the group's chart success in 1978.

POSTCARD FOR THE DAMNED
Printed by Walkerprint, London
February 1977
[dims unknown]

The Damned appear wearing eerie paper-bag masks alongside the Stiff Records logo.

FLYER FOR EATER AND GBH AT THE ROXY
23 February 1977
29.8 x 20.9 cm, 11¾ x 8¼ in

FLYER FOR THE ROXY, LONDON
March 1977
33 x 21.5 cm, 13 x 8½ in

Upcoming shows include Siouxsie and the Banshees, Chelsea, X-Ray Spex, the Drones, Shakin' Street, the Zips, the Jam, the Adverts, the Boys, Eater, the Lurkers, Slaughter & the Dogs, Johnny Moped, the Cortinas, the Beastly Cads, Sham 69, Kubie & the Rats and the Stranglers.

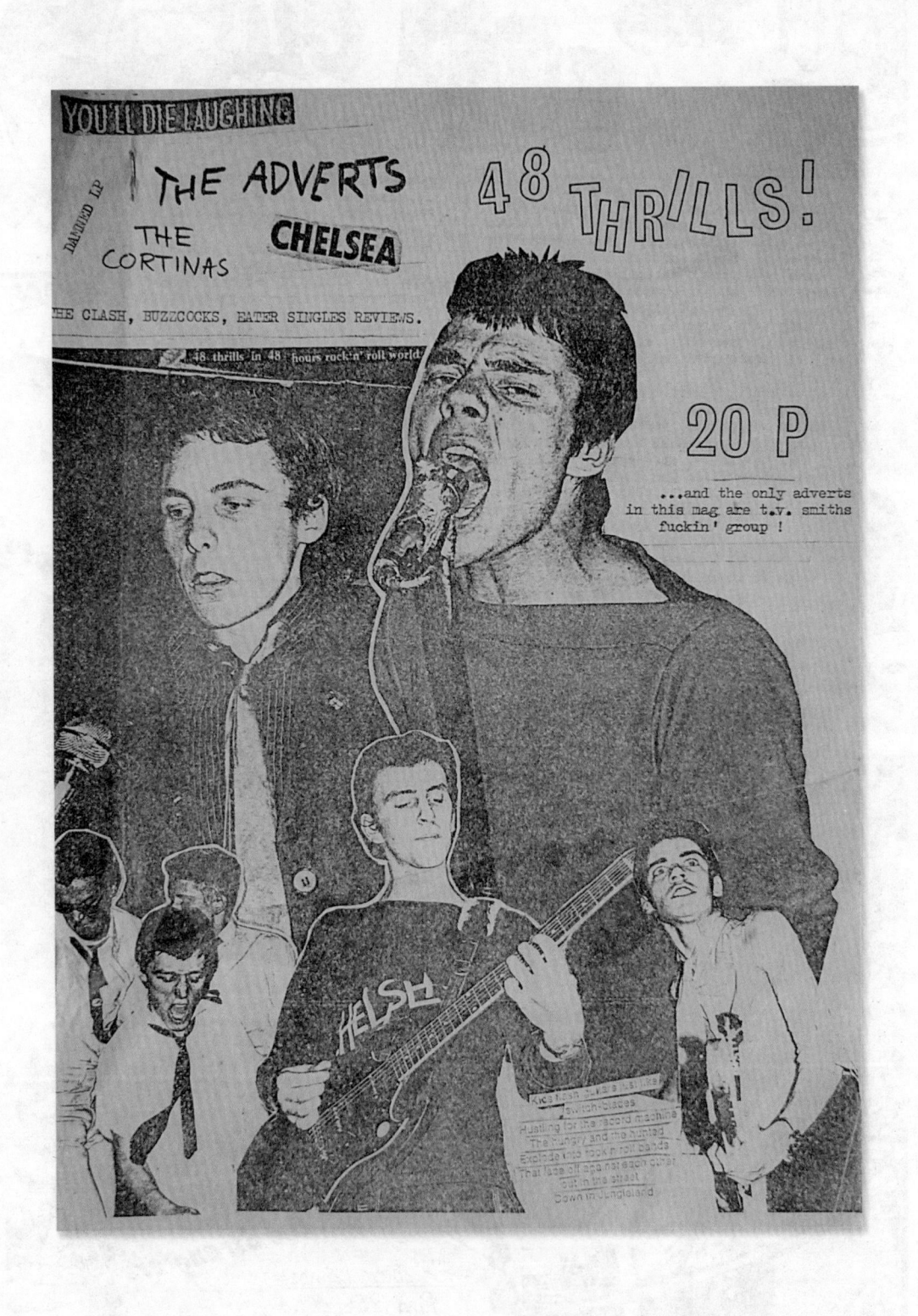

48 THRILLS #3
Adrian Thrills
March 1977
29.8 x 20.9 cm, 11¾ x 8¼ in

This zine includes articles on the Adverts, the Cortinas and a Chelsea concert in Stevenage.

WHITE STUFF #2
Sandy Robertson
March 1977
[dims unknown]

Features Patti Smith, Lenny Kaye, the Runaways and Kim Fowley.

SNIFFIN' GLUE #8
Mark Perry
March 1977
29.8 x 20.9 cm, 11¾ x 8¼ in

This issue on the 'New York Invasion!' highlights Johnny Thunders & the Heartbreakers, Cherry Vanilla and Wayne County. Buzzcocks, the Jam and the Clash are also featured.

CRIPES #1
Bruce Findlay, Brian Hogg
March 1977
29.2 x 20.9 cm, 11½ x 8¼ in

This first issue features the Rezillos.

FLYER FOR WAYNE COUNTY AT THE ROXY
4 March 1977
33 x 20.9 cm, 13 x 8¼ in

Most flyers for the Roxy were produced in black and white, making this a rare colour reproduction. Jayne County (born Wayne Rogers) became rock's first transsexual singer, after performing as Wayne County. Her career as a performer, musician and actress has spanned several decades.

POSTER FOR EATER'S SINGLE 'OUTSIDE VIEW'
11 March 1977
34.2 x 46.3 cm, 13½ x 18¼ in

Producer Dave Goodman recalls putting up posters near schools for the debut of 'Outside View'. Goodman said, 'It was a very direct form of advertising but it worked a treat. It meant that at least another 20,000 school kids would become aware of Eater, and that was a start.'

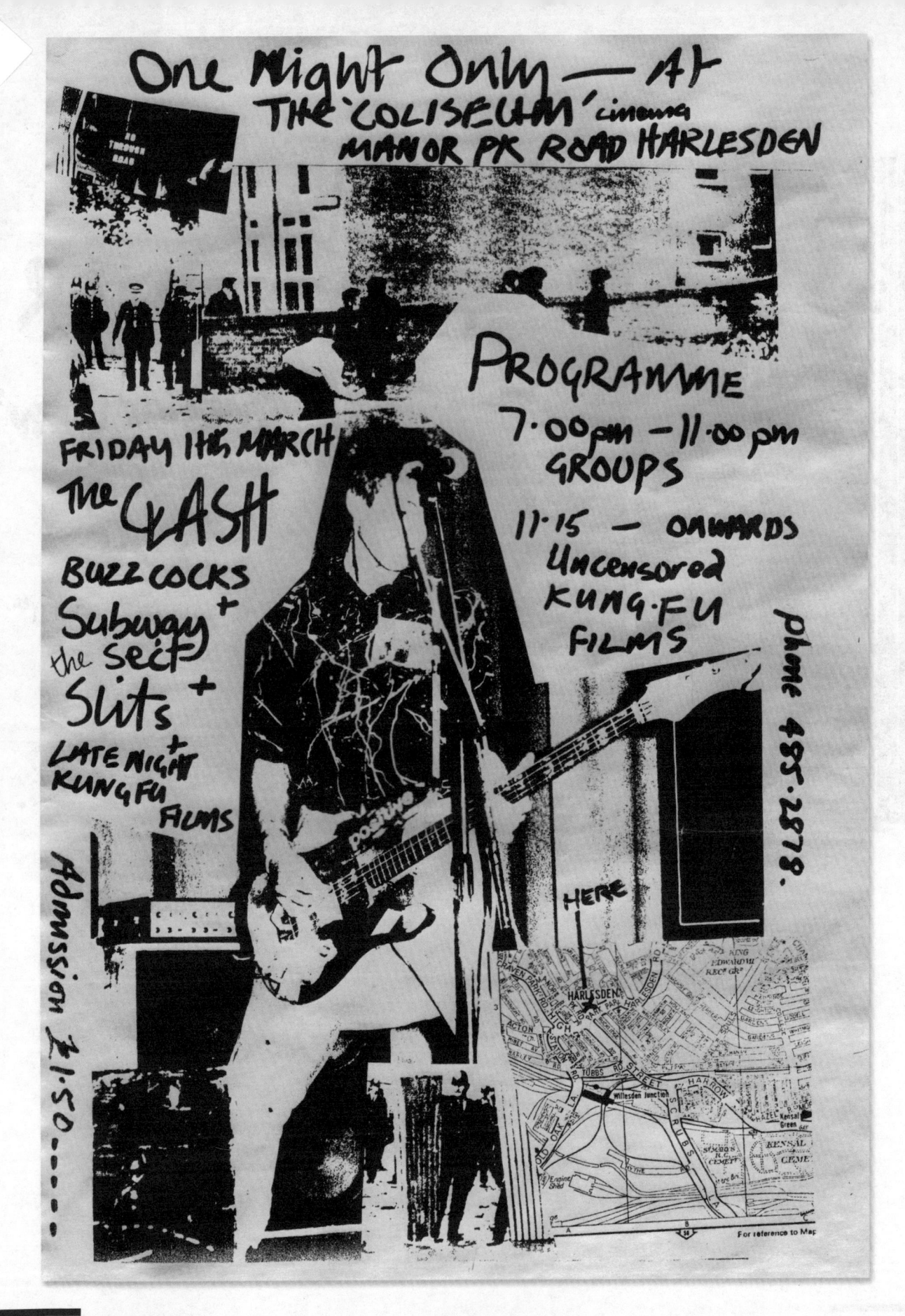

POSTER FOR THE CLASH, BUZZCOCKS,
SUBWAY SECT AND THE SLITS
AT COLISEUM CINEMA, HARLESDEN
11 March 1977
[dims unknown]

**FLYER FOR SIOUXSIE AND THE BANSHEES
AND THE SLITS AT THE ROXY, LONDON**
Barry Jones
26 March 1977
20.9 x 33 cm, 8¼ x 13 in

Barry Jones, a part owner of the Roxy, contributed to posters for the venue; he created this photocopied flyer at a slightly larger than standard A4 size.

FLYER FOR GENERATION X AT THE MARQUEE
Jon Savage
31 March 1977
28.5 × 20.3 cm, 11¼ × 8 in

This date was the band's first at the Marquee, a venue they would play six more times that year. The flyer was designed by Jon Savage, an English writer, broadcaster and music journalist best known for his 1991 book, *England's Dreaming*, an award-winning history of the Sex Pistols and punk.

The NEW WAVE magazine 2

```
INSIDE : S T R A N G L E R S  INTERVIEW
         I G G Y  REVIEW

         and so much more !!
```

THE NEW WAVE MAGAZINE #2
[March] 1977
28.5 x 21.5 cm, 11¼ x 8½ in

Includes an interview with the Stranglers, review of Iggy Pop and more.

CHELMSFORD'S DEAD #1
[after March] 1977
29.8 x 21.5 cm, 11¾ x 8½ in

Contains stories on the Clash, the Slits and Subway Sect and an interview with the Prefects.

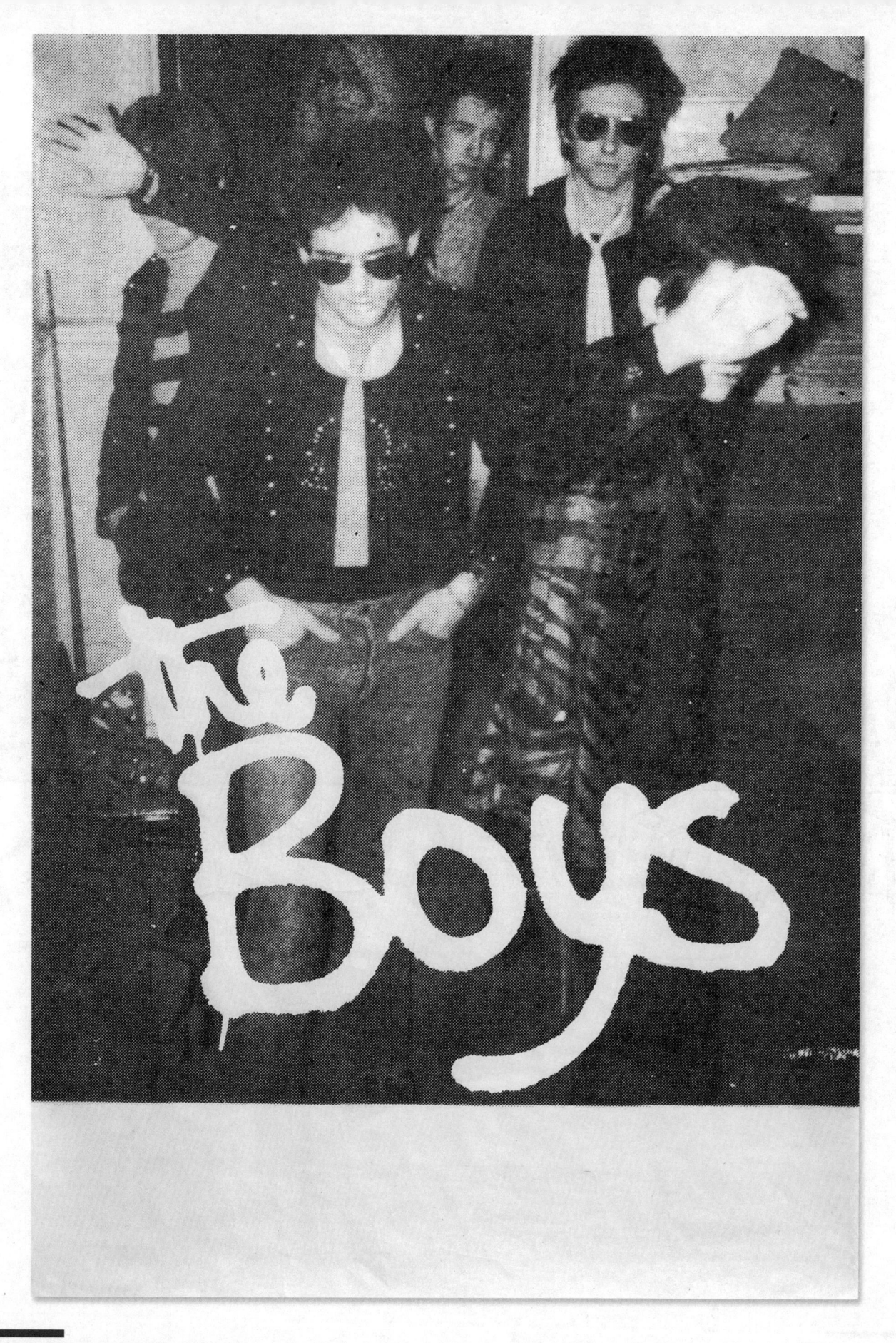

POSTER FOR THE BOYS' SINGLE 'I DON'T CARE'
1 April 1977
74.9 x 48.2 cm, 29½ x 19 in

FLYER FOR SHAM 69 AT THE ROXY
1977
20.9 x 26 cm, 8¼ x 10¼ in

**POSTER FOR THE DAMNED'S ALBUM
DAMNED DAMNED DAMNED**
1977
76.2 x 50.8 cm, 30 x 20 in

Features Peter Gravelle's photographs of the band members with custard pies in their faces. A well-known photographer for *Vogue* and *Harper's Bazaar*, Gravelle adopted the surname Kodick in the late 1970s, while shooting artists such as the Sex Pistols, Billy Idol and Elvis Costello.

The NEW WAVE magazine 3

INSIDE : D A M N E D INTERVIEW
A D V E R T S INTERVIEW
IGGY, MC5, JOHN CALE

and very little else...

THE NEW WAVE MAGAZINE #3
[April] 1977
29.2 x 20.9 cm, 11½ x 8¼ in

Interviews with the Adverts and Dave Vanian of the Damned, and reviews of the Clash's 'White Riot' and Iggy Pop's *The Idiot*.

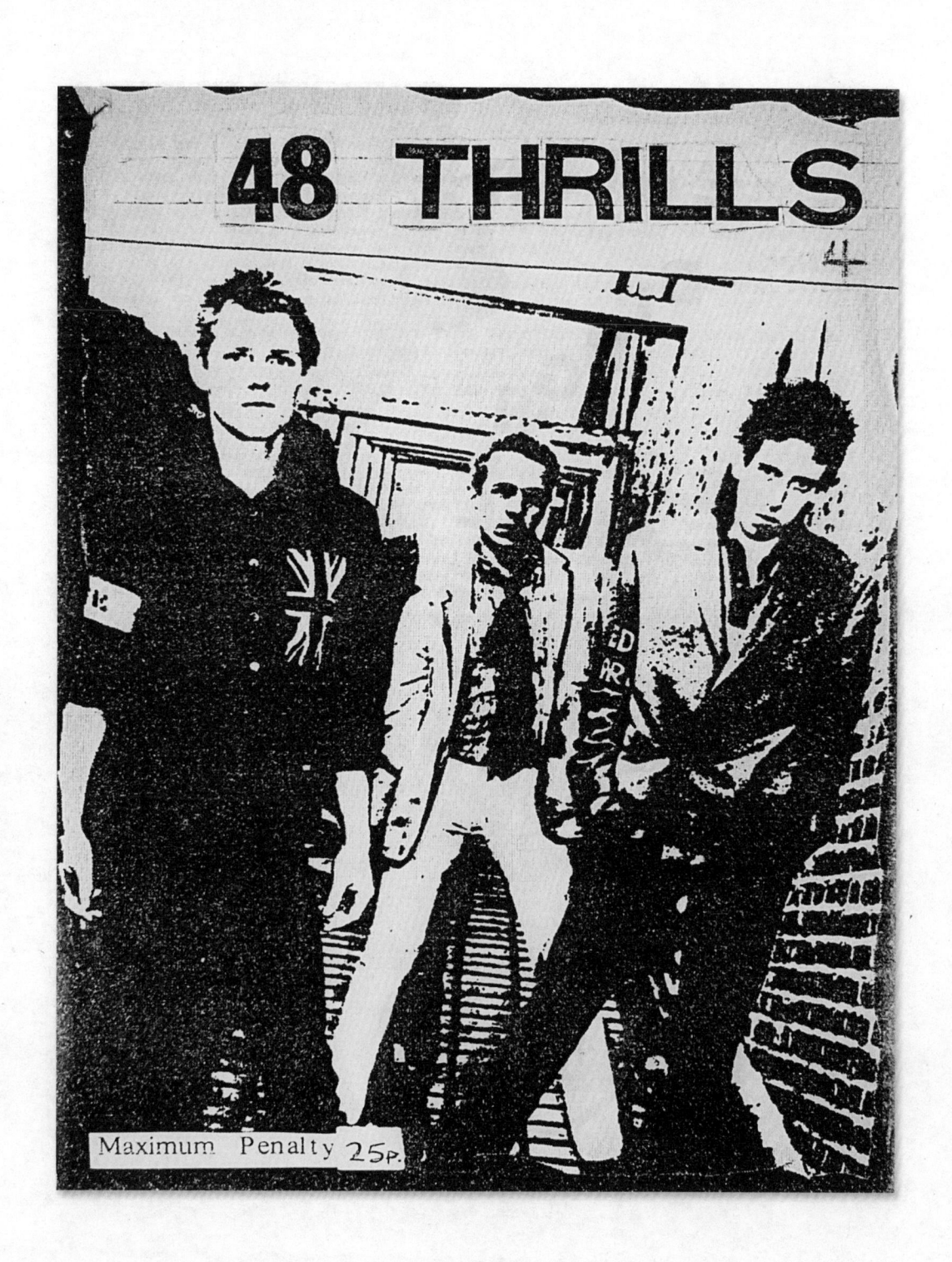

48 THRILLS #4
Adrian Thrills
April 1977
29.2 x 20.9 cm, 11½ x 8¼ in

Contains an article on the Clash, with a review and song lyrics.

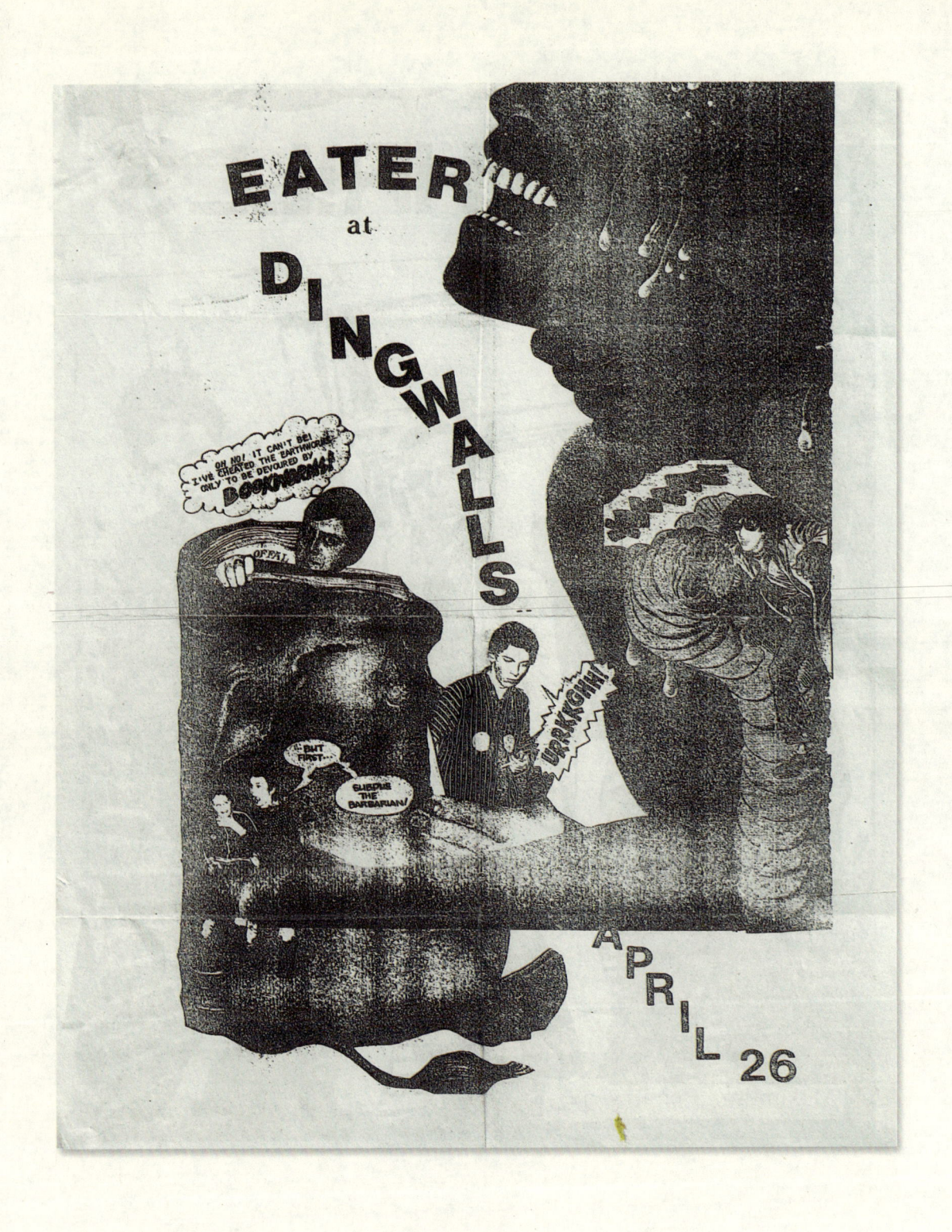

FLYER FOR EATER AT DINGWALLS
26 April 1977
26.6 x 20.3 cm, 10½ x 8 in

Eater released one album and five singles before splitting up. With an average age of 16, Eater band members were students by day and punk rockers by night. Johnny Thunders & the Heartbreakers' manager Leee Childers took an interest in the group, creating one-off concert flyers for the band.

MORE-ON #4
Sarah Shosubi
April 1977
33 x 20.3 cm, 13 x 8 in

Unique for its use of colour stock covers and an oversized format.

LIVE ALBUM
THE ROXY LONDON WC2 (Jan - Apr 77)

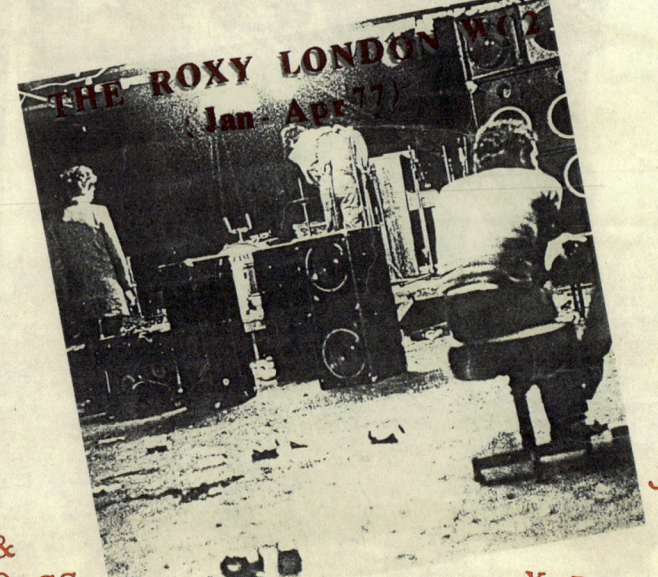

Slaughter & The Dogs
The Unwanted
Wire

The Adverts
Johnny Moped
Eater
X-Ray Spex
Buzzcocks

Between January and April this year, the Roxy Club devoted itself entirely to new wave music. There was nowhere else for the groups to play. This is the album of the club.

POSTER FOR THE ROXY LONDON WC2 COMPILATION ALBUM
1977
76.8 x 50.8 cm, 30¼ x 20 in

Promoters Andrew Czezowski and Susan Carrington officially opened the Roxy on 1 January 1977; following a dispute over the rent, their involvement ended four and a half months later with a parting gig by Siouxsie and the Banshees. The album features Wire, Eater, Johnny Moped and Buzzcocks, amongst others. It's unclear who is in the Barry Jones photograph on the sleeve and poster: some say it's the Damned, while others say it's the Police packing up their equipment after a gig with Cherry Vanilla.

STRANGLED #2
April 1977
29.8 x 20.9 cm, 11¾ x 8¼ in

Featuring the Jam, Squeeze, Ian Dury and a review of the Stranglers' *Rattus Norvegicus*. Early in 1977, Tony Moon's *Sideburns* metamorphosed into *Strangled* when the Stranglers' PR man, Alan Edwards, asked Moon to devote a zine exclusively to the group.

Working alongside the band, Edwards and Moon shifted the publication from a photocopied mish-mash into a glossy enthuzine. In addition to covering the Stranglers and their music, the zine also addresses controversial topics in which the band took an interest.

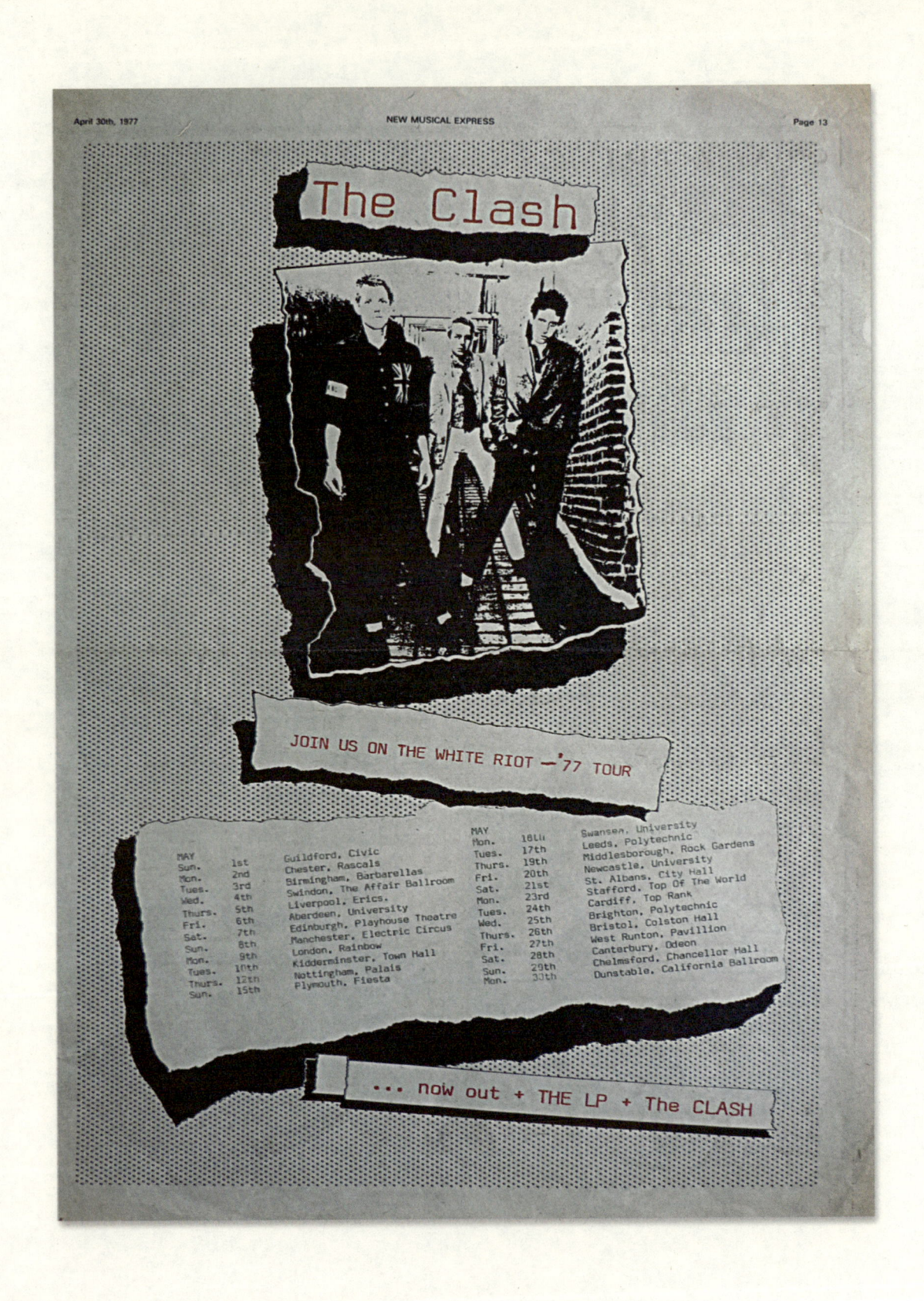

**ADVERTISEMENT IN NEW MUSICAL EXPRESS
FOR THE CLASH'S 'WHITE RIOT' TOUR**
30 April 1977
41.9 x 29.2 cm, 16½ x 11½ in

SNIFFIN' GLUE #9
Mark Perry
April/May 1977
29.8 x 20.9 cm, 11¾ x 8¼ in

Features the Models and the Damned, with a cover that showcases the Cortinas.

TEMPORARY HOARDING

An occasional zine-style paper published by Rock Against Racism into the early '80s, *Temporary Hoarding* focused on RAR gigs and regional political issues. It regularly featured interviews with punk and new wave figures and bands, including Johnny Rotten, Aswad, Carol Grimes, the Clash, Tom Robinson Band, Poly Styrene, Mark Perry, John Cooper Clarke, Tony Wilson and Mark E. Smith. The magazine was, in RAR co-founder Roger Huddle's words, 'the only really revolutionary cultural paper in Britain then or at any time'.

TEMPORARY HOARDING #1
May 1977
62.8 x 41.9 cm, 24¾ x 16½ in

Contains left-wing writer David Widgery's manifesto for RAR: 'We want rebel music, street music. Music that breaks down people's fear of one another. Crisis music. Now music. Music that knows who the real enemy is. Rock against racism.' The issue also offers information for prospective RAR concert organisers, a graphic addressing David Bowie's apparent flirtation with fascism during his 'Thin White Duke' period, pictures of the Clash and lyrics to Tom Robinson Band's 'The Winter of '79'.

what is Racism?

105

TEMPORARY HOARDING #3, CARNIVAL ISSUE
1977
31.8 x 22.2 cm, 12½ x 8¾ in

Features include '12 Months Under Heavy Manners', on police oppression, plus Elvis and Lewisham.

TEMPORARY HOARDING #4
1977
32.3 x 22.8 cm, 12¾ x 9 in

POSTER FOR THE VIBRATORS' SINGLE 'BABY BABY'
May 1977
38.1 x 25.4 cm, 15 x 10 in

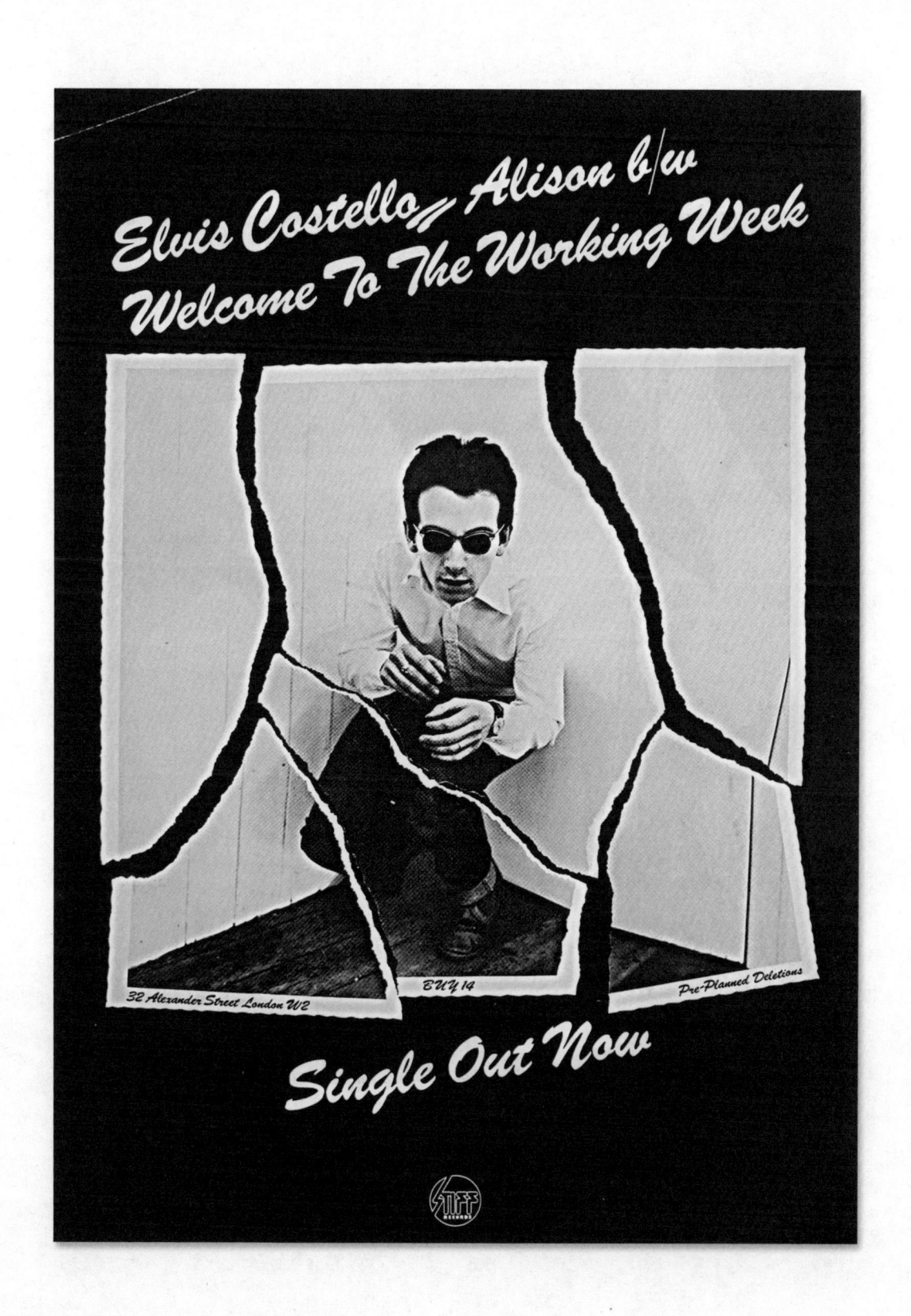

POSTER FOR ELVIS COSTELLO'S SINGLE 'ALISON'
May 1977
37.4 x 25.4 cm, 14¾ x 10 in

Released as a single on Stiff Records with the B-side 'Welcome to the Working Week'.

48 THRILLS #5
May 1977
29.8 x 20.9 cm, 11¾ x 8¼ in

Articles on the Sex Pistols, Generation X, the Jam and others.

ADVERTISEMENT FOR THE CLASH
1977
[dims unknown]

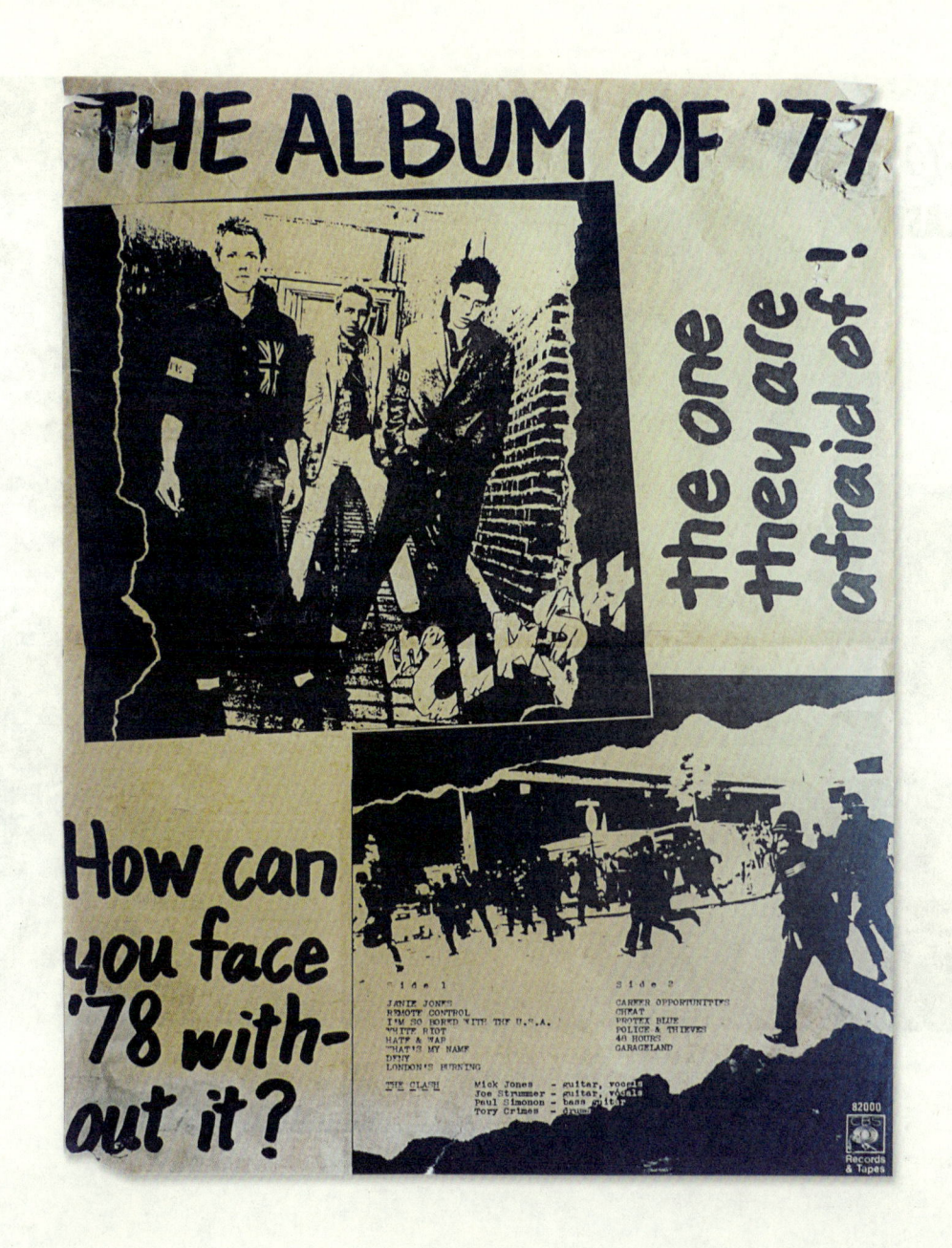

**PIN-UP POSTER OF THE CLASH,
OH BOY! MAGAZINE**
1977
21.5 x 29.2 cm, 8½ x 11½ in

POSTER FOR THE CLASH'S 'WHITE RIOT' TOUR
May 1977
99.6 x 76.2 cm, 39¼ x 30 in

On the 'White Riot' tour, the Clash was supported by the Jam, Subway Sect, the Slits and Buzzcocks. The silkscreened poster for the tour adapted photographer Kate Simon's famous shot from the sleeve of the band's debut album. The blank strip at the bottom, complete with torn graphics, allowed for concert details to be added later (in this case, at the Edinburgh Playhouse).

The NEW WAVE magazine 4

30p

INSIDE : J A M INTERVIEW
V I B R A T O R S INTERVIEW
CLASH, LOU REED, STRANGLERS
and nothing much else...

THE NEW WAVE MAGAZINE #4
[May] 1977
29.2 x 20.9 cm, 11½ x 8¼ in

Interviews with the Jam and the Vibrators; stories about the Clash, Lou Reed and the Stranglers.

**FLYER FOR JOHNNY MOPED
AT BRIGHTON POLYTECHNIC**
7 May 1977
36.1 x 25.4 cm, 14¼ x 10 in

Noteworthy for having once included Chrissie Hynde of the Pretenders and Captain Sensible of the Damned, Johnny Moped were one of the pioneering, if short-lived, punk bands to play live in the first few months of the Roxy.

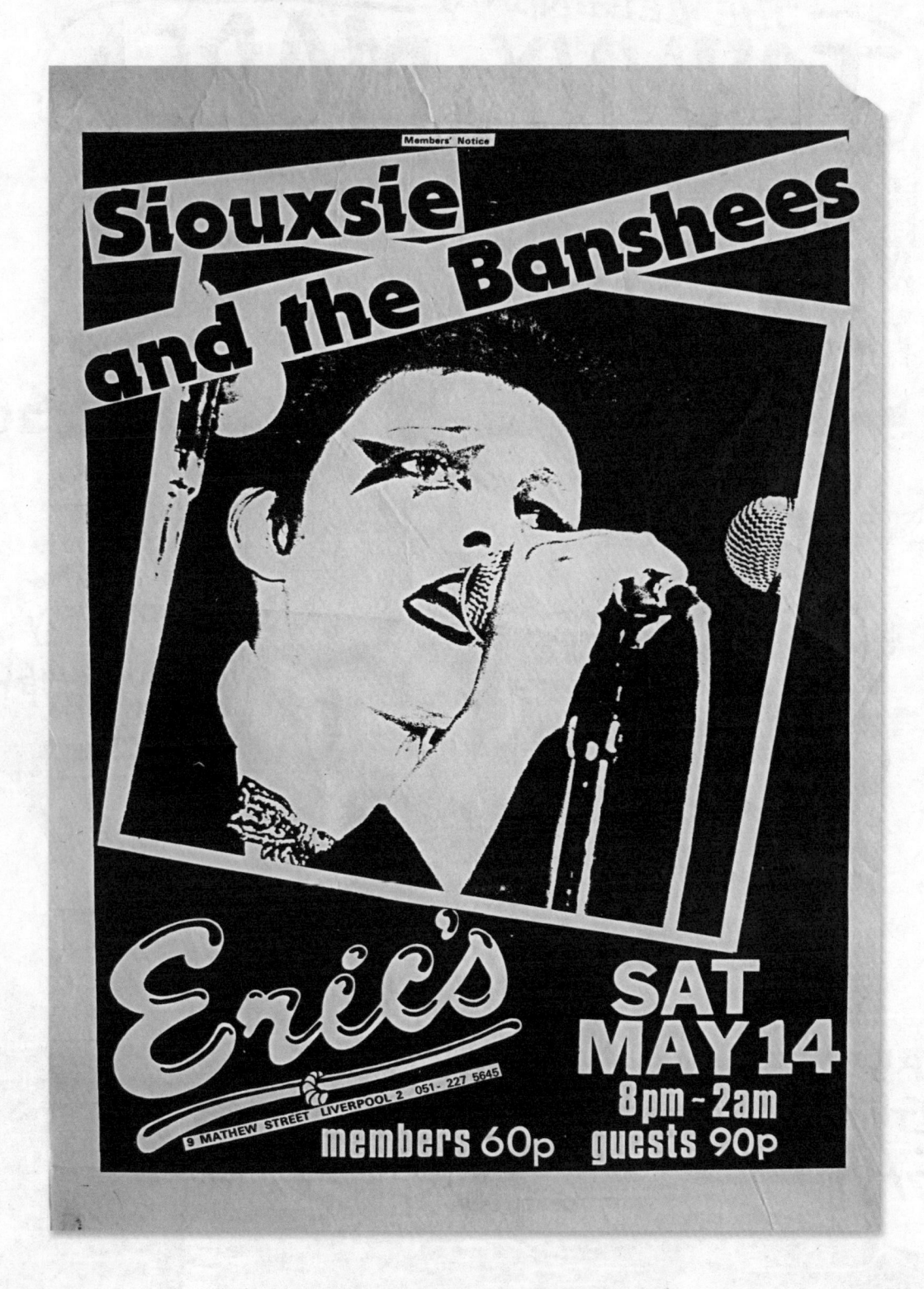

**POSTER FOR SIOUXSIE AND THE BANSHEES
AT ERIC'S, LIVERPOOL**
14 May 1977
63.5 x 44.4 cm, 25 x 17½ in

**FLYER FOR JOHNNY MOPED
AT THE BUCCANEER, BRIGHTON**
16 May 1977
33 × 21.5 cm, 13 × 8½ in

This offset lithography flyer carries promotional text: 'He's got a band behind him that he, and you, can really sweat too [sic]. Dave – drums, or that should be DRUMS, Fred Burk – bass and Slimey Toad – guitar. Altogether they're as tight as a fist.'

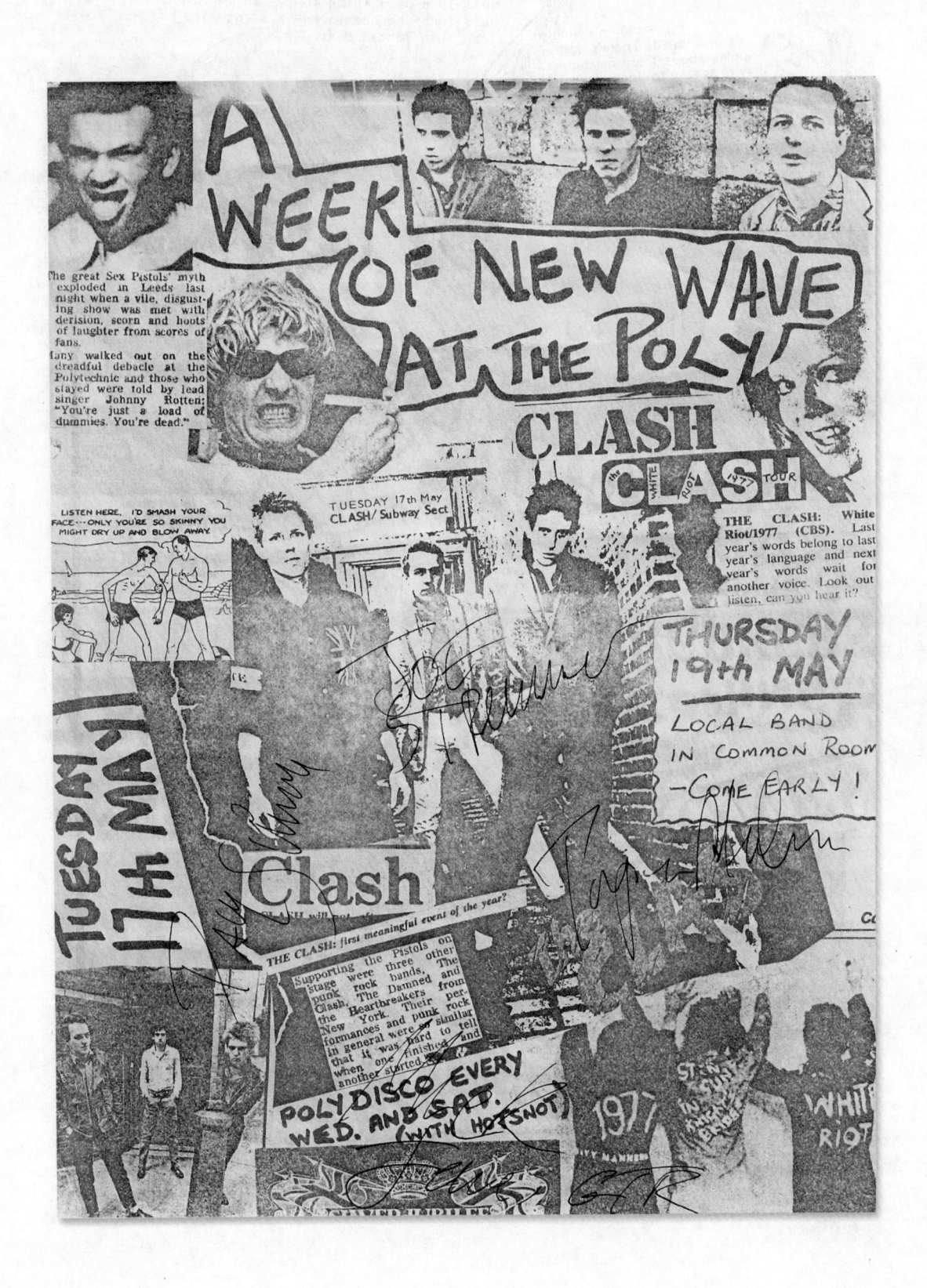

**AUTOGRAPHED FLYER FOR THE CLASH
AT LEEDS POLYTECHNIC**
17 May 1977
29.2 x 20.9 cm, 11½ x 8¼ in

This double-sided flyer advertises 'a week of New Wave at the Poly' and gigs that include the Clash, the Ramones and Johnny Thunders & the Heartbreakers. The flyer was autographed by the Clash after the performance.

Jubilee: official
THE SURFACE WORLD WILL BE MINE!!
Ramones drop 'sniff' track
RAMONES
"I REMEMBER YOU" THE RAMONES
SINGLE AVAILABLE NOW 6078 603
phonogram
RAMONES
FRIDAY 20th May
RAMONES/TALKING HEADS
THE RAMONES
FRIDAY 20th MAY
TALKING HEADS
COMING....
PUNK ROCK!
HEARTBREAKERS
JUNE 3rd
A BONE-CHILLING, NERVE-FRYING EPIC.. WILL KEEP YOU SCREAMING FOR DAYS!"
REX REED, NEW YORK DAILY NEWS
THERE MUST FOREVER BE A GUARDIAN AT THE GATES OF HELL...
She was young. She was beautiful. She was next!
the sentinel
GOD SAVE THE QUEEN
CLASH
SNIFFIN GLUE... AND OTHER ROCK'N' ROLL HABITS!

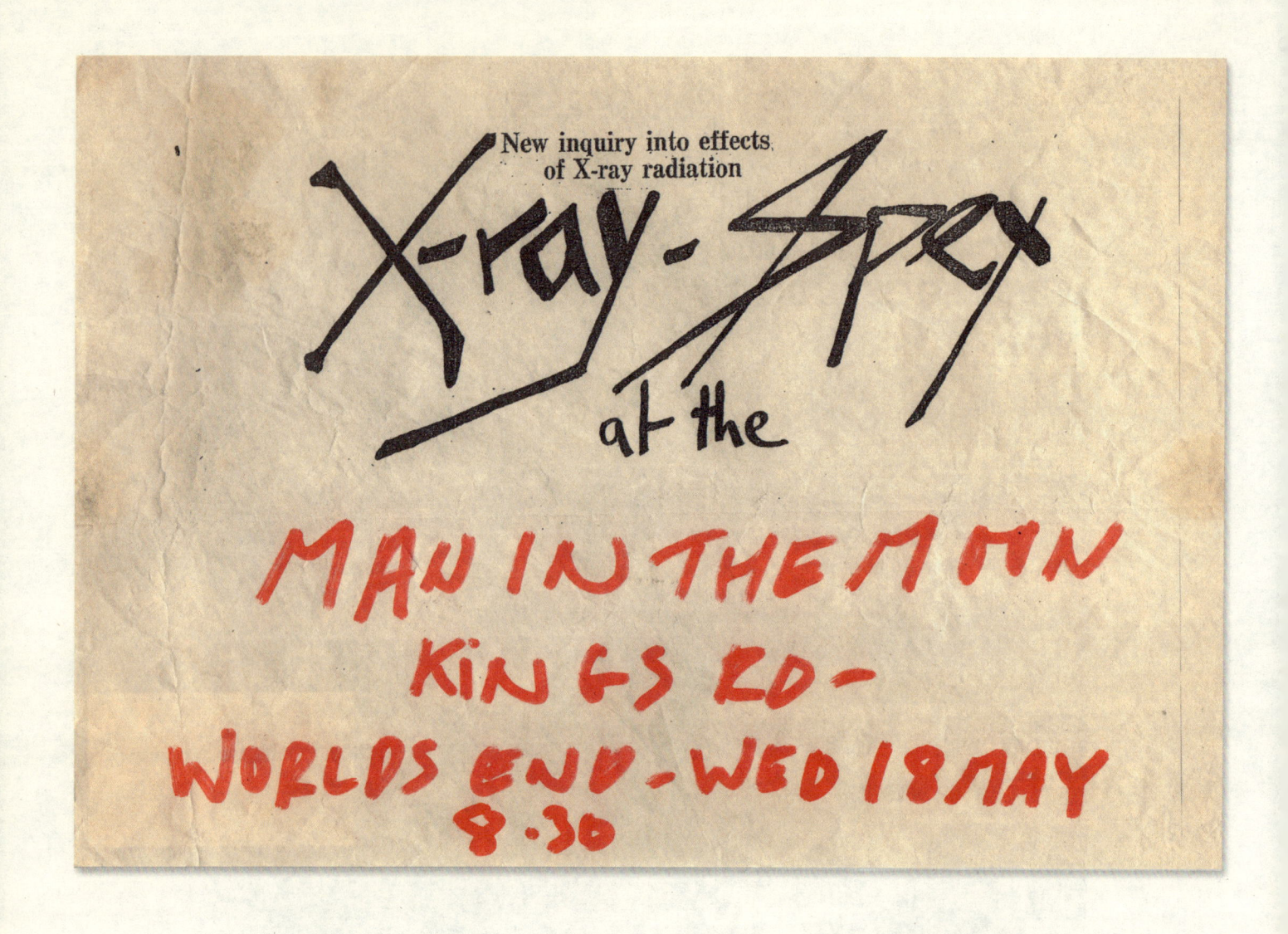

**FLYER FOR X-RAY SPEX
AT THE MAN IN THE MOON, LONDON**
18 May 1977
20.9 × 29.8 cm, 8¼ × 11¾ in

The Man in the Moon was a theatre on Kings Road, where acts such as Adam and the Ants performed. *Sounds* magazine wrote about this concert, describing the venue as 'a smallish basement room, low-ceilinged, with a bar along one wall, and quite plush – tonite healthily full with about 100 people. A stopgap scene – relaxed – I mean you gotta have somewhere to go nights now the Roxy's closed.'

**POSTER FOR THE CLASH'S SINGLES
'REMOTE CONTROL' AND 'LONDON'S BURNING'**
20 May 1977
29.8 x 20.9 cm, 11¾ x 8¼ in

ADVERTISEMENT FOR THE DAMNED AND THE ADVERTS IN MELODY MAKER
28 May 1977
41.9 × 29.2 cm, 16½ × 11½ in

Listing all the June tour dates and information about the Damned's single 'Neat Neat Neat' and the album *Damned Damned Damned*, the flyer also reads, 'The Damned can now play three chords. The Adverts can play one.'

POSTER FOR THE JAM'S 'IN THE CITY'
1977
71.1 x 49.5 cm, 28 x 19½ in

The wall behind the band was constructed in the studio for this photo shoot with Martyn Goddard. Bill Smith's graffiti was so striking, it was often displayed behind the band when they performed.

'GOD SAVE THE QUEEN' ARTWORK

The image of Queen Elizabeth II covered in Jamie Reid's ransom-note lettering is perhaps the best-known Pistols artwork. The original photograph is an official 1977 Silver Jubilee portrait by Royal photographer Peter Grugeon. Reid created two versions: the one seen here, with the band's name over the Queen's face, and another with swastikas over the Queen's eyes and a safety pin through her lips.

In 1970 Reid had co-founded *Suburban Press*, which developed into a political forum for Situationist slogans and allegations of local corruption. There he honed the unique style he would later employ for punk graphics, which used photocopiers with saturated colours, litho reproduction and unconventional typography. Reid created many images for the Sex Pistols, including the cover for *Never Mind the Bollocks, Here's the Sex Pistols*.

**POSTER FOR THE SEX PISTOLS' SINGLE
'GOD SAVE THE QUEEN'**
Jamie Reid
May 1977
69.2 x 98.4 cm, 27¼ x 38¾ in

**STICKER FOR THE SEX PISTOLS' SINGLE
'GOD SAVE THE QUEEN'**
Jamie Reid
1977
12.7 x 10.1 cm, 5 x 4 in

This sticker depicts Queen Elizabeth II with a cup of tea placed irreverently on her head. This is the rarer of the two issued designs.

**STICKER FOR THE SEX PISTOLS' SINGLE
'GOD SAVE THE QUEEN'**
Jamie Reid
May 1977
20.9 × 14.6 cm, 8¼ × 5¾ in

This sticker includes the caption 'She Ain't No Human Being', lifted from the song's lyrics.

**POSTER FOR THE SEX PISTOLS' SINGLE
'GOD SAVE THE QUEEN'**
Jamie Reid
May 1977
61.5 x 44.4 cm, 24¼ x 17½ in

When the image of the queen with swastikas on her eyeballs was originally submitted to A&M as the cover for the single, it was banned. It appeared later on a poster issued in Spain.

**FRENCH POSTCARD FOR THE SEX PISTOLS'
SINGLE 'GOD SAVE THE QUEEN'**
Jamie Reid
1977
13.9 x 10.7 cm, 5½ x 4¼ in

TRASH-77 #3
Craig Campbell
[May] 1977
29.8 x 20.9 cm, 11¾ x 8¼ in

Craig Campbell started this Glasgow-based zine to fill the gap left when Tony Drayton moved *Ripped & Torn* to London. This issue includes an interview with Joe Strummer of the Clash and reviews the group's appearance in Edinburgh on 7 May. The cover refers to the Sex Pistols' single 'God Save the Queen'.

ARTWORK FOR THE ONLY ONES' SINGLE 'LOVERS OF TODAY'
1 June 1977
75.5 x 50.1 cm, 29¾ x 19¾ in

This rejected artwork was originally intended for the cover of the Only Ones' debut single 'Lovers of Today'. The final artwork features a black-and-white image of the band.

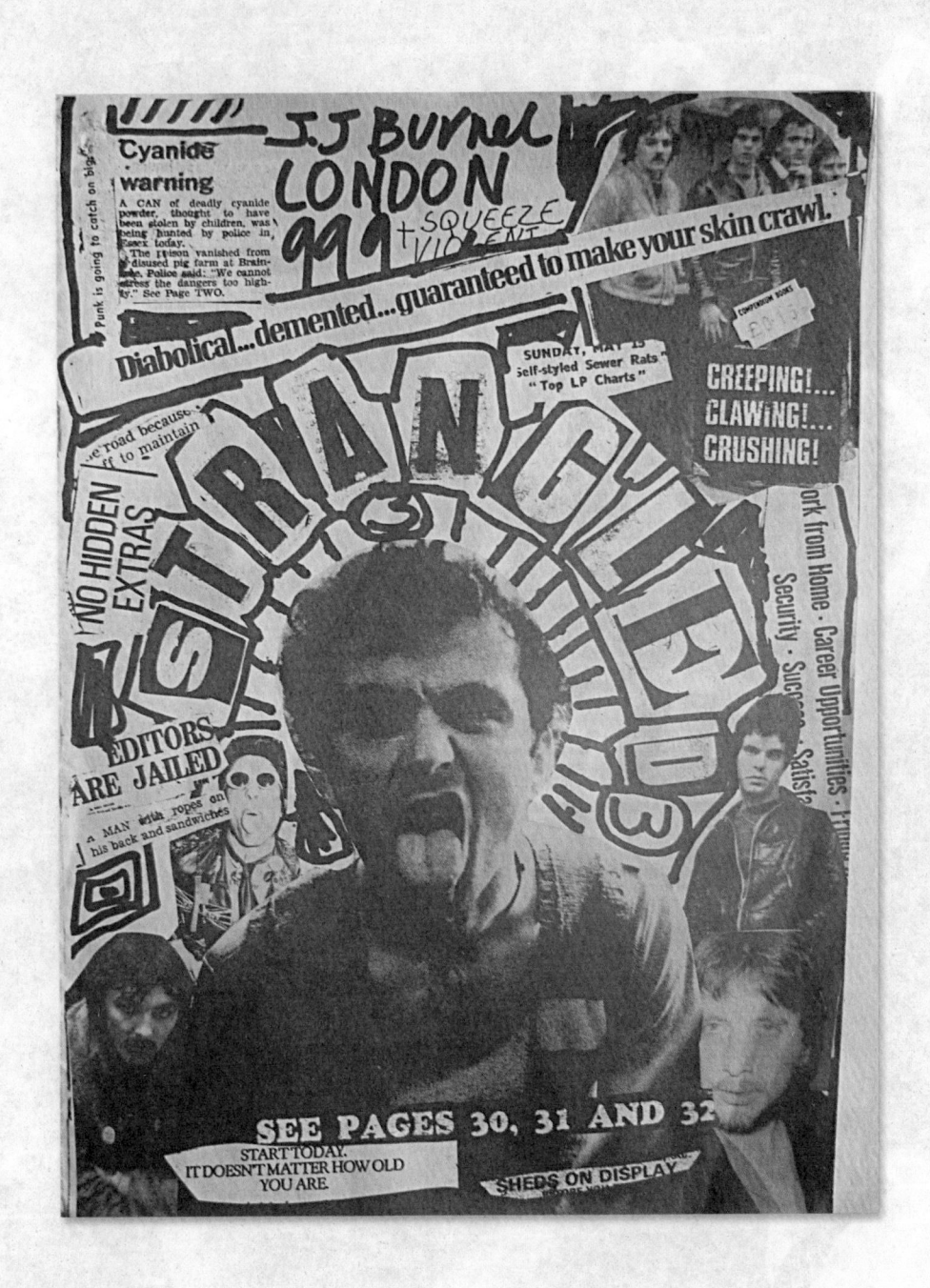

STRANGLED #3
1977
[dims unknown]

Includes Squeeze and 999.

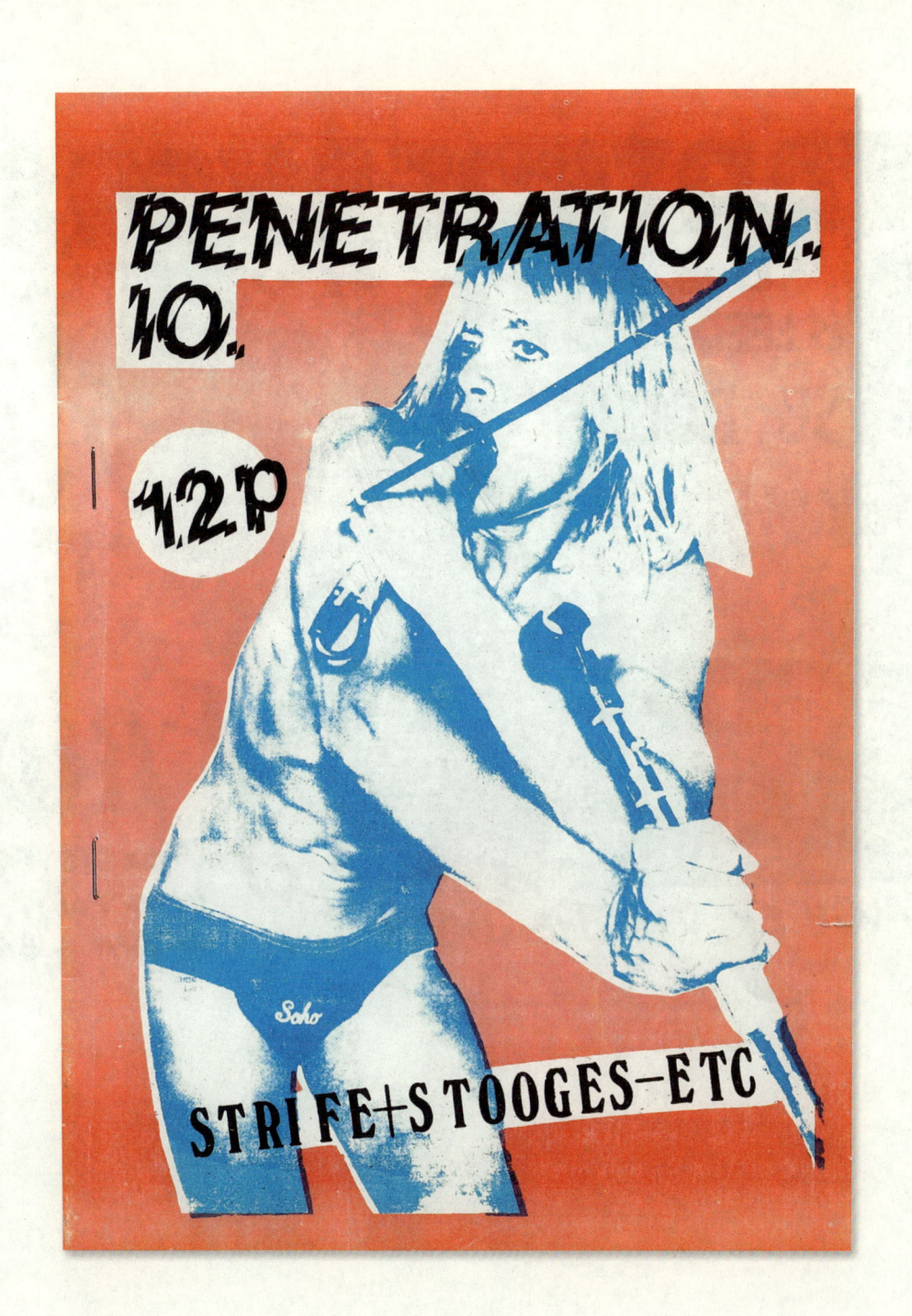

PENETRATION #10
Paul Welsh
1977
24.1 x 16.5 cm, 9½ x 6½ in

Features Iggy Pop, Buzzcocks and Strife.

**FLYER FOR THE HEARTBREAKERS
AT LEEDS POLYTECHNIC**
3 June 1977
20.9 × 29.2 cm, 8¼ × 11½ in

The New York punk group had relocated in 1976 to the UK, where they enjoyed some success. In 1977, Johnny Thunders & the Heartbreakers released their only album, *LAMF* (an abbreviation for 'like a motherfucker'), and went on to tour the US and the UK. This flyer promotes the Heartbreakers' singles 'Chinese Rocks' and 'Born to Lose'.

SNIFFIN' GLUE #10
Mark Perry
June 1977
29.8 x 20.9 cm, 11¾ x 8¼ in

Features articles on Chelsea, Johnny Moped and John Cale and information on the Clash's 'White Riot' tour.

The NEW WAVE magazine 5

LAST TIME I wrote about the current crop of fanzines, I was sent a Patti Smith bootleg by *Panache* and involved in a public scuffle with *New Wave*. I can only hope that a multitude of fights and free albums will result from the following Shock Horror Probe...

New Wave is as boringly wimpy and wet as ever. The 30p this would set you back could get you three copies of the *News Of The World!*

Ramones interview

30p

THE NEW WAVE MAGAZINE #5
[June] 1977
29.2 x 22.2 cm, 11½ x 8¾ in

Includes a Ramones interview.

LOOK AT THE [FUCKING] TIME #1
June 1977
33 x 20.3 cm, 13 x 8 in

According to text inside this issue: 'The magazine used to be called NFA, but as you can see we've changed the name to *Look at the Fucking Time*. It seems that some people thought we were a National Front mag, but in fact NFA stood for No Fixed Abode. Really, then, this is the 2nd issue.' Contains reviews of the Jam in Cambridge and the Transmitters at the Roxy. The last page is a rant about the demise of punk: 'The whole thing has become commercialised ... the groups are getting worse ... I thought it was gonna be all different but I was stupid and naive.'

SILVER JUBILEE

The Silver Jubilee of Elizabeth II in 1977 marked the 25th anniversary of the Queen's ascension to the throne. The occasion was celebrated throughout the year with large parties and parades in the United Kingdom and Commonwealth, culminating in June with 'Jubilee Day', which coincided with the Queen's birthday. (The actual anniversary of her ascension on 6 February was observed with church services throughout the month.) In Britain Jubilee Day – 7 June 1977 – was a national bank holiday.

**EVENING NEWS' PROMOTIONAL BOARD,
'LONDON'S BIG JUBILEE STREET PARTIES'**
June 1977
73 x 43.8 cm, 28¾ x 17¼ in

QUEEN ELIZABETH II SILVER JUBILEE
DUFEX PRINTS
F. J. Warren Ltd
1977
15.8 x 20.9 cm, 6¼ x 8¼ in

SILVER JUBILEE CARRIER BAG
1977
46.3 x 39.3 cm, 18¼ x 15½ in

Jubilee celebrations have long been the occasion for commemorative items, the most popular being stamps, coins and ceramics. The earliest royal mementoes date back to the Restoration of Charles II in 1660. Queen Elizabeth II's Silver Jubilee inspired a whole new range of keepsakes, including plates, socks, jigsaw puzzles, T-shirts and shopping bags.

141

CAMP TIMES
June–July 1977
[dims unknown]

This is the first cover of *Camp Times*, the UK gay liberation magazine. This edition features a parody of the celebratory publications produced for the Jubilee.

**POSTER FOR THE VIBRATORS' ALBUM
PURE MANIA**
June 1977
100.9 x 75.5 cm, 39¾ x 29¾ in

The Vibrators were singer-guitarist Ian 'Knox' Carnochan, bassist Pat Collier, guitarist John Ellis and drummer Eddie (aka John Edwards). The group formed in February '76 and supported groups like the Sex Pistols, the Stranglers and Iggy Pop. With Robin Mayhew as co-producer, Epic released *Pure Mania*, which cracked the Top 50 in the UK.

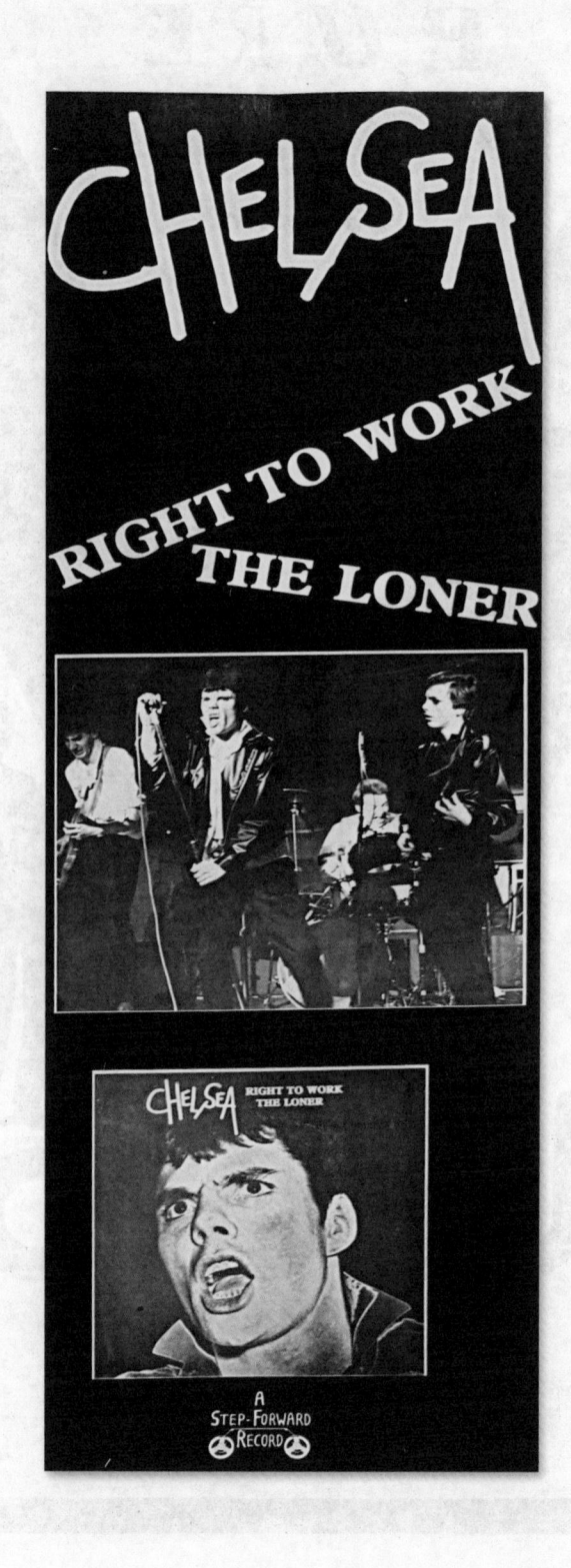

**POSTER FOR CHELSEA'S SINGLE
'RIGHT TO WORK'**
June 1977
73 x 24.7 cm, 28¾ x 9¾ in

Step Forward Records in-store promo.

ADVERTISEMENT FOR MUSIC WEEK'S TOP 50 SINGLES
11 June 1977
[dims unknown]

Shows the Sex Pistols' 'God Save The Queen' at No. 2 in the charts, despite the widely held view at the time that the record reached the top spot.

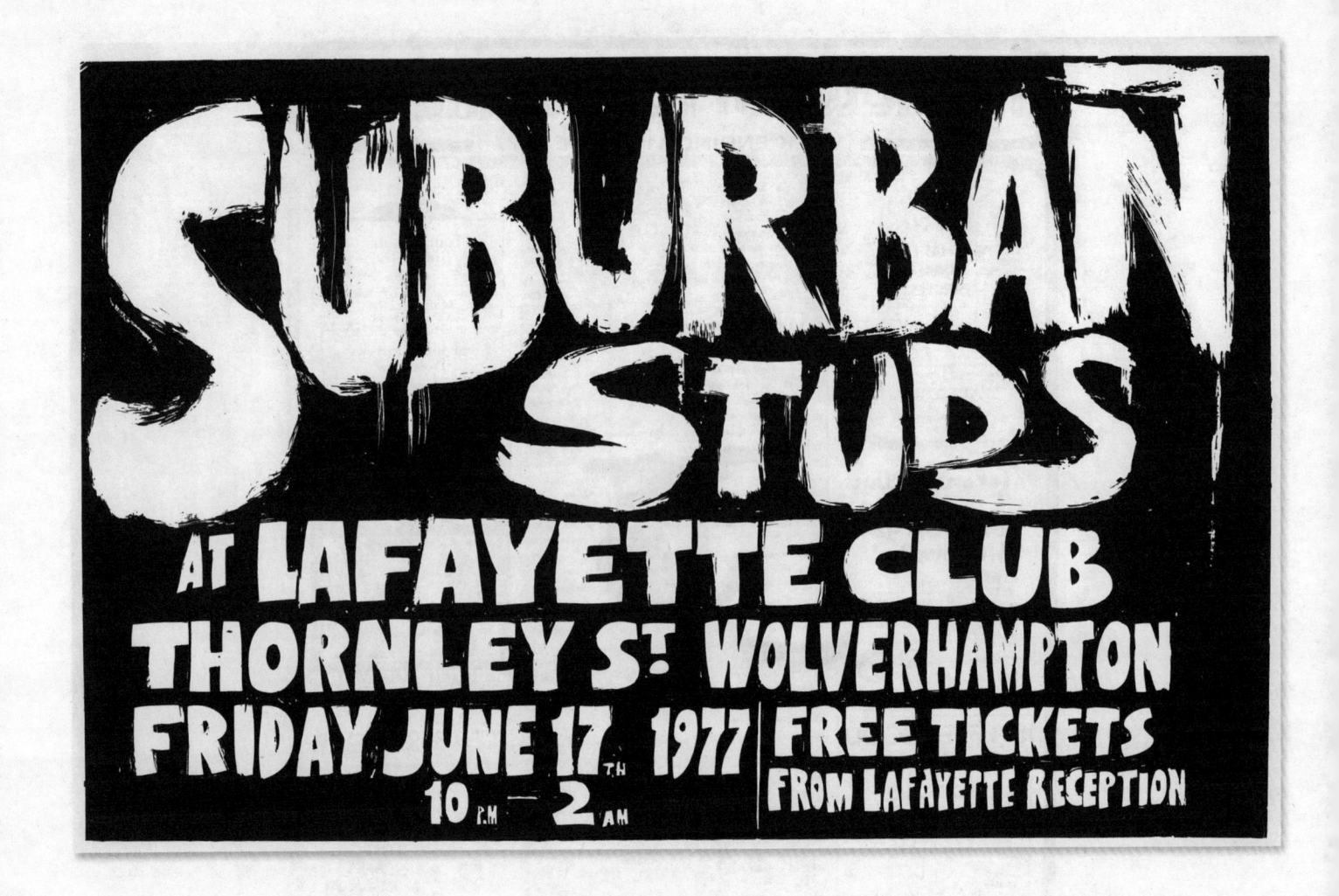

**POSTER FOR SUBURBAN STUDS
AT THE LAFAYETTE CLUB, WOLVERHAMPTON**
17 June 1977
51.4 x 76.2 cm, 20¼ x 30 in

Suburban Studs was one of the first punk bands to sign to an independent label, Pogo Records, and market themselves via a major label, WEA Records. The band's only record, *Slam*, was released the same year.

SOUNDS MAGAZINE
18 June 1977
40 x 30.4 cm, 15¾ x 12 in

This issue of *Sounds* – a weekly publication similar to *NME* – details the Sex Pistols' infamous trip on the River Thames to promote the single 'God Save the Queen' during Queen Elizabeth II's Silver Jubilee celebration.

147

**FLYER FOR THE JAM
AT THE OUTLOOK, DONCASTER**
20 June 1977
29.8 × 20.9 cm, 11¾ × 8¼ in

ROCK AGAINST RACISM'S RIGHT TO WORK CAMPAIGN POSTER WITH BUZZCOCKS AND THE VERBALS
25 June 1977
64.1 x 45 cm, 25¼ x 17¾ in

The Fall also played but are not listed on the poster. Rock Against Racism linked with the Right to Work Campaign 1977, which sought to advocate on behalf of the unemployed in Great Britain.

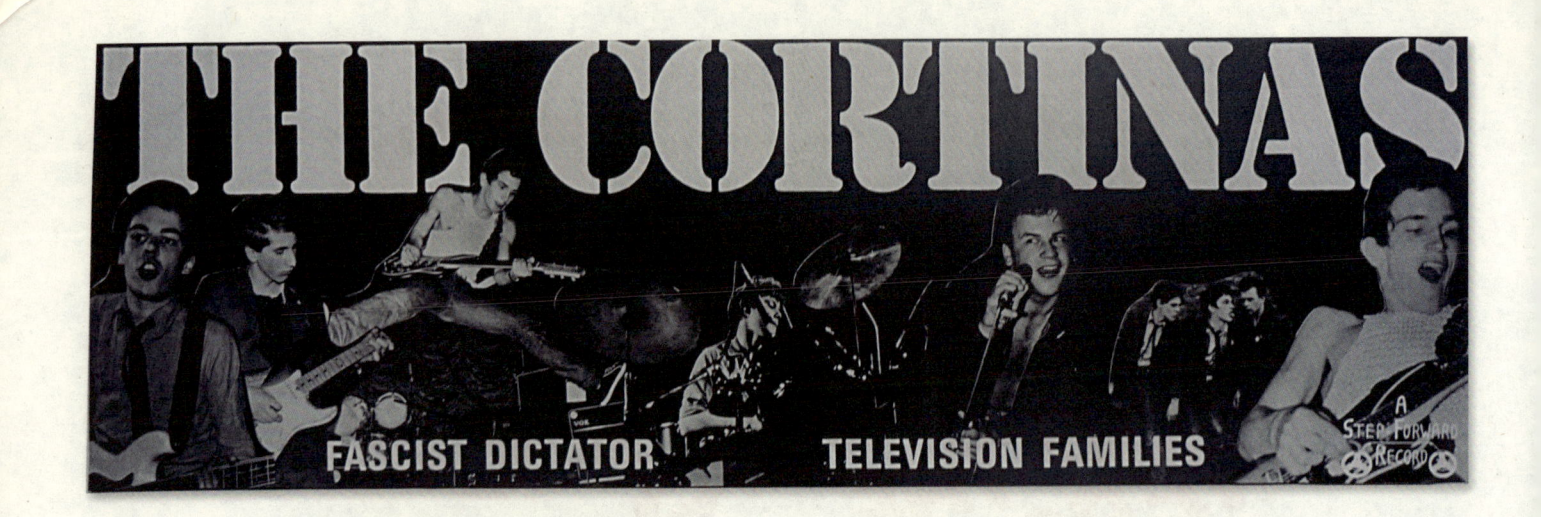

**POSTER FOR THE CORTINAS' EP
'FASCIST DICTATOR'**
June 1977
[dims unknown]

Rough Trade in-store promo.

POSTER FOR THE VIBRATORS' LIVE SINGLE 'LONDON GIRLS'
June 1977
50.8 x 30.4 cm, 20 x 12 in

The single's B-side, 'Stiff Little Fingers', would later inspire the group of the same name.

**POSTER FOR THE DAMNED AND THE ADVERTS
AT THE UNIVERSITY OF LANCASTER**
27 June 1977
75 x 50.1 cm, 29½ x 19¾ in

**FLYER FOR THE VIBRATORS, THE SLITS
AND OTHERS AT LEEDS POLYTECHNIC**
30 June 1977
29.2 x 20.9 cm, 11½ x 8¼ in

The Vibrators' 'Pure Mania' tour dates are printed on the reverse of the flyer, which incorporates images from the group's debut album.

POSTER FOR SUBURBAN STUDS' SINGLE 'QUESTIONS'
June 1977
75.6 x 50.8 cm, 29¾ x 20 in

LIVE WIRE #7
July 1977
29.2 x 20.9 cm, 11½ x 8¼ in

Includes articles and photos of the Sex Pistols, the Adverts, Generation X and Chelsea, and material on the Roxy.

WHITE STUFF #4
July 1977
29.8 x 20.9 cm, 11¾ x 8¼ in

BORED STIFF #1
C. Terry et al., Tyneside Free Press
July 1977
[dims unknown]

The inaugural issue of the zine includes articles on the Jam and the Sex Pistols, as well as a lengthy interview with Penetration's Pauline Murray.

POSTER FOR THE SEX PISTOLS' SINGLE 'PRETTY VACANT'
Jamie Reid
1 July 1977
69.2 x 99.6 cm, 27¼ x 39¼ in

The crowd photographs were taken from a film shot at the Sex Pistols' concert on 3 April 1977 at the Screen on the Green in Islington, the first concert in which Sid Vicious played with the band.

POSTER FOR THE SEX PISTOLS' SINGLE 'PRETTY VACANT'
Jamie Reid
July 1977
72.3 x 100.9 cm, 28½ x 39¾ in

Reid's image of two buses – both originally with 'nowhere' as their terminus – originated in 1972 with Suburban Press. San Francisco Situationist group Point-Blank picked up the image the following year for a pamphlet about the city's transit policy. It appeared again in 1976 in the Sex Pistols' *Anarchy* zine, and in its final form (with 'Nowhere' and 'Boredom' as the destinations) on the back of the picture sleeve for the single 'Pretty Vacant'.

**BANNER FOR THE SEX PISTOLS'
SINGLE 'PRETTY VACANT'**
Jamie Reid
1977
[dims unknown]

Virgin Records in-store promo.

SNIFFIN' GLUE #11
Mark Perry
July 1977
29.8 x 20.9 cm, 11¾ x 8¼ in

Features Johnny Rotten, the Clash and the Damned, all on the cover; an ad for Throbbing Gristle; and a review of the Modern Lovers.

THE NATIONAL FRONT

The National Front was formed in 1967 from the remnants of the League of Empire Loyalists, the British National Party and the Racial Preservation Society. The NF supported institutionalised racism in the name of reducing competition for jobs and lowering unemployment. Candidates for local election campaigned on the group's nationalist, anti-immigrant platform into the late '70s, but the group fell apart after 1979 when none of its candidates won seats.

NATIONAL FRONT, 'AN INTRODUCTION TO THE NATIONAL FRONT'
1970s
30.4 x 20.9 cm, 12 x 8¼ in

The group's two most identifiable logos are a torch with the Union Jack emblazoned on its flame and the same flag cut, like a puzzle piece, into the conjoined letters 'NF'.

**NATIONAL FRONT POSTER,
'HANG IRA MURDERERS'**
1970s
56.5 x 43.8 cm, 22¼ x 17¼ in

**NATIONAL FRONT POSTER,
'WORK NOT DOLE NOW'**
1970s
44.4 x 29.8 cm, 17½ x 11¾ in

'Work Not Dole Now' was amongst the slogans used by the NF when increasing oil prices led to stagflation and unemployment started to rise.

ANTI-NAZI LEAGUE BADGES
1977
4.4 cm, 1¾ in diameter

ANTI NAZI LEAGUE

Are you unemployed ? a school leaver with no hope of getting a job ? or are you stuck in a deadend low paid job because there are no others ? It's a story that has been repeated since the twenties all over Europe but it's a story that has different endings.

In Germany in the twenties many people, usually those not organised in bodies like trade unions, gave their votes to the Nazi Party because they offered a solution to a desperate economic situation. Their solution was to prepare the country for war by making weapons (and therefore profits) and shoving down wages by mass murder and terror. Jews were scapegoats for the crisis.

The National Front and the British Movement, who are recruiting young people to their ranks, are open supporters of Hitler's ideas. They blame black people for the economic crisis. (You may be forgiven for thinking this view is shared by Labour and Conservative governments who have competed to introduce tougher immigration laws.)

The Nazi National Front got walked all over at the last election. Now they are turning to street violence and intimidation of Blacks, Asians and anybody who disagrees with them. They would have us believe that Blacks cause unemployment. But it's not Blacks that close down factories. If profits are not high enough the BOSSES shut down plants or save money by paying fewer workers.

British bosses, bankers, judges and police chiefs are not OUR people. Racism works to their advantage and divides working people when the need for unity to fight for jobs is more important than ever.

Fascism is not just a threat to Blacks and Jews, but to all working people. Let's stop the NF and BM

SAY NO TO NAZIS.

Get them out of the football grounds and shopping centres

If you want more details about the Anti Nazi League send to

P O BOX 51
LONDON SW 10

ANTI-NAZI LEAGUE
1970s
28.5 x 20.3 cm, 11¼ x 8 in

Unemployment and race were politically charged issues in the 1970s. The Anti-Nazi League argued that blame for high levels of unemployment should be laid at the feet of the 'bosses, bankers, judges and police chiefs' rather than racial minorities in the country.

DANGER!
NAZIS AT WORK

AN OPENLY RACIST PARTY IS ASKING FOR YOUR SUPPORT — WITHOUT DISCLOSING WHAT THEY REALLY STAND FOR

IN PUBLIC THEY DENY THE NAZI LABEL

But in private they reveal the truth, as Tyndall did in a letter to an American Nazi:
"To be frank, I do not believe that a movement with an open Nazi label has a hope of winning national power either in Britain or the UK in the forseeable future. I have therefore sought to modify the form of our programme though not of course the essence of our ideology...Our strategy is to use the moderate elements, to work behind them for as long as is necessary, but to effectively control them."
"We are busy building a well-oiled Nazi machine in this country" (National Organiser Martin Webster)

THEY CLAIM THEY ARE 'JUST PATRIOTIC'

A closer look at their 'patriotism' reveals rife and strident anti-semitism.
"The Jew is like a poisonous maggot feeding on a body in an advanced state of decay." John Tyndall
And,
"We did not fight for our own freedom (in the Second World War), we fought for the freedom of the parasitic Jew to leech unmolested." Tyndall

THEY SAY THEY ARE FOR LAW AND ORDER

But they have a record for crimes of violence unmatched by any other organisation — except that of professional criminals. Listen to Wandsworth organiser, Ken Hampton:
"We've got some really vicious bastards. I'd never cross a couple of them...My branch is the biggest gang of thugs in London. We've got one guy who's done 18 months for nicking new cars. I've got numerous cases of burglaries and I think there's even a couple of cases of armed robbery!"

DON'T BE FOOLED! SAY NO TO RACISM!

Anti Nazi League

P&P NORWICH ANTI-NAZI LEAGUE, C/O BOX 151, LONDON.

ANTI-NAZI LEAGUE LEAFLET, 'DANGER! NAZIS AT WORK'
Mid-1970s
29.8 x 20.9 cm, 11¾ x 8½ in

Fearful that the National Front was gaining political clout in the country, the Anti-Nazi League distributed nearly nine million leaflets between 1977 and 1979.

THE NAZIONAL FRONT...

this is the truth

"We are busy setting up a well-oiled Nazi machine in this country"

MARTIN WEBSTER
National Activities Organiser
of the National Front

ANTI-NATIONAL FRONT LEAFLET
The National Committee Against Fascism
1970s
31.75 x 20.9 cm, 12½ x 8¼ in

The NEW WAVE magazine 6

INSIDE: BUZZCOCKS INTERVIEW
with Pete Shelley
HEARTBREAKERS INTERVIEW
with Walter Lure
and Stranglers, Damned, X-Ray Spex...

30p

THE NEW WAVE MAGAZINE #6
[July] 1977
29.2 × 20.9 cm, 11½ × 8¼ in

Contains interviews with Buzzcocks and Johnny Thunders & the Heartbreakers and articles about the Stranglers, the Damned and X-Ray Spex.

PUNKTURE #2
July 1977
29.2 x 20.9 cm, 11½ x 8¼ in

Featuring the Clash, the Vibrators and the Rezillos.

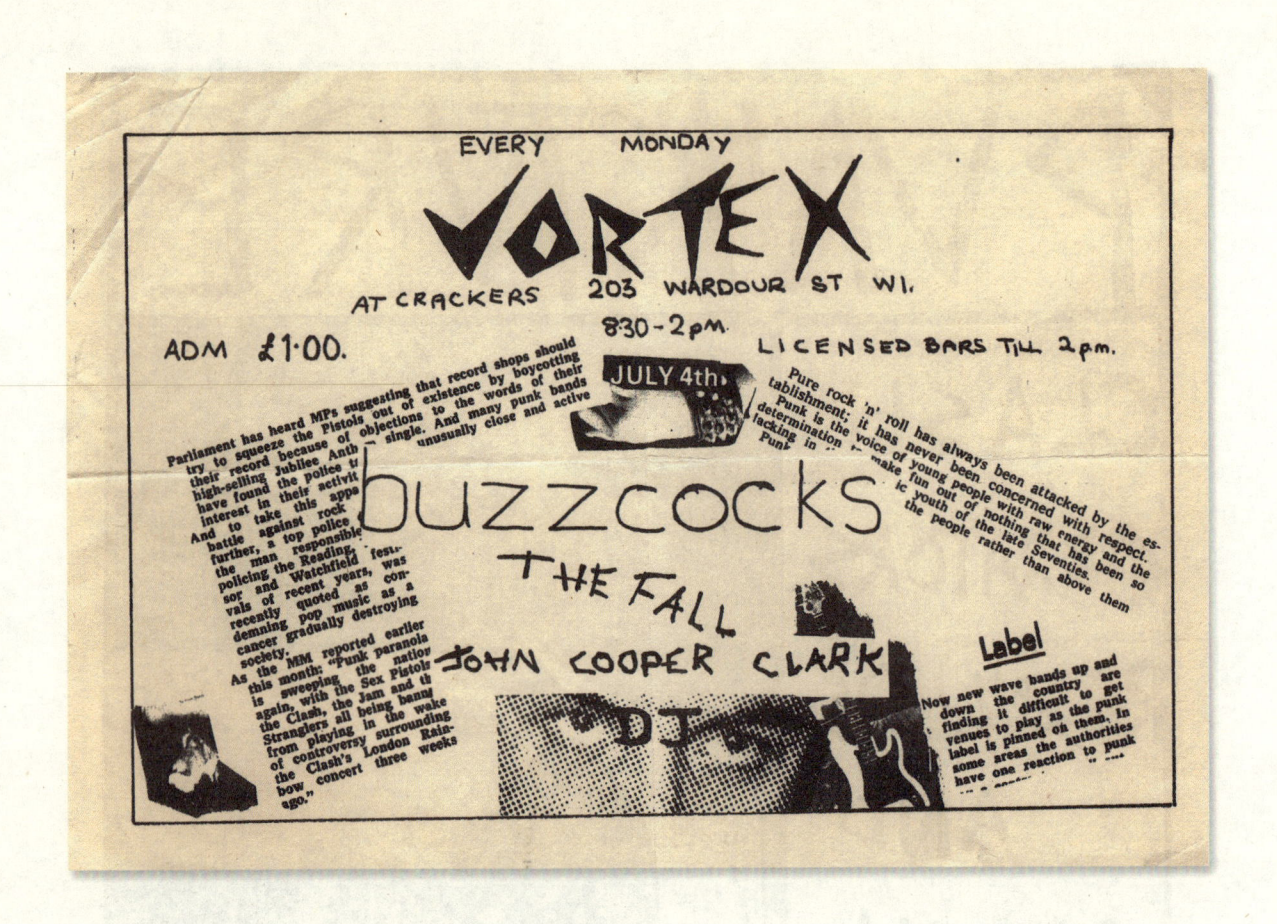

FLYER FOR BUZZCOCKS, THE FALL AND JOHN COOPER CLARKE AT CRACKERS, LONDON
4 July 1977
15.2 x 22.2 cm, 6 x 8¾ in

This flyer advertises the first concert organised by Vortex at Crackers in London on 4 July 1977. Buzzcocks, the Fall and John Cooper Clarke played the event alongside an unscheduled appearance by Johnny Thunders (born John Anthony Genzale Jr) and his group the Heartbreakers.

THE SEX PISTOLS IN MELODY MAKER
9 July 1977
45.7 x 33 cm, 18 x 13 in

The paper depicts Johnny Rotten next to the words 'Pistols Retreat', and the article reads, 'Anti-punk violence came to a head this week when the Sex Pistols went into hiding after continuous attacks on them over the last few weeks.'

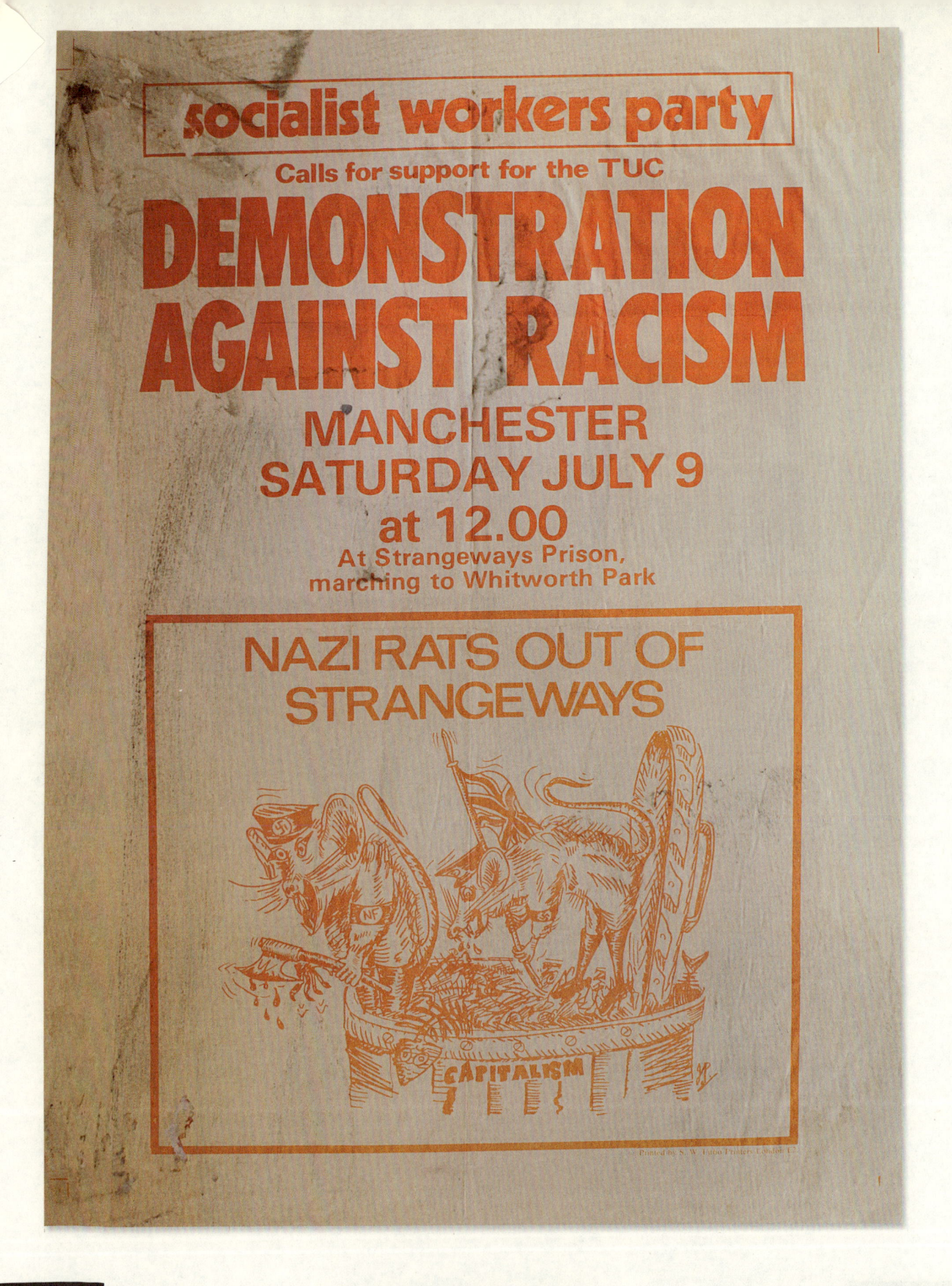

**SOCIALIST WORKERS PARTY,
'DEMONSTRATION AGAINST RACISM' POSTER**
9 July 1977
63.5 x 45 cm, 25 x 17¾ in

The Socialist Workers Party opposed war, capitalism and globalisation, as well as racism, and held a Demonstration Against Racism in July '77. The rats in the poster wear 'NF' for National Front on their armbands. Later, in *The National Front*, Nigel Fielding describes 'arrests of NF members in Manchester at a counter-demonstration against a union-backed racial harmony march', which was likely this SWP event.

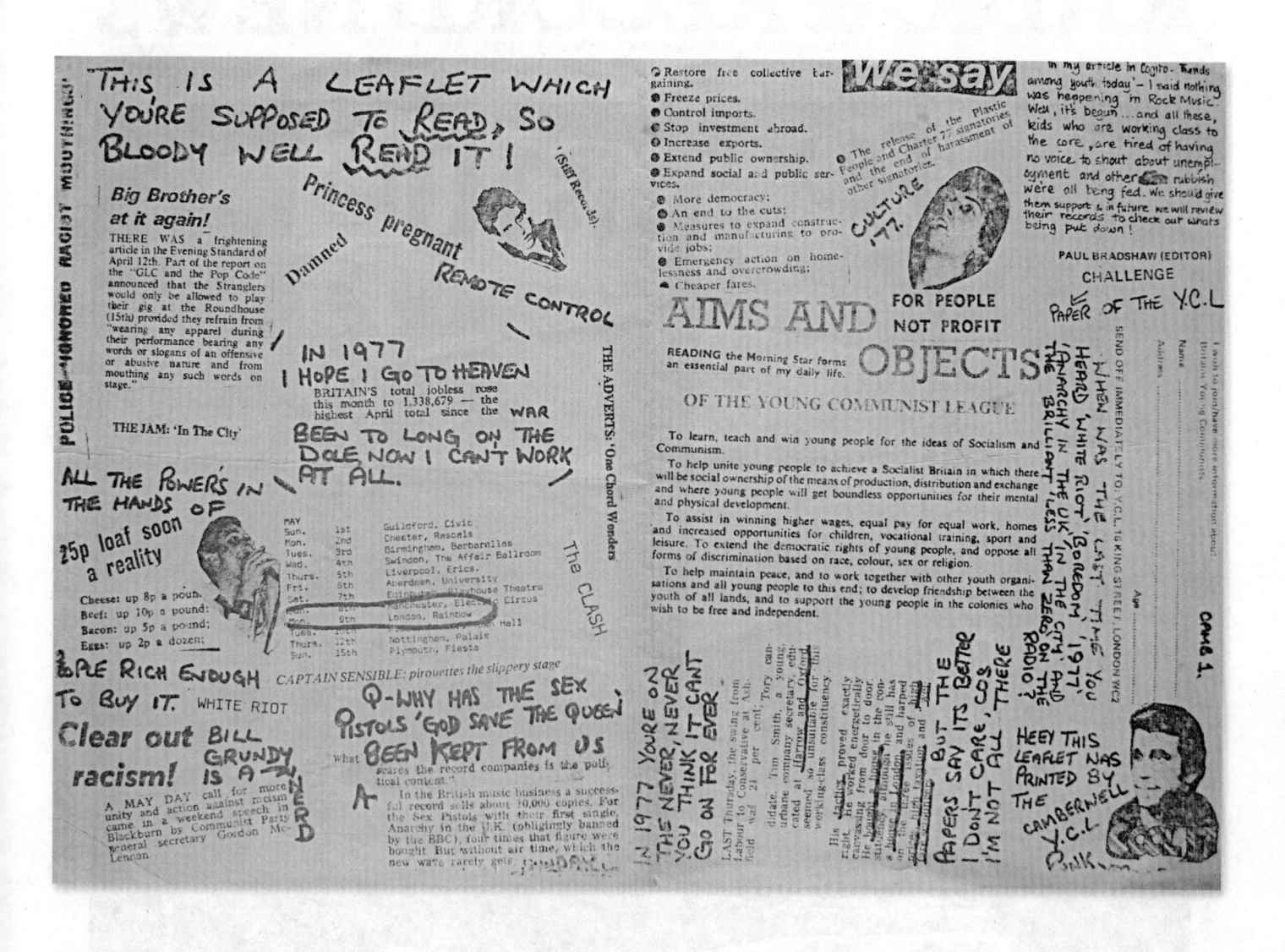

YOUNG COMMUNIST LEAGUE LEAFLET
Printed by the Camberwell YCL
1977
[dims unknown]

RADIO & RECORD NEWS
Incorporating NEEDLETIME : EVERY TUESDAY
Tuesday 12 July 1977
60p

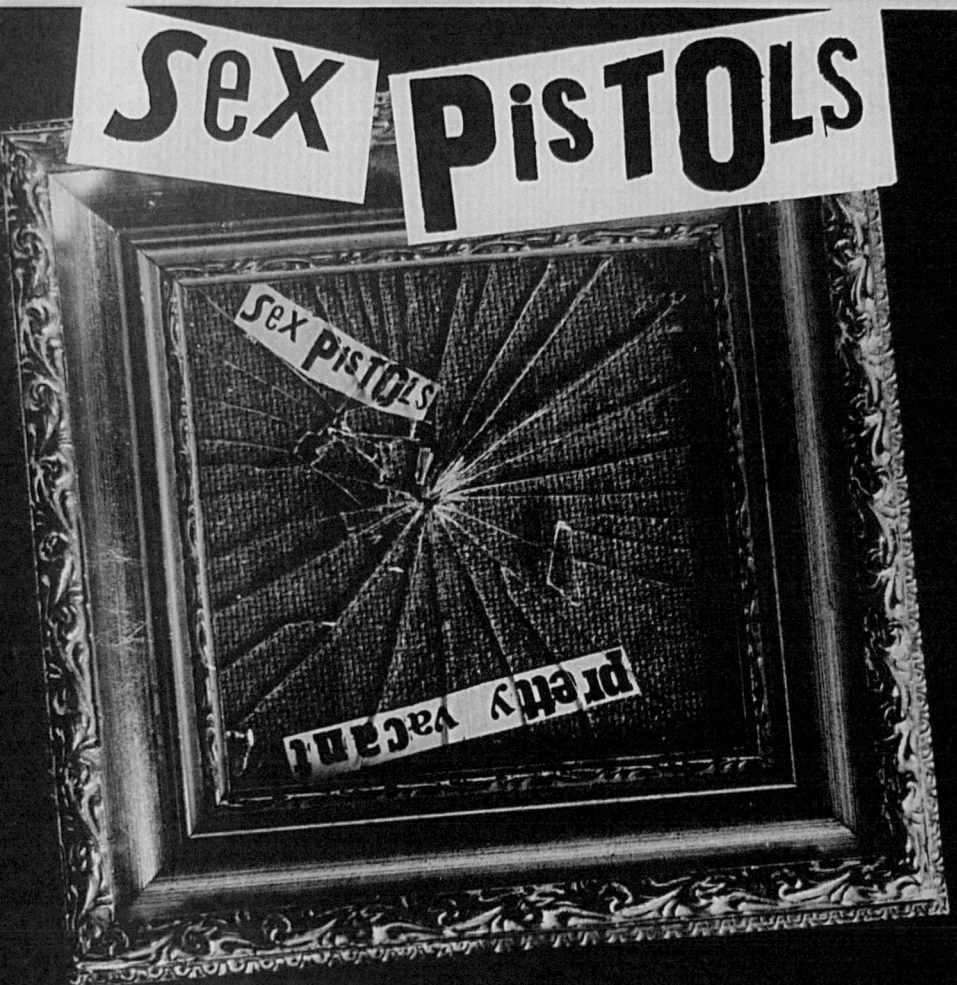

Sex Pistols

pretty vacant

VS 184

Pretty Vacant. A brand new, rush-released, highly non-controversial, innocent, friendly, loud and utterly fantastic three minutes of rock and roll that nobody, and that probably includes 'Top Of The Pops', nobody could possibly object to.
Pretty Vacant. Sex Pistols' incredible new single. Out and staying out on Virgin Records.
Pretty Vacant. Sex Pistols. Play it.

RADIO & RECORD NEWS
12 July 1977
[dims unknown]

Highlights the Sex Pistols and their single 'Pretty Vacant'.

REJECT PROMOTIONS
PRESENTS

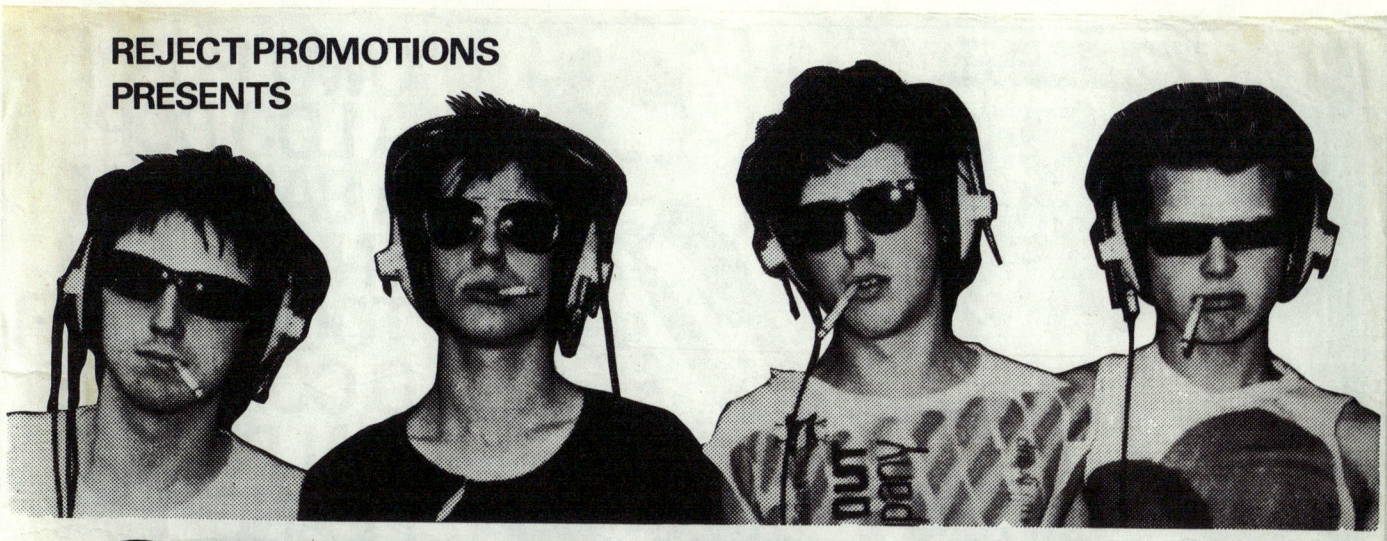

GENERATION X
+ SUPORT AT
FROM 9 p.m. - 1 a.m.   ON
TICKETS £1.25 FROM ANY HALF DECENT RECORD SHOP

CONCERT POSTER FOR GENERATION X
1977
50.8 x 76.2 cm, 20 x 30 in

Features large headshots of the band members, each with a dangling cigarette, sunglasses and headphones. A space for listing the venue is left blank.

"OWO POP A LOO BOP A BAM BAM SNUFF TOOTY STIFFI O CORPSEY MALBERG IN PLANO" WHO?

REVERSE OF FLYER FOR ALBERTO Y LOST TRIOS PARANOIAS' SLEAK AT THE ROYAL COURT THEATRE, LONDON
[July] 1977
15.2 x 34.2 cm, 6 x 13½ in

Double-sided flyer for the stage play *Sleak*, which starred Gordon Kaye and Julie Walters. The musical, written by C. P. Lee, is the story of a fictitious rock singer named Norman Sleak who commits suicide onstage. It premiered in May '77 as *Razor Blades and Round Shot*, and went on to have several runs in London and Rotterdam. The show played in the US shortly after the shooting of John Lennon, at a time when the American public had little appetite for a play about a pop star's suicide. The band's independently produced 'Snuff Rock', referenced on the reverse of the flyer, contains four tracks related to the musical.

THE SUNDAY TIMES *magazine*

JULY 17, 1977

A happy group of punks enjoying a joke at a punk ball

GORDON BURN, 'GOOD CLEAN PUNK',
SUNDAY TIMES MAGAZINE
17 July 1977
29.8 x 24.7 cm, 11¾ x 9¾ in

RIPPED & TORN #6
Tony Drayton
Summer 1977
29.2 x 20.9 cm, 11½ x 8¼ in

Includes interviews with the Electric Chairs and the Lurkers, as well as a poster of the Ramones. The cover replicates the cover of the Sex Pistols' single 'God Save the Queen', but replaces the face of Queen Elizabeth II with that of Johnny Rotten.

**ADVERTISEMENT FOR THE CLASH ET AL
AT THE BIRMINGHAM RAG MARKET (NME)**
Sebastian Conran
17 July 1977
[dims unknown]

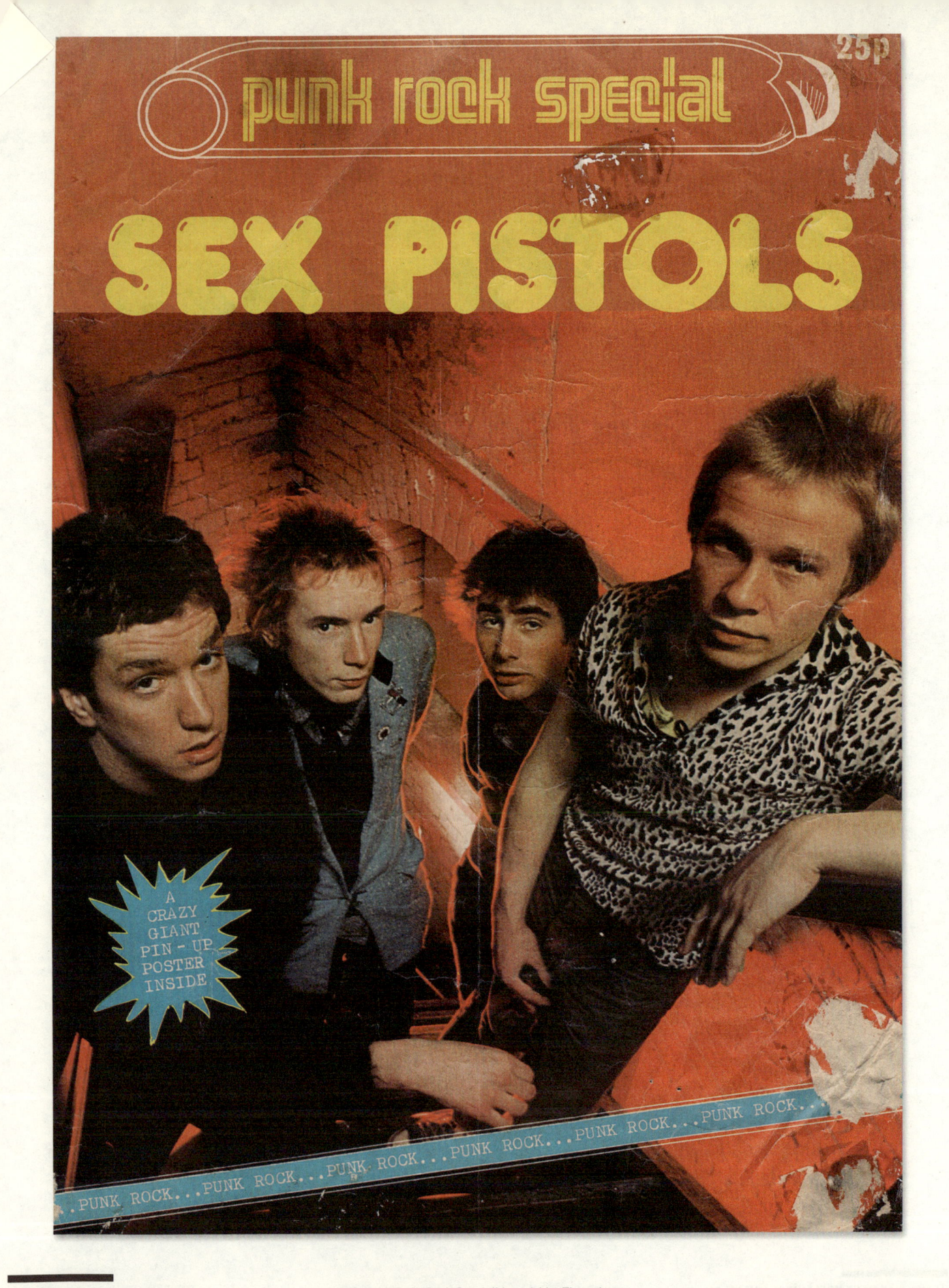

POSTER FOR THE SEX PISTOLS
Printed by Pepperwell Ltd
1977
59.6 x 41.9 cm, 23½ x 16½ in

A triple-fold 'Punk Rock Special' broadside. The colour photo of the Sex Pistols was taken in the Denmark Street studio. Apart from recording at this location, the Sex Pistols also lived above a nearby shop.

**FLYER FOR THE CORTINAS AND THE POLICE
AT LEEDS POLYTECHNIC**
14 & 21 July 1977
29.2 x 20.9 cm, 11½ x 8¼

One of the only shows where the newly formed Police performed as a four-piece, with two guitarists; a month later the band would only consist of Andy Summers, Stewart Copeland and Sting. Jill Furmanovsky took the photo of the Cortinas for an *NME* magazine interview.

POSTER FOR ELVIS COSTELLO
[July] 1977
101.6 x 75.5 cm, 40 x 29¾ in

Elvis Costello (born Declan Patrick MacManus) performed as 'D. C. Costello' until he signed to Stiff Records and his manager Jake Riviera suggested he take the name Elvis. The poster's photo is in the same style as the cover image from his debut album, *My Aim Is True*, on which Costello appears with oversized glasses that give him a resemblance to Buddy Holly.

**INSERT FROM COCK SPARRER'S SINGLE
'WE LOVE YOU'**
1977
17.7 x 25.4 cm, 7 x 10 in

FLYER FOR CHELSEA, THE CORTINAS, THE LURKERS AND SHAM 69 AT ACKLAM HALL, LONDON
21 July 1977
28.5 x 20.9 cm, 11¼ x 8¼ in

Acklam Hall, located off Portobello Road, was popular amongst post-punk bands. In 1979, journalist Chris Westwood told the *Record Mirror*, 'The Acklam Hall stinks. Like some scummy old school hall, it lacks atmosphere, facilities, everything. Ironically, it remains one of the solitary few places in the big city where crowds of little known quality bands can assemble and present their ideas to open-minded punters.' By the summer of 1977, bands like Chelsea and Sham 69 were attracting a following of skinheads.

**POSTER FOR THE LURKERS AND THE JOLT
AT THE MANIQUI, FALKIRK**
28 July 1977
33.6 × 24.1 cm, 13¼ × 9½ in

CONCERT FLYER FOR CHELSEA AND THE CORTINAS IN 'NEW WAVE RAVE'
27–29 July & 1 Aug 1977
20.9 x 13.9 cm, 8¼ x 5½ in

PUNKTURE #3
August 1977
29.8 x 20.9 cm, 11¾ x 8¼ in

Promotes the Midlands' punk scene. There are stories on the Sex Pistols, 999, the Stranglers and French punk, as well as 'Depressions – and other scandals'.

GENERATION X, THE LURKERS, STEEL PULSE AND ART ATTACKS AT THE VORTEX
1–2 August 1977
23.4 x 17.7 cm, 9¼ x 7 in

Run by ex-Roxy owner Andy Czezowski, the disco Crackers devoted its Monday and Tuesday nights to punk at the Vortex. The nightclub lasted nine months and opened London's first 24-hour punk venue, on Hanway Street. Dave Woods of March Artists booked the Vortex, where £1 purchased entry to see bands such as Generation X, the Lurkers, Steel Pulse and the Art Attacks. Vortex manager John Miller recalls the DIY attitude of bands: 'They'd turn up with their own sound equipment, their own lighting, they'd play for nothing and they'd spend all week sticking up fly posters all over town advertising their appearance at the club.'

ZIGZAG #75
August 1977
29.2 × 20.9 cm, 11½ × 8¼ in

Includes Blondie's Debbie Harry, Eddie and the Hotrods, the Slits, MC5 and others.

RIPPED & TORN #7
Tony Drayton
August 1977
29.8 × 20.9 cm, 11¾ × 8¼ in

Articles on the Sex Pistols, the Clash and New York Dolls, amongst others. The cover photograph shows the Sex Pistols with new bass guitar player Sid Vicious.

The NEW WAVE magazine 7

INSIDE : G E N E R A T I O N X
         INTERVIEW....
with Billy Idol & Tony James

& DEAD FINGERS TALK
& W I R E INTERVIEWS......

30p

THE NEW WAVE MAGAZINE #7
[August] 1977
29.2 x 20.9 cm, 11½ x 8¼ in

Interview with Generation X, and articles about Billy Idol and Tony James.

POSTER PROGRAMME FOR IAN DURY & THE BLOCKHEADS
Barney Bubbles
August 1977
59 x 83.8 cm, 23¼ x 33 in

Ian Dury & the Blockheads quickly gained a reputation as one of the best live acts to emerge from the new wave. When it released, their first single 'Sex and Drugs and Rock 'n' Roll' was both banned by the BBC and named Single of the Week by *NME*.

195

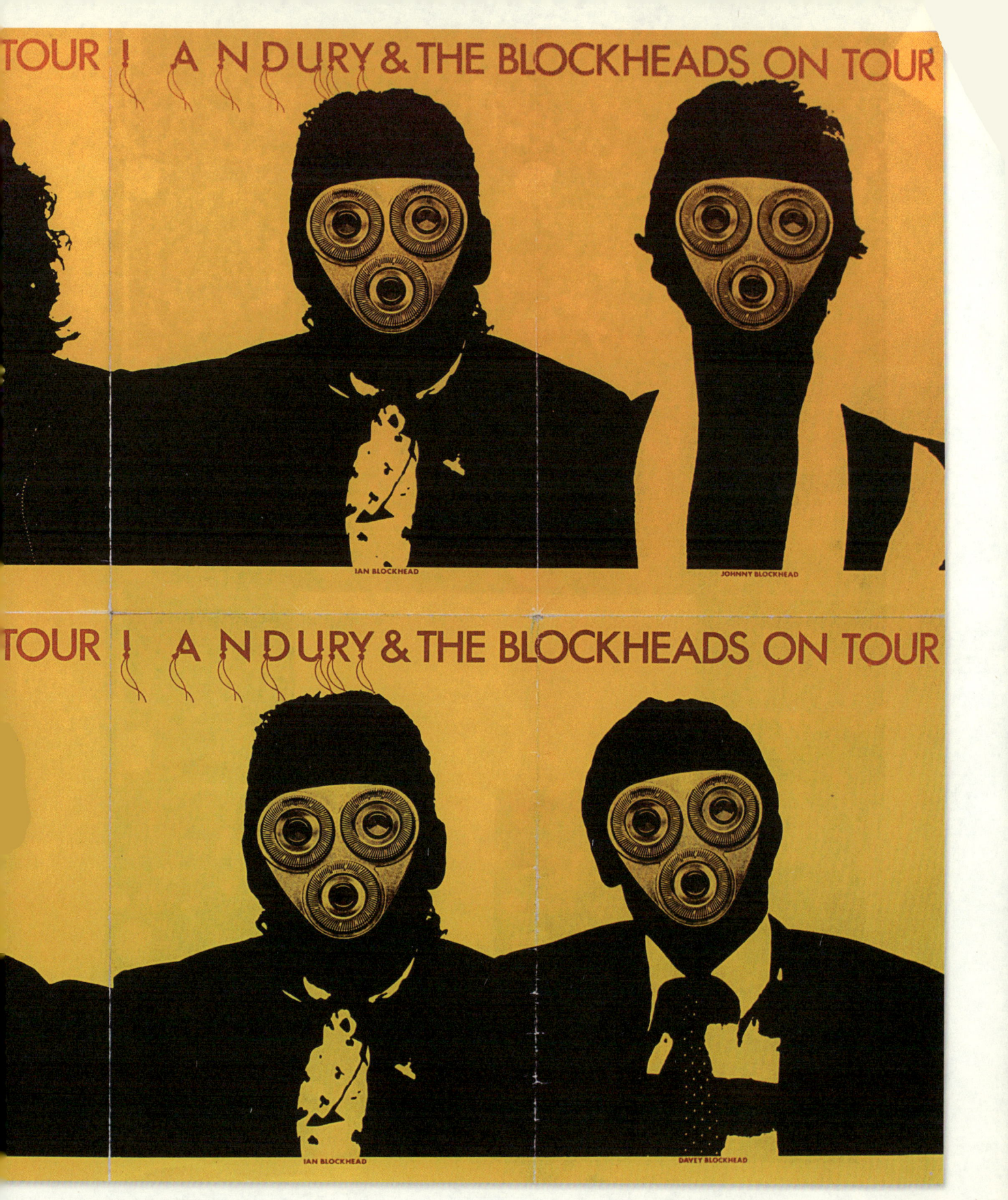

**POSTER FOR THE BOYS' ALBUM
THE BOYS**
August 1977
[dims unknown]

RUFF EDGES #3
August 1977
[dims unknown]

Interviews and features on Squeeze and Generation X.

**DOUBLE-SIDED POSTER FOR
THE BOOMTOWN RATS**
Adrian Boot
1977
84.4 x 59.6 cm, 33¼ x 23½ in

POSTER FOR THE ADVERTS' SINGLE 'GARY GILMORE'S EYES'
12 August 1977
55.8 x 43.1 cm, 22 x 17 in

Reproduced from the record's picture sleeve, the poster shows the band with blacked-out eyes. The Adverts' vinyl debut came about after performing B-side 'Bored Teenagers' on Harvest's live compilation album recorded at the Roxy.

PUNK MAGAZINE POSTER FEATURING THE SEX PISTOLS
1977
59.6 x 92 cm, 23½ x 36¼ in

Double-sided poster for *Punk* magazine with the Sex Pistols, the Clash, the Damned, the Stranglers, the Saints, the Jam, the Vibrators and Johnny Thunders & the Heartbreakers.

CLASH
The Clash are the most political of today's Punk groups.
THE DAMNED
The Damned are a group who love to have fun . . . and they do just that!
VIBRATORS
POSTER MAGAZINE
35p
PUNK
FEATURING
SEX PISTOLS·
THE CLASH
·STRANGLERS·
DAMNED·SAINTS
·JAM·VIBRATORS·
JOHNNY THUNDER+
THE HEARTBREAKERS
AND
OTHERS
INSIDE
FULL COLOUR
36 x 24 POSTER OF
SEX PISTOLS

NEW WAVE NEWS #3
1977
29.8 x 20.9 cm, 11¾ x 8¼ in

Comes with a fold-out poster of the Stranglers, with news and photographs of Sham 69, the Boomtown Rats and the Slits.

FLYER FOR THE CORTINAS AND THE POP GROUP AT THE MARQUEE CLUB
17 August 1977
20.9 x 29.8 cm, 8¼ x 11¾ in

In an interview with Bristol Archive Records, the Cortinas' drummer Daniel Swan describes the significance of playing the Marquee: 'I remember in June 1977 we had our first headlining show at the Marquee Club. Other than the Roxy and some opening shows, this was our first time in a legitimate London rock club. After soundcheck we came back to the club to find a long line of people waiting to get in. We could not believe it.'

CANDYBEAT 504
30 August 1977
29.8 x 20.9 cm, 11¾ x 8¼ in

Features stories about a Siouxsie and the Banshees concert in Plymouth, 30 August 1977, as well as Elvis Costello, Sham 69, Wire and X-Ray Spex.

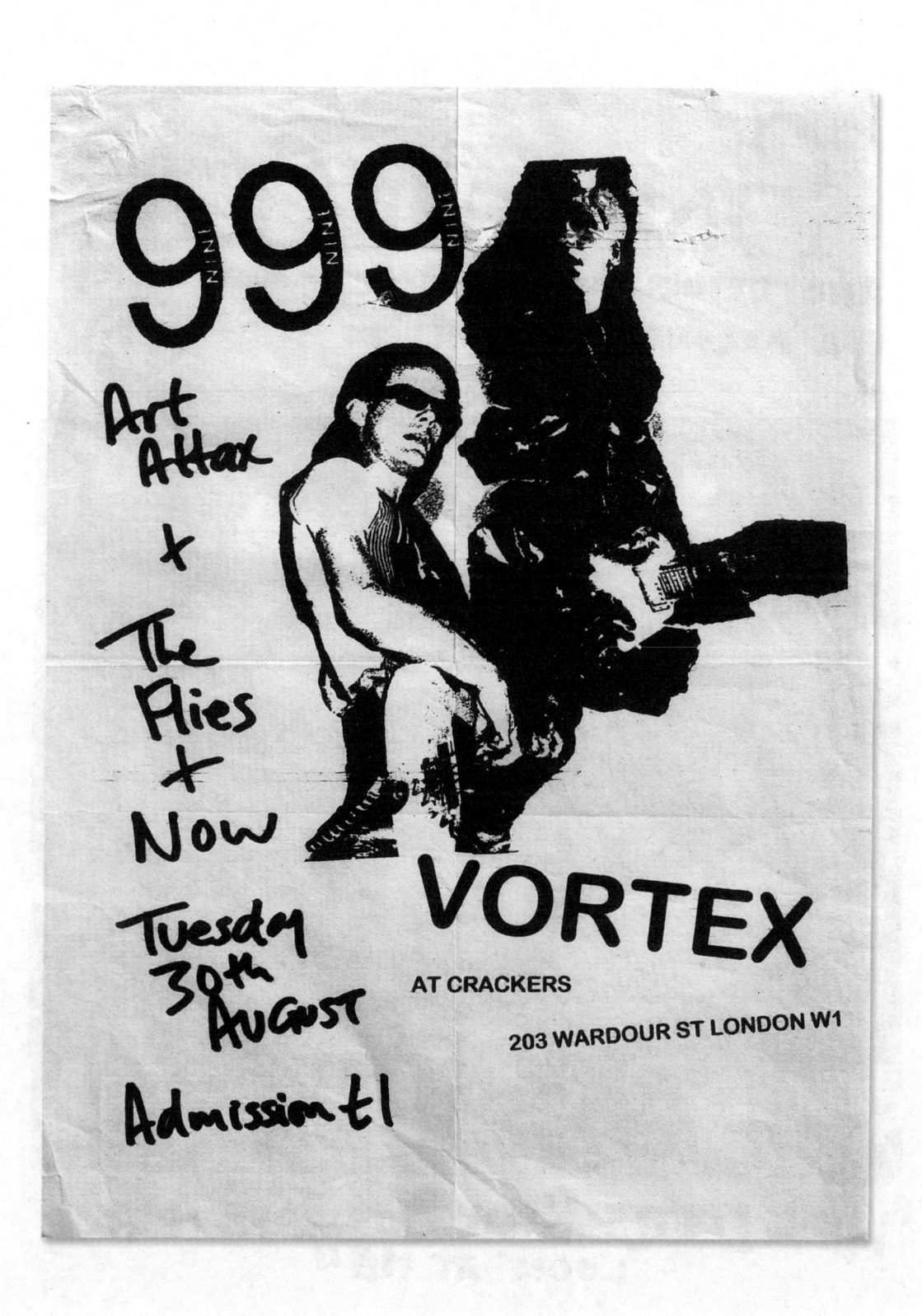

FLYER FOR 999, ART ATTACKS, THE FLIES AND NOW AT THE VORTEX
30 August 1977
29.2 x 20.3 cm, 11½ x 8 in

On Monday and Tuesday nights, disco club Crackers became the Vortex. According to *Record Mirror* journalist Jane Suck, 'Crackers is designed like a sewer. One path leads to the toilets, one path leads to the bar, and if you're lucky you'll find the stage in half an hour.'

SNIFFIN' GLUE #12
Mark Perry
August/September 1977
29.8 x 20.9 cm, 11¾ x 8¼ in

The zine's final issue includes a full-page photograph of the Clash by Jill Furmanovsky and a flexi-disc single for Alternative TV's 'Love Lies Limp'. Articles discuss Generation X, Chiswick Records and 'A Night at the Vortex'.

ALTERNATIVE T.V.

LOVE LIES LIMP

ALTERNATIVE GIG

I thought it'd be worth mentioning an unusual venture taking place at the Rat Club, 328 Grays Inn Road, London.

The club, which usually features only avant garde acts is gonna be the scene for a gig by Alternative TV, the band started by Mark P.

The group, one of the most inventive of the New wavers, will be putting on a special show and there will also be a US drag queen film! Starts at 9pm, a quid to get in.

The twelfth issue of *sniffin' Glue* is on sale at 30p and, as an anniversary bonus, features a giveaway flexi-disc featuring Alternative TV's 'Love lies Limp' taken from the band's first demo session. 15,000 copies have been printed.

POSTER FOR THE BOOMTOWN RATS' DEBUT ALBUM
Geoff Halpin
September 1977
66.6 x 50.1 cm, 26¼ x 19¾ in

With photography by Hannah Sharn, the cover for the Boomtown Rats' eponymous debut album has a moody and theatrical feel that matches the disc's dark themes.

CENTREFOLD POSTER OF GAYE ADVERT IN THE RECORD MIRROR
3 September 1977
59.6 x 40.6 cm, 23½ x 16 in

The poster's reverse is a letters page, where readers mourn the death of Elvis Presley on 16 August.

POSTER FOR THE VIBRATORS
1977
50.8 x 76.2 cm, 20 x 30 in

the rators

POSTERS FOR IAN DURY'S ALBUM NEW BOOTS AND PANTIES!!
Barney Bubbles; September 1977
75.5 x 50.8 cm, 29¾ x 20 in
74.9 x 50.1 cm, 29½ x 19¾ in

The album's title refers to the two items of clothing Dury said he always bought new. He formed his supporting band, the Blockheads, to promote the album on tour. Dury worked closely with legendary designer Barney Bubbles, who created many of the band's album covers.

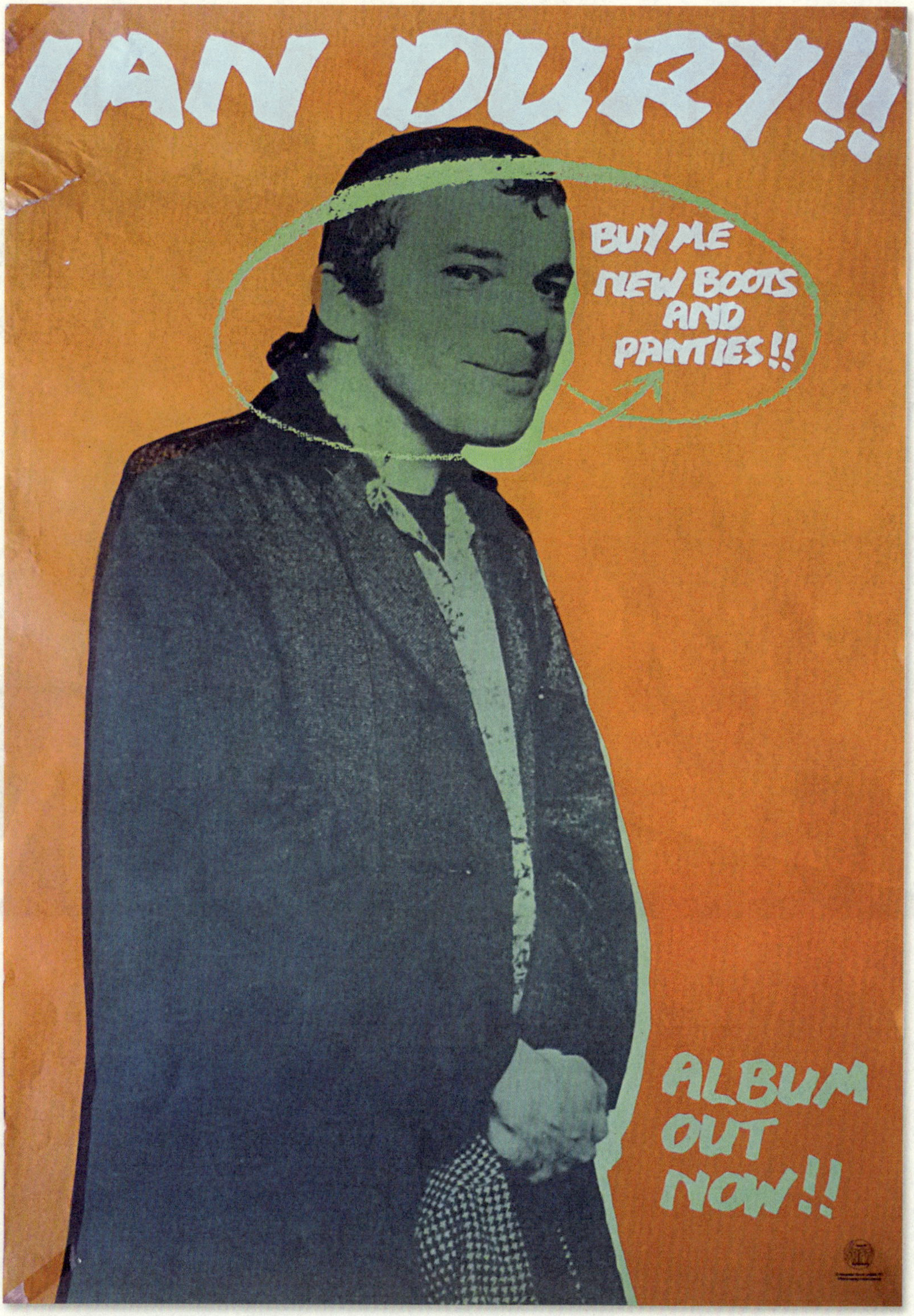
IAN DURY!!
BUY ME NEW BOOTS AND PANTIES!!
ALBUM OUT NOW!!

**POSTER AND FLYER FOR GENERATION X'S
SINGLE 'YOUR GENERATION'**
September 1977
[dims unknown]

Generation X new single
Your Generation Day by Day CHS 2165

generation   generation
 generation   generation
  generation   generation
   generation   generation
    generation   generation
      generationgeneration
       generatigeneration
        generagenaration
         genegenenation
          gegeneratioon
            generation
          gegeneratioon
         genegenenation
        generagenaration
       generatigeneration
      generationgeneration
     generation   generation
    generation   generation
   generation   generation
  generation   generation
 generation   generation

Chrysalis
Mail order copies from Rough Trade Records
202 Kensington Park Road. London W.11 (7274312)
70p + 10p P&P

STRANGLED #4
Tony Moon, Alan Edwards
September 1977
29.8 x 20.9 cm, 11¾ x 8¼ in

The special summer issue contains features on the Who, the Lurkers and Dr Feelgood, amongst others.

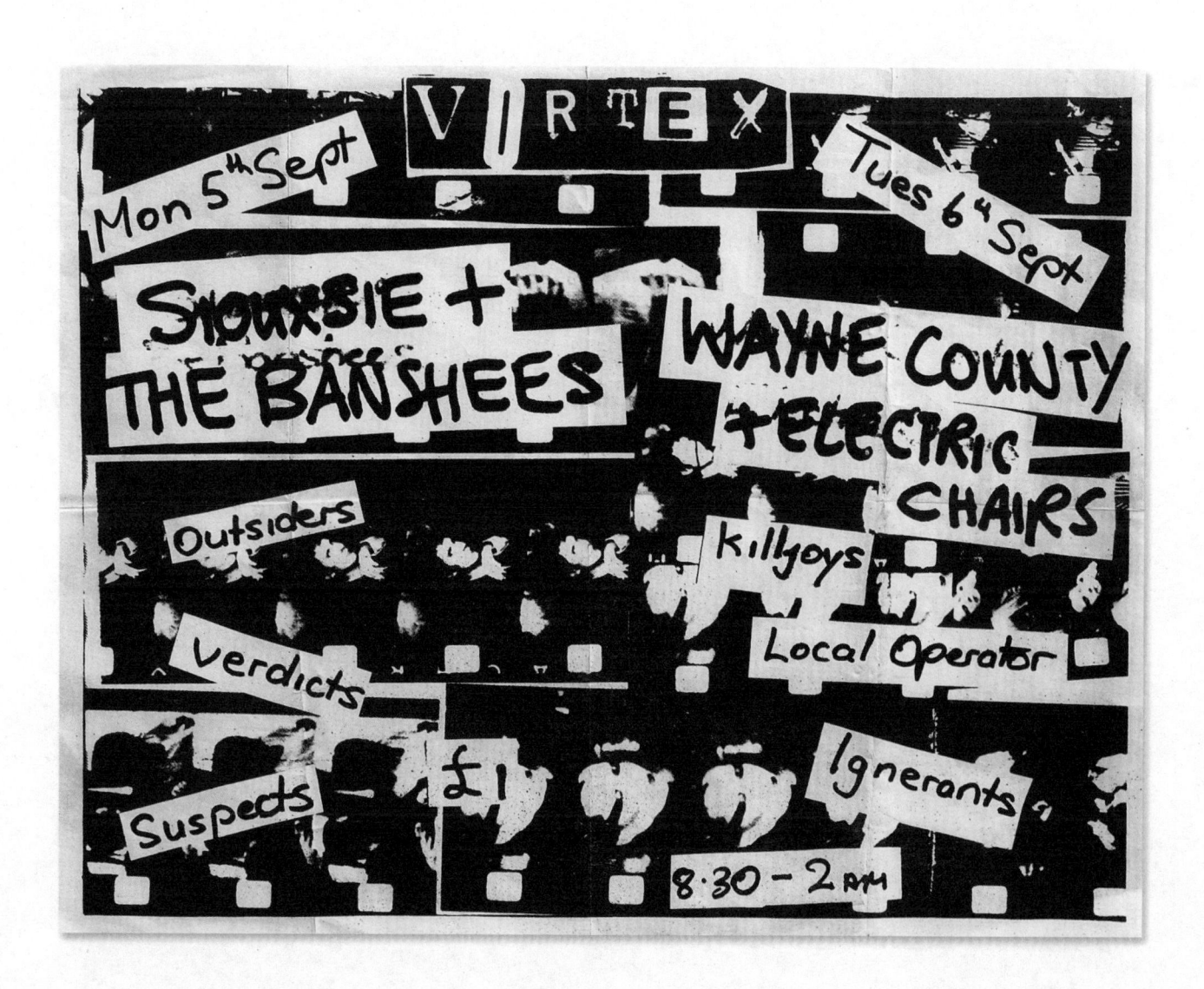

**FLYER FOR SIOUXSIE AND THE BANSHEES
AND WAYNE COUNTY & THE ELECTRIC CHAIRS
AT THE VORTEX**
5–6 September 1977
20.3 × 24.7 cm, 8 × 9¾ in

POSTER FOR GENERATION X AT THE WINDMILL CLUB, ROTHERHAM
8 September 1977
21.5 x 29.2 cm, 8½ x 11½ in

Image-conscious frontman Billy Idol (William Broad) left the band in 1981 to pursue a solo career. Idol refashioned his punk persona into pop music appeal and even appeared in popular teen magazines.

FLYER FOR PENETRATION AND DOCTORS OF MADNESS AT THE VORTEX, LONDON
13–14 September 1977
20.9 × 29.8 cm, 8¼ × 11¾ in

The two-day event featured Penetration, the Unwanted, New Hearts, Meat, Doctors of Madness, Jolt and Sham 69.

FLYER FOR ALTERNATIVE TV AT THE RAT CLUB
14 September 1977
20.9 x 29.8 cm, 8¼ x 11¾ in

On the back are annotations by *Ripped & Torn*'s Tony Drayton. Alternative TV, writes Drayton, was stopped on the way home from Dingwalls by the police, who were interested in his 'Sex, Drugs and Rock 'n' Roll' badge.

POSTER FOR THE ADVERTS AT THE WINDMILL CLUB, ROTHERHAM
15 September 1977
27.9 x 21.5 cm, 11 x 8½ in

POSTER FOR SLAUGHTER & THE DOGS' SINGLE 'WHERE HAVE ALL THE BOOT BOYS GONE?'
16 September 1977
73 x 97.7 cm, 28¾ x 38½ in

Silkscreened in-store promo for the band's debut single on Decca Records. Slaughter & the Dogs were one of the first UK punk bands to sign with a major label.

FLYER FOR THREE-DAY EVENT AT THE ROXY
19–21 September 1977
[dims unknown]

Shows by the Outsiders, Goats, Automatics, Wasps, the Shoplifters, the Tickets, Métal Urbain, the Tarts and Blunt Instrument

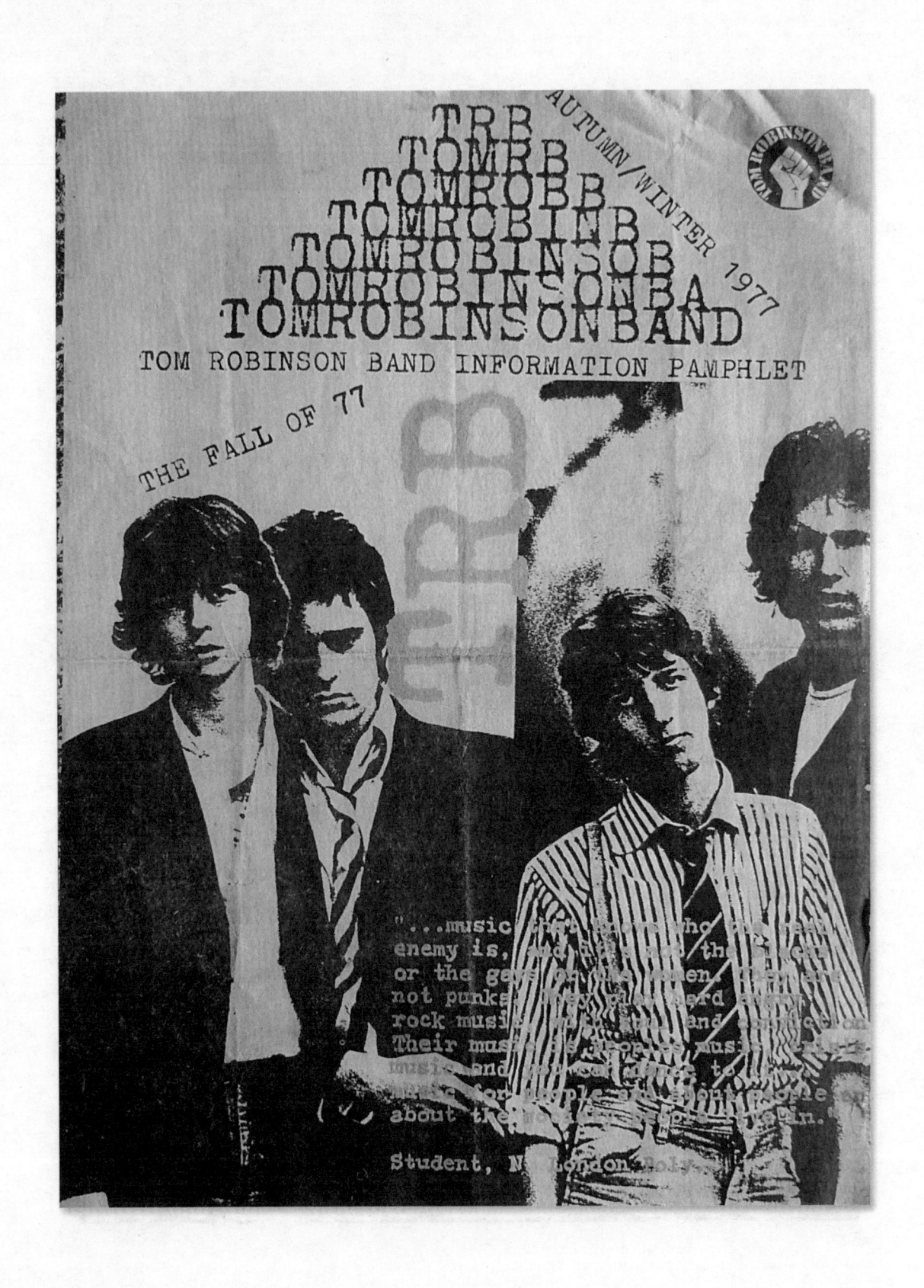

TOM ROBINSON BAND INFORMATION PAMPHLET
Autumn/Winter 1977
29.8 x 21.5 cm, 11¾ x 8½ in

The pamphlet offers information on Rock Against Racism, Release, *Spare Rib*, Gay Switchboard, the National Abortion Campaign and George Ince.

UP AGAINST THE WALL

Darkhaired dangerous schoolkids
Vicious suspicious sixteen
Jet black blazers at the bus stop
Sullen unhealthy and mean
Teenage guerillas on the tarmac
Fighting in the middle of the road
Supercharged PSIEs on the asphalt
The kids are coming in from the cold

High wire fencing on the playground
High rise housing all around
High rise prices on the high street
Ain't time to pull them down
White boys kicking in a window
Straight girls watching where they gone
Never trust a copper in a crime car
Just whose side are you on?

Consternation in Mayfair
Rioting in Notting Hill Gate
Fascists marching on the High Street
Cutting back the welfare state
Operator get me the hotline
Father can you hear me at all
Telephone kiosk out of order
Sprayean writing on the wall

CHORUS
Look out listen can you hear it
Panic in the Country now
Look out listen can you see it
Whitehall up against the wall
Up against the wall

the tom robinson band have a monthly duplicated news
bulletin which is distributed at gigs. copies available free
from linda cooke, 25 montpelier grove, LONDON NW5
and include information on ROCK AGAINST
RACISM, RELEASE, SPARE RIB, GAY
SWITCHBOARD, NATIONAL ABORTION
CAMPAIGN and GEORGE INCE.

press enquiries to EMI press office: 01-486-4488
management enquiries to colin bell: 01-624-4898
booking enquiries to cowbell agency: 01-262-7253

Designed and produced by
Rentamob graphics

POSTER FOR THE CLASH'S SINGLE 'COMPLETE CONTROL'
September 1977
29.8 × 20.9 cm, 11¾ × 8¼ in

POSTER FOR ULTRAVOX AT THE WINDMILL CLUB, ROTHERHAM
22 September 1977
29.2 x 41.2 cm, 11½ x 16¼ in

In February, Ultravox had released its debut album; the follow-up would come in October on the heels of this concert. The Windmill was one of two South Yorkshire venues to offer a home to the punk scene in the late '70s.

NOW 4 IDIOT 6
September 1977
29.8 × 20.9 cm, 11¾ × 8¼ in

Features John Otway, Buzzcocks, 999 and the Worst, with interviews, reviews and pictures.

POSTER FOR LONDON'S LIMITED-EDITION EP 'NO TIME'
September 1977
53.3 x 39.3 cm, 21 x 15½ in

Despite being picked up by major label MCA and managed by Simon Napier-Bell, who later managed bands such as Wham! and Ultravox, London only lasted two years, playing its final concert in December '77.

FLYER FOR THE DAMNED AT LEEDS POLYTECHNIC
23 September 1977
27.9 × 20.9 cm, 11 × 8¼ in

The image on the flyer is from the shoot for the cover of the band's second single, 'Neat Neat Neat'.

**POSTER FOR THE STRANGLERS' ALBUM
NO MORE HEROES**
23 September 1977
76.2 x 50.8 cm, 30 x 20 in

The Stranglers' second album, *No More Heroes*, was produced by Martin Rushent. The album became one of the band's highest-charting releases, peaking at No. 2 on the UK album chart.

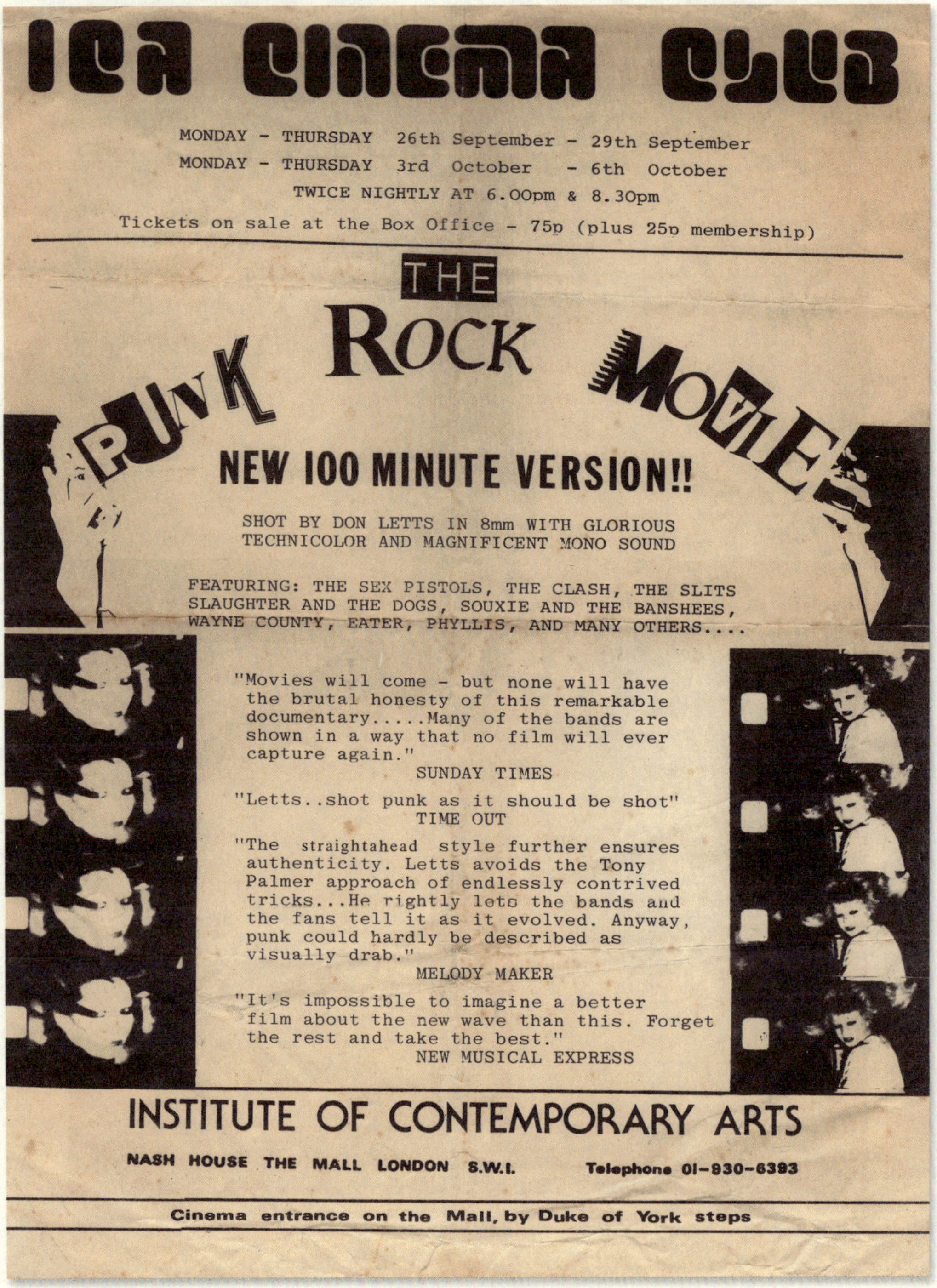

FLYER FOR DON LETTS'S THE PUNK ROCK MOVIE PREMIERE AT THE INSTITUTE OF CONTEMPORARY ARTS CINEMA CLUB
September/October 1977
30.4 x 20.9 cm, 12 x 8¼ in

Don Letts continued to edit the film after this showing, and an 86-minute version premiered in New York 10 months later. Letts shot this definitive London punk documentary on 8mm film at the Roxy in Covent Garden. Featured in the film are some of the earliest performances by the Clash, the Sex Pistols, Wayne County, Johnny Thunders and Billy Idol. Also includes the Slits, Slaughter & the Dogs, Siouxsie and the Banshees and Eater.

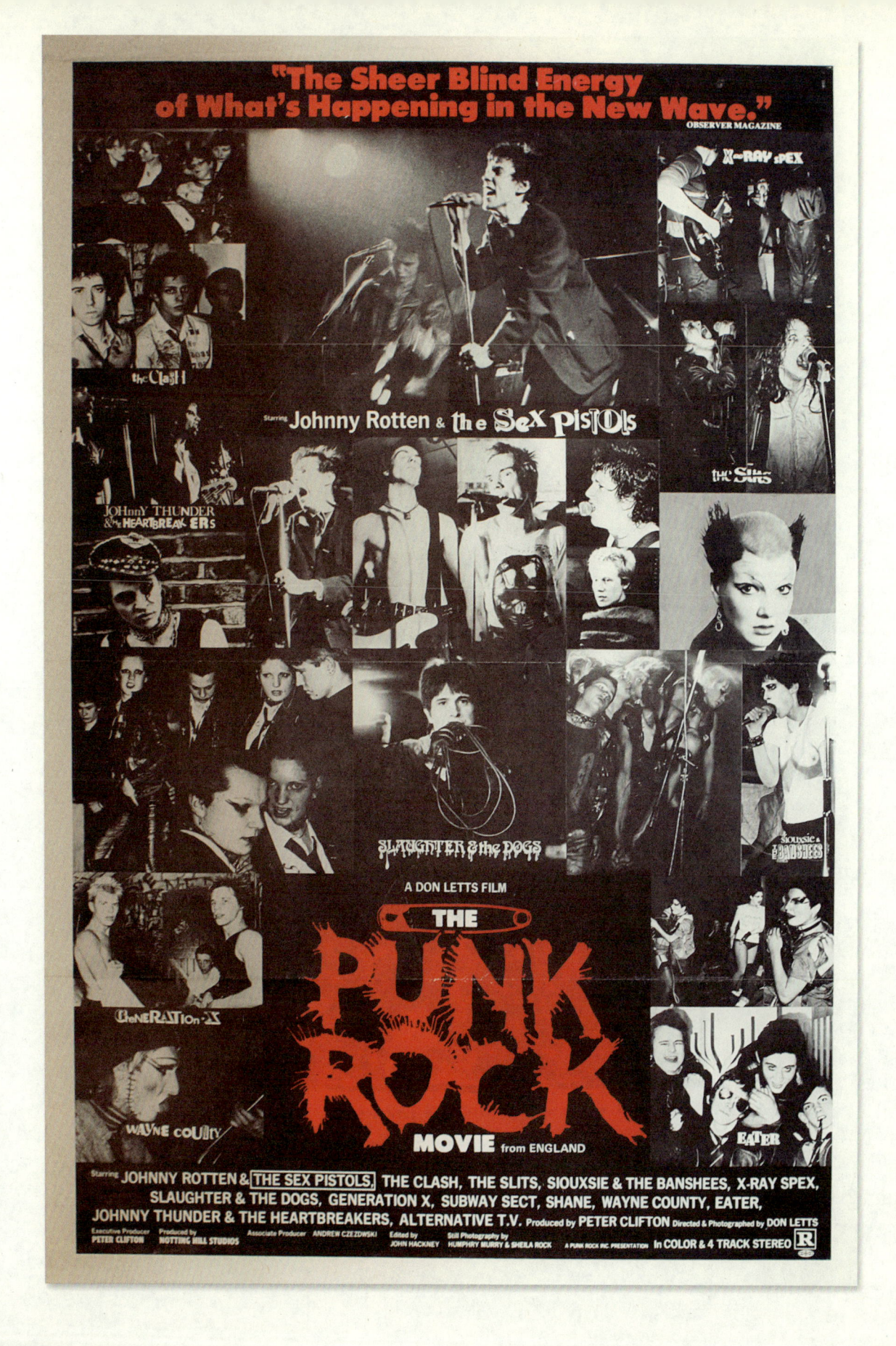

POSTER FOR DON LETTS'S
THE PUNK ROCK MOVIE
1977
[dims unknown]

WHITE STUFF #5
Sandy Robertson
September/October 1977
29.8 x 20.9 cm, 11¾ x 8¼ in

**POSTER FOR ULTRAVOX'S HA! HA! HA!
ALBUM AND TOUR**
[October] 1977
73 x 48.2 cm, 28¾ x 19 in

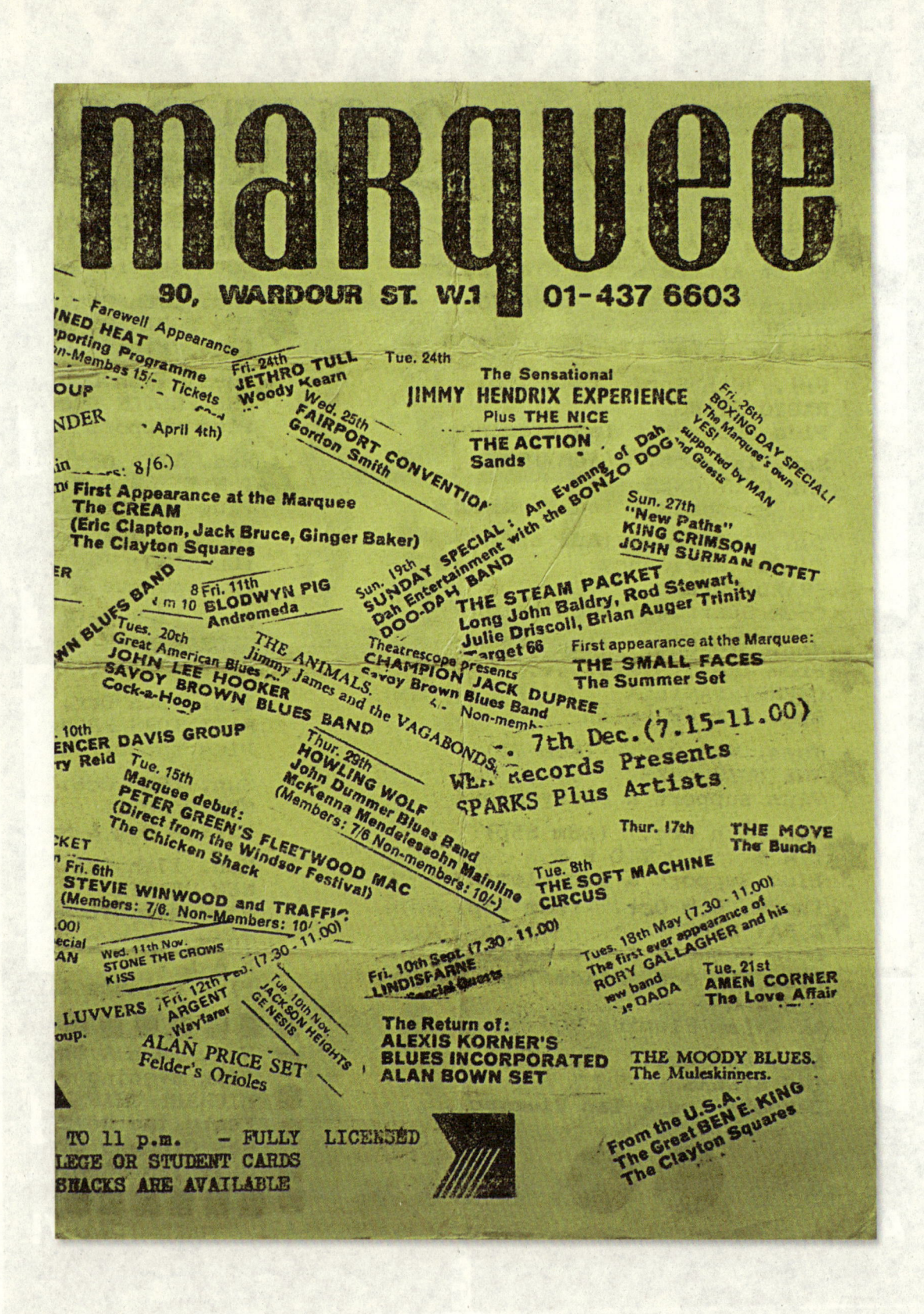

PROGRAMME FOR THE MARQUEE CLUB
October 1977
20.9 × 14.6 cm, 8¼ × 5¾ in

Bands include the Motors, the Only Ones, Cherry Vanilla, Buzzcocks, X-Ray Spex and Sham 69.

OCTOBER 77

Wed. 28th Sep. (Adm 75p)
★ THE MOTORS
Heart Attack & Ian Fleming

Thurs. 29th Sep. (Adm 70p)
GIGGLES
Smiler & Ian Fleming

Fri. 30th Sep. (Adm 75p)
RADIO STARS
Plus support & Ian Fleming

Sat. 1st Oct. (Adm 75p)
THE ONLY ONES
The Bazoomis & Ian Fleming

Sun. 2nd Oct. (Adm 65p)
Sunday Residency
GRAND HOTEL
Cock Sparrow & Nick Leigh

Mon. 3rd Oct. (Adm £1)
★ From the U.S.A.......
CHERRY VANILLA
Rage & Nick Leigh

Tues. 4th Oct. (Adm £1)
★ THE BUZZCOCKS
Plus support & Jerry Floyd

Wed. 5th Oct. (Adm 85p)
★ THE MOTORS
Plus support & Ian Fleming

Thurs. 6th Oct. (Adm 75p)
★ X RAY SPEX
Dole Queue & Ian Fleming

Fri. 7th Oct. (Adm 75p)
HERON
Al & Ian Fleming

Sat. 8th Oct. (Adm 75p)
THE STUKAS
Bazooka Joe & Ian Fleming

Sun. 9th Oct. (Adm 65p)
GRAND HOTEL
Cock Sparrow & Nick Leigh

Mon. 10th Oct. (Adm £1)
★ TOM ROBINSON BAND
Plus friends & Nick Leigh

Tues. 11th Oct. (Adm 85p)
★ THE FOSTER BROTHERS
Plus support & Jerry Floyd

Wed. 12th Oct. (Adm 85p)
★ THE MOTORS
Plus guests & Ian Fleming

Thurs. 13th Oct. (Adm 75p)
ILLUSION
Plus guests & Ian Fleming

Fri. 14th Oct. (Adm 75p)
GLORIA MUNDI
Plus support & Ian Fleming

Sat. 15th Oct. (Adm 75p)
RADIATORS FROM SPACE
Plus support & Ian Fleming

Sun. 16th Oct. (Adm 65p)
GRAND HOTEL
Prarie Dog & Nick Leigh

Mon. 17th Oct. (Adm 65p)
NEW HEARTS
Plus support & Nick Leigh

Tues. 18th Oct. (Adm 75p)
SALT
Plus friends & Jerry Floyd

Wed. 19th & Thurs. 20th Oct.
Folk Evening with.......
MICHAEL CHAPMAN & BAND
Featuring Keef Hartley &
Ray Clemens plus friends
D.J. Ian Fleming (Adm £1)

Fri. 21st Oct. (Adm 75p)
SHAM 69
Killjoy & Ian Fleming

Sat. 22nd Oct. (Adm 75p)
ADVERTISING
The Members & Ian Fleming

Sun. 23rd Oct. (Adm 65p)
GRAND HOTEL
Plus support & Nick Leigh

Mon. 24th Oct. (Adm £1)
★ TOM ROBINSON BAND
Plus friends & Nick Leigh

Tues. 25th Oct. (Adm 70p)
TYLA GANG
VHF & Jerry Floyd

Wed. 26th Oct. (Adm 75p)
★ X RAY SPEX
The Jolt & Ian Fleming

Thurs. 27th Oct. (Adm 75p)
QUANTUM JUMP
Plus support & Ian Fleming

Fri. 28th Oct. (Adm 75p)
GLORIA MUNDI
Plus support & Ian Fleming

Sat. 29th Oct. (Adm 75p)
PLUMMET AIRLINES
Sore Throat & Ian Fleming

Sun. 30th Oct. (Adm 65p)
GRAND HOTEL
Smiler & Nick Leigh

Mon. 31st Oct. & Tues. 1st Nov.
THE SAINTS
Plus support & Ian Fleming
(Admission £1)

**TOM ROBINSON BAND, TRB NEWS SHEET
'LIVE AS BROTHERS OR PERISH AS FOOLS'**
Fall 1977
29.2 x 20.9 cm, 11½ x 8¼ in

Double-sided sheet features a list of gigs.

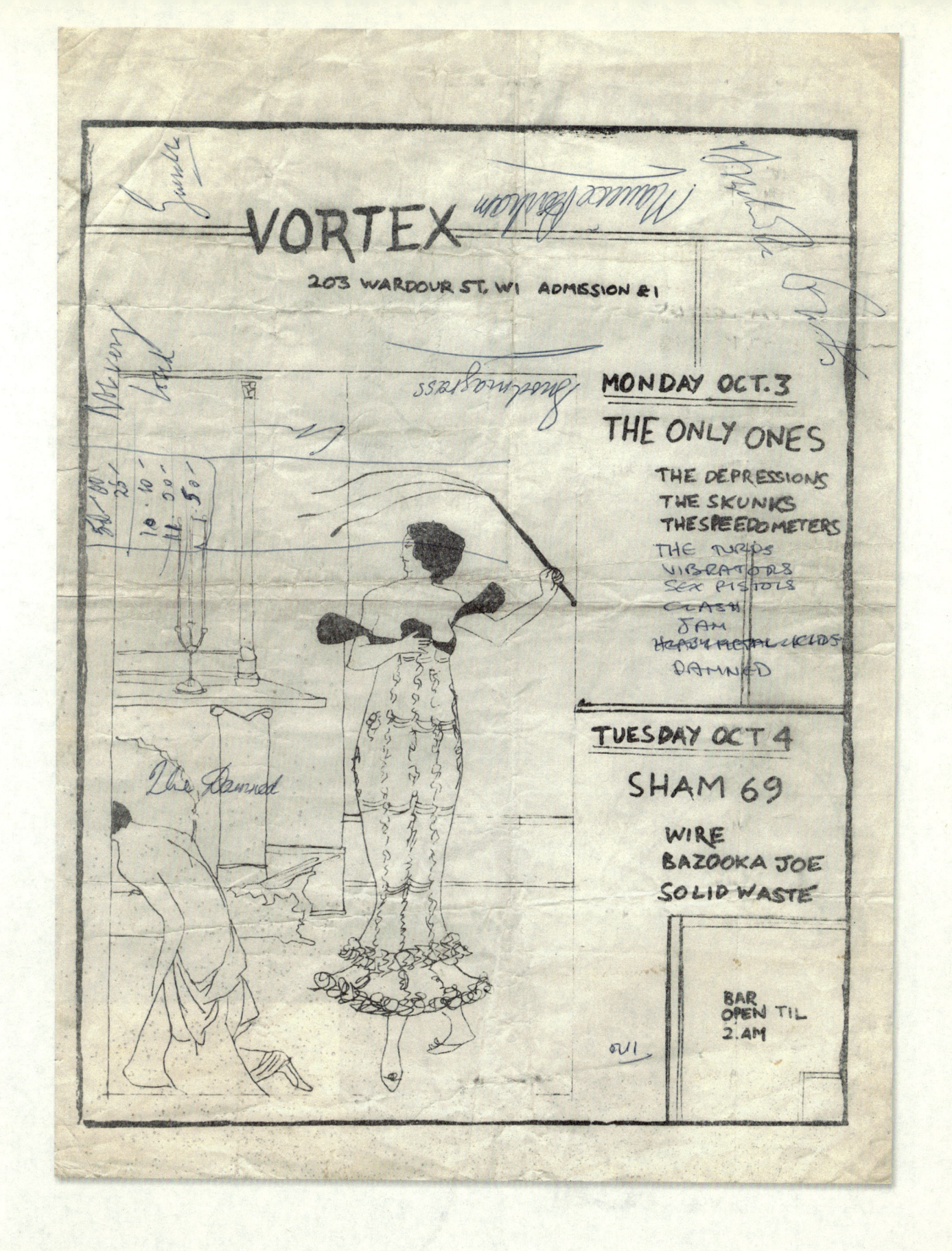

FLYER FOR THE ONLY ONES, THE DEPRESSIONS, SHAM 69, WIRE, BAZOOKA JOE, SOLID WASTE, AMONGST OTHERS AT THE VORTEX
3–4 October 1977
29.2 x 20.9 cm, 11½ x 8¼ in

THE NEW WAVE MAGAZINE #8
[October] 1977
29.2 × 20.9 cm, 11½ × 8¼ in

Contains stories on Poly Styrene, Generation X and John Otway.

POSTER FOR X-RAY SPEX'S SINGLE 'OH BONDAGE, UP YOURS!'
October 1977
60.9 x 43.1 cm, 24 x 17 in

The photo of Poly Styrene on the sleeve was taken at the Roxy. Styrene describes how she achieved the effect: it 'was a black-and-white photo, and then I ran it through a colour Xerox, which gives it that tone'. This single is regarded as the band's most enduring artefact. With its first line, 'Some people think little girls should be seen and not heard – but I think, oh bondage, up yours!' the song can be viewed as a harbinger of the riot grrrl movement, although Styrene has suggested that it was intended more as an anti-capitalist jingle.

**FLYER FOR JOHNNY THUNDERS
& THE HEARTBREAKERS' ALBUM
LAMF AND UK TOUR**
October 1977
[dims unknown]

POSTER FOR 999'S SINGLE 'NASTY! NASTY!'
October 1977
48.2 x 74.9 cm, 19 x 29½ in

The in-store promo features the 'raffle ticket'-style logo, designed by George Snow, often used to promote early 999 gigs on the London club circuit. Snow's work with 999 and the Stranglers led to more work for publications, including *Vogue* and the *Sunday Times*.

**POSTER FOR THE DEAD BOYS' ALBUM
YOUNG, LOUD AND SNOTTY**
[October] 1977
91.4 x 60.9 cm, 36 x 24 in

In a 1977 issue of the fanzine *Search & Destroy*, band member Stiv said the album was put together in three days as a demo, but was remixed and released, with this cover photo, without the band's knowledge while they were on tour.

VORTEX #1
October 1977
33 x 21.5 cm, 13 x 8½ in

The inaugural issue of the zine, produced by the club of the same name, features Sham 69's Jimmy Pursey on the cover and contains articles on Sham 69, the Radiators, the Models, the Boomtown Rats, Outsiders, Jolt and record reviews.

what 'ave we got?

SHAM 69

PANDA ARTISTS 01-727-8636

POSTER FOR SHAM 69'S 'SONG OF THE STREETS (WHAT 'AVE WE GOT?)'
[October] 1977
76.2 x 50.1 cm, 30 x 19¾ in

The phrase 'What 'Ave We Got?' is a verse to 'Song of the Streets', one of Sham 69's early numbers. In concert, the line invariably elicited the response 'Fuck all!' from audiences. Sham 69 were known for their rousing, self-consciously cockney-tinged, anthemic singles. The poster depicts singer Jimmy Pursey's arrest outside the Vortex in London. The band had signed on to perform on the roof of the club for its opening in late September, only to discover later that they had played on the roof next door. Sham 69's brief set consisted of 'I Don't Wanna', 'George Davis is Innocent' and 'Ulster' before police cut off the power and arrested Pursey for disturbing the peace.

DESIGN FOR THE SEX PISTOLS' SINGLE 'HOLIDAYS IN THE SUN'
Jamie Reid
October 1977
69.2 x 69.8 cm, 27¼ x 27½ in

The Sex Pistols' management company Glitterbest wanted to give the single 'Holidays in the Sun' a strong, eye-catching graphic. Reid found a Belgian tourist brochure in a travel agency, and added the words of the song to create a bright poster that contrasted the song's political hysteria. The Belgian tourist company sued, and Reid had to destroy the artwork in front of their lawyers.

**POSTER FOR THE SEX PISTOLS' SINGLE
'HOLIDAYS IN THE SUN'**
Jamie Reid
October 1977
69.8 x 99.6 cm, 27½ x 39¼ in

The monochrome image of a crowded beach was taken from the Christopher Gray book *Leaving the 20th Century*.

NOW I'VE GOT A REASON
NOW I'VE GOT A REASON
I'M STILL WAITING
AT THE BERLIN WALL
COS NOW I'VE GOT
A REASONABLE ECONOMY
HAD NO REASON TO BE
THERE AT ALL
THEY'RE STARING ALL NIGHT
AND STARING ALL DAY
BUT NOW I'VE GOT
REASON, NO REAL
REASON TO BE
AT THE BERLIN WALL
CHEAP DIALOGUE
CHEAP ESSENTIAL SCENERY
A CHEAP HOLIDAY
OTHER PEOPLES MISERY!
SEX PISTOLS
VIRGIN RECORDS VS191

FLYER FOR KILLJOYS, SPITFIRE BOYS, JAH WOOSH, THE CRABS AND OTHERS AT THE VORTEX
24–25 October 1977
[dims unknown]

**POSTER FOR THE ADVERTS' SINGLE
'SAFETY IN NUMBERS'**
28 October 1977
59 x 41.2 cm, 23¼ x 16¼ in

Silkscreened in-store promotional poster for the Adverts' single 'Safety in Numbers'.

BANNER FOR THE SEX PISTOLS' ALBUM NEVER MIND THE BOLLOCKS, HERE'S THE SEX PISTOLS
1977
29.2 x 87.6 cm, 11½ x 34½ in

The Sex Pistols guitarist Steve Jones said he picked up the phrase 'never mind the bollocks' from two fans who often said it to one another. The group's singer, Johnny Rotten, explained it as a working-class expression for 'stop talking rubbish'. When the phrase was judged an 'indecent advertisement', only Virgin's legal efforts, helped by barrister and author Sir John Mortimer, allowed the band to keep it in the title.

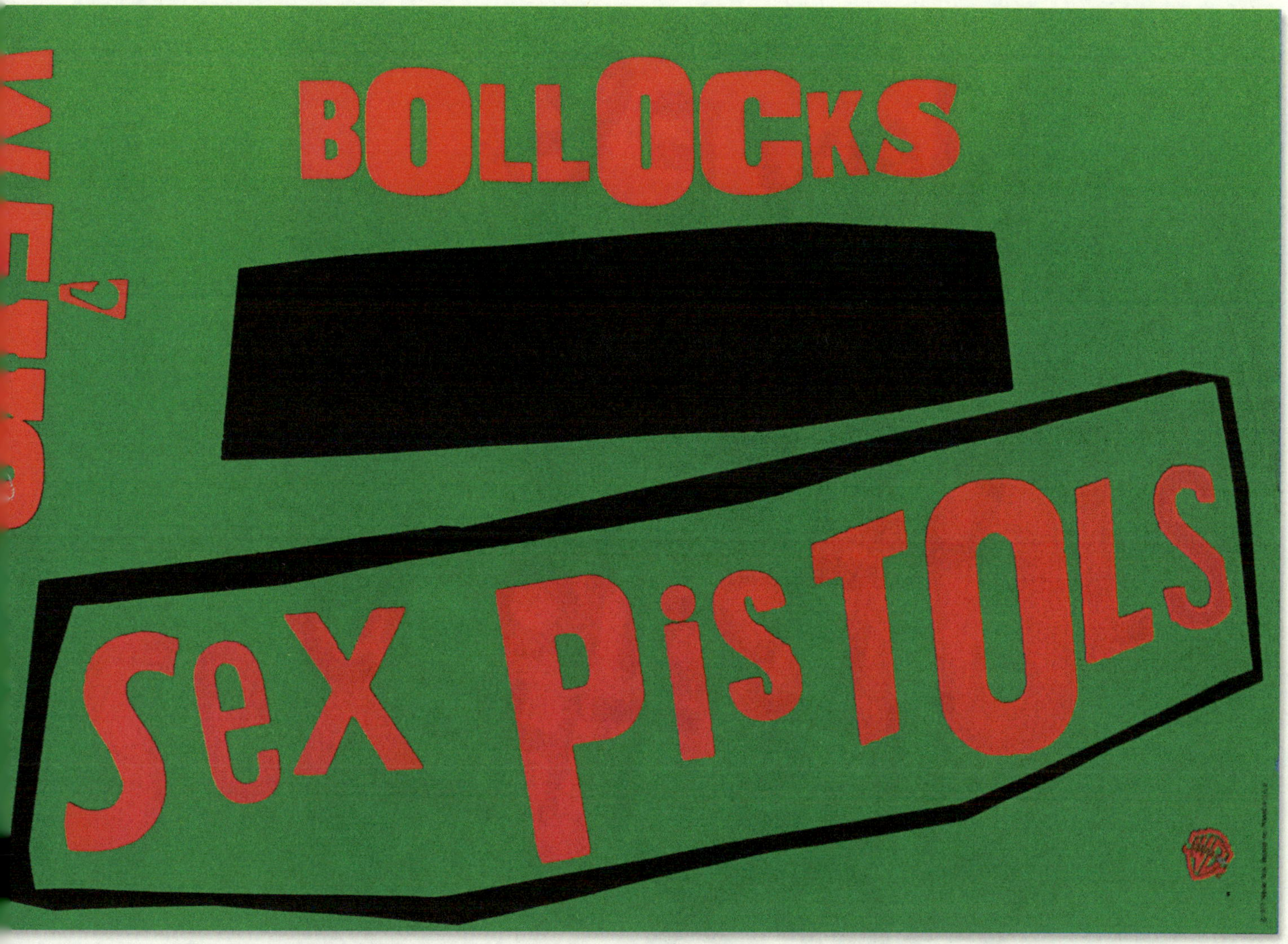
BOLLOCKS
SEX PISTOLS

**TOILET PAPER PROMO FOR THE SEX PISTOLS'
ALBUM NEVER MIND THE BOLLOCKS, HERE'S
THE SEX PISTOLS**
1977
19.6 x 12 cm, 7¾ x 4¾ in

Part of Warner Bros. US promotional material for the album.

FLYER FOR SIOUXSIE AND THE BANSHEES, ADAM AND THE ANTS, AUNTIE PUS AND THE VOID AT THE VORTEX, LONDON
31 October 1977
[dims unknown]

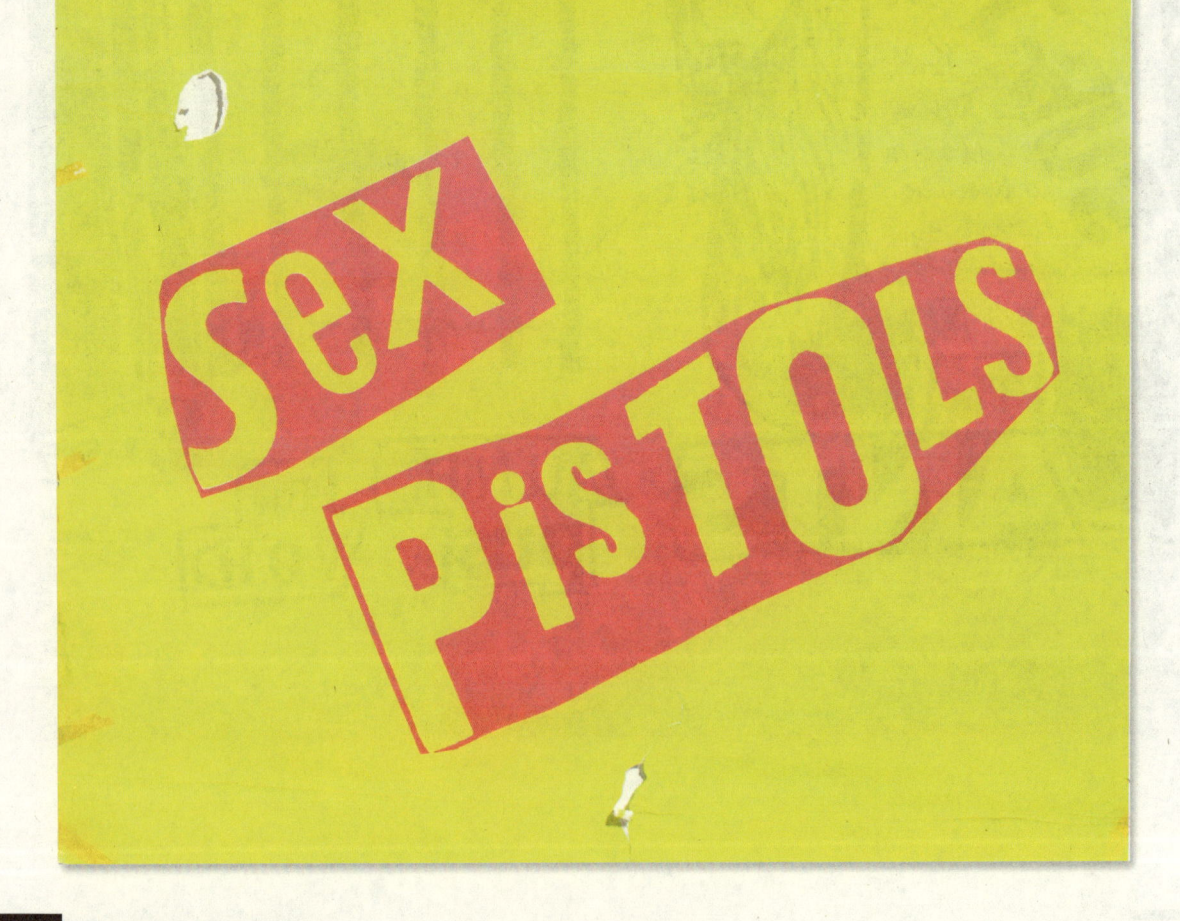

POSTER FOR THE SEX PISTOLS' ALBUM NEVER MIND THE BOLLOCKS, HERE'S THE SEX PISTOLS
Jamie Reid
1977
152.4 x 90.8 cm, 60 x 35¾ in

**POSTER FOR RICHARD HELL & THE VOIDOIDS'
'BLANK GENERATION' ON THE CLASH'S 'OUT
OF CONTROL' TOUR**
October/November 1977
70.4 x 49.5 cm, 27¾ x 19½ in

Richard Hell was unimpressed with Sire Records' poster, which he deemed inappropriate to an art-punk band and better matched to the sci-fi/horror movies of Hammer Films. Hell said, 'At the time the poster really annoyed me. It's interesting just as an artefact of the record companies' mentalities and their shaky take on what bands were doing, but it's still dumb as shit.'

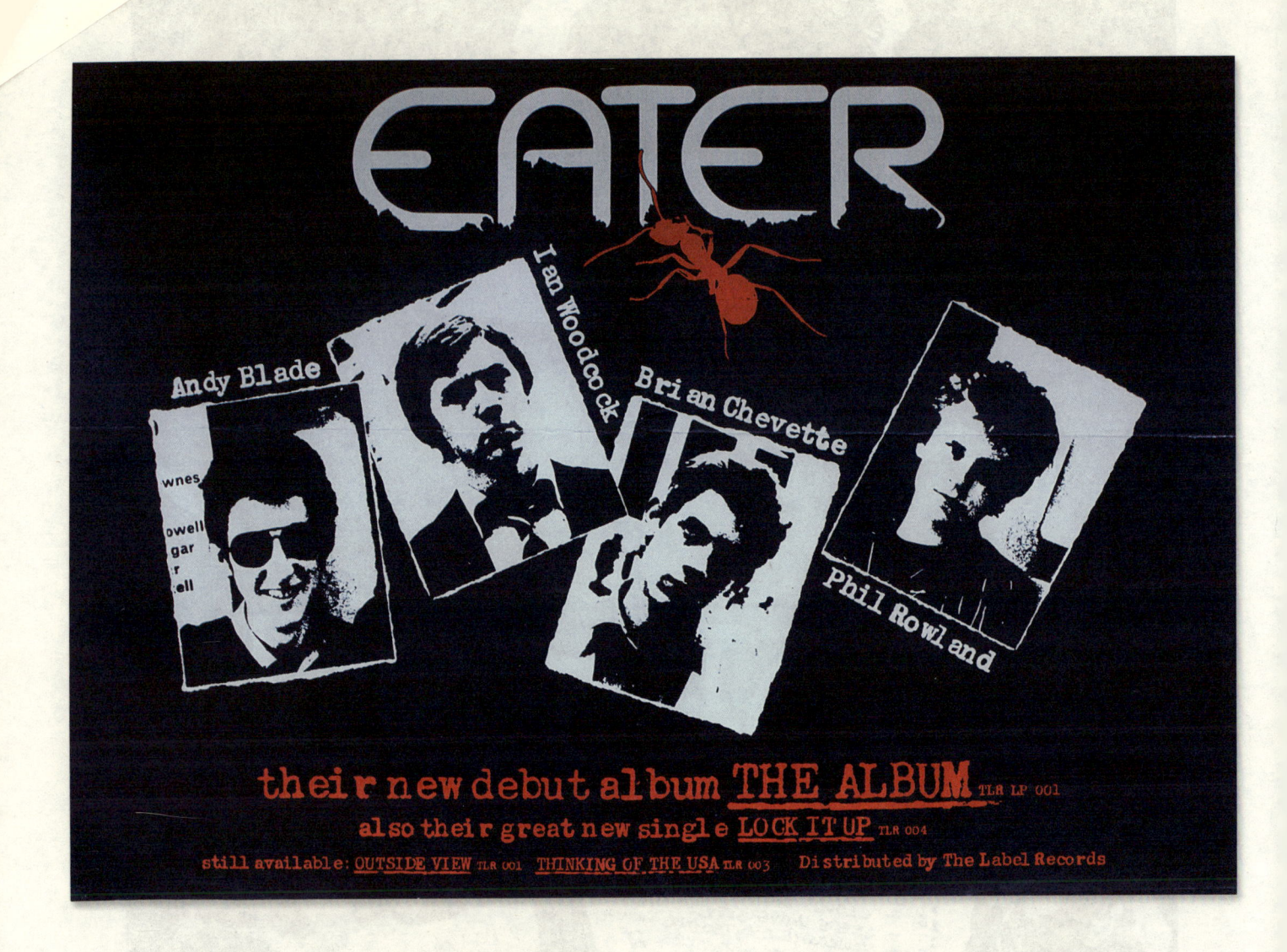

POSTER FOR EATER'S DEBUT THE ALBUM
November 1977
42.5 x 59 cm, 16¾ x 23¼ in

Silkscreened in-store promo, distributed by The Label Records.

**FLYER FOR IAN DURY & THE BLOCKHEADS'
SINGLE 'SWEET GENE VINCENT'**
November 1977
34.9 × 23.4 cm, 13¾ × 9¼ in

From the album *New Boots and Panties!!*, the song is a tribute to singer Gene Vincent; the B-side is 'You're More Than Fair'.

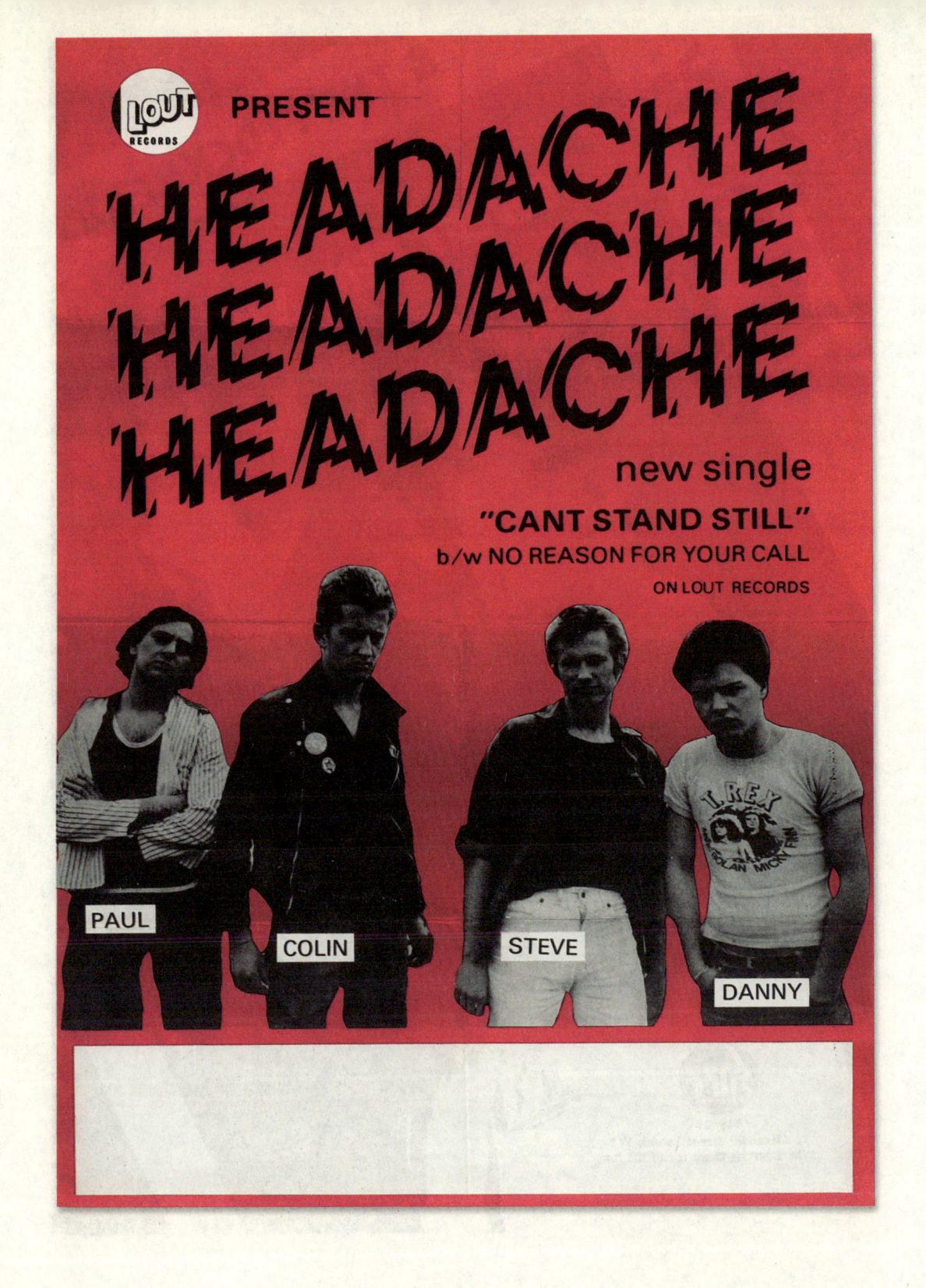

POSTER FOR HEADACHE'S SINGLE 'CAN'T STAND STILL'
November 1977
50.8 x 34.9 cm, 20 x 13¾ in

Silkscreened in-store promotional poster for 'Can't Stand Still', Headache's only single. One photo shoot supplied the images of the band for the poster and the single.

THE NEW WAVE MAGAZINE #9
[November] 1977
29.2 x 20.9 cm, 11½ x 8¼ in

Features the Radiators from Space and the Desperate Bicycles.

RIPPED & TORN #9
Tony Drayton
November 1977
29.8 x 20.6 cm, 11¾ x 8½ in

This one-year anniversary issue includes articles on the Sex Pistols, Dead Fingers, the Weirdos and others, with Johnny Rotten on the cover.

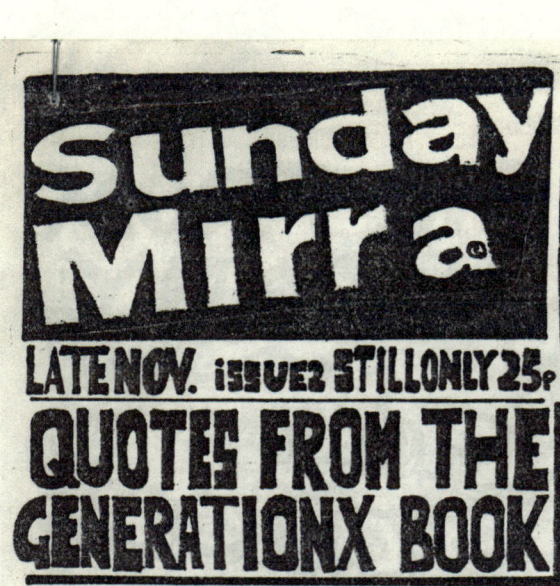

SUNDAY MIRRA #2
November 1977
29.8 × 20.9 cm, 11¾ × 8¼ in

Highlights Sham 69, Wire and the Sex Pistols.

TOUR PROGRAMME FOR THE TUBES AT THE HAMMERSMITH ODEON
November 1977
29.8 x 20.9 cm, 11¾ x 8¼ in

This four-page programme includes photos, a discography, liner notes and lyrics to the song 'White Punks on Dope'.

UP 'N' COMING #4
November 1977
20.3 x 16.5 cm, 8 x 6½ in

Features Warren Harry, Buster Crabbe, Amazorblades, Grand Hotel and Clayson and the Argonauts.

**PROMO FOR BLONDIE'S SINGLE
'RIP HER TO SHREDS'**
November 1977
29.8 x 20.9 cm, 11¾ x 8¼ in

Blondie's first single on Chrysalis Records in the UK was issued in 12" and 7" formats. The B-sides, 'In the Flesh' and 'X Offender', had both previously been issued as A-side singles by Private Stock Records.

STICK THIS ON YOUR WALL

POSTER FOR GENERATION X AT KING'S COLLEGE, LONDON
4 November 1977
57.1 x 75.5 cm, 22½ x 29¾ in

In 1976, Generation X were the first band to play at the Roxy. The group performed their debut single, 'Your Generation', on *Marc*, a music-based television programme hosted by Marc Bolan of T. Rex, the day before they appeared at King's College. Bolan's death on 16 September, however, delayed the show's broadcast until later that month.

POSTER FOR THE CLASH'S 'OUT OF CONTROL' TOUR, WITH RICHARD HELL & THE VOIDOIDS
Sebastian Conran
8–9 November 1977
101.6 × 76.2 cm, 40 × 30 in

Conran recollects working on the poster: 'I was at college (Central), being a roadie for the Clash and doing general design work on their posters, record sleeves, T-shirts, etc. Joe Strummer and I shared a house with photographer Roco Macauley; we had a darkroom in the basement … The artwork for the poster and sleeve were about the size of a postcard, which I prepared in my bedroom. It was a great feeling arriving in a town on the tour-bus and seeing the posters pasted all over the place … It was mainly on the strength of this work, which Michael Wolff liked, that I got my first job with Wolff Olins.'

FLYER FOR SLAUGHTER & THE DOGS, SPIZZ 77, RAPED AND MÉTAL URBAIN AT THE VORTEX
14 November 1977
29.2 x 20.3 cm, 11½ x 8 in

ADVERTISEMENT FOR THE SEX PISTOLS' NEVER MIND THE BOLLOCKS, HERE'S THE SEX PISTOLS IN MELODY MAKER
19 November 1977
41.9 x 29.2 cm, 16½ x 11½ in

A collage of newspaper clippings, with details about the album.

NOV 1977 — $1.50/75p (UK)

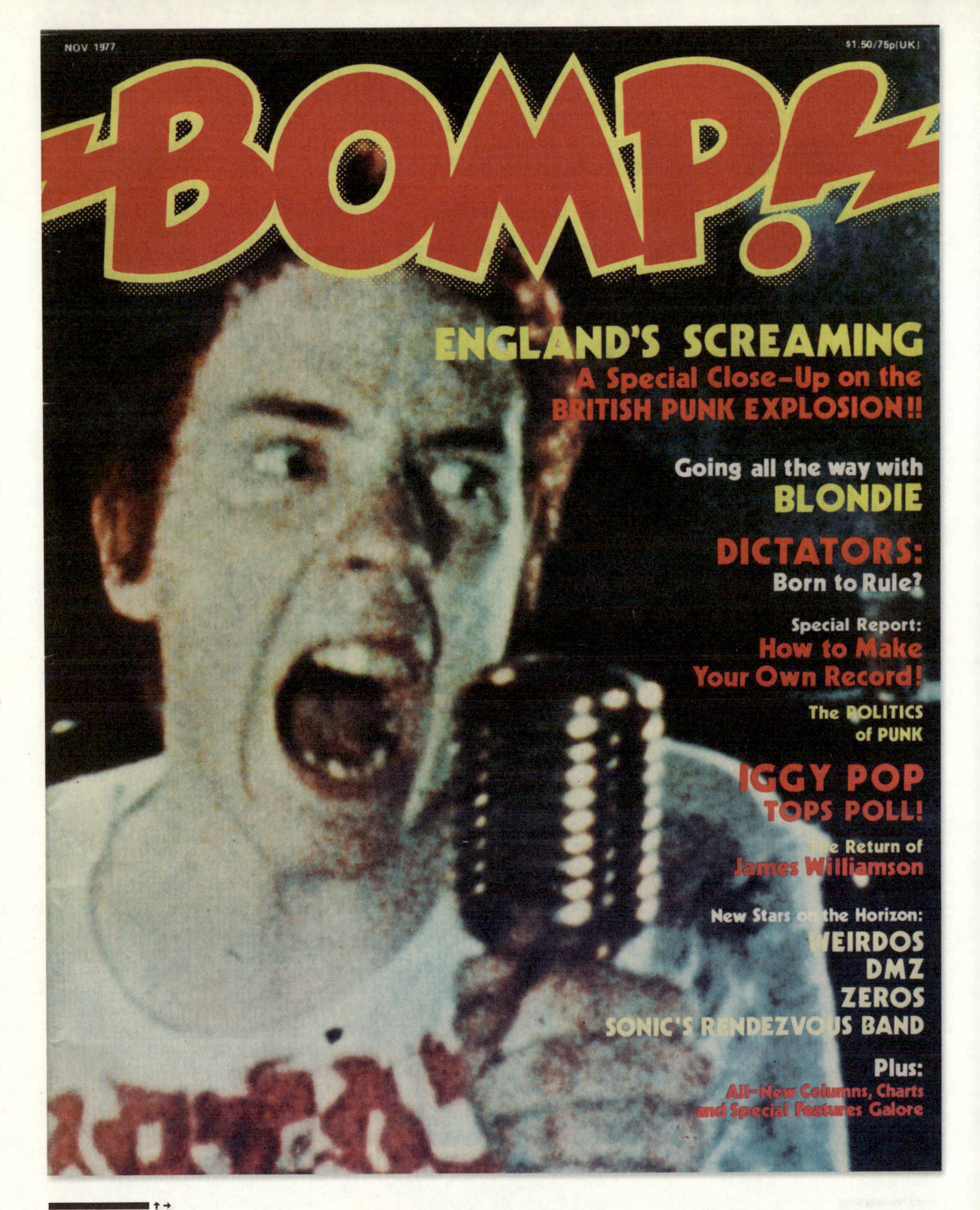

BOMP!

ENGLAND'S SCREAMING
A Special Close-Up on the BRITISH PUNK EXPLOSION!!

Going all the way with BLONDIE

DICTATORS: Born to Rule?

Special Report: How to Make Your Own Record!

The POLITICS of PUNK

IGGY POP TOPS POLL!

The Return of James Williamson

New Stars on the Horizon:
WEIRDOS
DMZ
ZEROS
SONIC'S RENDEZVOUS BAND

Plus:
All-New Columns, Charts and Special Features Galore

BOMP!
November 1977
[no other info]

The full title was *Who Put the Bomp*, but it became known as simply *Bomp!* This issue features 'England's Screaming', a detailed chronological account of British punk by Don Hughes and Greg Shaw with help from *NME*. Spanning glam, pub rock and the early punk scene of the 101'ers, the Sex Pistols and *Sniffin' Glue*, this article is an example of early punk navel-gazing.

ENGLAND'S SCREAMING!

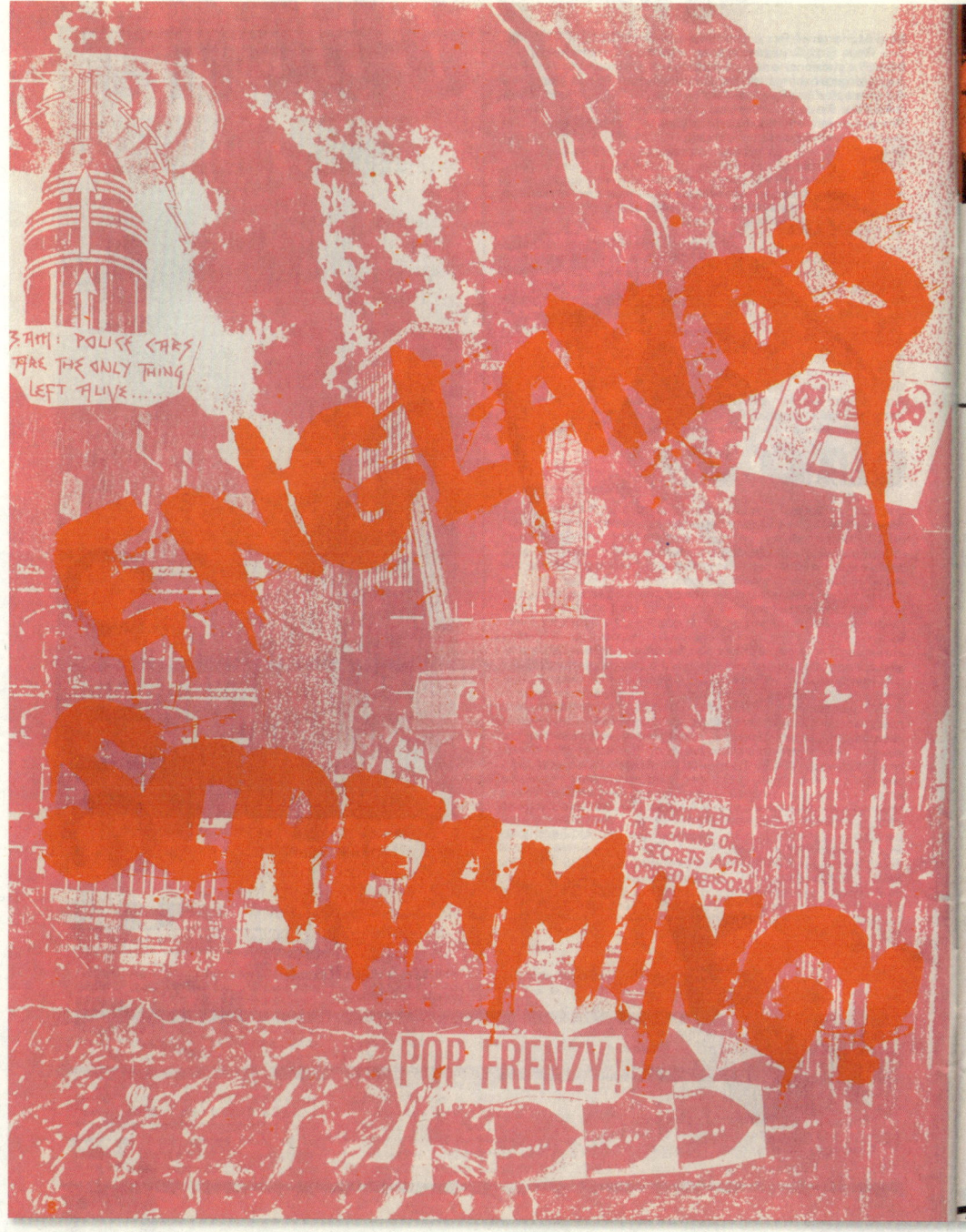

POP FRENZY!

3AM: POLICE CARS ARE THE ONLY THING LEFT ALIVE...

ENGLAND. A year ago, wh[at]
A distant land full of fading superstar[s]
fan from Decatur to Dunedin is savi[ng]
of the ongoing revolution tha[t]
PUNK ROCK. At the start, it wasn't
cultural mulch of London's out-of-work
established order and a spectacle tha[t]
the fab moptops. By now the New Wa[ve]
something about the way they do it in
loose in the streets of London; it's out
we thought this might be a good time to

AS IT HAPPENED:
A CHRONOLOG OF THE U.K. PUNK SCENE

London—1973

With glitter rock, **Bowie, Elton, Zep, Floyd,** et al, at their peaks, rock concerts were very much a them & us situation. Throughout this year, older rock fans looked to the pubs for entertainment as the "stars" increasingly played fewer concerts and many left England entirely, as tax exiles. As the fans began to realize how impersonal it had all become, there was a desire to return to the basics, first seen in the Rockabilly revival groups that played in the London pubs: **Crazy Cavan, Rock Island Line, Shakin' Stevens, HWild Angels, Fumble.** These bands helped instigate a return to **fun** rock & roll, supported by the well-developed Teddy Boy scene (since the end of the '50s England has always had thousands of diehard greasers (or Teds as they call 'em) who dressed and acted in outrageous '50s punk style and lived in their own self-contained world) and as their legions grew, the Black Raven pub (opposite Petticoat Lane) was a mecca for the movement around this time.

London—1974

The pub-rock scene was by now well established, with all forms of music being performed on a "good-time" level, reaching a high-water mark by the end of the year. The Hope & Anchor had established itself as the leading venue for all pub-rock bands, the most successful at this time being **Dr. Feelgood** (R&B), **Kokomo** (soul), and **Chilli Willi & the Red Hot Peppers** (country rock). By December, **Feelgood** had a record contract and began to hit the provinces; the word soon got around that they were **the** band to see. December saw the release of "Roxette".

1975

JAN/FEB

The Naughty Rhythms Tour:

273

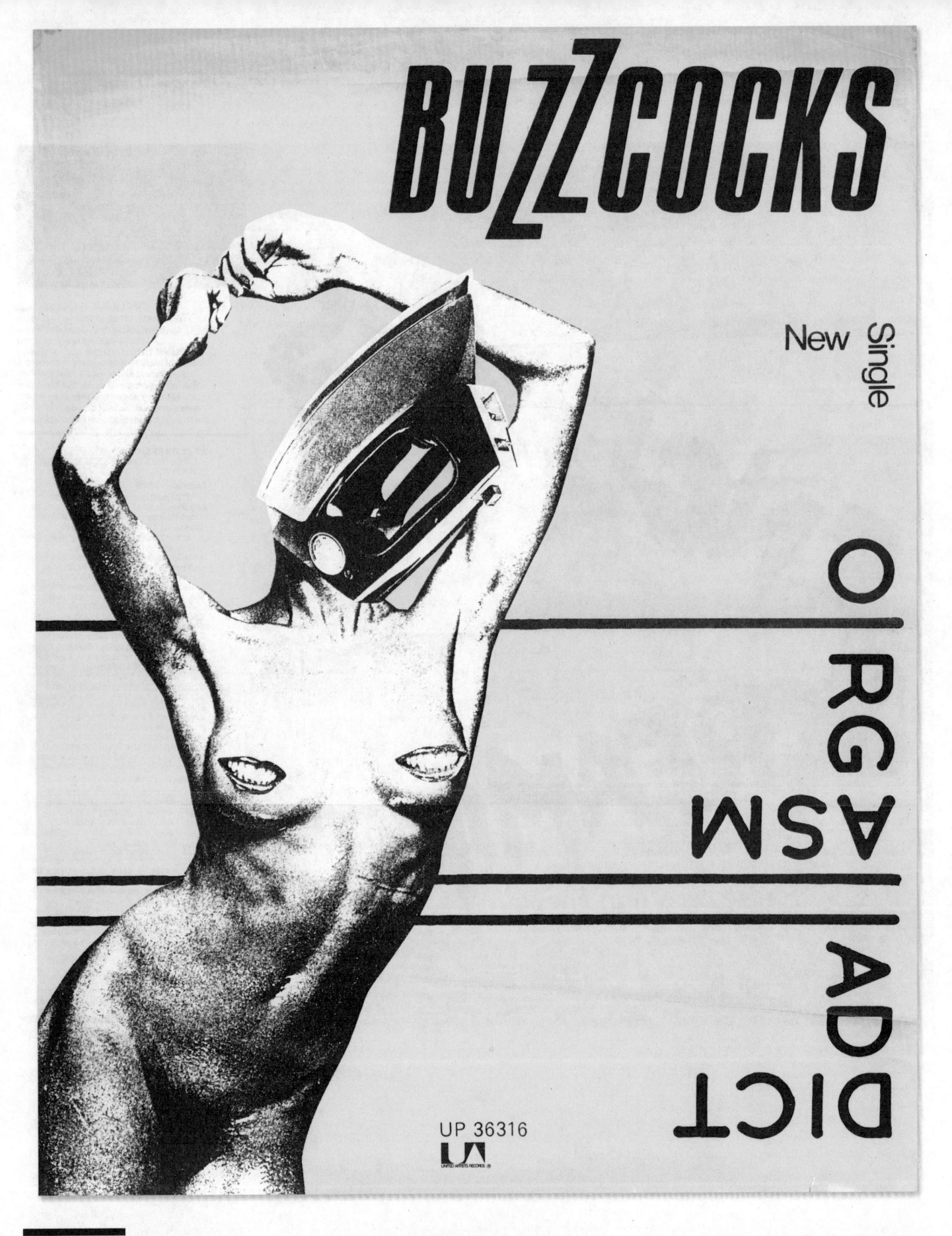

**POSTER FOR BUZZCOCKS' SINGLE
'ORGASM ADDICT'**
Linder Sterling, Malcolm Garrett
November 1977
99 × 73 cm, 39 × 28¾ in

'Orgasm Addict' was the band's first single with United Artists and without original frontman Howard Devoto. The poster is an expanded version of the single sleeve's confrontational collage. Sterling once described making the collage 'in a Salford bedroom; I had a sheet of glass, a scalpel and piles of women's mags... the iron came from an Argos catalogue and the female torso came from a photographic magazine called *Photo*'. Guitarist and singer Pete Shelley said, 'It's exactly what you want for a record sleeve. As soon as you see it, you can't get the image out of your head. It was all pretty top shelf back in 1977.'

PROMO CARD FOR THE CLASH
Sebastian Conran
1977
[dims unknown]

Sebastian Conran studied industrial design engineering at Central Saint Martins in London. Afterward, he worked with the Clash, designing clothes, posters, promotional materials, record sleeves and stage sets.

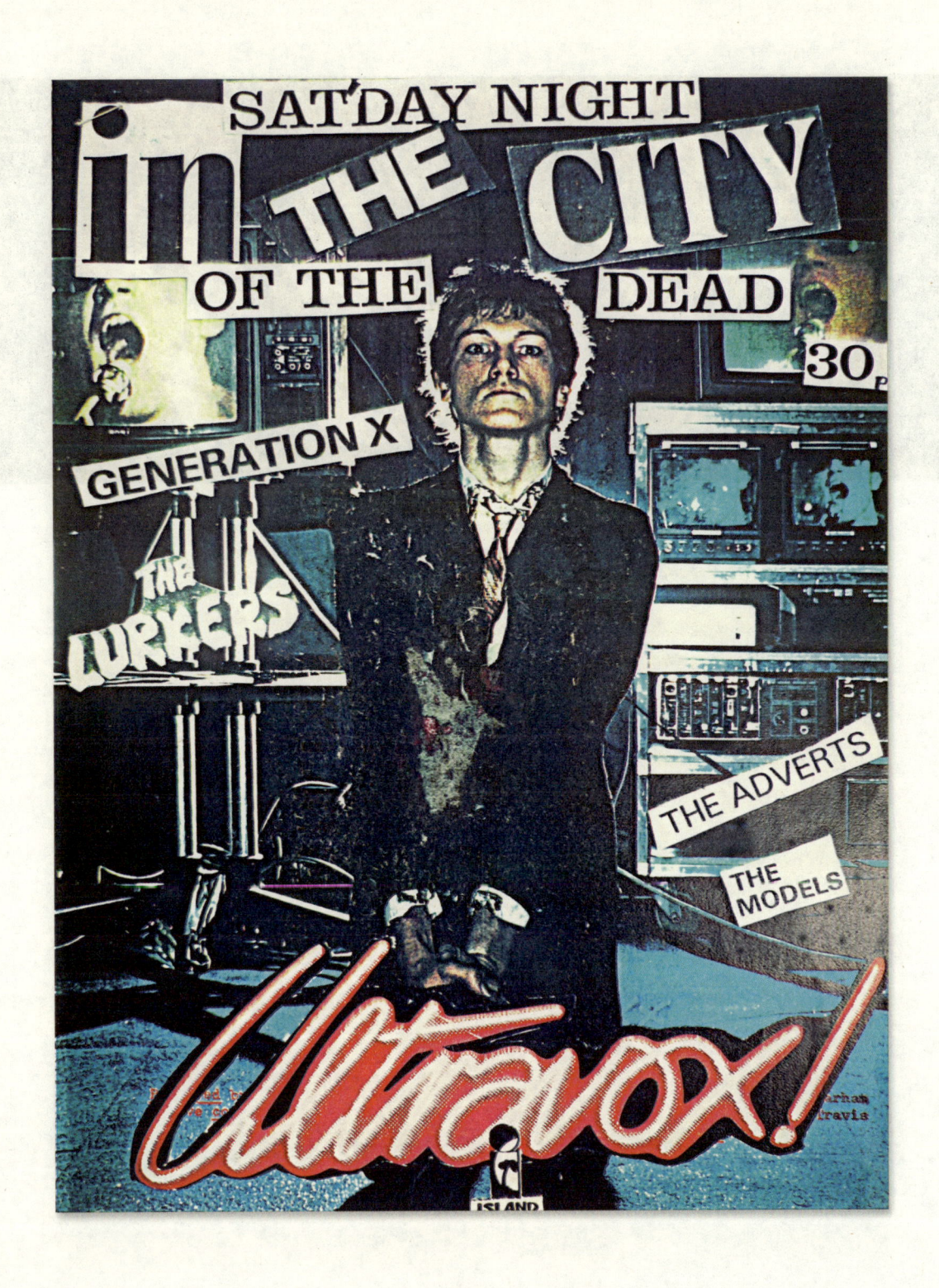

IN THE CITY #1
Francis Drake
1977
29.8 x 21.5 cm, 11¾ x 8½ in

Features Generation X, the Lurkers, the Adverts, the Models and Ultravox. Francis Drake produced this punk-new wave zine while he worked for Virgin Records in London. The majority of issues were 24 stapled pages, with reviews and interviews.

IN THE CITY #2
Francis Drake
1977
29.8 x 20.9 cm, 11¾ x 8¼ in

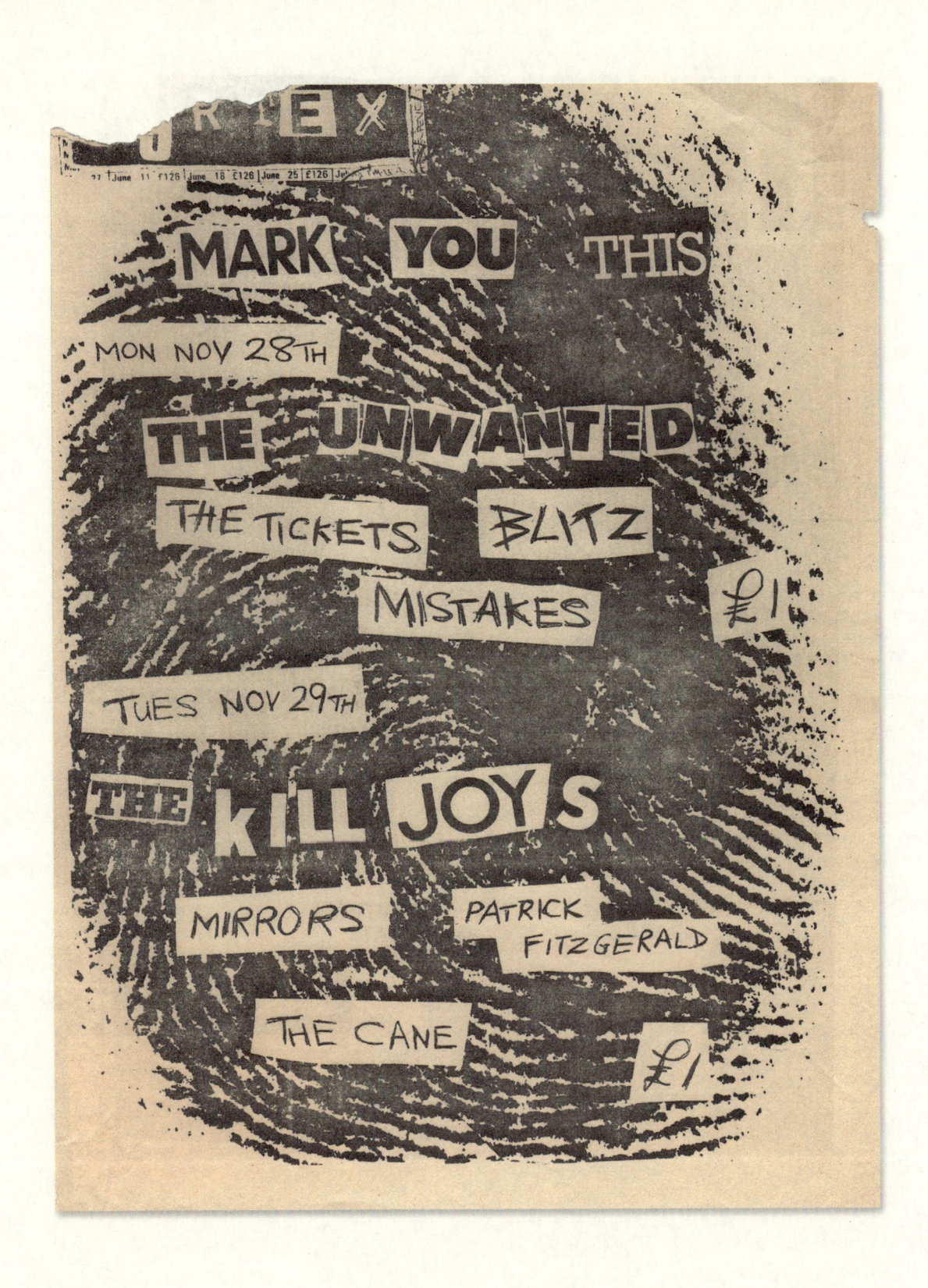

**FLYER FOR THE UNWANTED ET AL
AT THE VORTEX**
28–29 November 1977
27.9 x 20.3 cm, 11 x 8 in

The flyer emulates Jamie Reid's 'ransom note' typography, set against a thumbprint. In addition to the Unwanted, the bill included the Tickets, Blitz, Mistakes, Killjoys, Mirrors, Patrik Fitzgerald and Cane.

**POSTER FOR ALTERNATIVE TV'S SINGLE
'HOW MUCH LONGER'**
29 November 1977
75.5 × 50.8 cm, 29¾ × 20 in

Silkscreened poster for Alternative TV's single 'How Much Longer' with B-side 'You Bastard' on Deptford Fun City Records. The song criticised the trendiness of punk style: 'How much longer will people wear / Nazi armbands and dye their hair?'

POSTER FOR THE DEAD BOYS AND THE DAMNED'S 'UK INVASION' TOUR
November/December 1977
70.4 x 48.8 cm, 27¾ x 19¼ in

This poster also notes the Dead Boys' debut single 'Sonic Reducer'.

PANACHE
Mick Mercer
December 1977
[dims unknown]

With a penchant for goths and dark humour, Mick Mercer showed his talent for spotting the best new bands. The fanzine is a valuable reflection of the period between punk and the later tribal wars between youth subcultures.

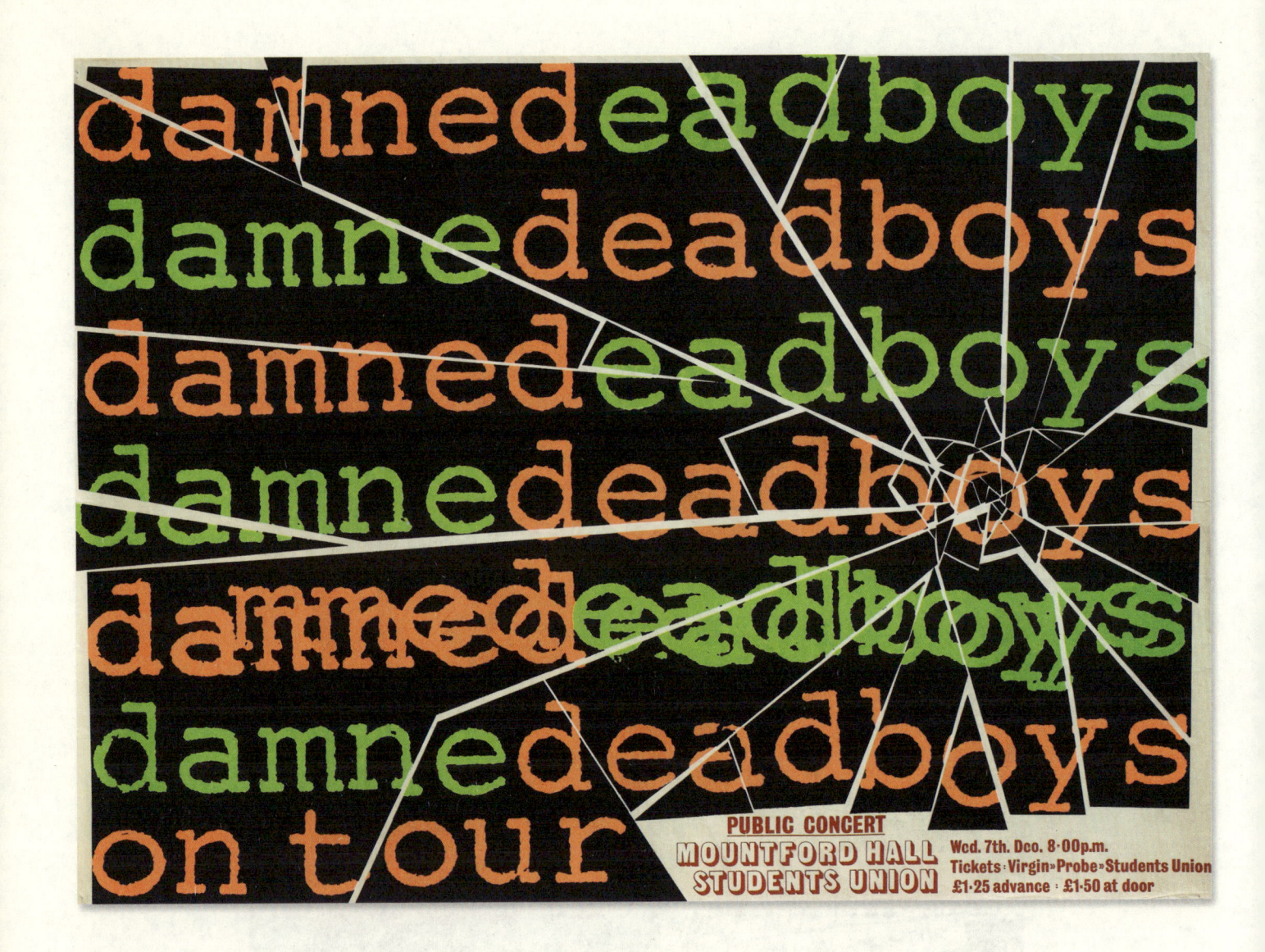

**POSTER FOR THE DAMNED AND DEAD BOYS
AT MOUNTFORD HALL, LIVERPOOL**
7 December 1977
99 x 98.4 cm, 29 x 38¾ in

Although formed after the Sex Pistols, the Damned released the first punk single, 'New Rose'. They also released an album before the Pistols, and were first to tour America. From Cleveland, Ohio, the Dead Boys evolved from the remnants of Rocket from the Tombs.

FLYER FOR THE DAMNED, DEAD BOYS
AND MATT VINYL & THE DECORATORS
AT CLOUDS, EDINBURGH
9 December 1977
[dims unknown]

**FLYER FOR X-RAY SPEX AT THE
HOPE & ANCHOR, LONDON**
10 December 1977
27.9 × 20.9 cm, 11 × 8¼ in

This gig was recorded, and the track 'Let's Submerge' appeared on the *Hope & Anchor Front Row Festival* double LP of live recordings. The flyer features the same image that appears on the sleeve for X-Ray Spex's single 'Oh Bondage, Up Yours!' released several months earlier.

FLYER FOR THE CORTINAS AND THE PIGS AT THE MARQUEE CLUB, LONDON
14 December 1977
29.8 × 20.9 cm, 11¾ × 8¼ in

The short-lived group the Cortinas released three singles and an album. Step Forward Records released the second single, 'Defiant Pose', two days after this concert. Drummer Daniel Swan recalls, 'By the end of 1977 it felt like the whole scene had a giant hangover and there was a feeling of "what are we going to do now."'

POSTER FOR THE CORTINAS' SINGLE 'DEFIANT POSE'
[December] 1977
75.5 x 50.8 cm, 29¾ x 20 in

Silkscreened in-store promo for the Cortinas' second single on Step Forward Records.

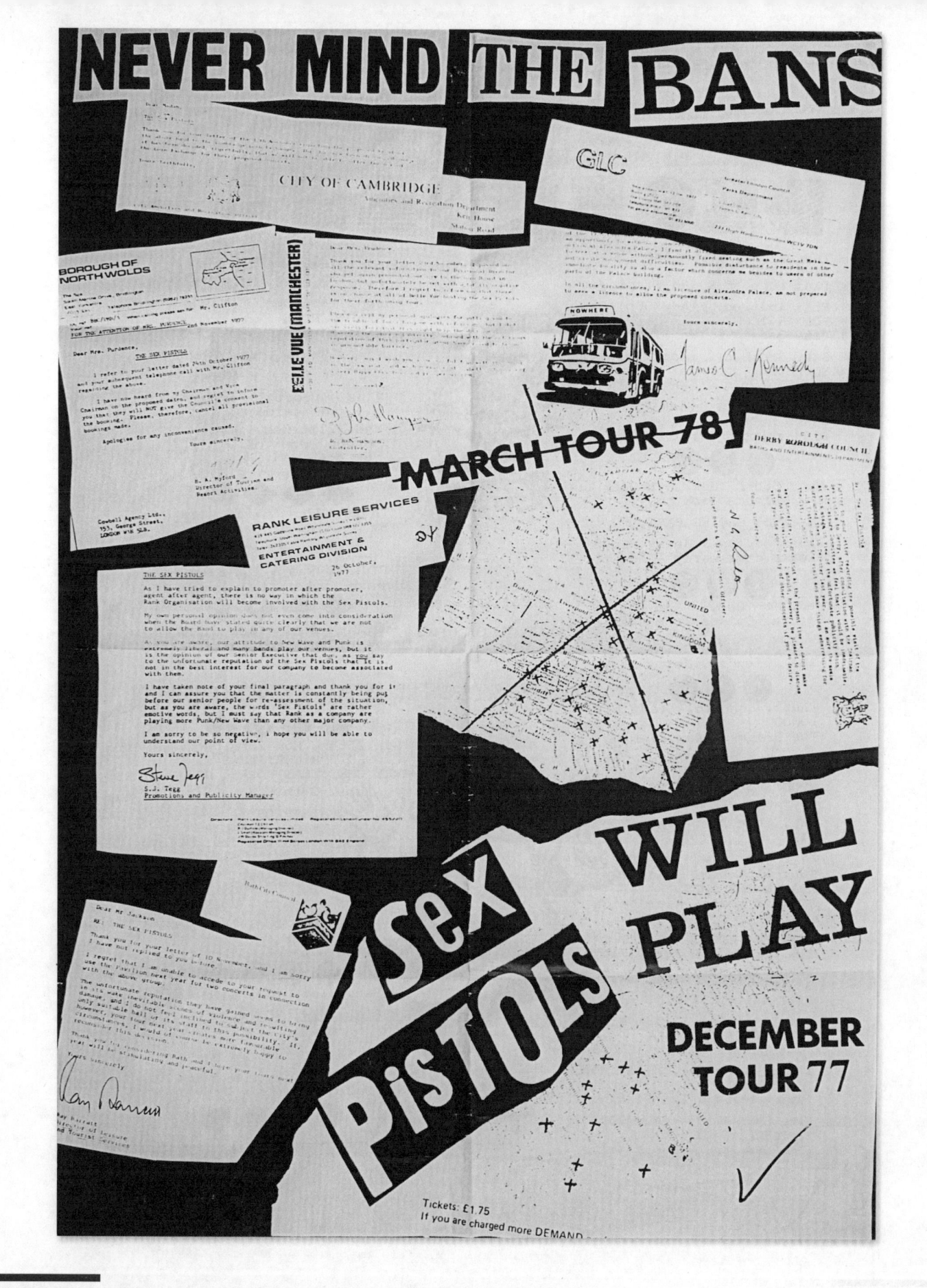

**PROMOTIONAL MATERIAL FOR THE SEX PISTOLS'
'NEVER MIND THE BANS' UK TOUR**
Jamie Reid
December 1977
95.8 x 64.1 cm, 37¾ x 25¼ in

The Sex Pistols' 'Never Mind the Bans' tour would be their last in the UK. The poster incorporates several letters of cancellation from promoters and local civic councils.

DECEMBER 77

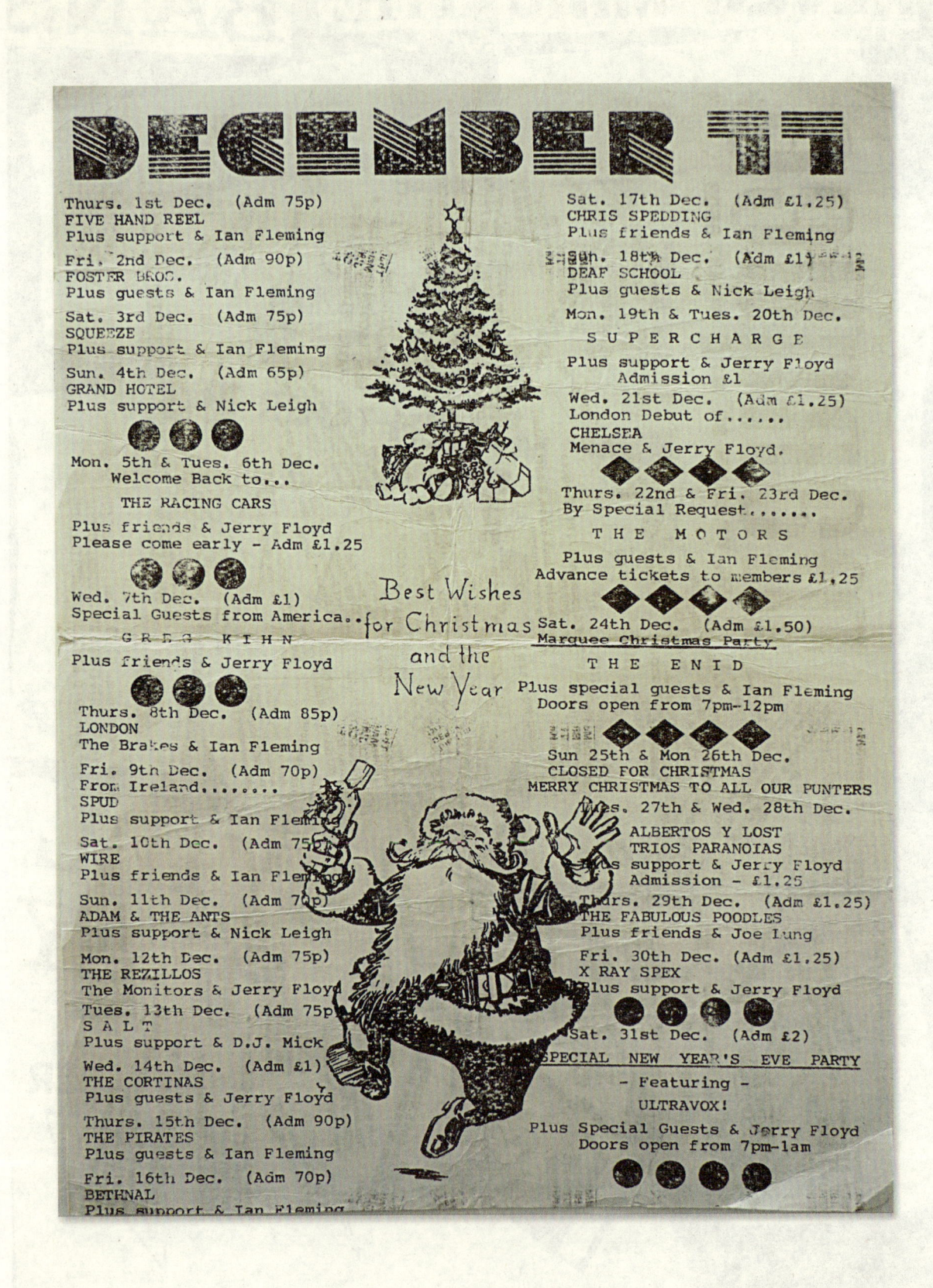

Thurs. 1st Dec. (Adm 75p)
FIVE HAND REEL
Plus support & Ian Fleming

Fri. 2nd Dec. (Adm 90p)
FOSTER BROS.
Plus guests & Ian Fleming

Sat. 3rd Dec. (Adm 75p)
SQUEEZE
Plus support & Ian Fleming

Sun. 4th Dec. (Adm 65p)
GRAND HOTEL
Plus support & Nick Leigh

Mon. 5th & Tues. 6th Dec.
Welcome Back to...
THE RACING CARS
Plus friends & Jerry Floyd
Please come early - Adm £1.25

Wed. 7th Dec. (Adm £1)
Special Guests from America..
GREG KIHN
Plus friends & Jerry Floyd

Thurs. 8th Dec. (Adm 85p)
LONDON
The Brakes & Ian Fleming

Fri. 9th Dec. (Adm 70p)
From Ireland........
SPUD
Plus support & Ian Fleming

Sat. 10th Dec. (Adm 75p)
WIRE
Plus friends & Ian Fleming

Sun. 11th Dec. (Adm 70p)
ADAM & THE ANTS
Plus support & Nick Leigh

Mon. 12th Dec. (Adm 75p)
THE REZILLOS
The Monitors & Jerry Floyd

Tues. 13th Dec. (Adm 75p)
S A L T
Plus support & D.J. Mick

Wed. 14th Dec. (Adm £1)
THE CORTINAS
Plus guests & Jerry Floyd

Thurs. 15th Dec. (Adm 90p)
THE PIRATES
Plus guests & Ian Fleming

Fri. 16th Dec. (Adm 70p)
BETHNAL
Plus support & Ian Fleming

Sat. 17th Dec. (Adm £1.25)
CHRIS SPEDDING
Plus friends & Ian Fleming

Sun. 18th Dec. (Adm £1)
DEAF SCHOOL
Plus guests & Nick Leigh

Mon. 19th & Tues. 20th Dec.
SUPERCHARGE
Plus support & Jerry Floyd
Admission £1

Wed. 21st Dec. (Adm £1.25)
London Debut of......
CHELSEA
Menace & Jerry Floyd.

Thurs. 22nd & Fri. 23rd Dec.
By Special Request.......
THE MOTORS
Plus guests & Ian Fleming
Advance tickets to members £1.25

Sat. 24th Dec. (Adm £1.50)
Marquee Christmas Party
THE ENID
Plus special guests & Ian Fleming
Doors open from 7pm-12pm

Sun 25th & Mon 26th Dec.
CLOSED FOR CHRISTMAS
MERRY CHRISTMAS TO ALL OUR PUNTERS

Tues. 27th & Wed. 28th Dec.
ALBERTOS Y LOST
TRIOS PARANOIAS
Plus support & Jerry Floyd
Admission - £1.25

Thurs. 29th Dec. (Adm £1.25)
THE FABULOUS POODLES
Plus friends & Joe Lung

Fri. 30th Dec. (Adm £1.25)
X RAY SPEX
Plus support & Jerry Floyd

Sat. 31st Dec. (Adm £2)
SPECIAL NEW YEAR'S EVE PARTY
- Featuring -
ULTRAVOX!
Plus Special Guests & Jerry Floyd
Doors open from 7pm-1am

Best Wishes for Christmas and the New Year

PROGRAM FOR THE MARQUEE CLUB
December 1977
20.9 x 14.6 cm, 8¼ x 5¾ in

Includes bands performing that month, including Adam and the Ants, the Cortinas, the Rezillos, the Motors, amongst others.

POSTER FOR SUICIDE'S DEBUT ALBUM SUICIDE
Timothy Jackson, Alan Vega
[December] 1977
58.4 × 39.3 cm, 23 × 15½ in

In-store promo for Suicide's eponymous album on Red Star Records. Suicide played its first gig in November 1970 at Vega's workshop space, the Project of Living Artists. Flyers announced that early performance as 'Punk Music by Suicide'. It appears to have been the first use of the word 'punk' to advertise a concert.

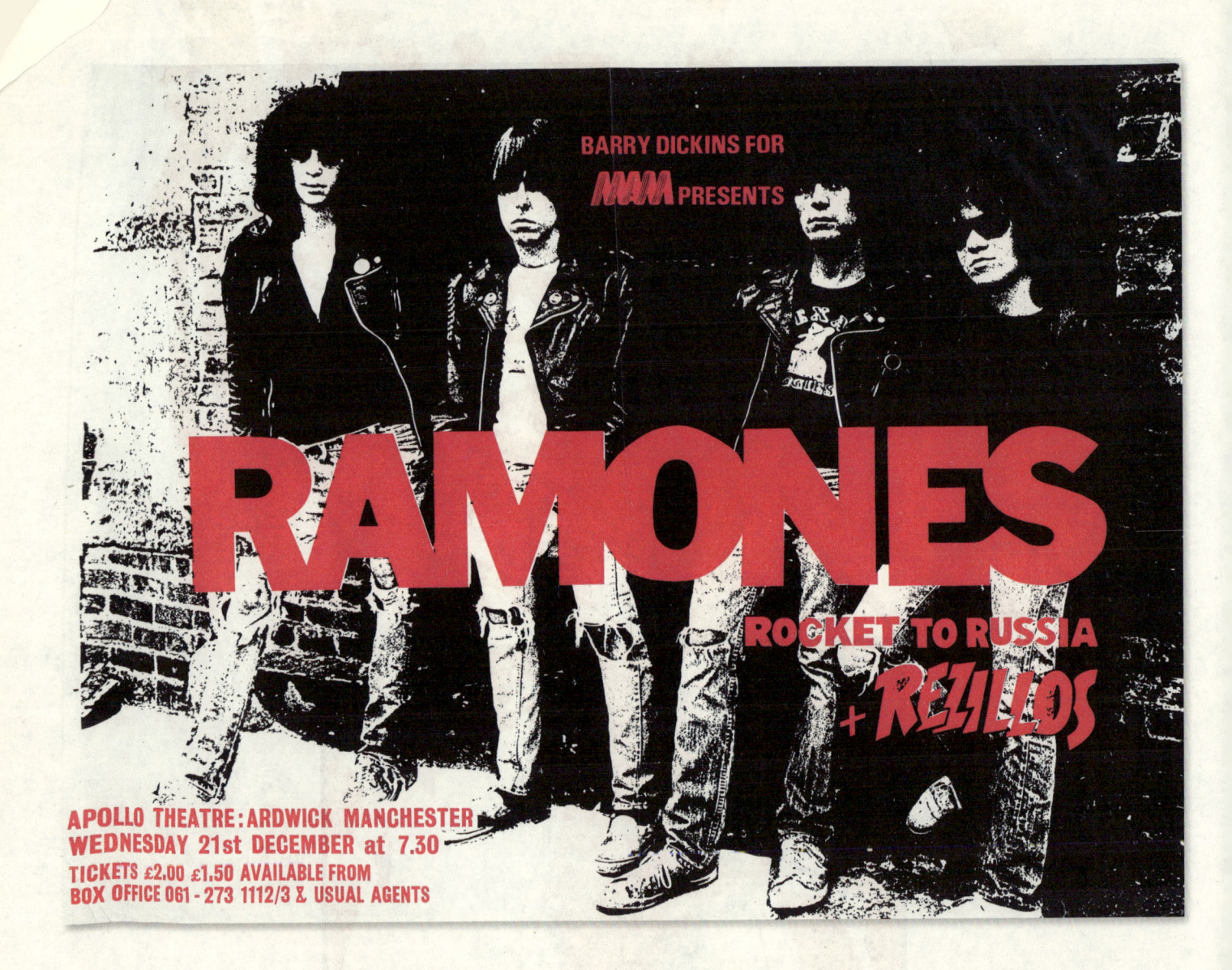

POSTER FOR THE RAMONES' 'ROCKET TO RUSSIA' TOUR AT THE APOLLO THEATRE, MANCHESTER
21 December 1977
75.5 x 97.7 cm, 29¾ x 38½ in

American photographer Roberta Bayley photographed the cover for the Ramones' third album, which was similar to their first. Support came from the Scottish band the Rezillos. The poster came with a copy of the programme and ticket stub for the show.

WHITE STUFF #6
Sandy Robertson
Christmas 1977
29.8 x 20.9 cm, 11¾ x 8¼ in

GRAHAM PARKER POSTER
Barney Bubbles
1977
99.6 x 74.9 cm, 39¼ x 29½ in

PUNK ROCK RULES OK?
Alison Edwards, Glynis Holland
Published by World Distributors, Manchester
1977
29.8 x 20.9 cm, 11¾ x 8¼ in

Punxploitation magazine featuring lurid photos and sinister captions.

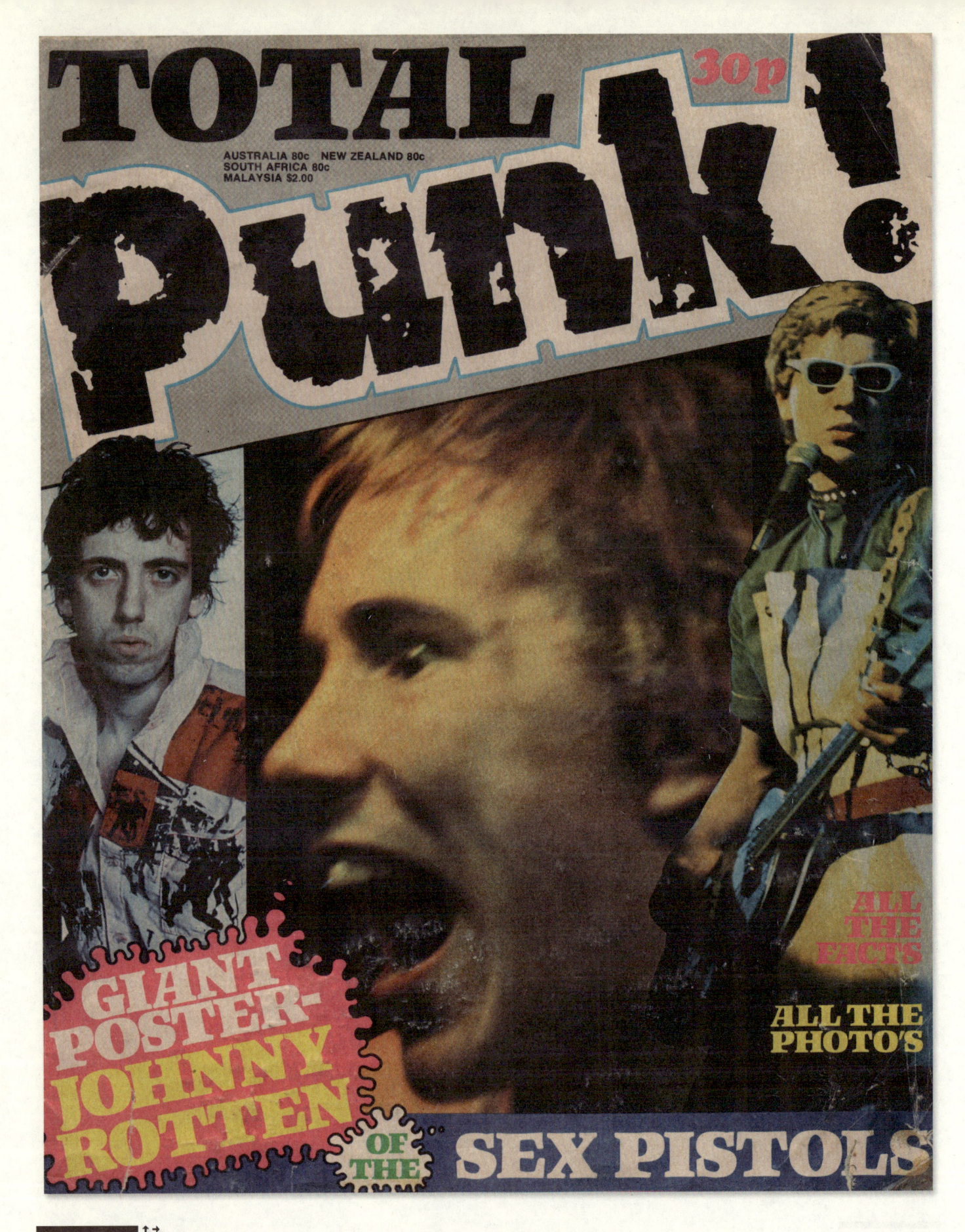

TOTAL PUNK! POSTER MAGAZINE
Produced by IPC Magazines
1977
[dims unknown]

QUOTES:

"We really are the blank generation — we've got nothing to say" — KNOX of the VIBRATORS

"I can remember going to concerts and seeing all those hippies being far out and together, maaaaaaaaaan, despising me because I was about 20 years younger than they were and having short hair. That's when I saw through their bullshit. A lot of punks are like that as well, which makes me really sick" — JOHNNY ROTTEN

Pistols

The Clash

The Jam

Finchley Mob

POSTER FOR GENERATION X'S SINGLE 'PERFECT HITS'
Jon Savage
1977
38.7 x 29.8 cm, 15¼ x 11¾ in

This poster was ripped off the wall of a Generation X gig in Bournemouth, April 1978. The self-released single 'Perfect Hits' had come out the previous year.

Ultravox!

ULTRAVOX ! ist da.
Ultra who ?
ULTRAVOX !

Selbst für Insider der britischen Musikszene ist diese Truppe noch ein weitgehend unbeschriebenes Blatt, denn keiner der fünf Musiker ist bislang - soweit bekannt - irgendwo im Showbusiness in Erscheinung getreten. Umso erstaunlicher mutet das Debüt-Album des Quintetts an. Ausgefeilte Arrangements, intelligente Songs, routinierte Handhabung von Instrument und Studiotechnik, Eigenschaften, über die manch arrivierter Musiker dankbar sein dürfte.

ULTRAVOX ! hieß ursprünglich Tiger Lily und steht ähnlich wie Roxy Music in der Tradition englischer Collegebands, intellektuellen Rockzirkeln, die ihr Personal vornehmlich an den Kunstakademien des Landes rekrutieren. Die fünf Musiker - keiner ist älter als 20 Jahre - kamen auf Initiative des Leadsängers und Hauptsonglieferanten John Foxx zusammen. Er ist die treibende Kraft des Ensembles. Im Sommer 1976 wurde ein Vertrag mit Island Records geschlossen. Danach zog sich die Truppe zurück und sammelte in aller Ruhe Material für ihren ersten Longplayer. Im Herbst schließlich begannen sie mit den Aufnahmesessions. Das Album wird bei uns in Kürze auf den Markt kommen.

/ 2

John Foxx
Stevie Shears
Warren Cann
Billy Currie
Chris Cross

GERMAN MEDIA MATERIALS FOR ULTRAVOX
Island Records
1977
29.8 x 20.9 cm, 11¾ x 8¼ in

To promote the debut release of *Ultravox!* Island sent information about the album and the band to select German media.

ROTTEN TO THE CORE #4
1977
[dims unknown]

Dave Chaos produced this zine in Nottingham when he was eighteen and advertised it as 'Recommended to Guttersnipes'.

THE DAMNED'S DISCIPLES SONG BOOK
1977
29.8 x 20.9 cm, 11¾ x 8¼ in

Published by Stiff Records and originally available by mail order only, the 28-page book contains handwritten lyrics, member information and pictures.

SITUATION #3
1977
29.8 x 21.5 cm, 11¾ x 8½ in

Advertises on its cover: 'If you thought the last issue was crap, wait till you read this one.'

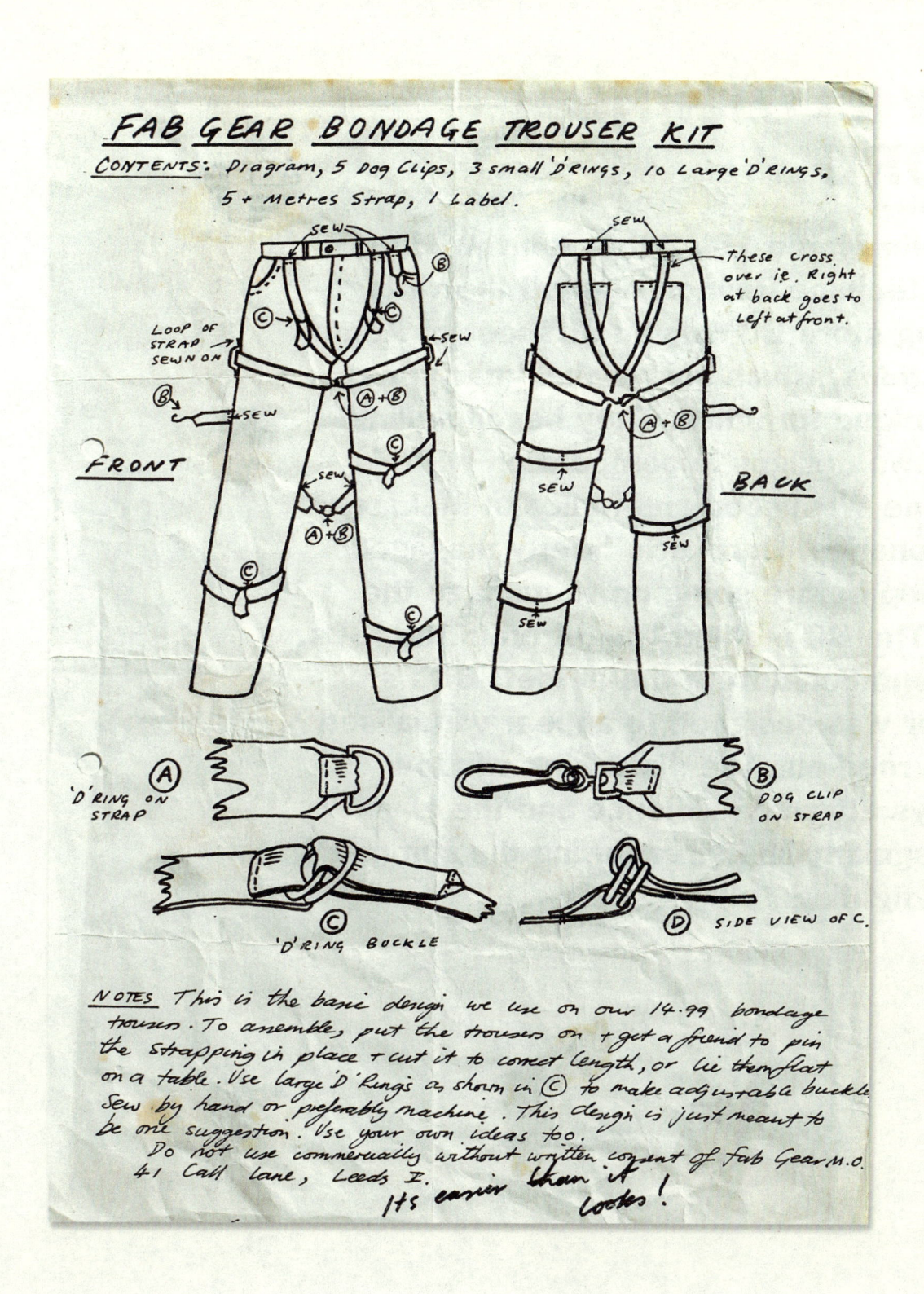

FAB GEAR'S BONDAGE TROUSER KIT FLYER
1970s
29.8 x 20.9 cm, 11¾ x 8¼ in

This instruction sheet on how to fit bondage straps to one's trousers could have been an inspiration to Vivienne Westwood, who opened her clothing boutique, Sex, on Kings Road in 1974, and specialised in bondage gear and other clothing that defined the punk aesthetic.

BOY CLOTHING STORE

It was in March 1977 that John Krivine, with Stephane Raynor, opened the vintage clothing store BOY as an offshoot of Acme Attractions, which sold pinball machines and antique furniture. They began selling their own designs in competition with Vivienne Westwood and Malcolm McLaren's Seditionaries. Don Letts briefly managed the shop before going on to manage the Slits. The BOY brand caught on in the '80s. Confrontational from the outset, BOY's interior was designed to appear vandalised and burned-out; the disturbing window displays attracted violence and the glass was regularly shattered during the summer's street fighting.

BOY POSTER, 'THE STRENGTH OF THE COUNTRY LIES IN ITS YOUTH'
Peter Christopherson
1978
59.6 x 41.9 cm, 23½ x 16½ in

This offset-litho poster, designed by Peter Christopherson, advertises the punk fashion shop using a photograph of a boy with a bloodied head lying in the street, two boot-shod youths standing over him. Some 200 posters were produced. According to John Krivine, 'the boy on the ground is John Hareward (Little John), and the quote is [John and Peter's]. I wasn't even consulted... I wouldn't have commissioned a poster: There was no money for a poster, and what do I do with a poster? I was shocked at the quote. The photo was fine, but the words were very deco, very 1930s. It was like a cheeky gift from them to me.'

**JOHNNY ROTTEN SHOPPING BAG,
BOY CLOTHING STORE**
1978
43.8 x 34.9 cm, 17¼ x 13¾ in

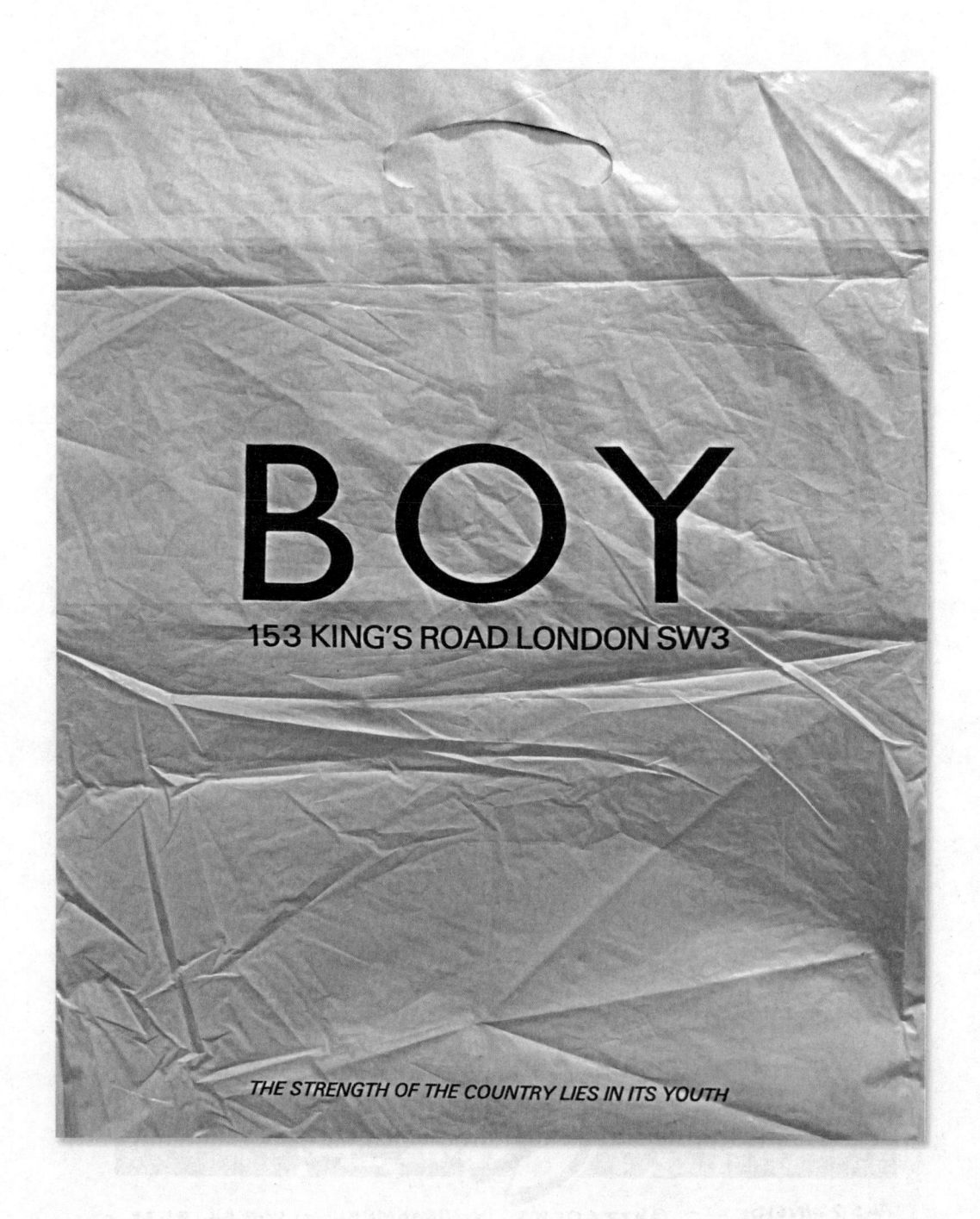

PLASTIC CARRIER BAG, BOY CLOTHING STORE
1978
45 x 35.5 cm, 17¾ x 14 in

CANDYBEAT 504 #4
1978
29.8 x 20.9 cm, 11¾ x 8¼ in

Signed by Fay Fife and Jo Callis of the Rezillos.

TANKIT #1
Published by the Teachers Club
1978
[unknown dims]

A number of specialised groups sprang up in the late '70s to combat the influence of the National Front, amongst them Teachers Against the Nazis (TAN), which produced resource packs for use in primary and secondary schools (TANkits).

NATIONAL FRONT STICKERS
1978
[various dims]

SOCIALIST WORKERS PARTY STICKERS
1978
[various dims]

SKAN #2
1978
31.1 x 21.5 cm, 12¼ x 8½ in

Like Teachers Against Nazis, Skools Against Nazis was the culmination of an Anti-Nazi League effort to influence targeted demographics. SKAN published its own 16-page magazine. This issue features interviews with reggae bands and poems by Leon Rosselson.

SKAN #3
1978
29.8 x 21 cm, 11¾ x 8¼ in

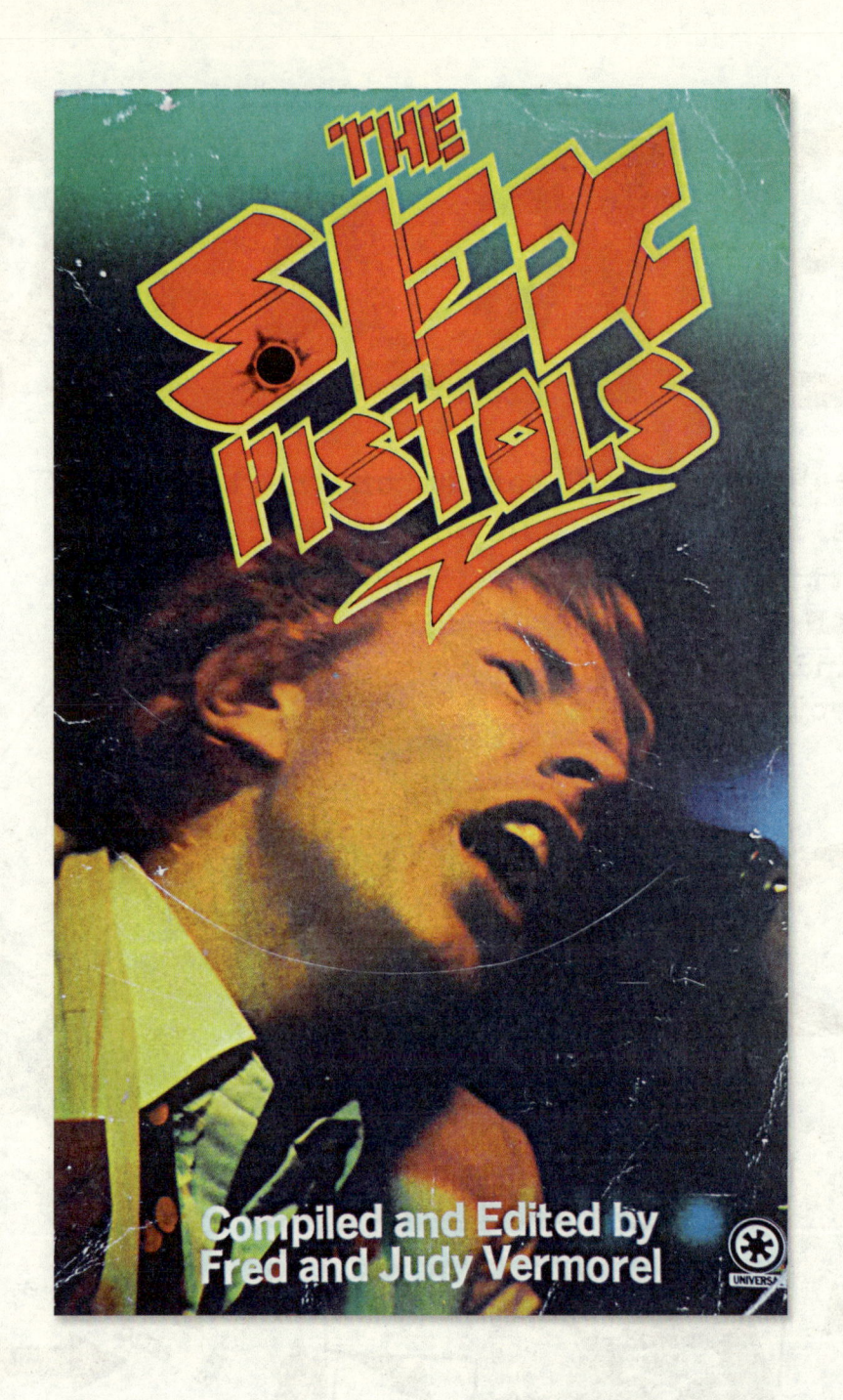

THE SEX PISTOLS
Fred and Judy Vermorel
Universal Books, 1978
18.4 x 10.7 cm, 7¼ x 4¼ in

Published by Universal Books, 224 pages, with eight pages of glossy black-and-white photos.

IN THE GUTTER
Val Hennessy
Quartet, 1978
25.4 × 20.3 cm, 10 × 8 in

This London publication surveys punk fashion and so-called primitive dress. Val Hennessy, a Fleet Street journalist, had limited experience with her subject and produced the book while creating a television programme about punk.

'THE BOY LOOKED AT JOHNNY': THE OBITUARY OF ROCK AND ROLL
Julie Burchill, Tony Parsons
Pluto Press, 1978
19.6 × 13.9 cm, 7¾ × 5½ in

Julie Burchill and Tony Parsons wrote their highly opinionated history of punk while working at *NME* magazine. They were hired after they'd answered an ad for 'two hip young gunslingers' to cover the emerging punk movement.

NOT ANOTHER PUNK BOOK!
Terry Jones, Isabelle Anscombe
Aurum Press, 1978
29.8 x 21.5 cm, 11¾ x 8½ in

This photobook offers a vivid account of the London punk scene.

SHOCKWAVE
Virginia Boston, Derek Ridgers
Plexus Publishing, 1978
[unknown dims]

Features almost 200 of Derek Ridgers's photographs of first-generation punk bands and their audiences between '76 and '77.

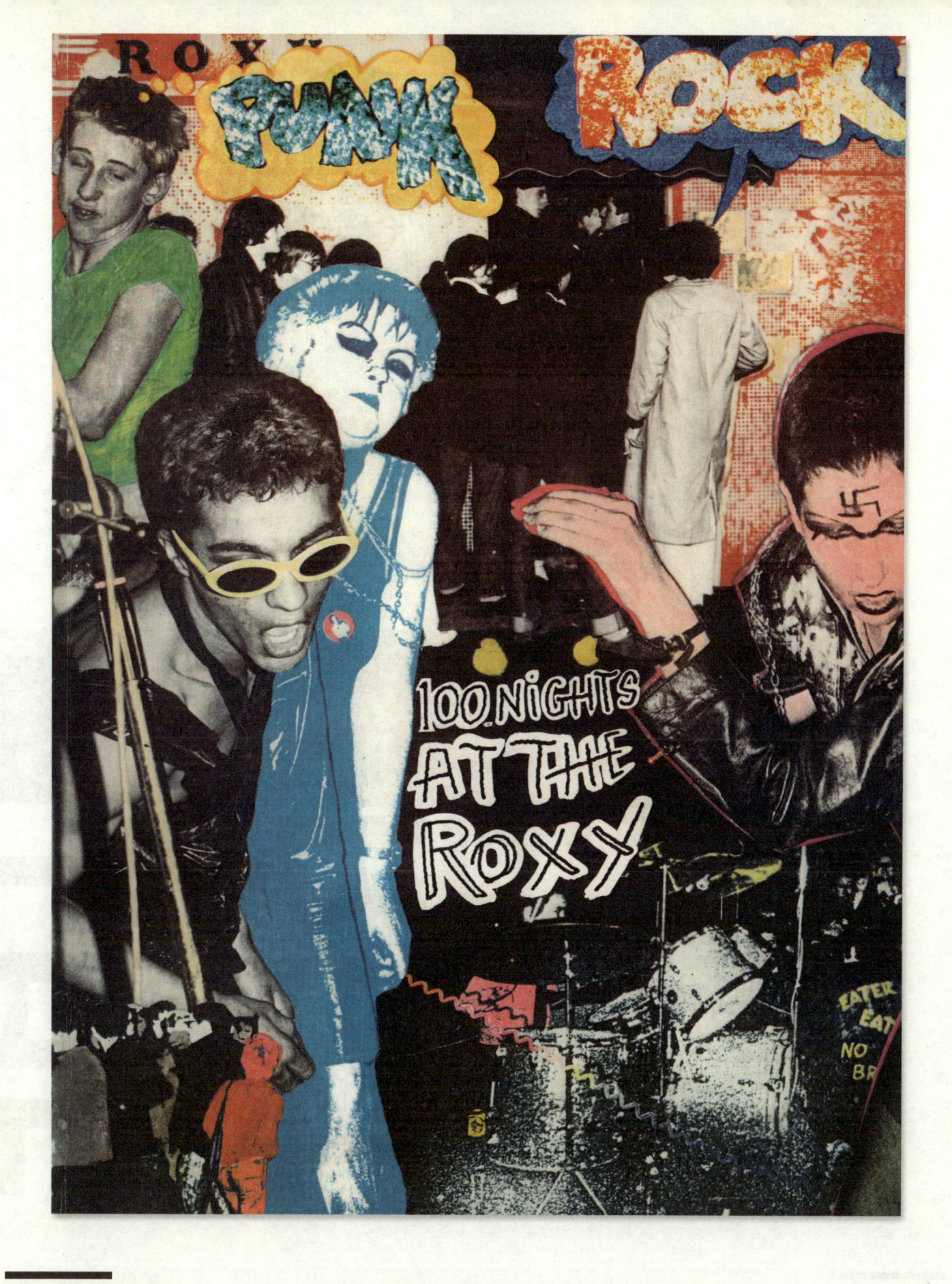

100 NIGHTS AT THE ROXY
Michael Dempsey
Big O Publishing, 1978
29.8 x 20.9 cm, 11¾ x 8¼ in

A pictorial account of the music and culture at the Roxy, compiled by the manager of the Adverts.

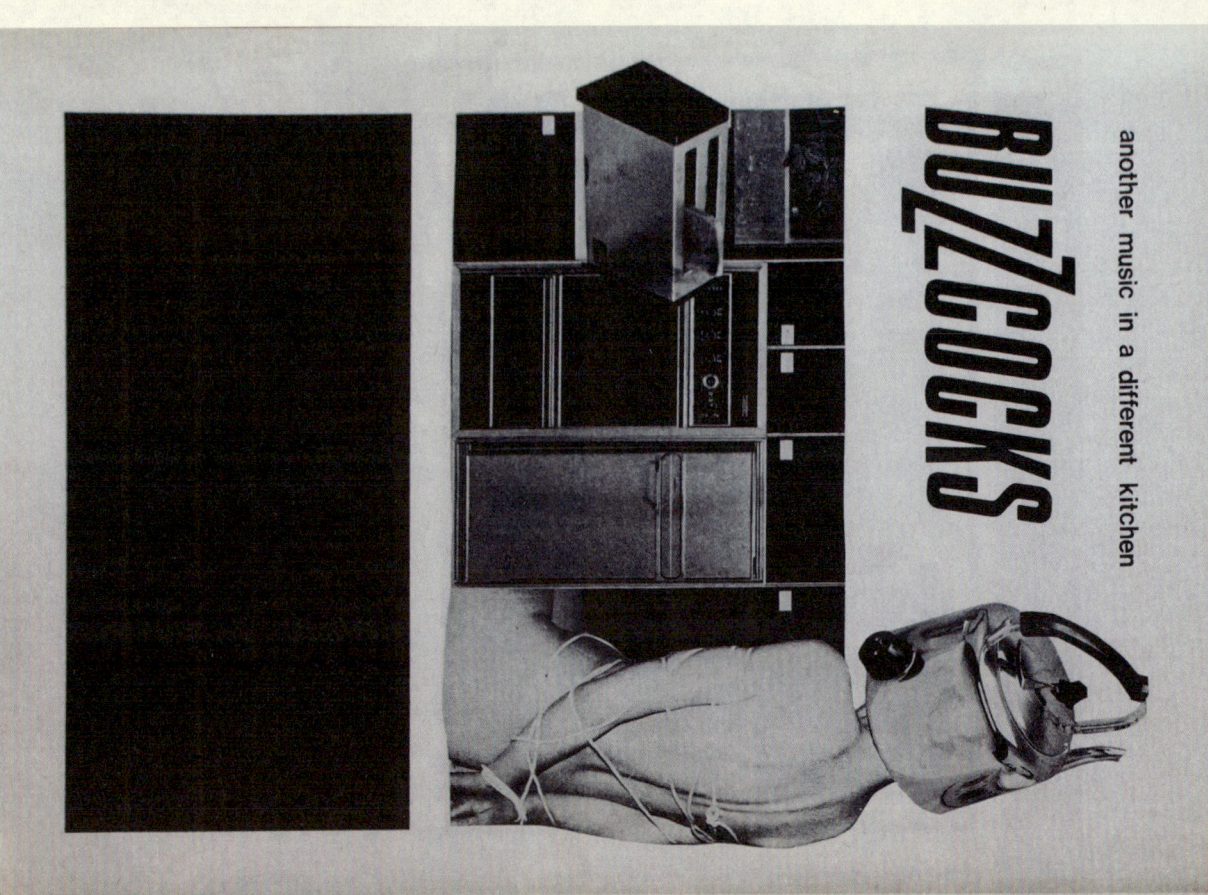

THE SECRET PUBLIC (ORG 2)
1978
41.9 × 59 cm, 16½ × 23¼ in

The Secret Public was a collaboration between Jon Savage and Linder Sterling. They printed the publication in Manchester in an edition of 1,000, and distributed copies through independent record shops. Savage told *Dazed and Confused* in 2010: 'It was certainly inspired by punk and it was just taking it a bit further. Neither of us were particularly interested in punk by numbers because that was as boring as the very thing that punk was reacting against in the first place. Certainly by the time we did it, which was '77, punk had become a cliché. Punk became a cliché very quickly, which is a shame, but it did.'

Strength & Health

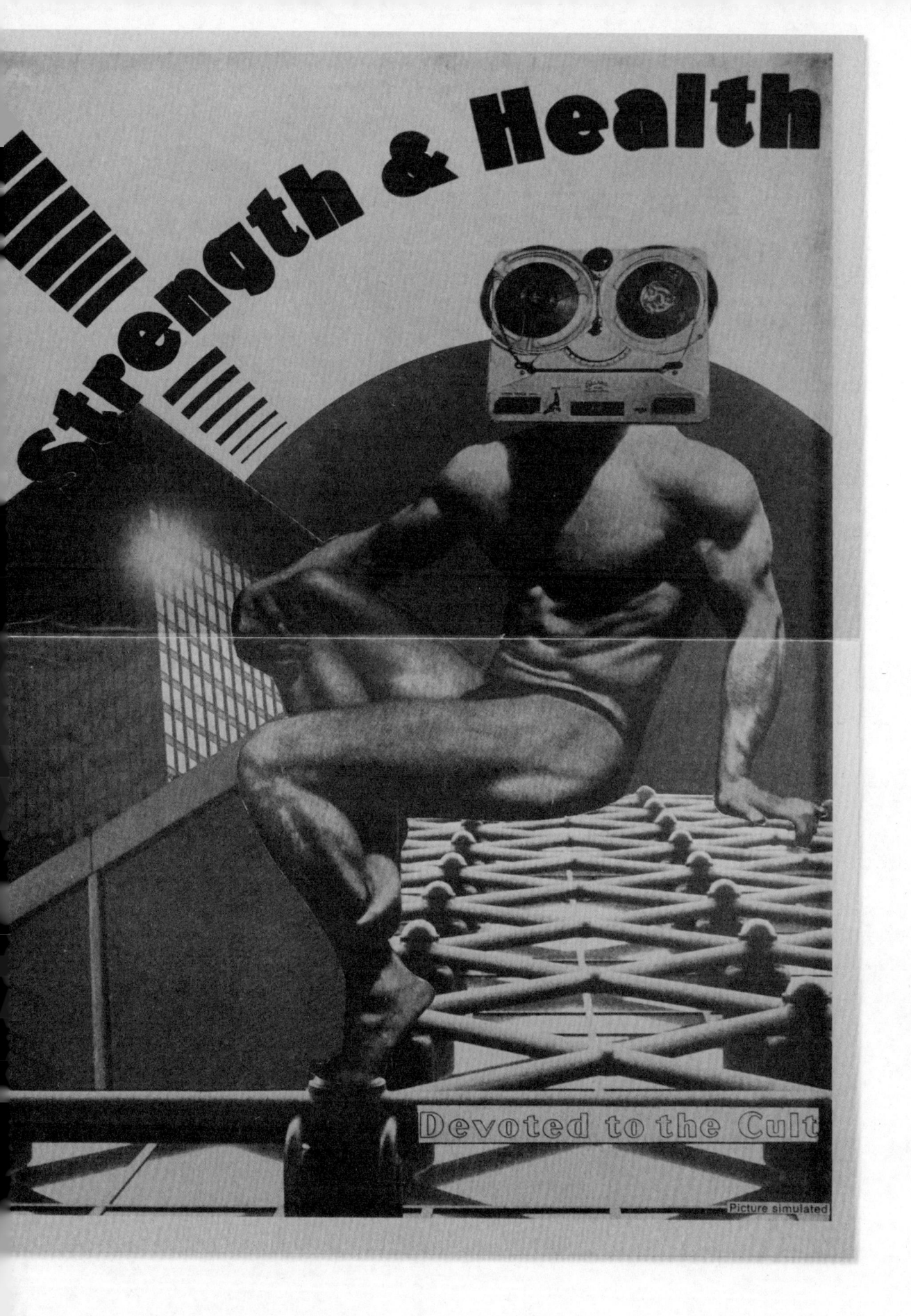

Devoted to the Cult

Picture simulated

There's PEP-PEP-PEP

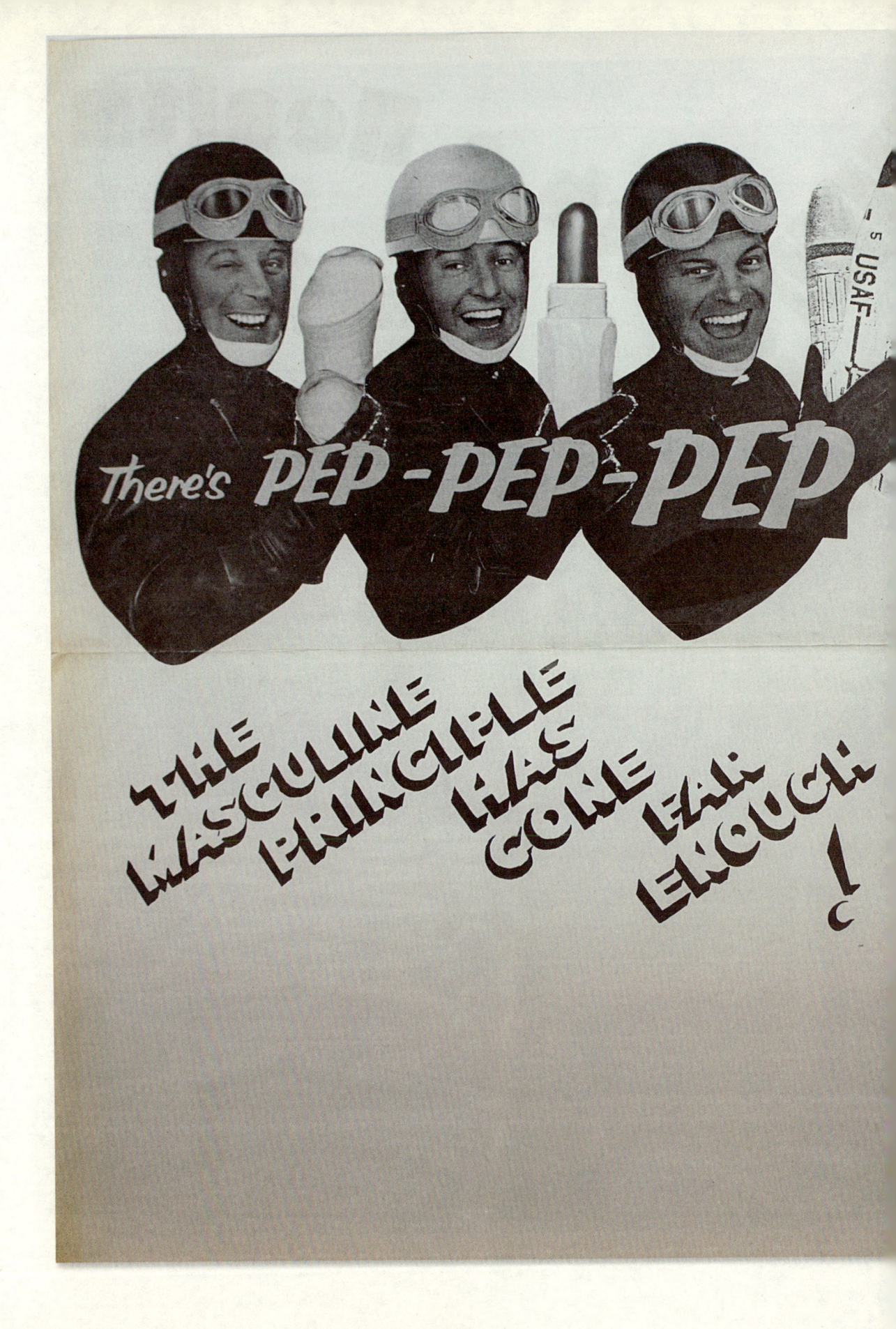

THE MASCULINE PRINCIPLE HAS GONE FAR ENOUGH!

ESQUIRE
BOOT POLISH
AUTOMAT
I am the passenger / & I ride & ride / I ride thru the city's ripped backsides
I need a car that can get me around / I need a city what it can shine

322

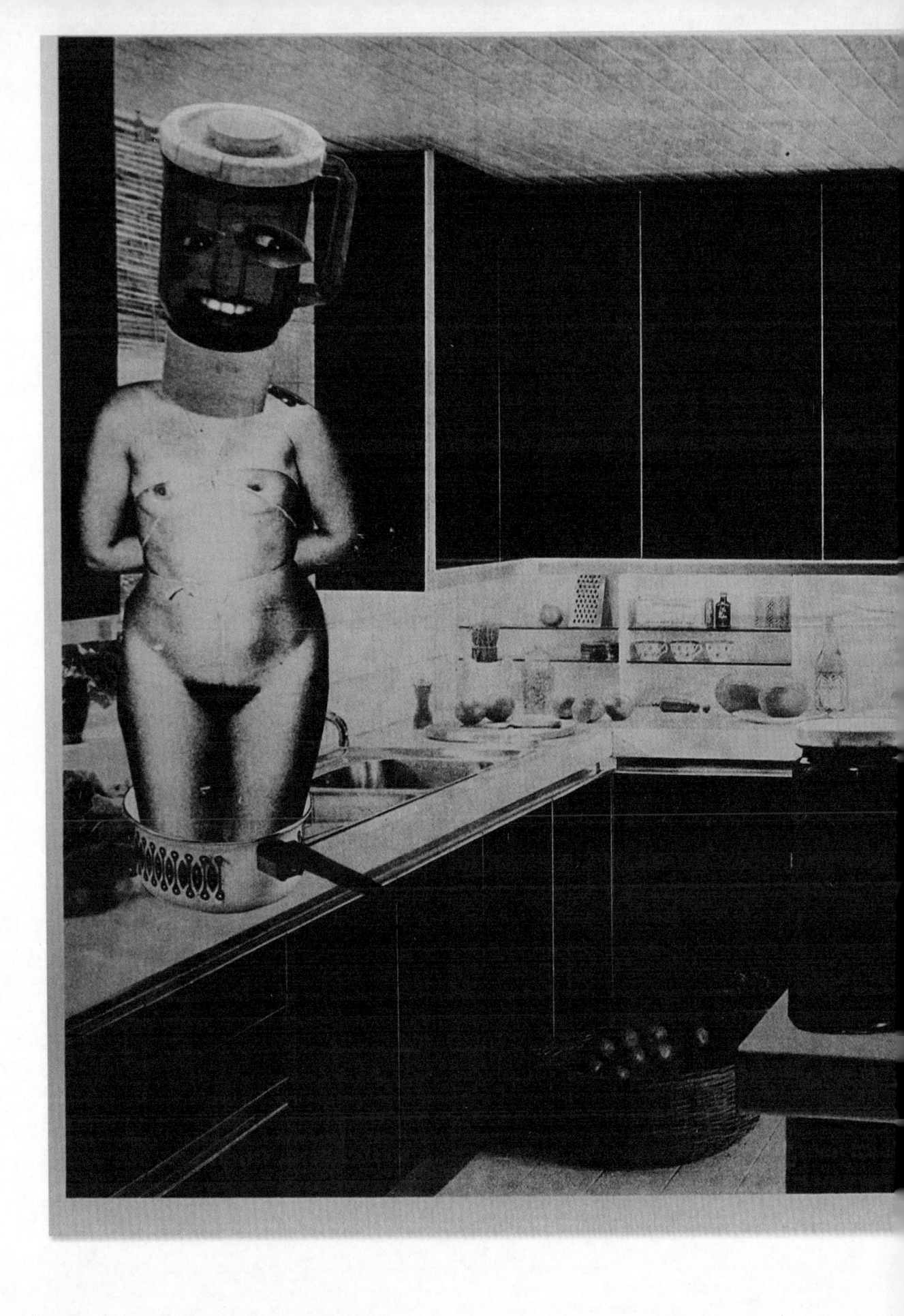

NEW HORMONES
bi product

¡GENERATION X!
Perfect Hits
Low-swung new look! Soft sprung new ride!
MARQUEE THUR MAR 31

pages
1,4,5,8,9
JON SAVAGE

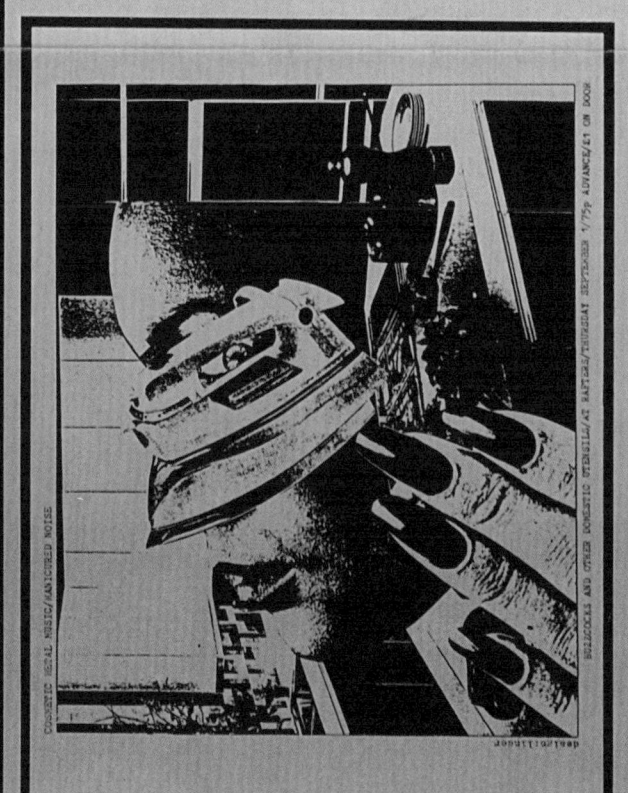

LINDER
pages
2,3,6,7,10,12

ORG 2

hanks to Richard Boon and Ruth Marten

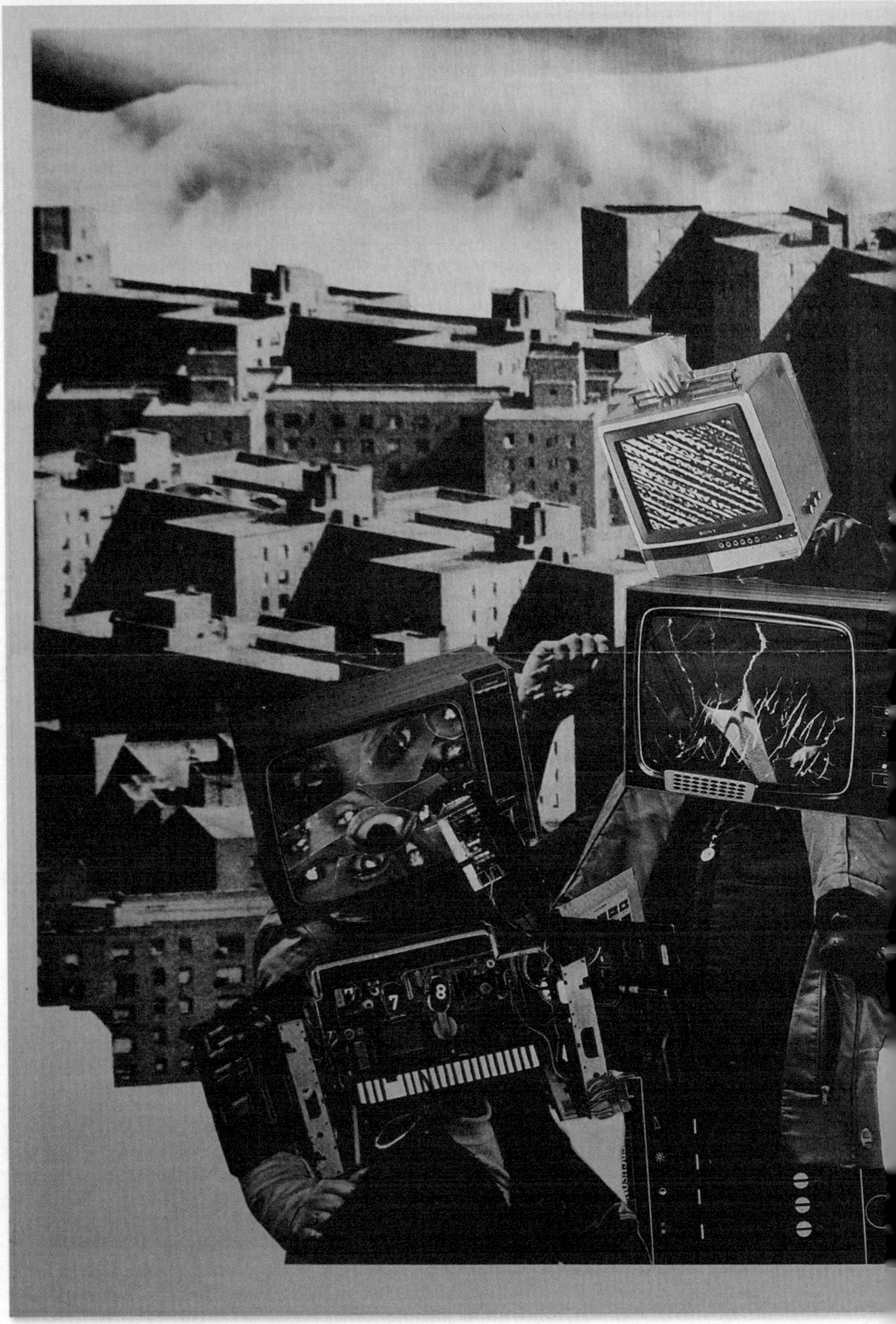

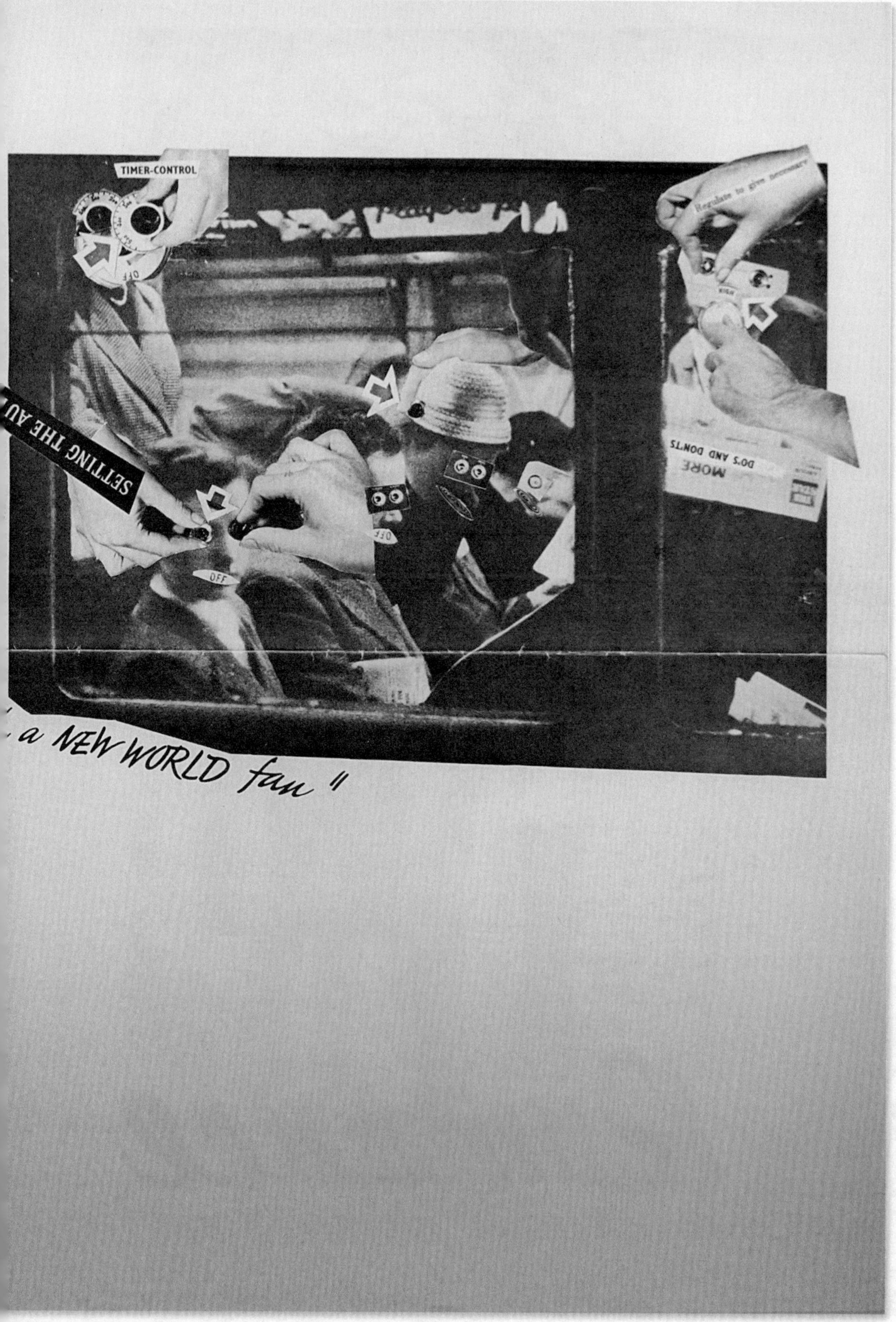
TIMER-CONTROL
SETTING THE AU
Regulate to give necessary
MORE
DO'S AND DON'TS
OFF
OFF
OFF
"a NEW WORLD fan"

Romance

327

AUTOPSY: film soundtrack

The magic is you. Girl's voice 'Well anyway'
I KNEW THEN WE HAD A WORKABLE BOMB
Band 'WHY NOT' ends 'You, you, you.
A-'The one they threw out of the aeroplane.'
S-'Yea, they threw his body out of the aeroplane, right, and then, so what did they do!'
A-'Thats where the Germans went and attacked them in Mogadishu or somewhere.'
S-'Yea and this bloke right, he hadn't a bit of rope or anything so they murdered him!'
A-'Isn't that the three of them that were all... Do you mean the Baader-Meinhof people in Germany is this. There were three of them who were meant to have killed themselves, and then yesterday they discovered, one of the ones who was meant to have killed themselves had been shot through the back of the head'.
Terror ist ultimatum from Mogadishu..
Kodak representative 'At 18 frames a second.'
An injection of Methadine or similar drug.
Would not in fact object if Russia built over its limit of submarine launched ballistic missiles.....And frankly I doubt it.
SUICIDE bass line
OPERATED ON THIS MORNING-..He's said to have died from stomach cancer...DR.GROVES PLEASE.
CRASS-'YOU find that it's not easy would you like to see me dead.'
Suicide bass line
CRASS-'You poke your knives into my brain You send me insane.'
TALKING HEADS-'PSYCHO KILLER qu'est ce que c'est.'
I KNEW THEN WE HAD A WORKABLE BOMB
CRASS-sections from four songs 'Is it working do you really believe in-I am a subject of useless, futureless, endless, mindless.
SECOND THOUGHTS? NO NO NO SECOND THOUGHTS.
D.J.'The Macestra Orchestra called the magic is you.'
Womans birth screams.
WELL I THINK HE'S GONNA HAVE TO CHANGE EITHER THAT OR FACE TOTAL AND UTTER DESTRUCTION.
CRASS-' I am a product, I am a symbol, of endless, hopeless, fruitless, aimless games. I'm a glossy package on a supermarket shelf, my contents ar'nt fit for human consumption, I could tragically injure your perfect health
My ingredients will sieze up your bodies function.
I am the dirt everyone walks on
I am the orphan nobody wants
I am the staircarpet everyone walks on
I am the leper nobody wants to touch
I am a sample I am a scapegoat of useless, futureless, endless, mindless ideas.'
Frankly I doubt it.
Terrorist ultimatum
KYOTO, RELIGIOUS, CULTURAL, CITY.
Machine gun, was shattered. Frankly I doubt it
AND HE ASKED ME IF WE WOULD SCRATCH THAT OFF THE LIST.
PIANO MUSIC.
DOCTOR HAS JUST RETURNED MOST ENTHUSIASTIC AND CONFIDENT THAT THE LITTLE BOY IS AS HUSKY AS HIS BIG BROTHER.
Orchestra with -'Touch me, hold me, and I'll never up and far away. Love me, touch me,
The magic is you.
CRASS-'Is it alright really, Is it working do you really believe in Thatcher. well I believe in me.
I SUPPOSE IN YEARS TO COME OTHER NATIONS OF IMPORTANCE WILL WANNA BUILD THIER OWN ATOMIC BOMBS? YES I DARE SAY THE TEMPTATION WILL BE

How far the neck of the womb has opened up or dilated as doctors say.
CRASS-'Securicor' 'I walk the pavement with my club and hat.
I deal in money you can't get at
You wanna use me co's i'm up for rent. Tough shit co's I'm real busy. You ought to know me co's I've been a cop, out of the army where I learned a lot some kids still chuckle when they see my van. Well it's not all money sonny, do you wanna come closer. Securicor cares.
THE ORDER HAS BEEN GIVEN
CRASS-'I can't stand it when they're preaching, I should be working. They fill you up with Jesus Christ, he's the biggest fucking heist. I can't stand it,
OPERATED ON THIS MORNING
DR. GROVES PLEASE.
CRASS-'Can't breathe, can't move, locked in can't get out wanna shout, wanna scream, Is this life or a dream, no lies no ties.
CRASS-'When you don't wanna hear, they will say you're full of vice
Do they owe us a living of course they do of course they fucking do
Just give you a small injection.
NIPPLE ERECTORS-'What a shame' 'Desperation.

+++++++++++++++++++++++++++++++++++++

SOUND SOURCES
- Orchestral pop songs—Radio
- American voice—President Truman Why he dropped the second bomb on Nagasaki; code expressions used referring to little boy.
- Terrorists at Mogadishu
- Birth screams; nurses voice for treatment.
- Hubert Humphries; Strategic Arms Limitation Treaty, american voice 'Frankly I doubt it.'
- Piano-Played by a woman whose life was saved in Nazi extermination camp by playing this piece.

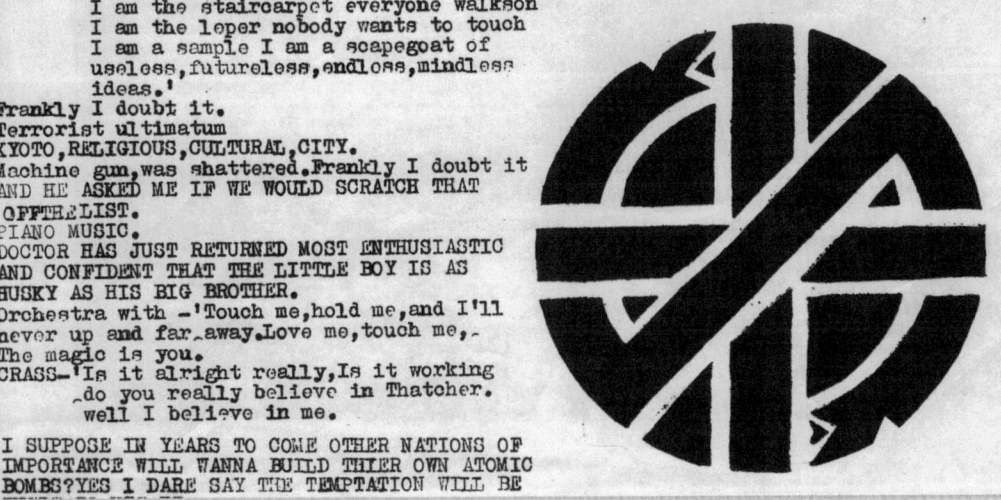

POSTER FOR CRASS AUTOPSY FILM PROJECT AND SOUNDTRACK
Gee Vaucher
1978
38.1 x 25.4 cm, 15 x 10 in

This large poster, hand-screened with heavy ink, promotes the Crass *Autopsy* film project. The poster contains lyrics and other informative text, and photocopies of the original art were distributed by the band.

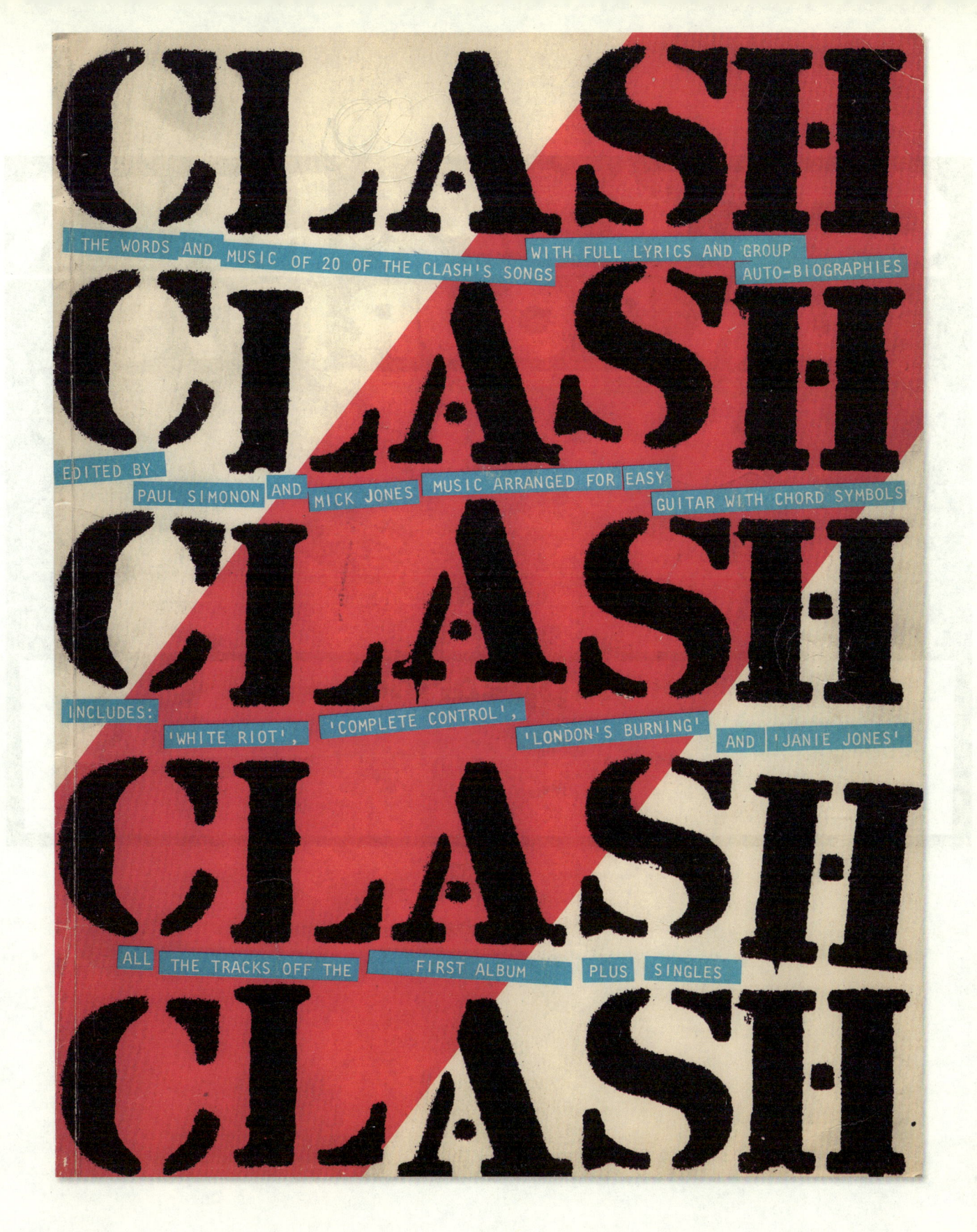

THE CLASH SONGBOOK
Paul Simonon, Mick Jones
1978
30.4 x 22.8 cm, 12 x 9 in

Featuring music and lyrics for 20 songs, including the first album, this songbook was edited by the Clash bassist Paul Simonon and guitarist Mick Jones.

POSTER FOR COCK SPARRER'S UK TOUR
1978
75.6 x 101.6 cm, 29¾ x 40 in

RAW POWER #2
Steve Marshal, South London
1978
29.8 x 20.9 cm, 11¾ x 8¼ in

NEVER MIND THE BOLLOCKS

HERE'S THE

Sex Pistols'

FIRST U.S. TOUR

NOWHERE | BOREDOM

nasty, yelling yelling and throwing things at the band, and 20% of the crowd clearly does not know what on earth is going on.......A mighty blow is struck for Punk Rock!!

PROGRAMME FOR THE SEX PISTOLS' 'NEVER MIND THE BOLLOCKS' US TOUR
January 1978
27.9 × 21.5 cm, 11 × 8½ in

Covers the Pistols' appearances in Atlanta, Georgia; Memphis, Tennessee; and San Antonio, Texas.

SUNDAY MIRRA #3
January 1978
29.8 × 20.9 cm, 11¾ × 8¼ in

The fanzine re-appropriated the negative, sensationalist coverage of punk in the tabloid press for its own ends.

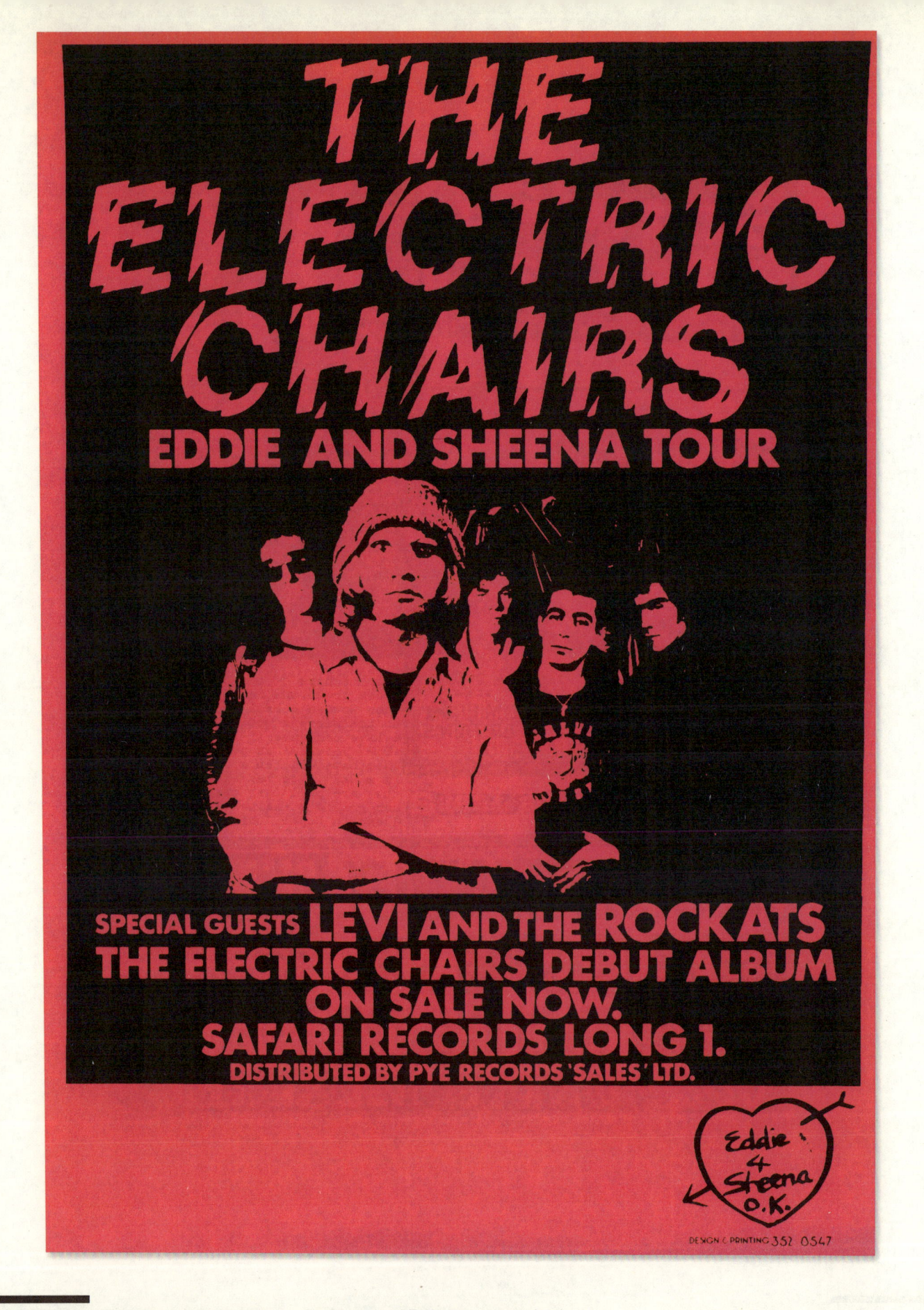

POSTER FOR THE ELECTRIC CHAIRS AND LEVI & THE ROCKATS ON THE 'EDDIE & SHEENA' TOUR
January 1978
75.5 x 50.8 cm, 29¾ x 20 in

The first-ever punk/Ted tour was named after the Electric Chairs' second single. Teds, or Teddy Boys, were a rival Kings Road youth subculture established in the '50s.

FLYER FOR THE ELECTRIC CHAIRS AND LEVI & THE ROCKATS ON THE 'EDDIE & SHEENA' TOUR
[January] 1978
28.5 x 20.9 cm, 11¼ x 8¼ in

The illustrated comic strip depicts a love affair between Eddie, a Teddy Boy, and Sheena, a punk.

PROS

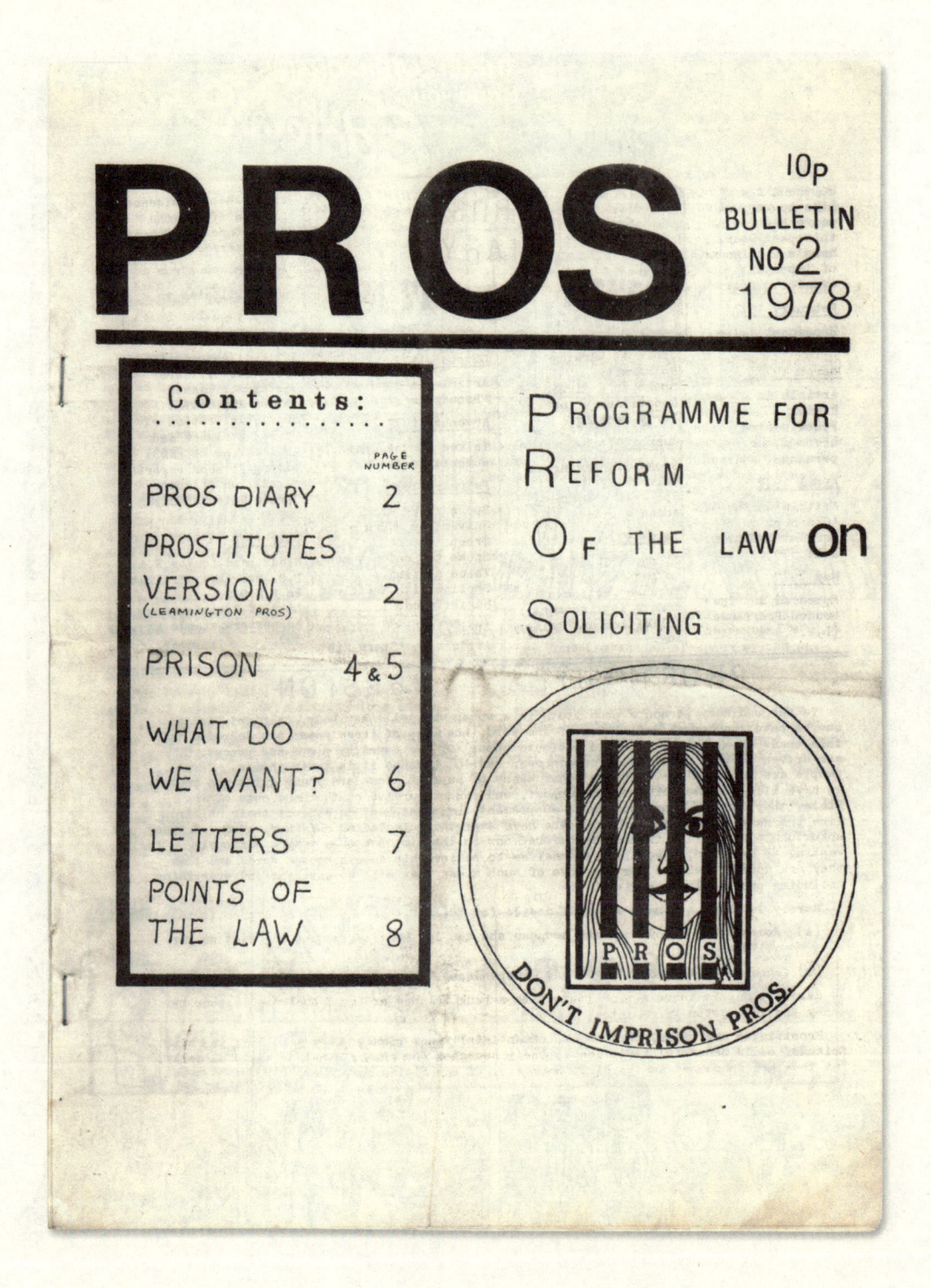

10p
BULLETIN
NO 2
1978

Contents:

	PAGE NUMBER
PROS DIARY	2
PROSTITUTES VERSION (LEAMINGTON PROS)	2
PRISON	4 & 5
WHAT DO WE WANT?	6
LETTERS	7
POINTS OF THE LAW	8

PROGRAMME FOR
REFORM
OF THE LAW on
SOLICITING

DON'T IMPRISON PROS.

PROS: PROGRAMME FOR REFORM OF THE LAW ON SOLICITING #2
1978
[Unknown dims]

Discusses issues faced by prostitutes and advocates the reform of laws, particularly related to prison sentences for loitering and soliciting for the purposes of prostitution.

READ

National Front
NEWS
10p

THE NEWSPAPER SUPPORTING THE
NATIONAL FRONT

SEND 30p FOR SAMPLE COPY TO: 50 PAWSONS ROAD, CROYDON, SURREY CRO2QF.

Printed and published by NFN Press, 50 Pawsons Road, Croydon, Surrey CRO 2QF

NATIONAL FRONT NEWS
1970s
21.5 x 28.5 cm, 8½ x 11¼ in

FLYER FOR SIOUXSIE AND THE BANSHEES, THE ADVERTS, MOTORHEAD, THE VIBRATORS, GENERATION X AND BUZZCOCKS AT THE GREYHOUND, CROYDON
February/March/April 1978
21.5 x 13.9 cm, 8½ x 5½ in

The back of this flyer warns against 'pogo dancing', a style of dance that involves vigorous jumping. It was so popular amongst punks that, in 1976, the Vibrators recorded the song 'Pogo Dancing'.

PLEASE NOTE

We are very sorry but

POGO DANCING
OR SIMILAR
IS NOT ALLOWED DUE TO
ACCIDENTS & INJURIES
DURING RECENT WEEKS

FOX ENTERPRISES

**FLYER FOR THE VIBRATORS
AT 400 BALLROOM, TORQUAY**
14 February 1978
13.9 x 20.9 cm, 5½ x 8¼ in

POSTER FOR THE VIBRATORS' SINGLE 'AUTOMATIC LOVER'
February 1978
50.8 x 35.5 cm, 20 x 14 in

The only single from their album *V2*, the Vibrators' 'Automatic Lover' cracked the UK's Top 40 at No. 35. The in-store poster made distinctive use of photomontage.

**POSTER FOR SHAM 69'S ALBUM
TELL US THE TRUTH**
February 1978
34.2 x 31.1 cm, 13½ x 12¼ in

POSTER FOR WRECKLESS ERIC'S SINGLE 'RECONNEZ CHERIE'
February 1978
37.4 x 25.4 cm, 14¾ x 10 in

Wreckless Eric writes: 'When I was at art school up in Hull, I discovered Cajun music via an album on the Oval label called *Another Saturday Night*. It was later re-released on Stiff, just after "Reconnez Cherie" came out in fact, and they put out "Promised Land" by Johnnie Allan as a single. On the strength of a couple of radio plays, they transferred all the promotion from "Reconnez Cherie" and got Johnnie Allan over for a holiday. He wasn't a musician anymore, he was a schoolteacher and all he was interested in was whisky and poontang. It was ironic that the album that inspired me to write "Reconnez Cherie" ended up being the reason that the song failed to chart.'

POSTERS FOR THE CLASH'S SINGLE 'CLASH CITY ROCKERS'
17 February 1978
102.8 x 76.2 cm, 40½ x 30 in

In-store promotional poster was distributed in both colour and black-and-white.

CLASH CITY ROCKERS

the CLASH
CBS 5834

c/w *Jail Guitar Doors*

For release February 17th

Order from CBS Order Desk Tel: 01-960 2155, CBS Distribution Centre, Barlby Road, London W10

POSTERS FOR DEAF SCHOOL'S 'ENGLISH BOYS: WORKING GIRLS' UK TOUR
18 February 1978
74.9 × 49.5 cm, 29½ × 19½ in

This silkscreened poster advertises Deaf School's gig at Loughborough University; it uses a striking image of vocalist Bette Bright, who was married to Suggs, the singer-songwriter from the band Madness.

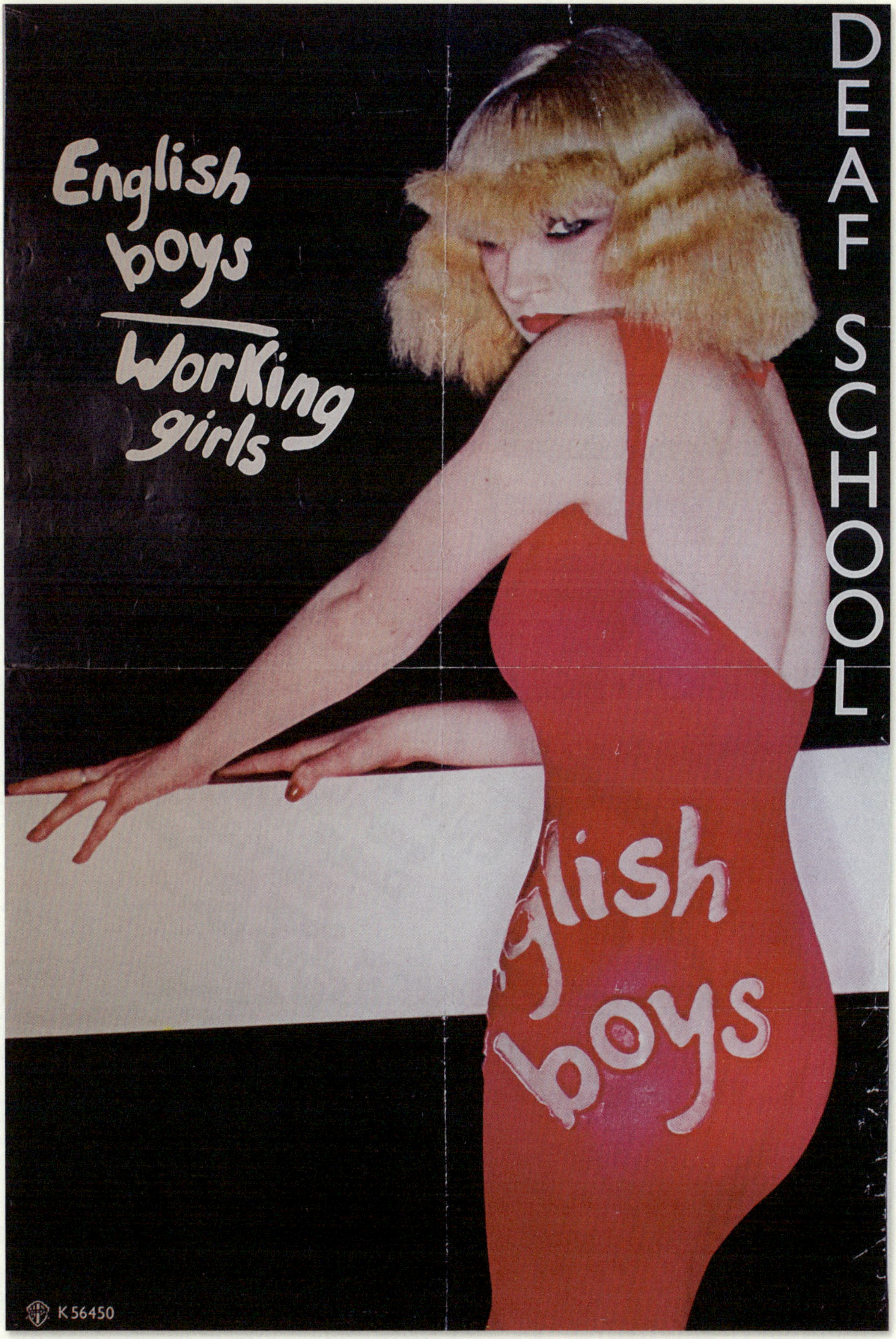
English boys
Working girls
DEAF SCHOOL
glish boys
K 56450

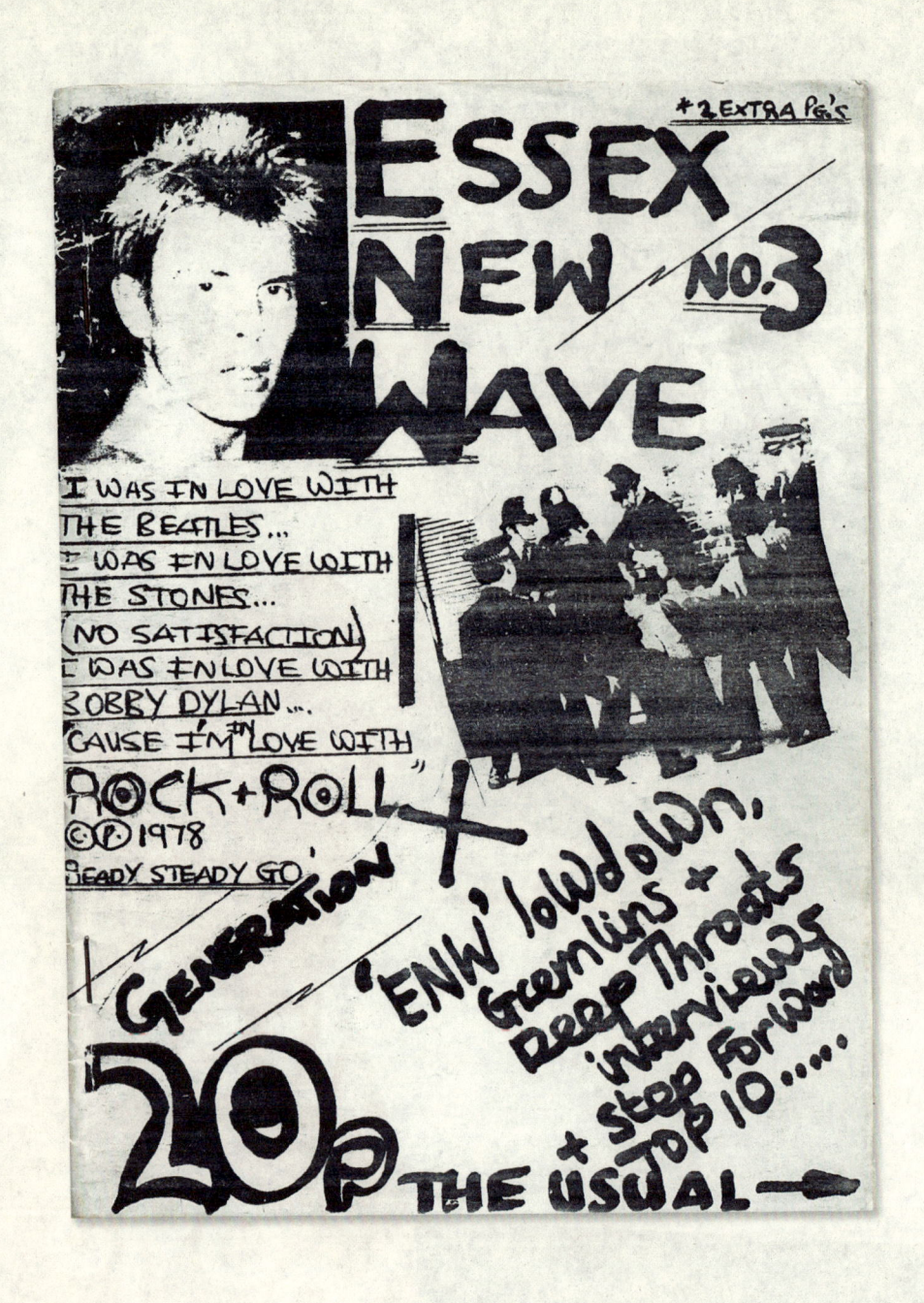

ESSEX NEW WAVE #3
February 1978
20.9 x 14.6 cm, 8¼ x 5¾ in

Contains interviews with Gremlins and Deep Throats.
The cover features lyrics from Generation X song
'Ready Steady Go'.

**POSTER FOR SUBURBAN STUDS
AT THE SUBSCRIPTION ROOMS, STROUD**
24 February 1978
60.3 x 43.1 cm, 23¾ x 17 in

FLYER FOR ULTRAVOX'S LIVE EP 'RETRO'
24 February 1978
13.3 x 20.9 cm, 5¼ x 8¼ in

Ultravox released their first EP, 'Retro', with live versions of 'The Man Who Dies Everyday', 'Young Savage', 'The Wild, the Beautiful and the Damned' and 'My Sex', recorded with original lead singer John Foxx.

FLYER FOR ULTRAVOX
February 1978
20.9 x 29.2 cm, 8¼ x 11½ in

With a review of an Ultravox performance
at the Marquee Club.

FLYER FOR 'LONDON'S BEST SUNDAY PUNK SHOW' AT THE ROXY
26 February 1978
50.1 x 75.5 cm, 19¾ x 29¾ in

A Sunday punk show hosted by London promoter, DJ and manager Jock McDonald at the Roxy. The Roxy closed permanently in April 1978. At the end of the year McDonald tried to revive the club when he broke in and squatted in the space, only to be evicted.

**POSTER FOR BLONDIE'S 12-INCH SINGLES
'DENIS', 'CONTACT IN RED SQUARE' AND
'KUNG FU GIRLS'**
February 1978
42.5 x 30.4 cm, 16¾ x 12 in

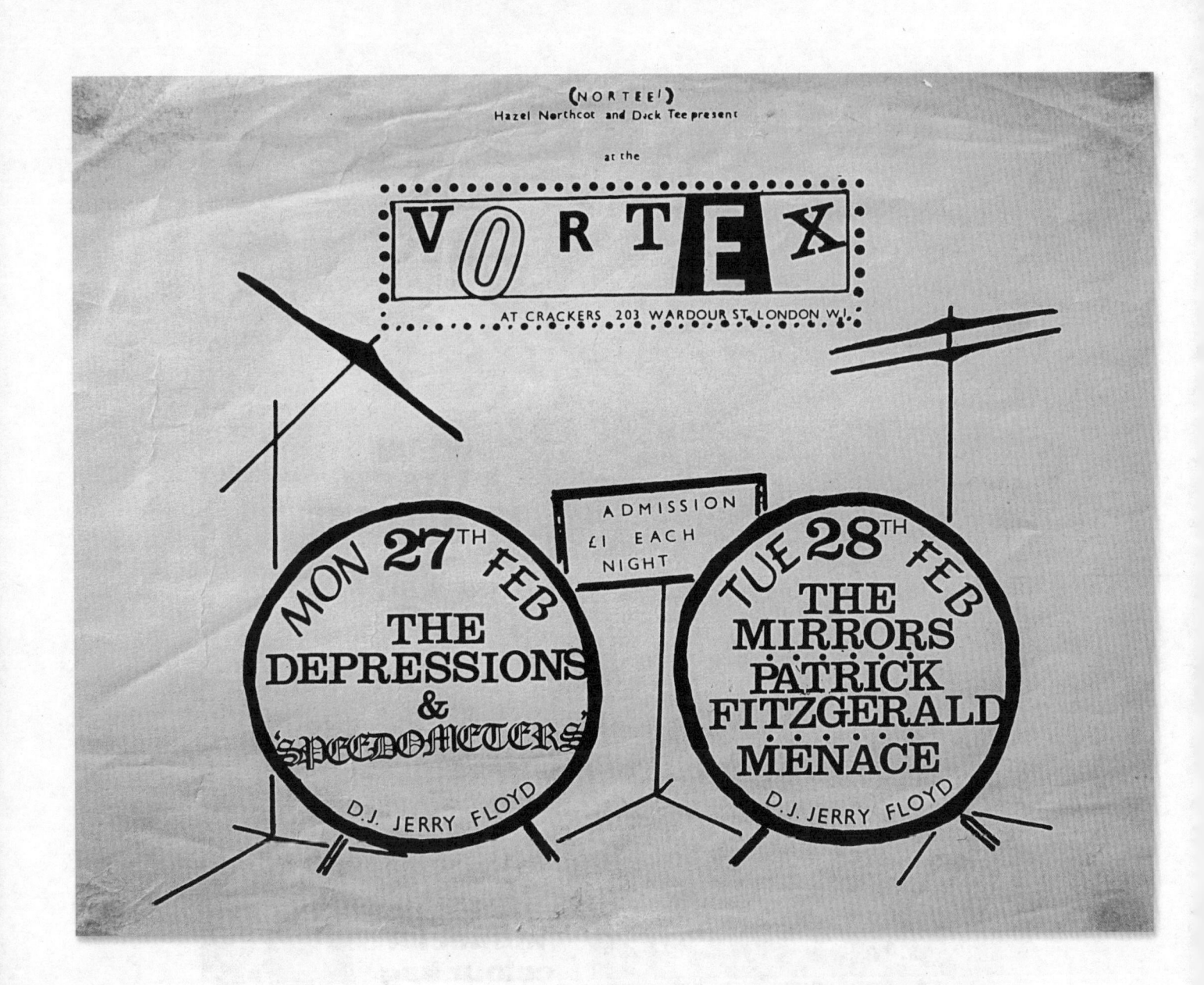

FLYER FOR THE DEPRESSIONS, SPEEDOMETERS, MIRRORS, PATRIK FITZGERALD AND MENACE AT THE VORTEX, LONDON
27–28 February 1978
20.3 x 25.4 cm, 8 x 10 in

**POSTER FOR GENERATION X'S SINGLE
'READY STEADY GO'**
March 1978
[unknown dims]

films and filming

Inside: Close Encounters of the Third Kind   march 1978   60p

ADAM ANT in Jubilee

ADAM ANT IN FILMS AND FILMING
March 1978
[unknown dims]

Adam Ant appears on the cover of trade magazine *Films and Filming* to promote his involvement in Derek Jarman's film *Jubilee*. Ant debuted as a recording artist with the song 'Deutscher Girls', which is on the film's soundtrack, and 'Plastic Surgery', which the band performed in the film itself.

**POSTER FOR BUZZCOCKS' ALBUM
ANOTHER MUSIC IN A DIFFERENT KITCHEN**
March 1978
29.8 x 20.9 cm, 11¾ x 8¼ in

The album included the hit single 'I Don't Mind', which reached No. 55 on the UK singles chart in May. This was Buzzcocks' second lineup, with vocals from Pete Shelley, after the departure of Howard Devoto.

FLYER FOR BUZZCOCKS AT THE PAVILION, HEMEL HEMPSTEAD
5 March 1978
20.9 x 14.6 cm, 8¼ x 5¾ in

**FLYER FOR SHAM 69 AT THE LOCARNO,
COVENTRY AND KING'S HALL, DERBY**
7 & 10 March 1978
29.8 x 20.9 cm, 11¾ x 8¼ in

References the football chant, 'There won't be many going home'.

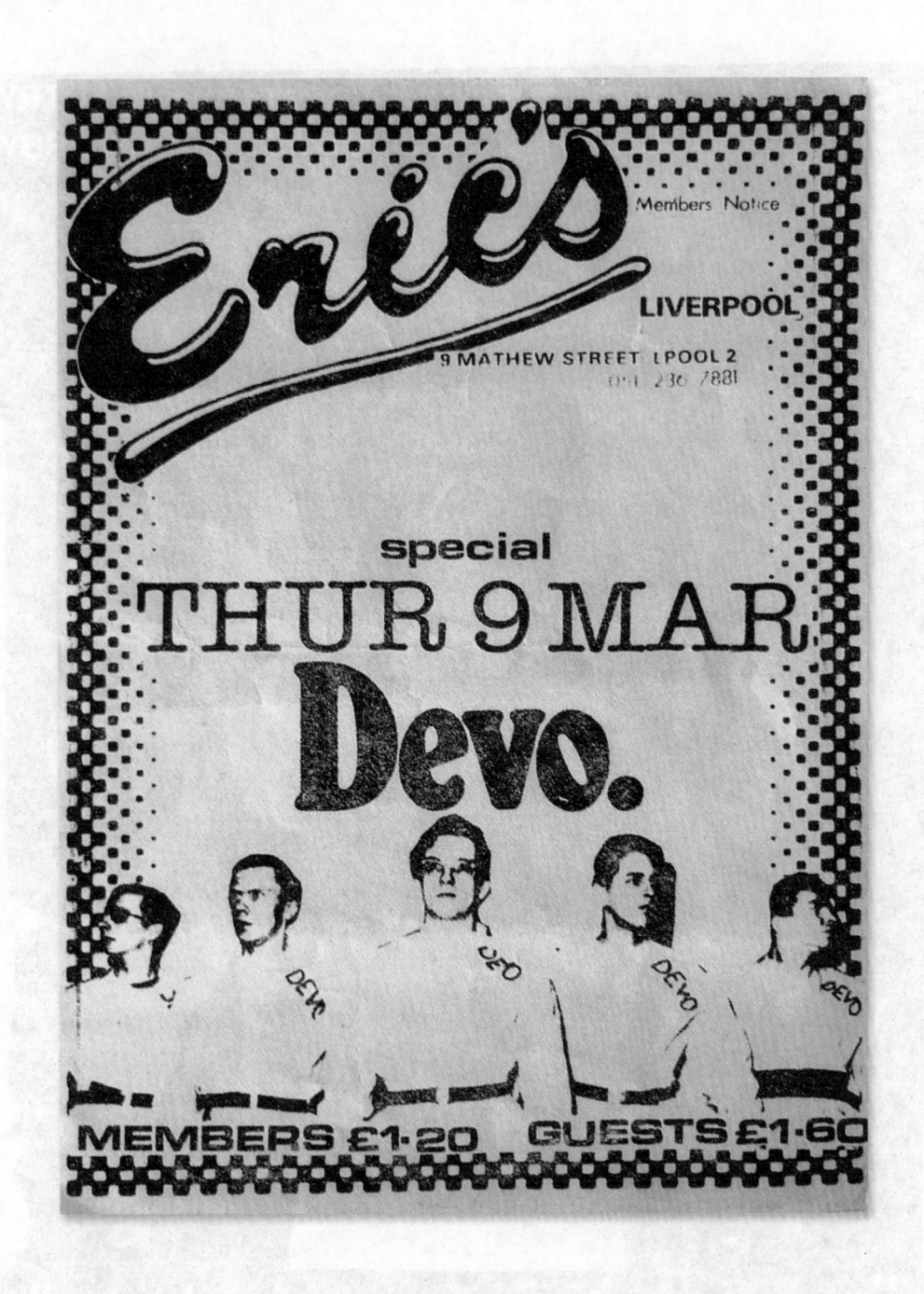

FLYER FOR DEVO AT ERIC'S, LIVERPOOL
9 March 1978
20.9 x 14.6 cm, 8¼ x 5¾ in

Eric's opened in Liverpool city centre on 1 October 1976. Although it closed after four years, the venue had a significant impact on the Merseyside music scene.

ANTI-NAZI LEAGUE POSTER, 'NEVER AGAIN'
1978
43.8 x 64.7 cm, 17¼ x 25½ in

Many of the ANL's posters were designed to be cut out and pasted on placards for demonstrations.

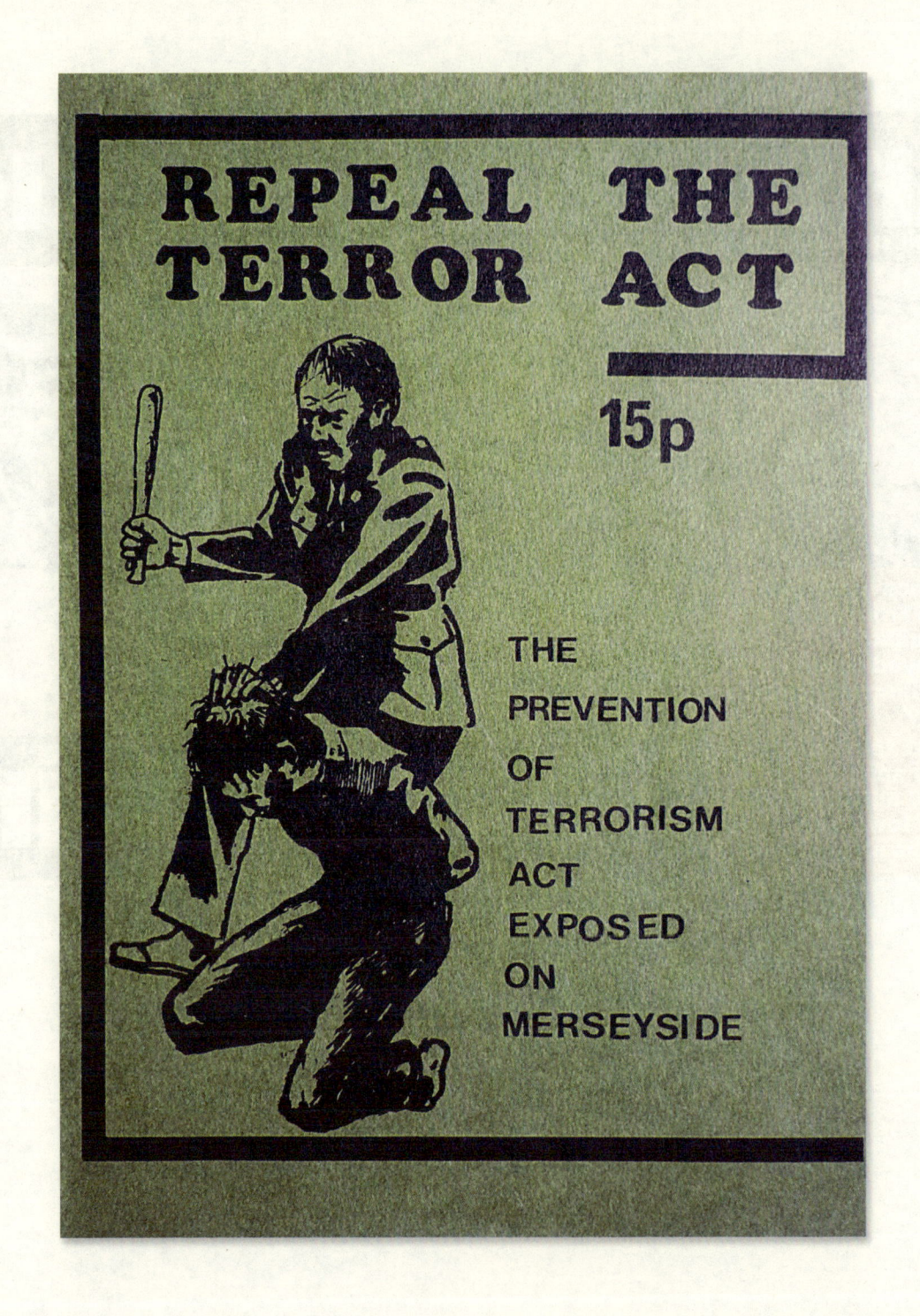

REPEAL THE TERROR ACT
United Troops Out Movement
20.9 x 14.6 cm, 8¼ x 5¾ in

**FLYER FOR SHAM 69 AND SUBWAY SECT
AT LOCARNO BALLROOM**
19 & 21 March 1978
20.9 × 14.6 cm, 8¼ × 5¾ in

**POSTER FOR BUZZCOCKS AND THE SLITS
AT THE VICTORIA HALL, HANLEY**
30 March 1978
74.9 x 100.3 cm, 29½ x 39½ x in

Designed to look like wrapping paper, the poster is from Buzzcocks' third UK tour.

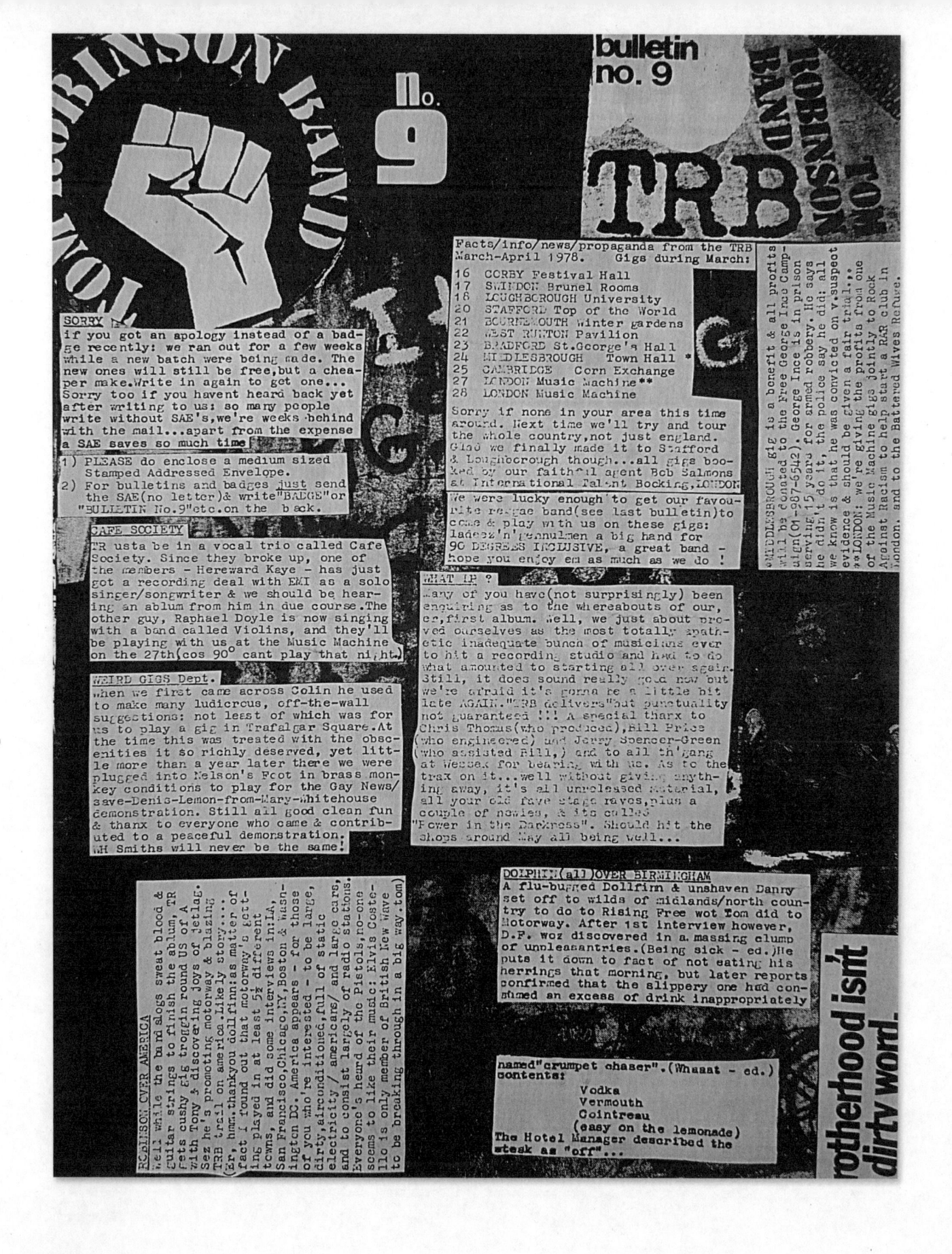

TOM ROBINSON BAND,
TRB NEWS SHEET BULLETIN #9
March/April 1978
31.1 x 21.5 cm, 12¼ x 8½ in

From the start, the Tom Robinson Band gave out free typewritten, stencilled news bulletins at gigs.

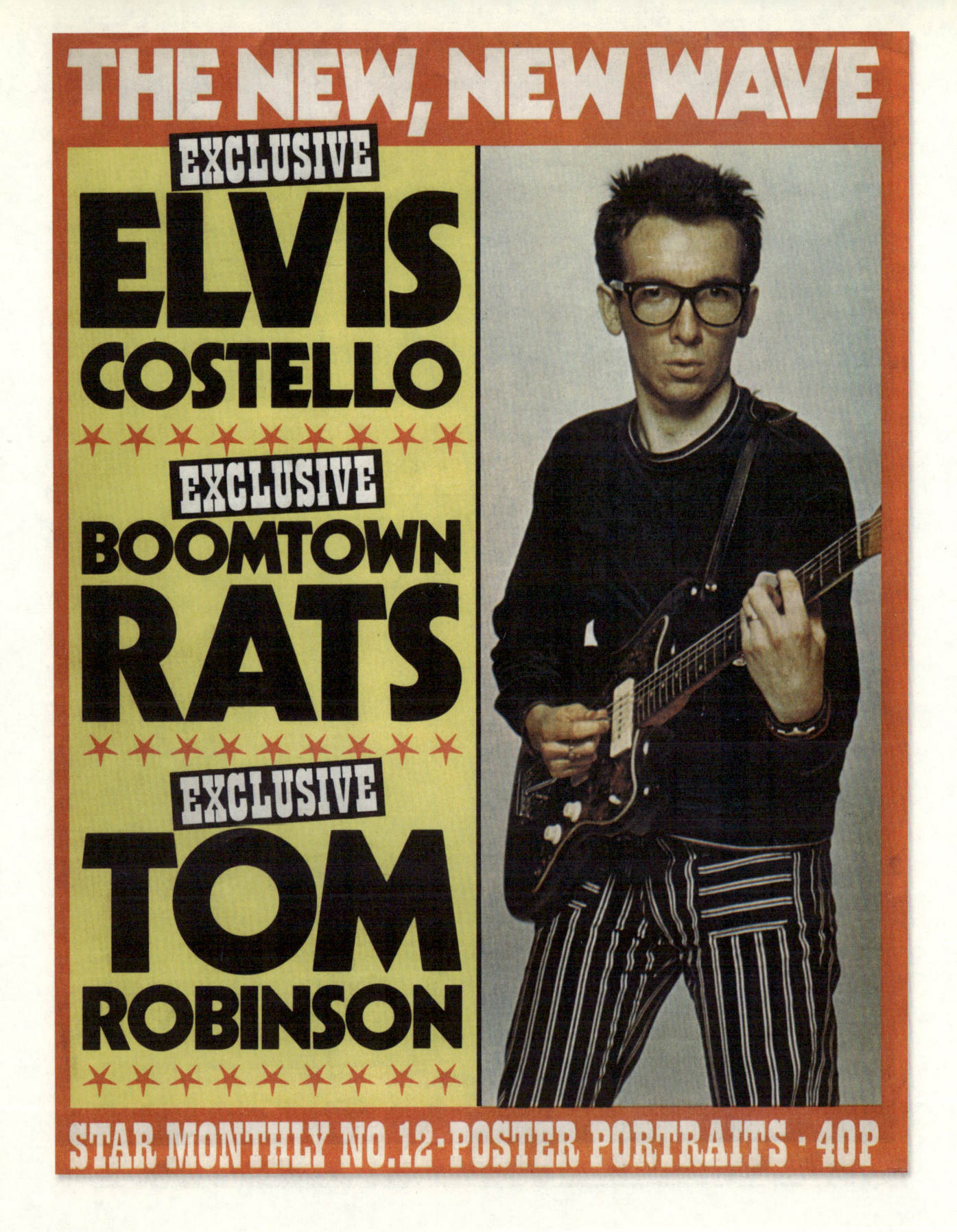

STAR MONTHLY #12
April 1978
31.1 x 24.1 cm, 12¼ x 9½ in

Sunday Mirra

MID APRIL ISSUE 5 25p ©

SOMETHING STRANGE? WIRE.

Dose are the group whom the Mirra has supported since its own Issue 1. On pages three and four is the interview with the four, that tells how they have come from being merely 'scouts' and members of the non-political organisation known to many as 'Church Lads Brigade', to being the aclaimed instigators of the renowned Hayes Wave. The interview reveals all, their loves, their hates, how they corrupted honest pub owners in order to secure their first gigs. Dose, the group with a song which, so they claim, mentions two swear words, (one of which is repeated twice). This is the group Mary Whitehouse warned us of, the group which turned Hillingdon Borough into an exciting area to live in once again, for the first time since the Opening Ceremony for the big Sainsbries Store in the Uxbridge High Street.etc.etc.etc.

MOPED MANIA

Moped Mania is here to stay. The album is out at last, Cycledelic, the lp reported to you in our first issue (Mirra gets repetitive), as our first interview, during the record's recording over 8 months ago. Inside are the latest mundane photos of the Mopeds. The album now high in the charts proves the general public are at last showing appreciation for the Croyden natives' music. As Slimey Toad put it in the SM1, "unfortunately, unless Johnny's a punk success he'll definartly end up in a looney home" Johnny Moped, the star: page sixteen.

SUNDAY MIRRA #5 (FINAL ISSUE)
April 1978
[unknown dims]

POSTER FOR X-RAY SPEX'S SINGLE 'THE DAY THE WORLD TURNED DAY-GLO'
April 1978
75.5 x 50.8 cm, 29¾ x 20 in

The poster uses the same bright globe found on the sleeve of the band's second single.

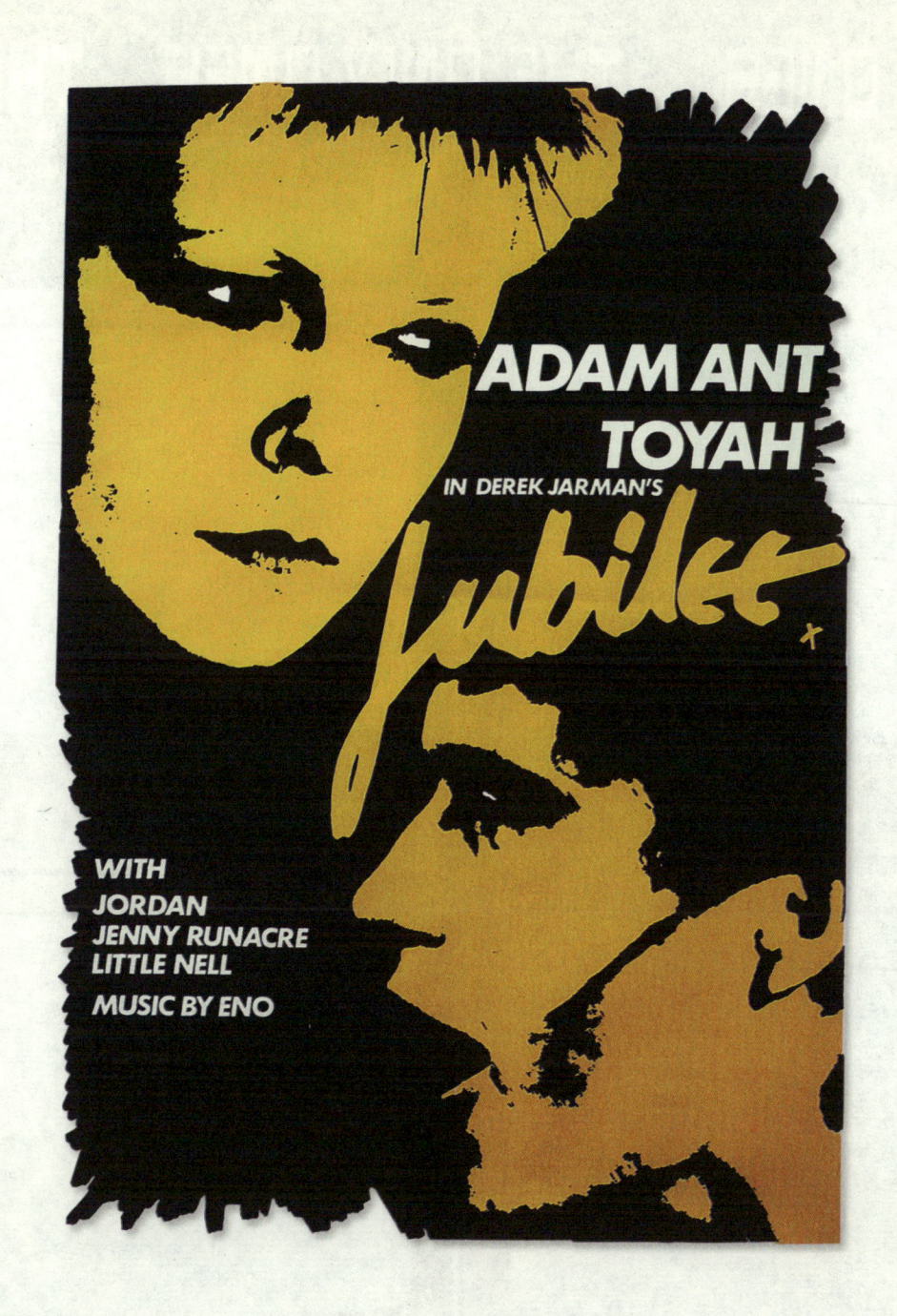

POSTER FOR DEREK JARMAN'S JUBILEE
1978
76.2 x 50.8 cm, 30 x 20 in

In Derek Jarman's film *Jubilee*, Queen Elizabeth I reappears during her namesake's Silver Jubilee in 1977. Many punk icons have a role in the film, including Toyah Willcox, Nell Campbell and Hermine Demoriane. The Slits, Wayne County, Adam and the Ants and Siouxsie and the Banshees all perform; the soundtrack is by Brian Eno.

**POSTER FOR THE ONLY ONES' SINGLE
'ANOTHER GIRL, ANOTHER PLANET'**
April 1978
50.8 x 38.1 cm, 20 x 15 in

This single, from the band's debut album, was issued in a UK limited edition.

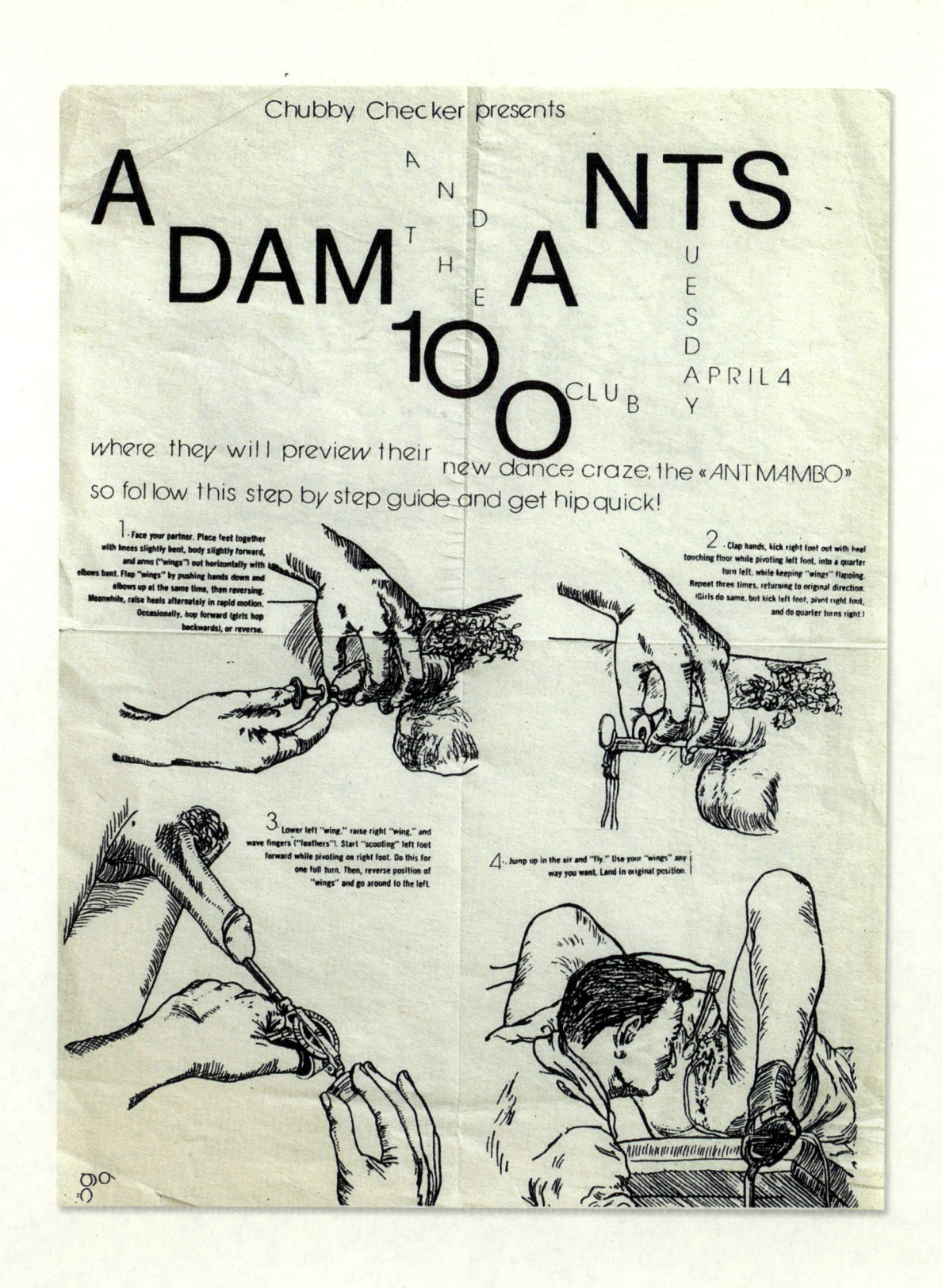

**FLYER FOR ADAM AND THE ANTS
AT THE 100 CLUB, LONDON**
Adam Ant
4 April 1978
28.5 × 20.9 cm, 11¼ × 8¼ in

Adam Ant designed his flyers using Letraset and stencils, with a distinct pop art sensibility informed by contemporary artists such as Allen Jones, who designed erotic furniture, and Eduardo Paolozzi, Adam's teacher at Hornsey College of Art. Adam often emphasised themes of bondage and domination – in this case, a medical textbook clipping that depicts a catheter being inserted.

ADAM AND THE ANTS' STICKER
1978
8.8 x 10.1 cm, 3½ x 4 in

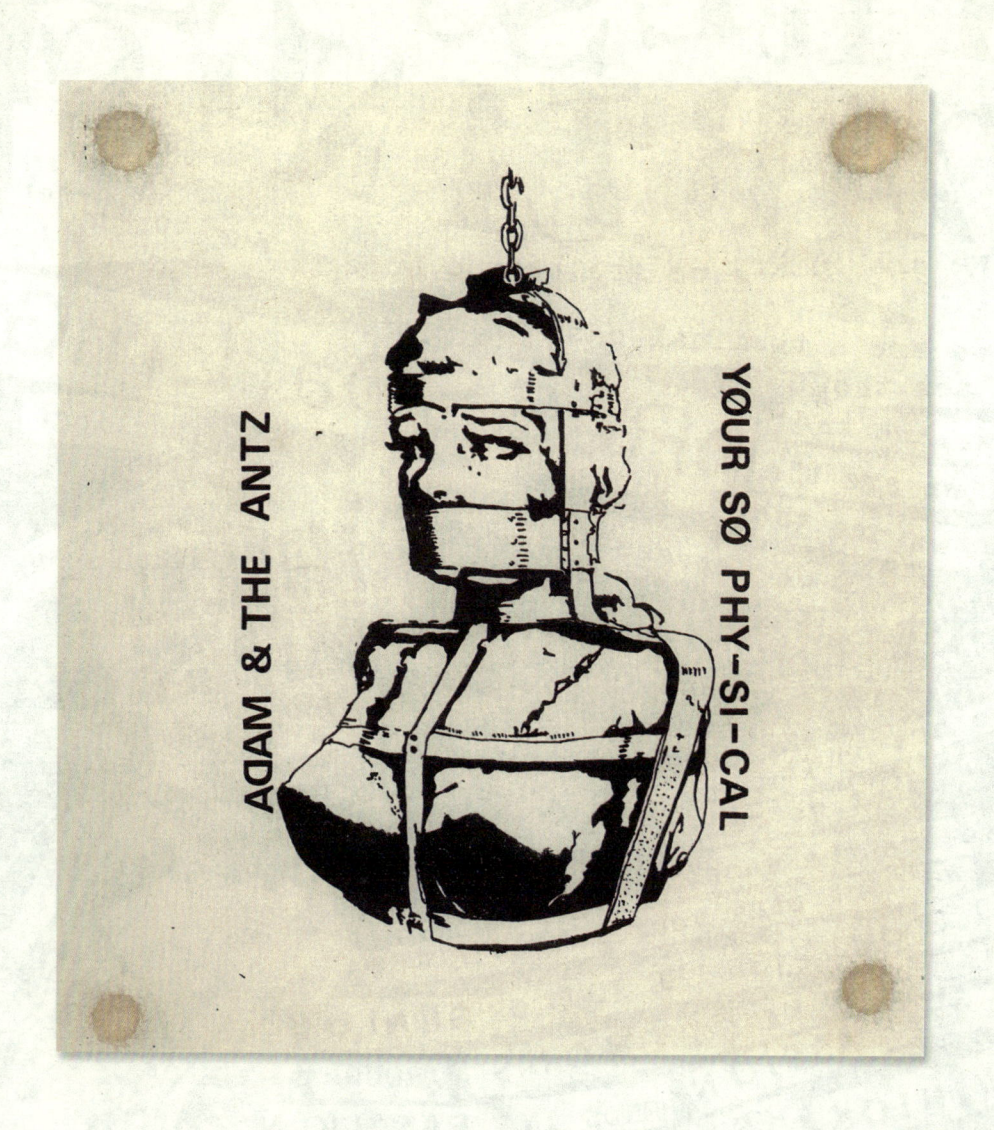

ADAM AND THE ANTS' STICKER, 'YOU'RE SO PHY-SI-CAL'
1978
12.7 x 11.4 cm, 5 x 4½ in

At concerts, Adam and the Ants gave away stickers like this one with lyrics from the song 'Physical (You're So)'. Adam used an extensive amount of bondage imagery in his promotional material.

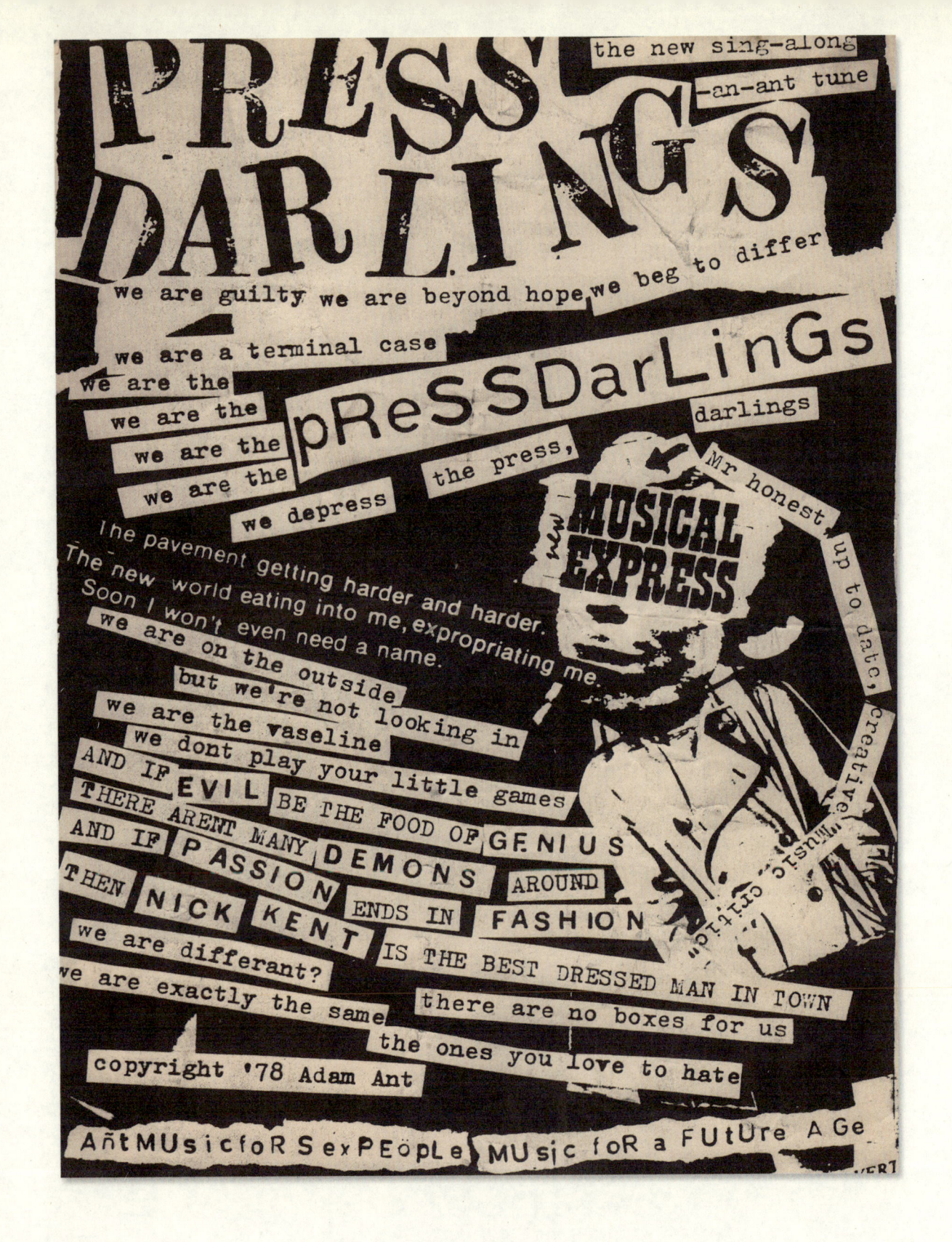

FLYER FOR ADAM AND THE ANTS' SONG 'PRESS DARLINGS'
1978
20.9 x 15.2 cm, 8¼ x 6 in

The song appears as the B-side of the single 'Kings of the Wild Frontier', released on CBS in 1980.

POSTER FOR ADAM AND THE ANTS
1978
27.9 x 31.8 cm, 11 x 12½ in

RECORD MIRROR
8 April 1978
40.6 × 29.8 cm, 16 × 11¾ in

The cover features Sid Vicious with his girlfriend Nancy Spungen. Prophetically, the caption reads, 'Why does Sid Vicious think he'll be dead in two years?' Several months later Vicious was arrested and charged with Spungen's murder. Out on bail, he overdosed and died on 2 February 1979.

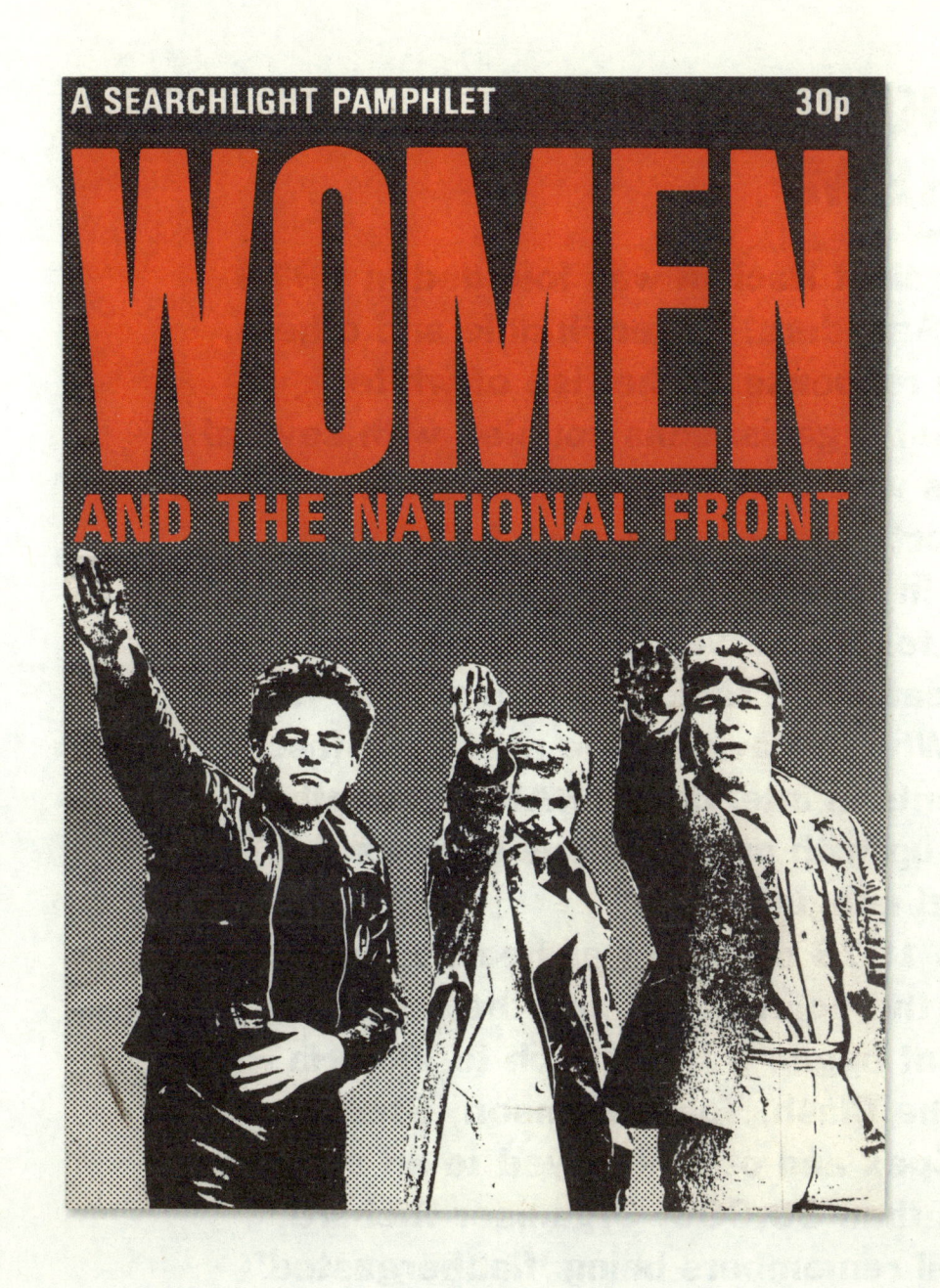

WOMEN AND THE NATIONAL FRONT, SEARCHLIGHT PAMPHLET
1978
20.9 x 14.6 cm, 8¼ x 5¾ in

Women and the National Front was written by Veronica Ware, who worked with the anti-fascist journal *Searchlight*. The publication explores fascist policies' effect on women; in particular, it examines the NF's fascist approach to women.

377

ROCK AGAINST RACISM

Rock Against Racism was founded in 1976 by Red Saunders, Roger Huddle and others, partly in response to the rise of white nationalist organisations coupled with several incidents where well-known musicians appeared to support right-wing causes. At a 1976 concert in Birmingham, Eric Clapton declared support for Conservative MP Enoch Powell and repeated the National Front slogan 'Keep Britain White'; David Bowie made pro-fascist statements in interviews. RAR frequently teamed up with organisations such as the Anti-Nazi League.

RAR's 1978 carnival was heavily publicised by both the political left and the music press. The event began with a march to Victoria Park, where the Clash, Tom Robinson, Steel Pulse, X-Ray Spex and others played to an audience of more than 80,000. Organiser Richard Buckwell remembers being 'flabbergasted' by the size of the event: 'We expected 10,000 or 20,000 people.'

ROCK AGAINST RACISM BADGES
1977
[various dims]

POSTER FOR ROCK AGAINST RACISM CARNIVAL, VICTORIA PARK
David King
30 April 1978
92.7 x 62.8 cm, 36½ x 24¾ in

The poster was printed before the bill was finalised and did not mention that the Clash or Patrik Fitzgerald would play.

ROCK AGAINST RACISM STICKERS
1978
22.2 x 19 cm, 8¾ x 7½ in

Amongst the slogans are 'Legalize it', 'Love Music, Hate Racism!', 'I Ain't Gonna Work on Maggie's Farm', 'The Government Never Resigns' and 'Right On Sister! Bondage Up Yours!'

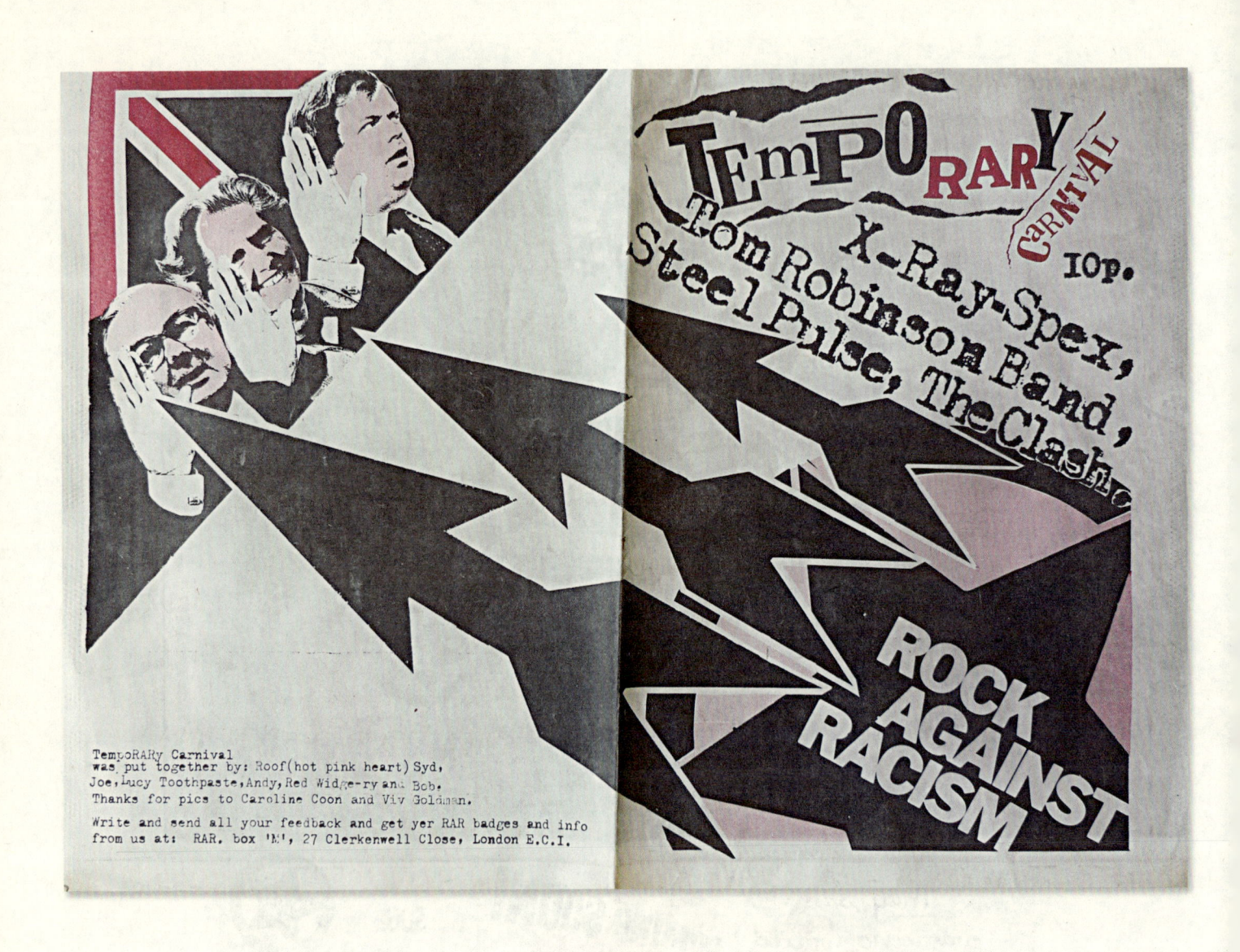

TEMPORARY HOARDING, ROCK AGAINST RACISM CARNIVAL ISSUE
30 April 1978
31.7 x 42.5 cm, 12½ x 16¾ in

This special edition of the magazine was sold at Victoria Park during the RAR carnival.

"IF 20,000 CAN COME TO THE CARNIVAL, WE WANT THEM ALL THERE TO DEMONSTRATE AGAINST THE NAZIS WHEN THEY MARCH."
Steel Pulse

"IF YOU HAVE TO HAVE AN ELITE, A WHITE ELITE PUTTING DOWN ANOTHER GROUP OF PEOPLE, THE BLACKS, THEY WILL BE READY TO PUT DOWN OTHER GROUPS OF PEOPLE; TRADES UNIONISTS, WOMEN, GAYS LIKE MYSELF, WHATEVER!"
Tom Robinson

"IF YOU ARE PICKED ON AND PICKED ON YOU HAVE TO TAKE A STAND"
Steel Pulse

"BLACK AND WHITE RACIAL DISHARMONY IS JUST A COVER STORY, CONCOCTED TO HIDE THE FACT THAT WORKING CLASS PEOPLE ARE STILL BEING KICKED ALL OVER THE PLACE"
Patrick Fitzgerald

"IF YOU WANT TO LIVE YOUR LIFE IN MINDLESS BONDAGE, JOIN THE NF. I YOU WANT TO BE YOUR SELF DONT BOTHER."
Poly Styrene

"FIRST ROCK, MEANING ROCK MUSIC, ROCK MUSIC AGAINST RACISM. SECOND, ROCK LIKE YOU'RE ROCKIN', LIKE DANCING AGAINST RACISM. THEN ITS LIKE ROCK, LIKE STONE, HARD LIKE A PEBBLE, PUT IT IN THE WATER AND NOTHING CAN WASH IT AWAY"
Steel Pulse

"I'M HALF JEWISH SO I SUPPOSE THE NF WILL TRY AND SEND HALF OF ME BACK TO LITHUANIA."
Mick Jones Clash

FUNDRAISING FLYER FOR ROCK AGAINST RACISM, 'LOVE MUSIC / HATE RACISM!'
1978
29.2 x 20.9 cm, 11½ x 8¼ in

ANTI-NAZI LEAGUE, 'STOP THE NAZI NATIONAL FRONT!'
David King
1978
45 x 63.5 cm, 17¾ x 25 in

David King gained fame for his work for the *Sunday Times Magazine* in the 1960s and '70s, adapting a 1920s modernism by using blocks of text and colour, type and image. King donated his time to the ANL and Anti-Apartheid Movement.

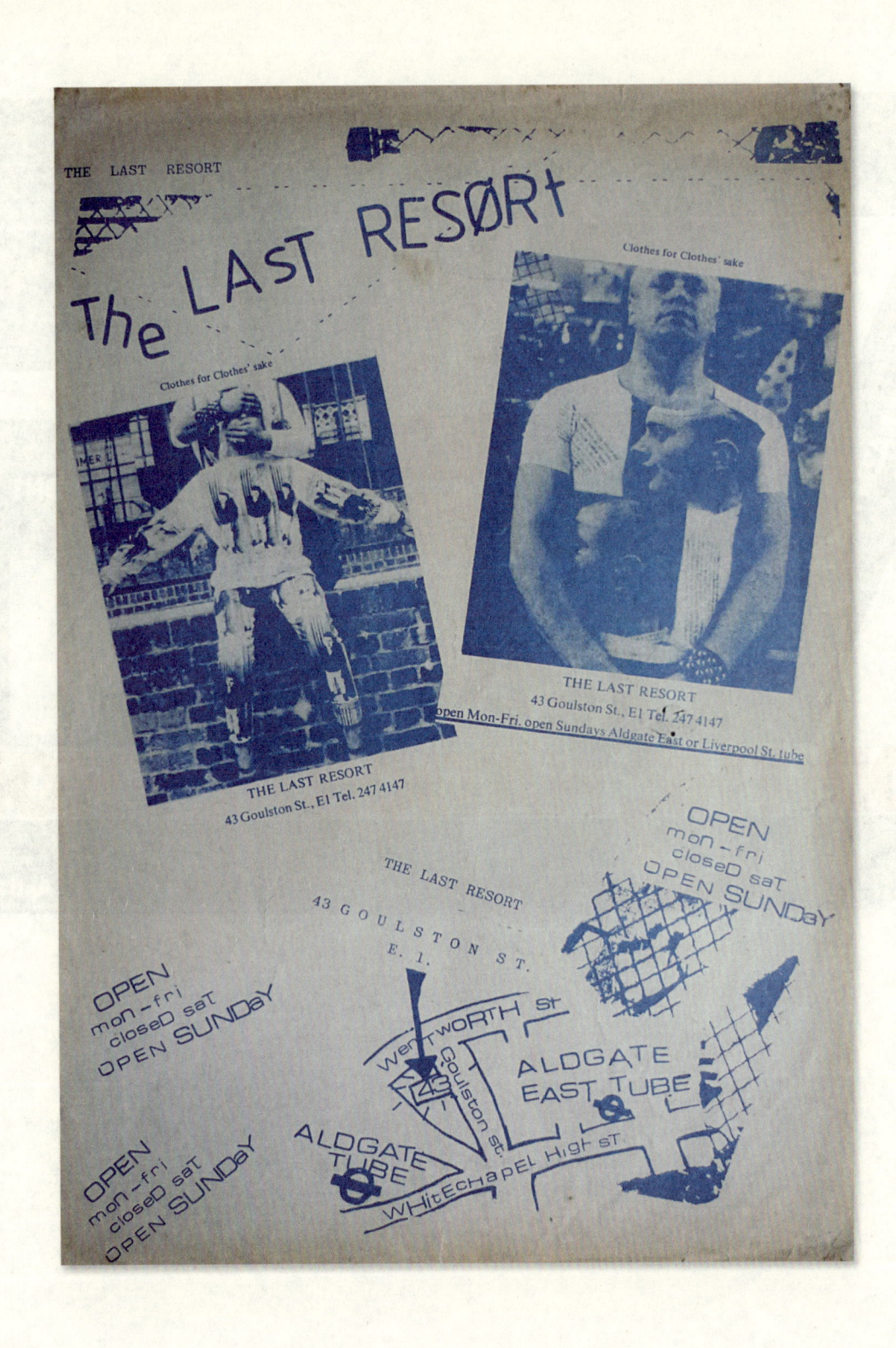

FLYER FOR THE LAST RESORT SHOP ON PETTICOAT LANE
1978
32.3 x 21.6 cm, 12¾ x 8½ in

The Last Resort shop was frequented by skinheads, including Skrewdriver frontman Ian Stuart Donaldson.

NATIONAL FRONT STATEMENT OF POLICY
1970s
30.4 x 15.2 cm, 12 x 6 in

Propounds the idea that British citizens were being deprived of political and economic power. The group's statement outlines major policy platforms, with topics ranging from foreign affairs, the economy and national defence to race and immigration, public health and the environment.

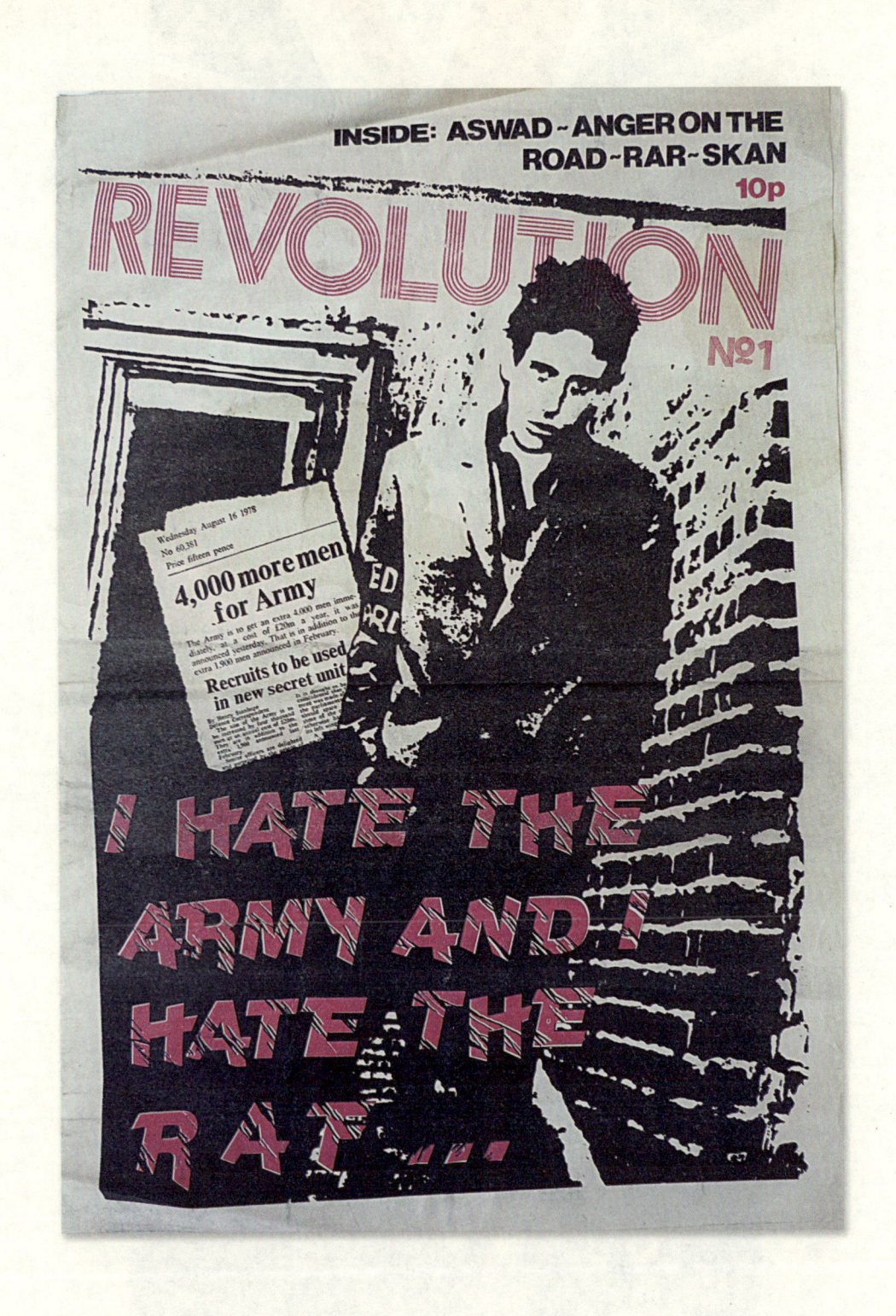

REVOLUTION #1
1978
40 x 27.9 cm, 15¾ x 11 in

Cover features Mick Jones of the Clash and lyrics from the band's song 'Career Opportunities', 'I hate the Army and I hate the RAF'.

REVOLUTION #3, 'FREE ABORTION ON DEMAND OK!'
1978
42.5 x 31.1 cm, 16¾ x 12¼ in

Features articles on unions, nurses and schools.

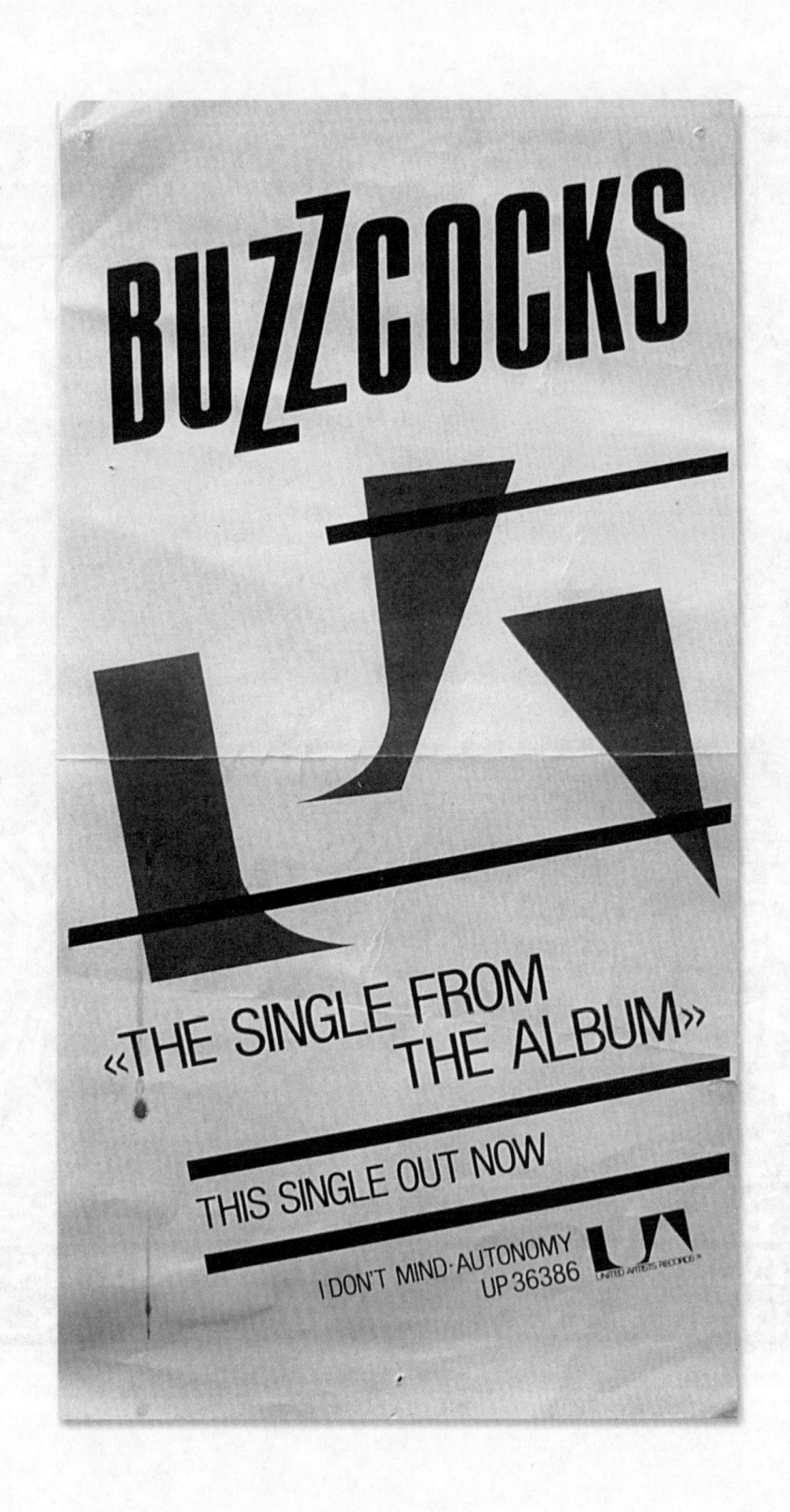

POSTER FOR BUZZCOCKS' SINGLE 'I DON'T MIND'
April 1978
35.5 x 17.7 cm, 14 x 7 in

**FLYER FOR SLAUGHTER & THE DOGS'
'DO IT DOG STYLE' TOUR**
April/May 1978
29.8 × 20.9 cm, 11¾ × 8¼ in

With support from Eater and Blitzkrieg Bop, the tour followed the release of the album.

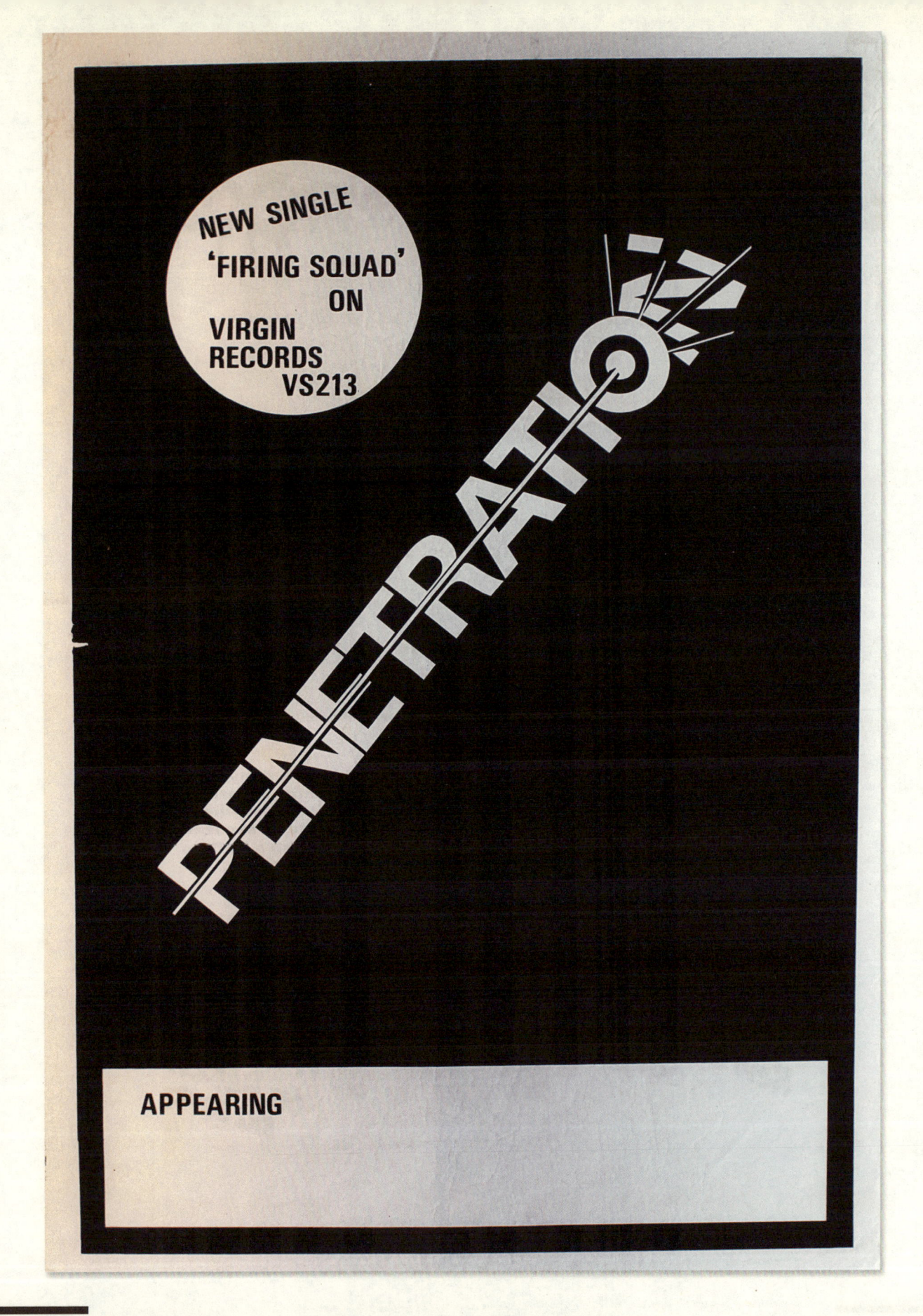

POSTER FOR PENETRATION'S SINGLE 'FIRING SQUAD'
May 1978
75.5 x 51.4 cm, 29¾ x 20¼ in

Penetration's second single. The letter 'o' in the group's name has been altered to resemble a target, in keeping with the single's title.

**POSTER FOR ALTERNATIVE TV'S SINGLE
'LIFE AFTER LIFE'**
May 1978
75.5 x 50.8 cm, 29¾ x 20 in

TEMPORARY HOARDING #6
Summer 1978
42.5 x 30.4 cm, 16¾ x 12 in

Articles on Patrik Fitzgerald, Peter Tosh, Jimmy Pursey, skinheads, Deptford Fun City Records, early Adam and the Ants and more.

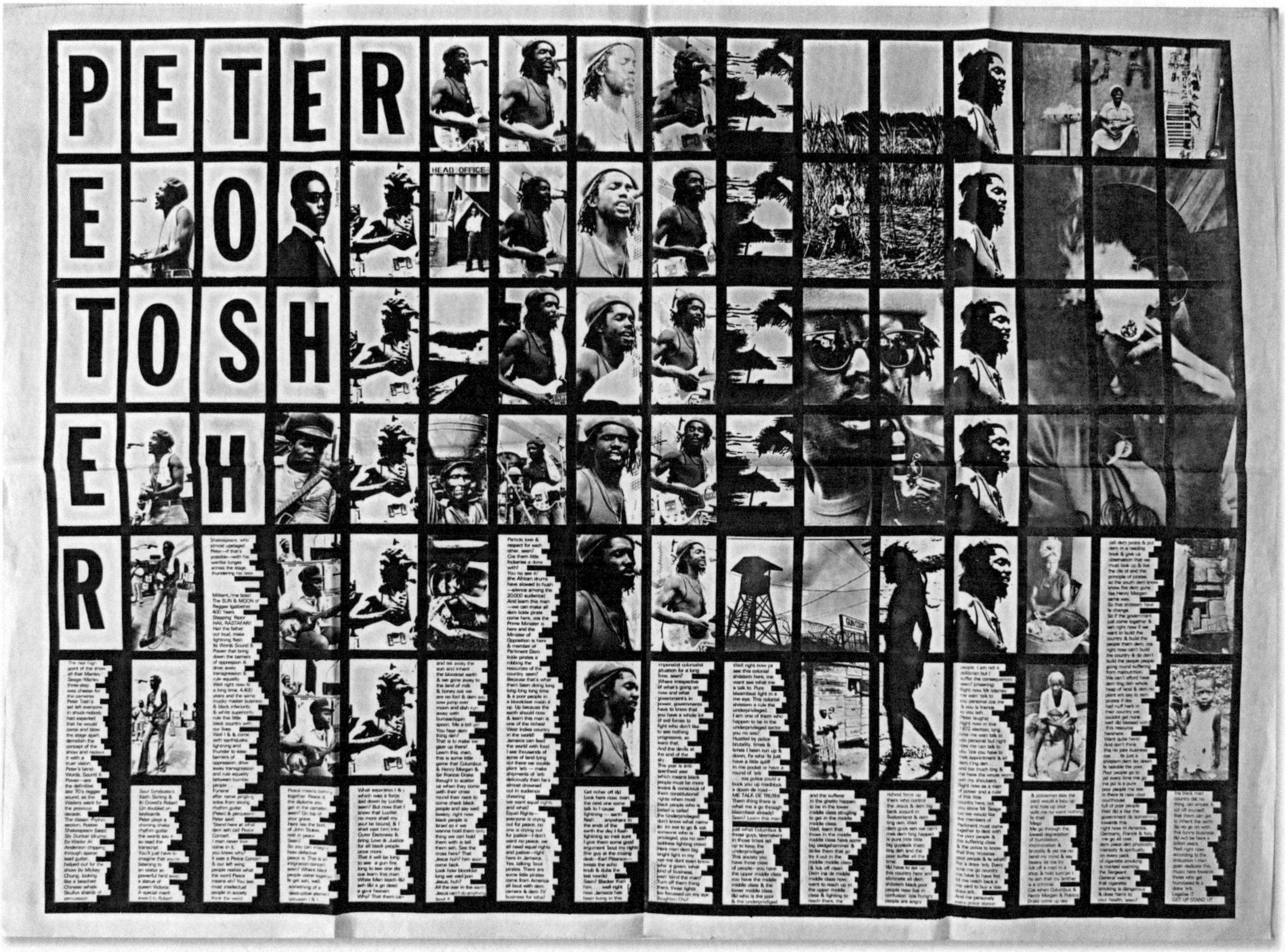
PETER
TOSH

THE LEVELLER #16
June 1978
29.8 x 20.9 cm, 11¾ x 8¼ in

This London political magazine described itself as 'an independent monthly socialist magazine'.

POSTER FOR PLASTIC BERTRAND'S ALBUM AN 1
1978
71.1 × 49.5 cm, 28 × 19½ in

AN 1 was the debut album of Plastic Bertrand (born Roger Jouret) and contained the single 'Ça Plane Pour Moi', which propelled Jouret to international fame. He would later tour Canada, Japan, Australia, Scandinavia, Europe and the US.

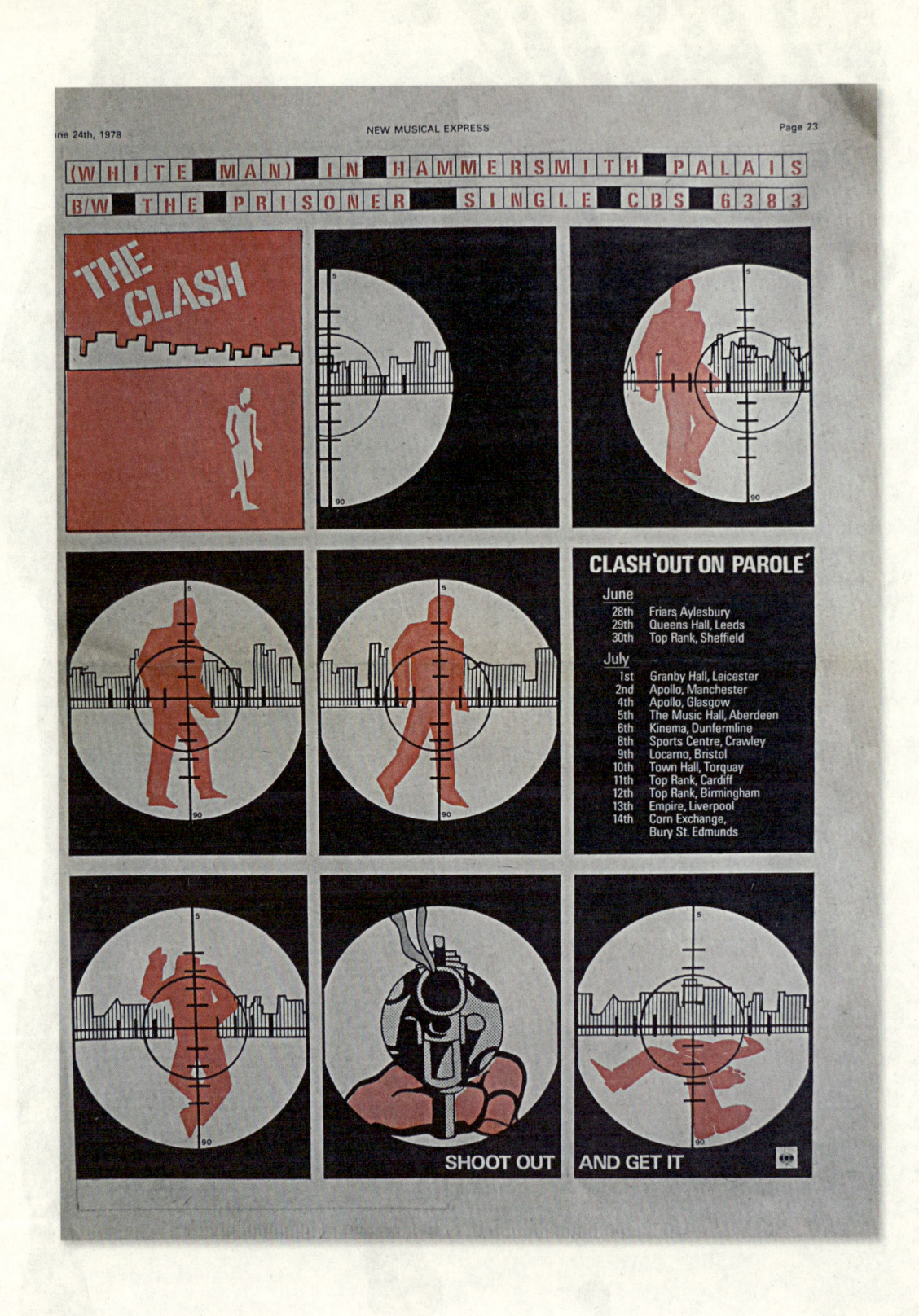

ADVERTISEMENT IN NME FOR THE CLASH'S 'OUT ON PAROLE' TOUR
24 June 1978
41.9 x 29.2 cm, 16½ x 11½ in

Advertises the Clash's tour and the single '(White Man) in Hammersmith Palais'.

**POSTER FOR THE SEX PISTOLS/SID VICIOUS
SINGLE 'MY WAY'**
Jamie Reid, John Tiberi
June 1978
69.8 x 46.9 cm, 27½ x 18½ in

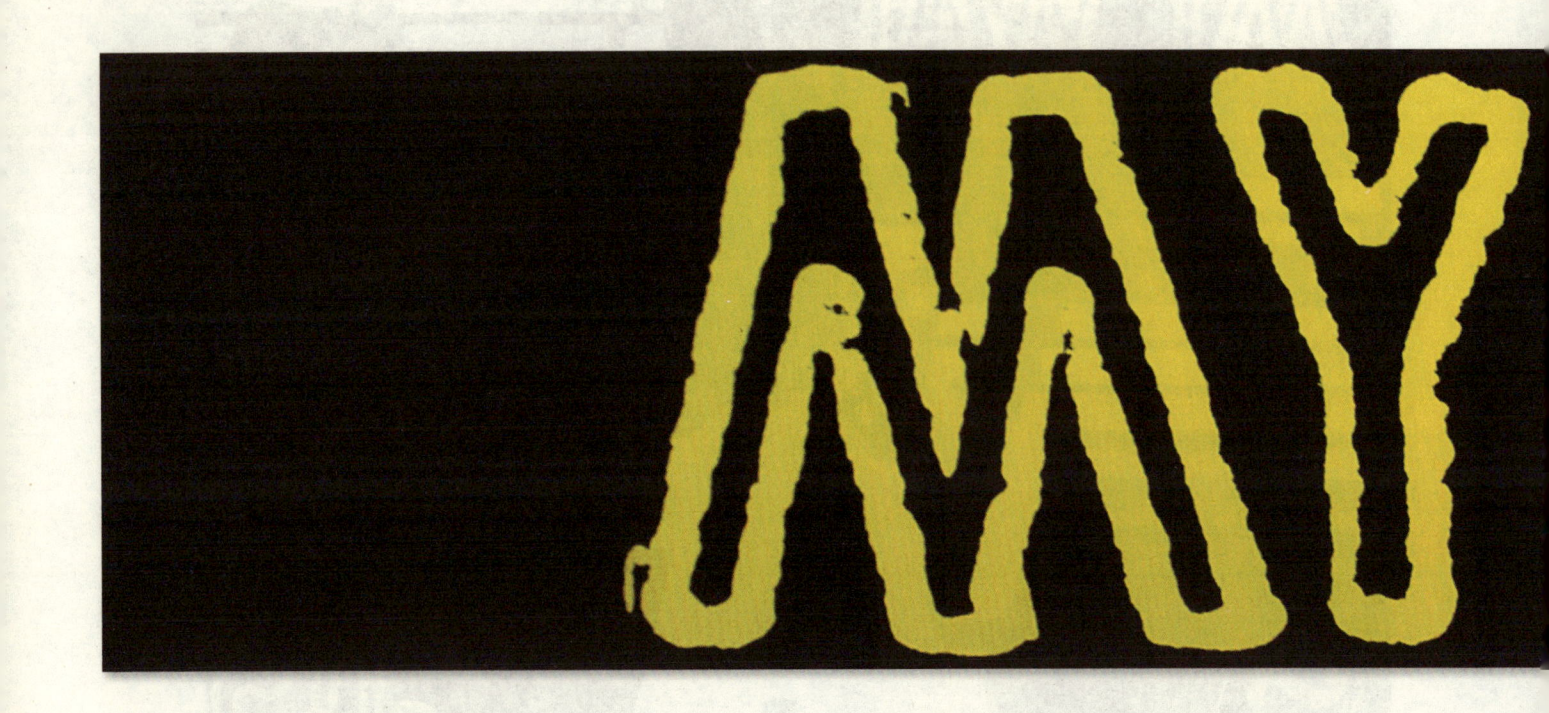

BANNER FOR THE SEX PISTOLS/SID VICIOUS SINGLE 'MY WAY'
30 June 1978
12 x 71.7 cm, 4¾ x 28¼ in

For his version of 'My Way', originally popularised by Frank Sinatra, Sid Vicious improvised many of the lyrics and sang to a more up-tempo arrangement. The single charted at No. 7 in the UK.

WAY

THE CLASH ON PAROLE

PLUS FROM THE U.S.A. **Suicide**
*EXCEPT ON THESE DATES

*Wed June 28   AYLESBURY FRIARS
*Thurs 29   LEEDS QUEENS HALL
*Fri 30   SHEFFIELD TOP RANK
Sat July 1   LEICESTER GRANBY HALL
Sun 2   MANCHESTER APPOLLO
Tues 4   GLASGOW APPOLLO
Wed 5   ABERDEEN MUSIC HALL
Thurs 6   DUNFERMLINE KINEMA
Sat 8   CRAWLEY SPORTS CENTRE
Sun 9   BRISTOL LOCARNO
Mon 10   TORQUAY TOWN HALL
Tues 11   CARDIFF TOP RANK
Wed 12   BIRMINGHAM TOP RANK
Thurs 13   LIVERPOOL EMPIRE
Fri 14   BURY ST EDMUNDS CORN EXCHANGE

POSTER FOR THE CLASH'S 'ON PAROLE' TOUR
June/July 1978
102.2 x 76.2 cm, 40¼ x 30 in

The Clash had released their second album and were out 'on parole' after Paul Simonon and Topper Headon were arrested on the roof of their Camden rehearsal studio for shooting at pigeons with air pistols (an incident that inspired the song 'Guns on the Roof').

The band played 26 concerts in 30 days on the tour, with supporting acts Suicide and the Specials. The Clash were often joined onstage by Steve Jones of the Sex Pistols, who had broken up earlier that year.

```
FROM:   PROGRAMME ORGANISER

TO:     ALL STAFF.                          6th July 1978


The new record by the Sex Pistols with Ronald Biggs is not
to be played under any circumstances.

                                        JIM BRADY
```

BBC INTERNAL MEMORANDUM ON THE SEX PISTOLS
6 July 1978
[unknown dims]

Informs BBC radio stations not to play the Sex Pistols' single 'No One Is Innocent', with vocals by train robber Ronnie Biggs.

Marquee History

1962 CHRIS BARBER HUMPHREY LYTTLETON ALEXIS KORNER

1963 ROLLING STONES, LONG JOHN BALDRY, SONNY BOY W...

1964 MANFRED MANN YARDBIRDS ROD STEWART

1965 THE WHO MOODY BLUES SPENCER DAVIS GROUP

1966 SMALL FACES SIMON & GARFUNKEL PINK FLOYD
STEVIE WONDER DAVID BOWIE LOVING SPOONFUL

1967 JEFF BECK CREAM FLEETWOOD MAC ANIMALS
JIMI HENDRIX TEN YEARS AFTER THE NICE P...

1968 JOE COCKER JETHRO TULL LED ZEPPELIN S...

1969 YES FREE BLACK SABBATH STEPPENWOLF K...

1970 GENESIS STATUS QUO THE FACES HUMBLE PIE

1971 WISHBONE ASH RORY GALLAGHER HAWKWIND U...

1972 NAZARETH AL STEWART FOCUS MAN MC5

1973 AVERAGE WHITE BAND THIN LIZZY CAMEL AC...

1974 SUPERTRAMP BE-BOP DELUXE COUNTRY JOE MacDO...

1975 KIKI DEE GONG BRAND X STREETWALKERS

1976 AC/DC EDDIE & THE HOT RODS AUTOMATIC MAN

1977 MOTORS GENERATION X THE JAM BUZZCOCKS
BOOMTOWN RATS JOHN CALE ULTRAVOX X RAY...

Fri 30th—Sat 1st—Sun 2nd & Mo...
Special Guests from Americ...

THE RUBINOOS
Plus friends & D.J.s
Advance tickets to members £1
Non-members at the door £1

Tues 4th July (Adm £1)
Special Independence Day
Celebrations with ...

THE MOVIES
Plus guests Joe Lung

Wed 5th & Thurs 6th July (Adm...

DIRE STRAITS
Plus guests & Ian Fleming

Fri 7th July (Adm 85p)
THE BRAKES
Plus support & Ian Fleming

Sat 8th July (Adm 75p)
APOSTROPHE
Plus guests & Ian Fleming

Sun 9th July (Adm £1.25)
MEALTICKET
Plus guests & Mandy H

Mon 10th July (Adm 75p)
WINDOW
Plus support & Jerry Floyd

Tues 11th July (Adm £1)
TONIGHT
Plus friends & Joe Lung

PROGRAMME FOR THE MARQUEE CLUB
July 1978
20.9 × 14.6 cm, 8¼ × 5¾ in

Two-sided flyer describes the venue and lists gigs and dates on the reverse, including performances by Johnny Moped, Suicide, the Adverts and others.

MARQUEE JULY 78.

Wed 12th July (Adm £1.50)
For one night only..
SONJA KRISTINA ex Curved Air
Plus support & Jerry Floyd

Thur 13th July (Adm 75p)
AUTOMATICS
Plus support & Ian Fleming

Fri 14th July (Adm £1)
★ NEW HEARTS
Plus friends & Ian Fleming

Sat 15th July (Adm 75p)
THE NEWS
Plus guests & Ian Fleming

Sun 16th July (Adm £1)
★ ERIC BELL ex Thin Lizzy
Plus friends & Mandy H

Mon 17th July (Adm £1.25)
★ JONNY MOPED
Plus guests & Jerry Floyd

Tues 18th July (Adm £1.50)
Special guests from U.S.A.
SUICIDE
Plus support & Joe Lung

Wed 19th July (Adm £1)
★ DEAD FINGERS TALK
Plus support & Jerry Floyd

☆ New membership cards available only 75p ☆

Thurs 20th & Fri 21st (Adm £1.50)
Special guest appearance
RADIO STARS
Plus friends & Ian Fleming

Sat 22nd July (Adm 85p)
BLAST FURNACE & THE HEATWAVES
Business &Ian Fleming

Sun 23rd July (Adm £1)
★ SUPERCHARGE
Plus guests & Mandy H

Mon 24th July (Adm £1.50)
From America we welcome
SHIRTS
Plus support & Jerry Floyd

Tues 25th July (Adm £1)
★ TONIGHT
Plus guests & Joe Lung

Wed 26th & Thurs 27th July
A Marquee Special Concert
THE ADVERTS
Plus guests & Jerry Floyd
Advance tickets to members £1.40
Non-members at the door £1.60

Fri 28th July (Adm £1.50)
★ CHELSEA
Plus friends & Ian Fleming

Sat 29th July (Adm 75p)
RUMBLE STRIP
Plus support & Ian Fleming

Sun 30th July (Adm £1)
THE BANNED
Plus guests & Mandy H

Mon 31st July (Adm 85p)
TOURISTs
Plus friends & Jerry Floyd

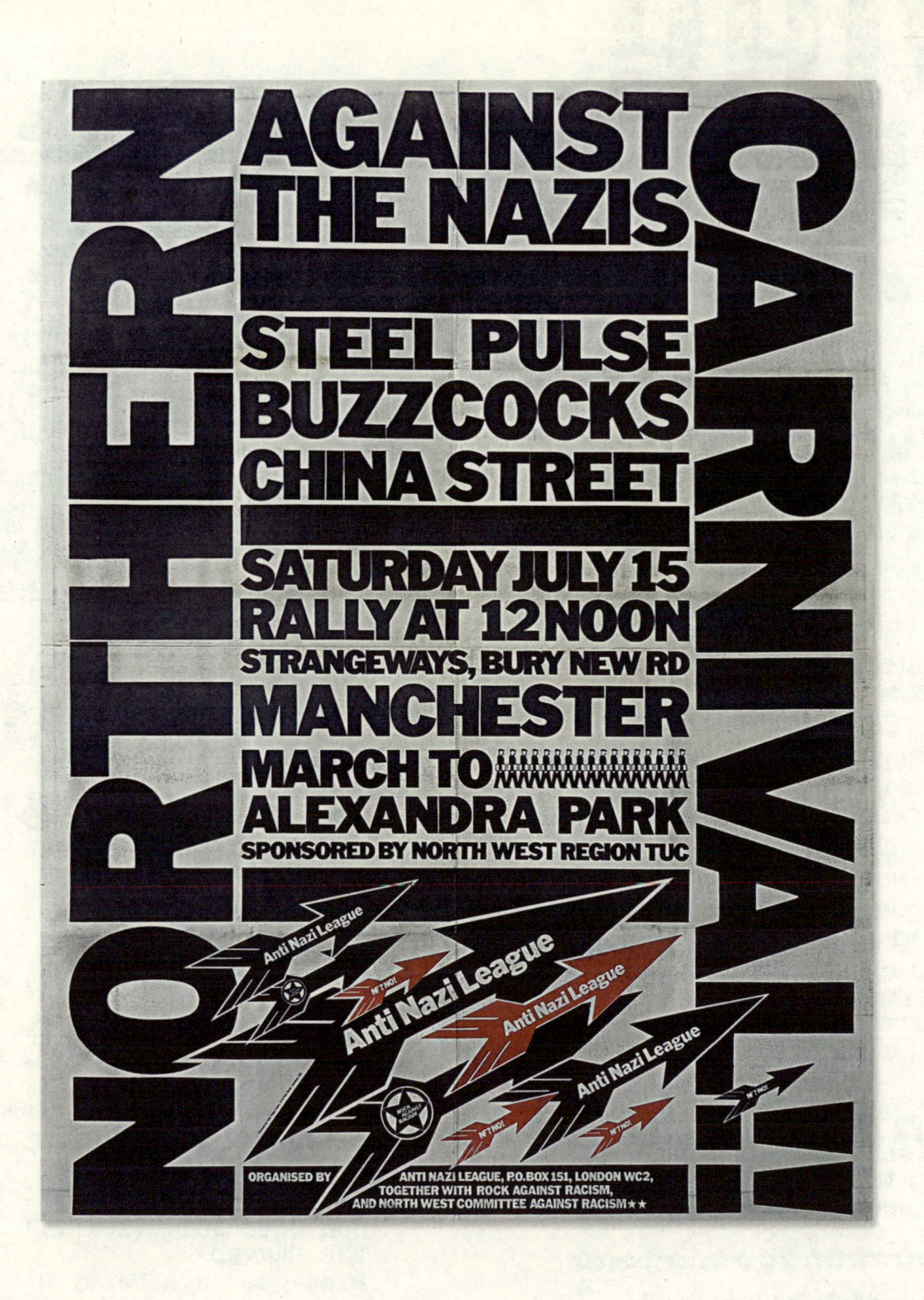

POSTER FOR NORTHERN CARNIVAL
AT ALEXANDRA PARK, MANCHESTER
David King
15 July 1978
86.3 x 62.8 cm, 34 x 24¾ in

POSTER WITH TOM ROBINSON BAND LOGO
David King
[July] 1978
72.3 x 47.6 cm, 28½ x 18¾ in

The logo appears on the cover of the group's debut album, *Power in the Darkness*. The raised fist is similar to that of the Socialist Workers Party.

FLYER FOR JOHNNY MOPED AT THE MARQUEE CLUB, LONDON
17 July 1978
20.3 x 14.6 cm, 8 x 5¾ in

Captain Sensible of the Damned made a guest appearance on stage, playing lead guitar.

FLYER FOR SIOUXSIE AND THE BANSHEES AND SPIZZOIL AT THE RUSSELL CLUB, MANCHESTER
20 July 1978
74.9 x 60.3 cm, 29½ x 23¾ in

Singer/guitar player Spizz (born Kenneth Spiers) was the chief force behind punk/new wave band Spizzenergi, aka Athletico Spizz 80, Spizzoil and the Spizzles – the band's annual name change was part of Spizz's abortive attempt to set a record for most recordings under different names. Spizzenergi's single 'Where's Captain Kirk?' was first to top the UK Indie Chart in early 1980.

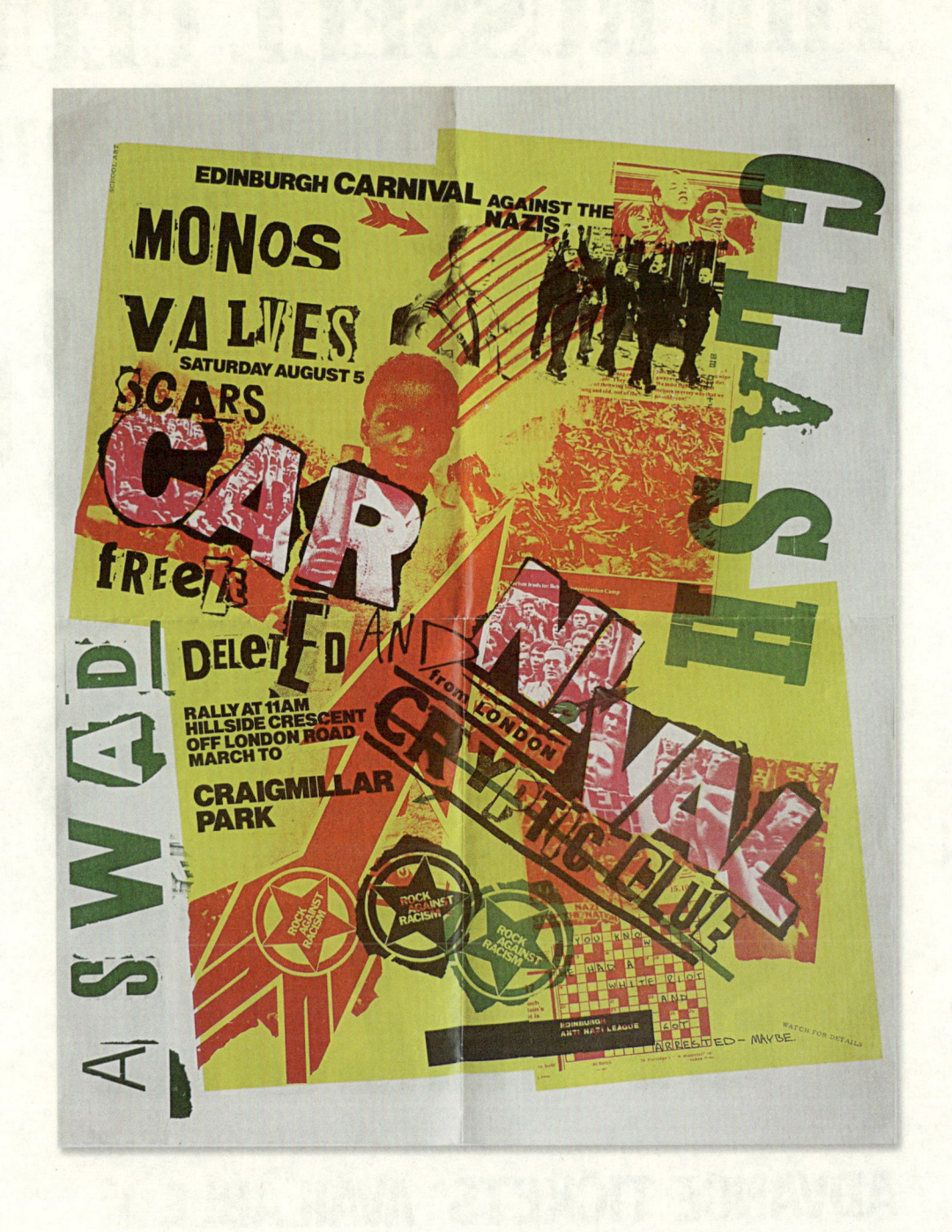

POSTER FOR CARNIVAL AGAINST THE NAZIS EVENT, EDINBURGH
5 August 1978
[unknown dims]

A five-colour silkscreen poster for a regional event in Edinburgh, which was to culminate in a concert headlined by the Clash. The Clash had to cancel at the last minute and were replaced by Aswad.

**POSTER FOR SIOUXSIE AND THE BANSHEES'
SINGLE 'HONG KONG GARDEN'**
August 1978
69.8 x 61.5 cm, 27½ x 24¼ in

The song takes its title from the Hong Kong Garden
Chinese takeaway in the Chislehurst High Street.

POSTER FOR BLONDIE'S SINGLE 'PICTURE THIS'
August 1978
43.1 x 50.8 cm, 17 x 20 in

From the album *Parallel Lines*, this track reached No. 12 in the UK singles chart; 'Fade Away and Radiate' is the B-side. In 2007, speaking of her onstage persona, Debbie Harry told the *Guardian*, 'I think one thing that's interesting about rock 'n' roll is that sexuality is a little bit more ambiguous. Mick Jagger was very fey, and I always liked that. I think that women who get up on stage in rock are manly in lots of ways – a certain ferocity.'

POSTER FOR WAYNE COUNTY & THE ELECTRIC CHAIRS' 'STORM THE GATES' TOUR
August 1978
76.2 x 50.8 cm, 30 x 20 in

The tour commenced after Wayne County's nose job, and the dates were timed to accommodate County's ongoing transition from male to female. The tour culminated with a major concert at Camden's Electric Ballroom in December 1978. The gig was filmed, but the footage has yet to be released.

RIPPED & TORN #13
Tony Drayton
August 1978
29.8 x 20.9 cm, 11¾ x 8¼ in

Features Suicide, X-Ray Spex and a page by Adam Ant; an advert for the Fall's 'Bingo Masters Breakout' EP; and pre-release photos from the Sex Pistols' film *The Great Rock 'n' Roll Swindle*. This was the first issue of *Ripped & Torn* to use saddle-stapling.

999 #1
1978
29.8 x 20.9 cm, 11¾ x 8¼ in

RECORD MIRROR WITH DEBBIE HARRY OF BLONDIE
9 September 1978
41.9 x 29.8 cm, 16½ x 11¾ in

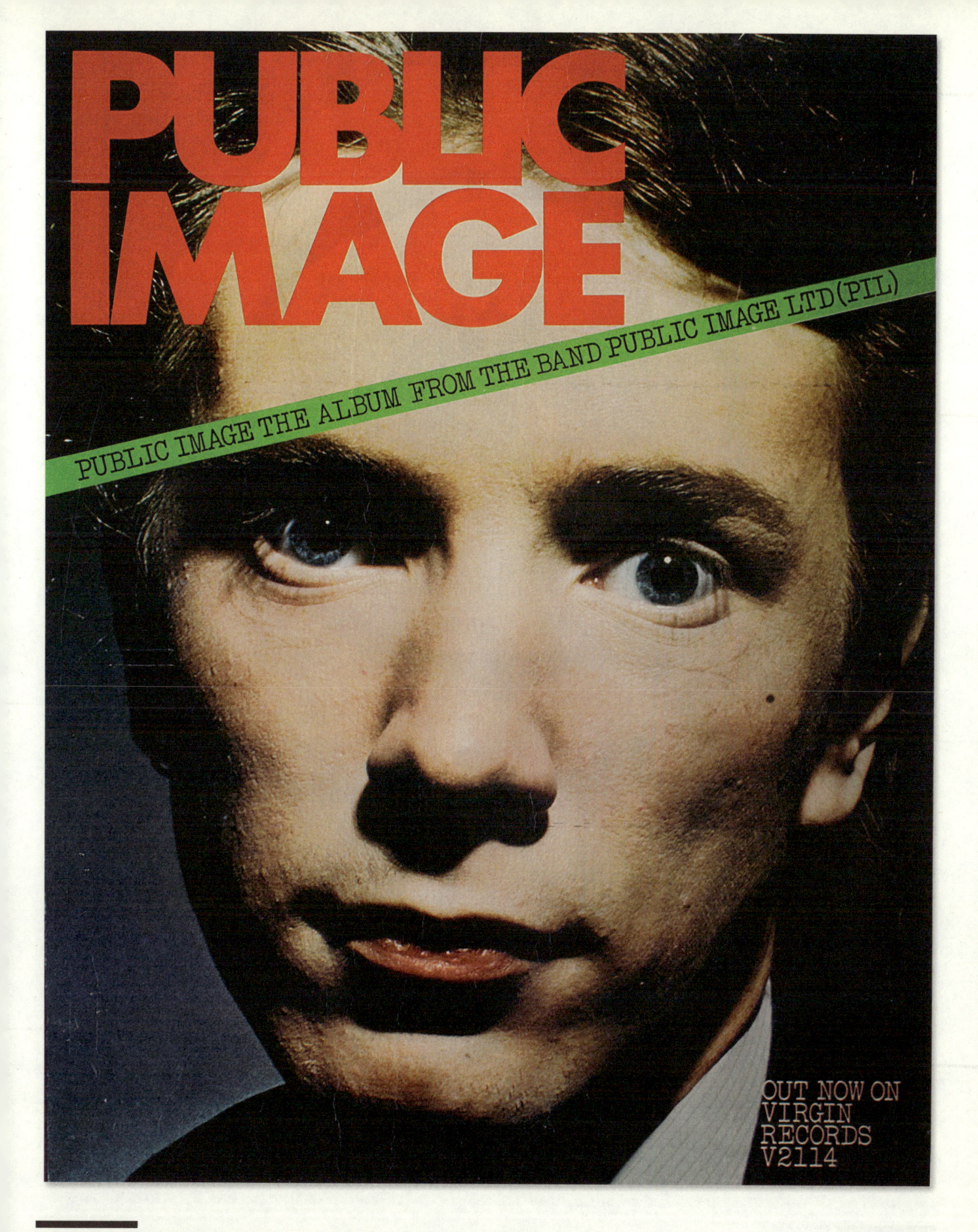

POSTER FOR PUBLIC IMAGE LTD'S SINGLE 'PUBLIC IMAGE'
Terry Jones, Dennis Morris
1978
56.5 x 41.9 cm, 22¼ x 16½ in

Features a graphic by Terry Jones and photography by Dennis Morris. John Lydon had seen Morris's photos of Bob Marley on tour, and recruited Morris to take the first official shots of the Sex Pistols after the band signed to Virgin Records. Morris photographed the band for a year, and continued to work with Lydon after he went on to form Public Image Ltd (PiL).

**POSTERS FOR ANTI-NAZI LEAGUE/
ROCK AGAINST RACISM'S CARNIVAL 2**
24 September 1978
85.7 × 62.8 cm, 33¾ × 24¾ in
62.8 × 85 cm, 24¾ × 33½ in

The second Anti-Nazi League Carnival took place in Brockwell Park, London, although it had been advertised as starting at Hyde Park. The event drew an even larger crowd than the first carnival, with an estimated 100,000 people in attendance. It was partly overshadowed by a National Front counterprotest in East London. Some on the left insisted that the ANL/RAR Carnival crowd cancel their event and go to East London to face the NF. As 250 NF marchers assembled in the East End, the ANL's response was badly organised, arrived late and failed to disperse the NF group.

CARNIVAL 2
ASWAD
SHAM69 MISTY
ELVIS COSTELLO
& THE ATTRACTIONS
11am • Sept 24 th •
Hyde Park •
March to Brixton
Anti Nazi League
ROCK
AGAINST
RACISM

**FLYER FOR ANTI-NAZI LEAGUE/
ROCK AGAINST RACISM'S CARNIVAL 2**
24 September 1978
20.3 x 29.8 cm, 8 x 11¾ in

POSTER FOR CHELSEA, THE FALL AND THE SNIVELLING SHITS AT THE MUSIC MACHINE, LONDON
25 September 1978
75.5 x 101.6 cm, 29¾ x 40 in

**FLYERS FOR THE SLITS ET AL
AT ACKLAM HALL**
19 & 26 September & 3 October 1978
20.9 × 14.6 cm, 8¼ × 5¾ in

Using stick figure drawings by the band, these flyers advertise appearances by the Slits at London's Acklam Hall in September and October 1978. Acklam Hall regularly hosted punk acts such as the Raincoats, Stiff Little Fingers, the Psychedelic Furs, Ruts and the Monochrome Set, along with reggae acts like Exodus and the Satellites.

tHe
Slits
have fun
and experience
the Slit
At
the aklam
Hall
tues 26th sept
+ THE DOLL
tues 3rd oct
+ innocents
+ THE DOLL
aklam rd.
Westbourn Park
Ladbroke Grove
WESTBOURNE
bar open til 12.

NEGATIVE REACTION #7
Jon Romney
September/October 1978
29.8 x 20.9 cm, 11¾ x 8¼ in

The zine *Negative Reaction* originated in Cambridge in February 1977. This issue features Wreckless Eric (Eric Goulden), a new wave artist who had recently released his second album, *The Wonderful World of Wreckless Eric*.

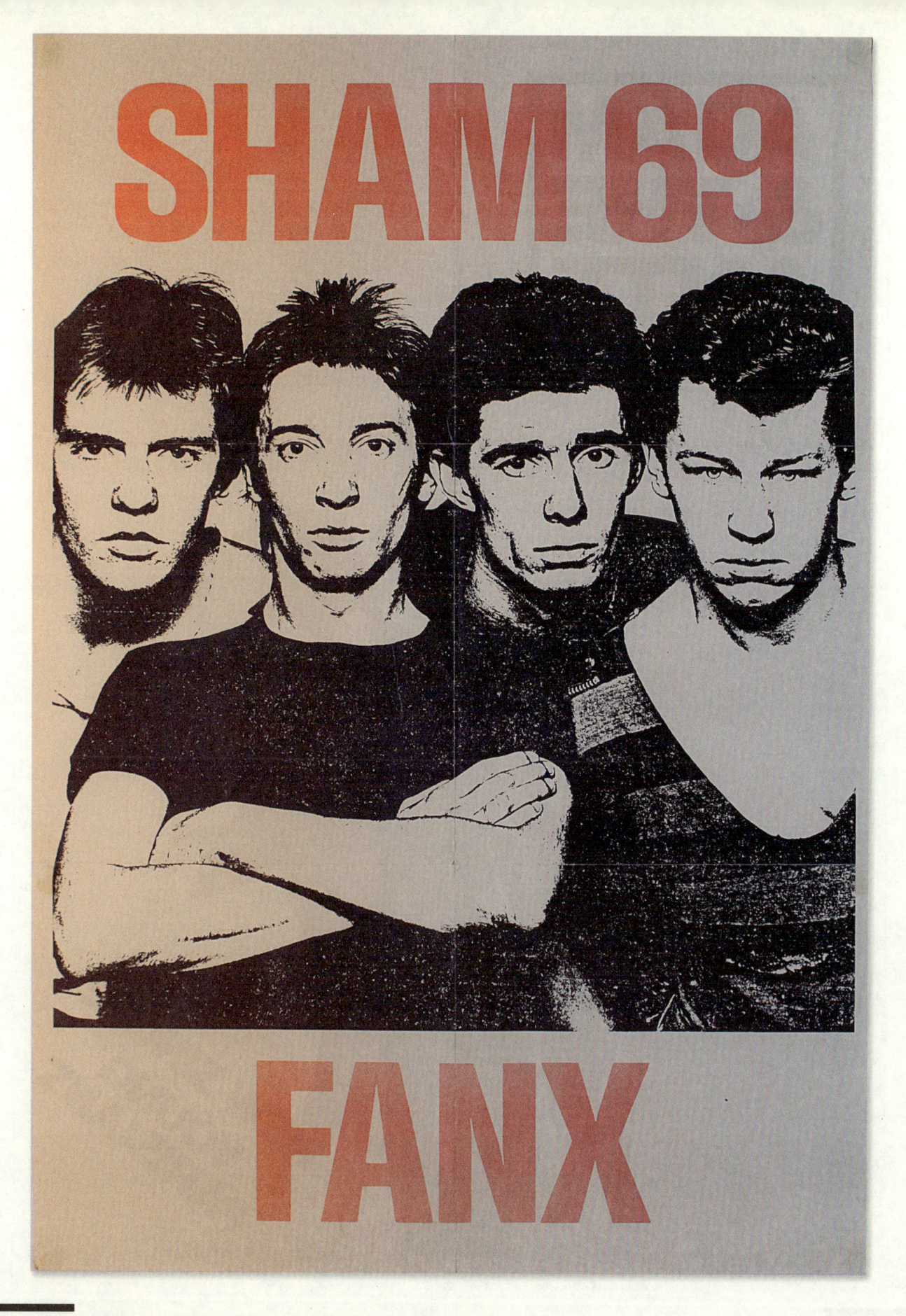

POSTER FOR SHAM 69, 'FANX'
October 1978
76.8 x 50.8 cm, 30¼ x 20 in

Included in the group's concept album *That's Life*, this poster bears the simple message 'Fanx' – which was also the message on the blank B-side of their 1977 single 'Song of the Streets'.

POSTER FOR ADAM AND THE ANTS' SINGLE 'YOUNG PARISIANS'
October 1978
86.3 x 60.9 cm, 34 x 24 in

Adam and the Ants debut single on Decca Records.

POSTER FOR PUBLIC IMAGE LTD'S SINGLE 'PUBLIC IMAGE'
October 1978
[unknown dims]

After the demise of the Sex Pistols, John Lydon formed Public Image Ltd with guitarist Keith Levene and bassist Jah Wobble. The song 'Public Image' was written while Lydon was still a member of the Sex Pistols.

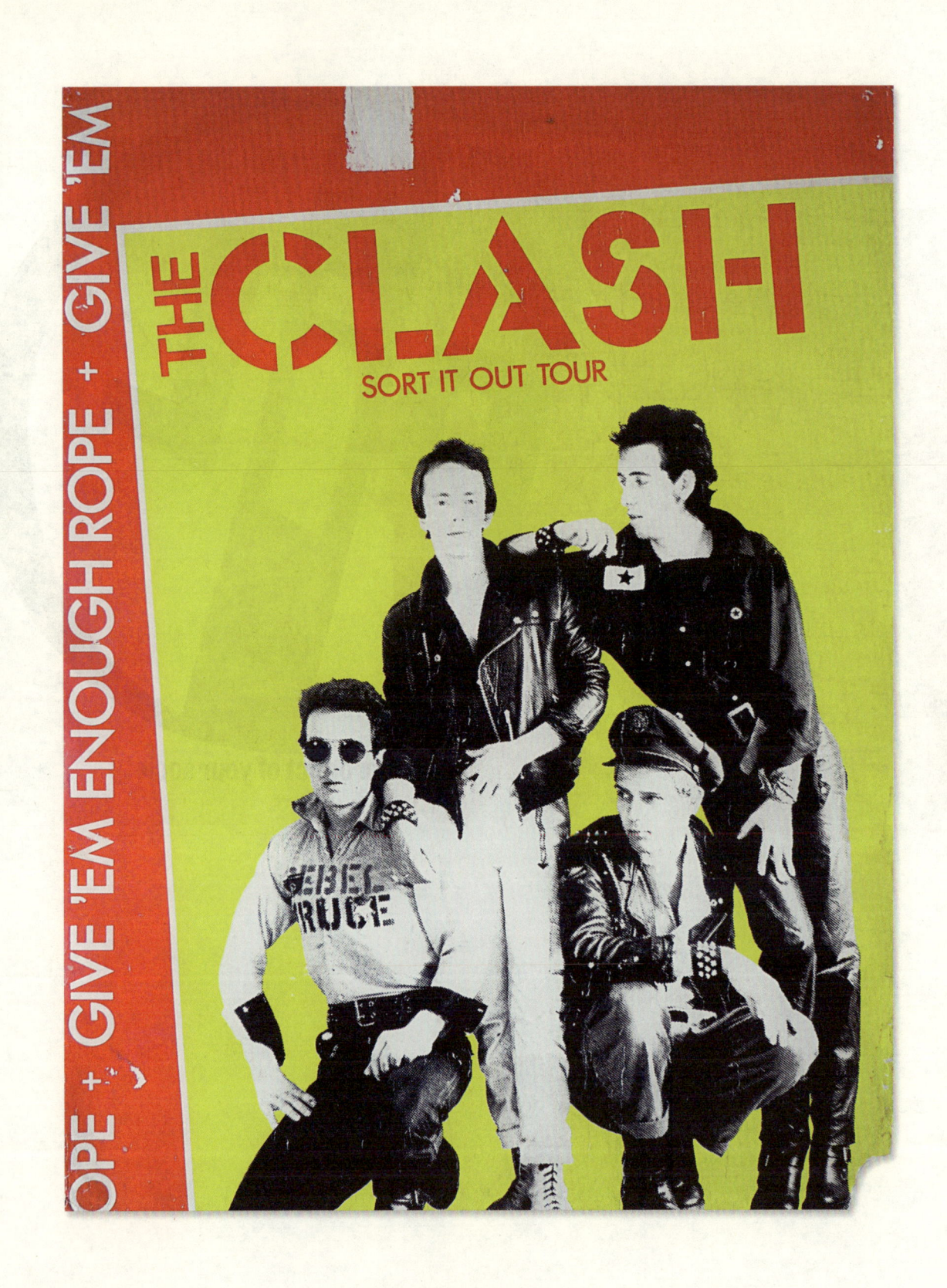

POSTER FOR THE CLASH'S 'SORT IT OUT' TOUR
October 1978
83.8 x 60.3 cm, 33 x 23¾ in

RIPPED & TORN #14
Tony Drayton
October 1978
29.8 x 20.9 cm, 11¾ x 8¼ in

24 pages featuring Adam and the Ants, Eraserhead, Buzzcocks, trash rock, the Clash, the Viletones, Wayne County, Public Image Ltd, Sham 69 and the Shades.

**FLYER FOR CHELSEA'S 'LAST EVER GIG'
AT THE ROXY**
6 October 1978
21.5 x 33 cm, 8½ x 13 in

POSTER FOR RAR CONCERT WITH THIRD WORLD AND JOHN COOPER CLARKE AT LANCASTER UNIVERSITY
19 November 1978
76.2 x 50.8 cm, 30 x 20 in

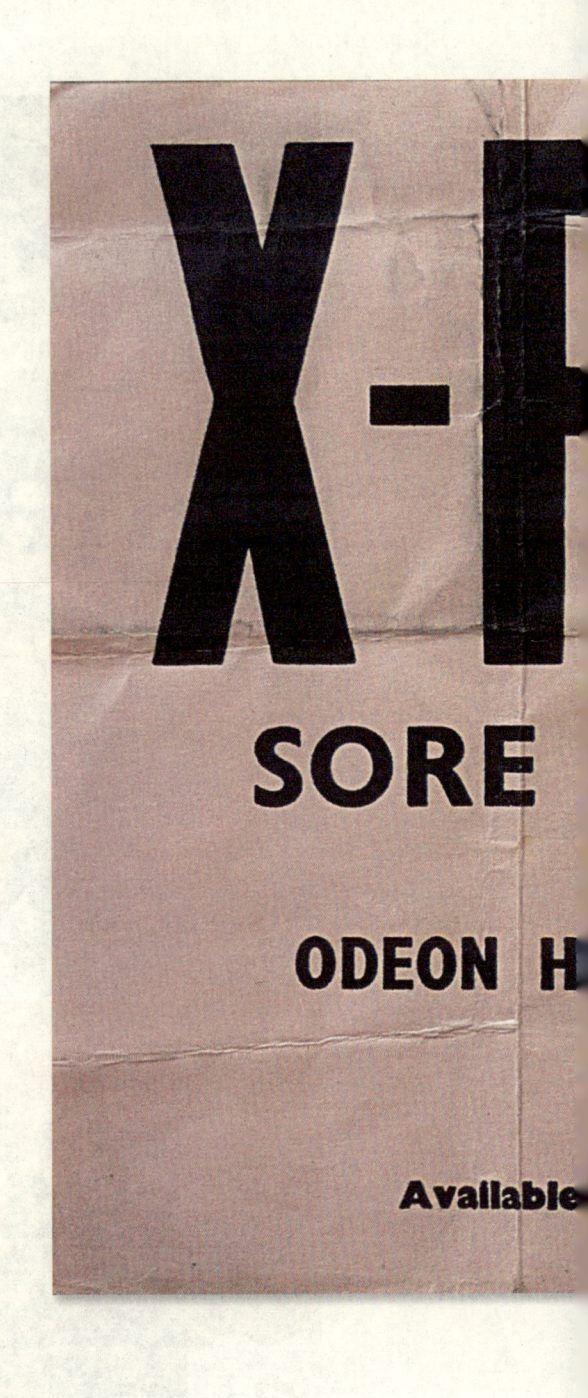

**FLYER FOR X-RAY SPEX, SORE THROAT
AND THE INVADERS AT HAMMERSMITH ODEON**
27 November 1978
13.9 x 24.1 cm, 5½ x 9½ in

...AY SPEX

...ROAT   THE INVADERS

...RTIN "MIGHTY MOUTH"

...ERSMITH on MONDAY, 27th NOVEMBER

AT 8.00 p.m.

...s: £3.00   £2.50   £2.00   £1.50

...e BOX OFFICE: 01-748 4081/2 and usual agents

**FLYER FOR SHAM 69 WITH THE CIMARONS
AT THE ELECTRIC BALLROOM, LONDON**
30 November & 1 December 1978
10.1 x 14.6 cm, 4 x 5¾ in

ANARCHY #28
December 1978
29.8 × 20.9 cm, 11¾ × 8¼ in

**FLYER FOR 'JOCK MCDONALD PRESENTS'
ADAM AND THE ANTS, UK SUBS AND THE PACK
AT THE RAINBOW THEATRE**
13 December 1978
20.9 x 29.8 cm, 8¼ x 11¾ in

In 1977 and '78, McDonald rented out the top floor of the Rainbow Theatre to put on gigs. According to a member of the Straps, 'The gig was cancelled as we were doing our sound check. We were told to get off stage and leave the venue immediately as Jock McDonald hadn't paid for the hire. There must have been at least 3,000 or 4,000 people outside waiting to come in.'

**FLYER FOR 'JOCK MCDONALD PRESENTS'
ADAM AND THE ANTS AT THE RAINBOW
THEATRE**
20 December 1978
20.9 x 14.6 cm, 8¼ x 5¾ in

Adam and the Ants, Human League, the Members, UK Subs and the Pack at the Rainbow Theatre in Finsbury Park.

POSTER FOR 999
1978
45 x 72.3 cm, 17¾ x 28½ in

POSTER FOR PENETRATION
1978/79
71.7 x 50.1 cm, 28¼ x 19¾ in

Renowned photographer Paul Slattery shot many of the concert photos of the group on this poster. Slattery became a rock photographer in 1975 and documented legendary acts, including the Sex Pistols, the Ramones and the Clash.

**POSTER FOR THE DAMNED
AT ERIC'S, LIVERPOOL**
1979
74.9 x 49.5 cm, 29½ x 19½ in

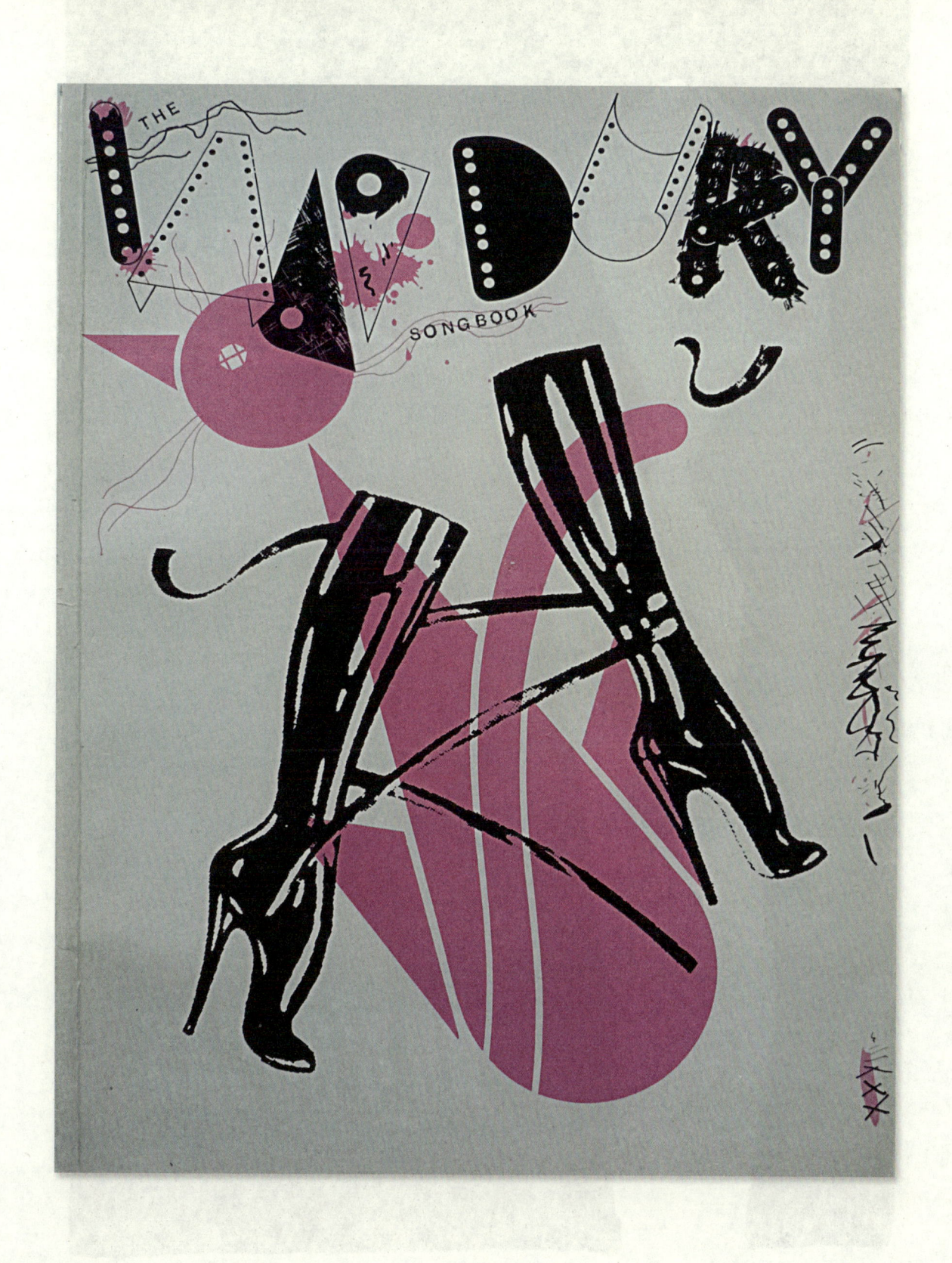

THE IAN DURY SONGBOOK
Barney Bubbles, Blackhill Music
1979
30.4 x 22.8 cm, 12 x 9 in

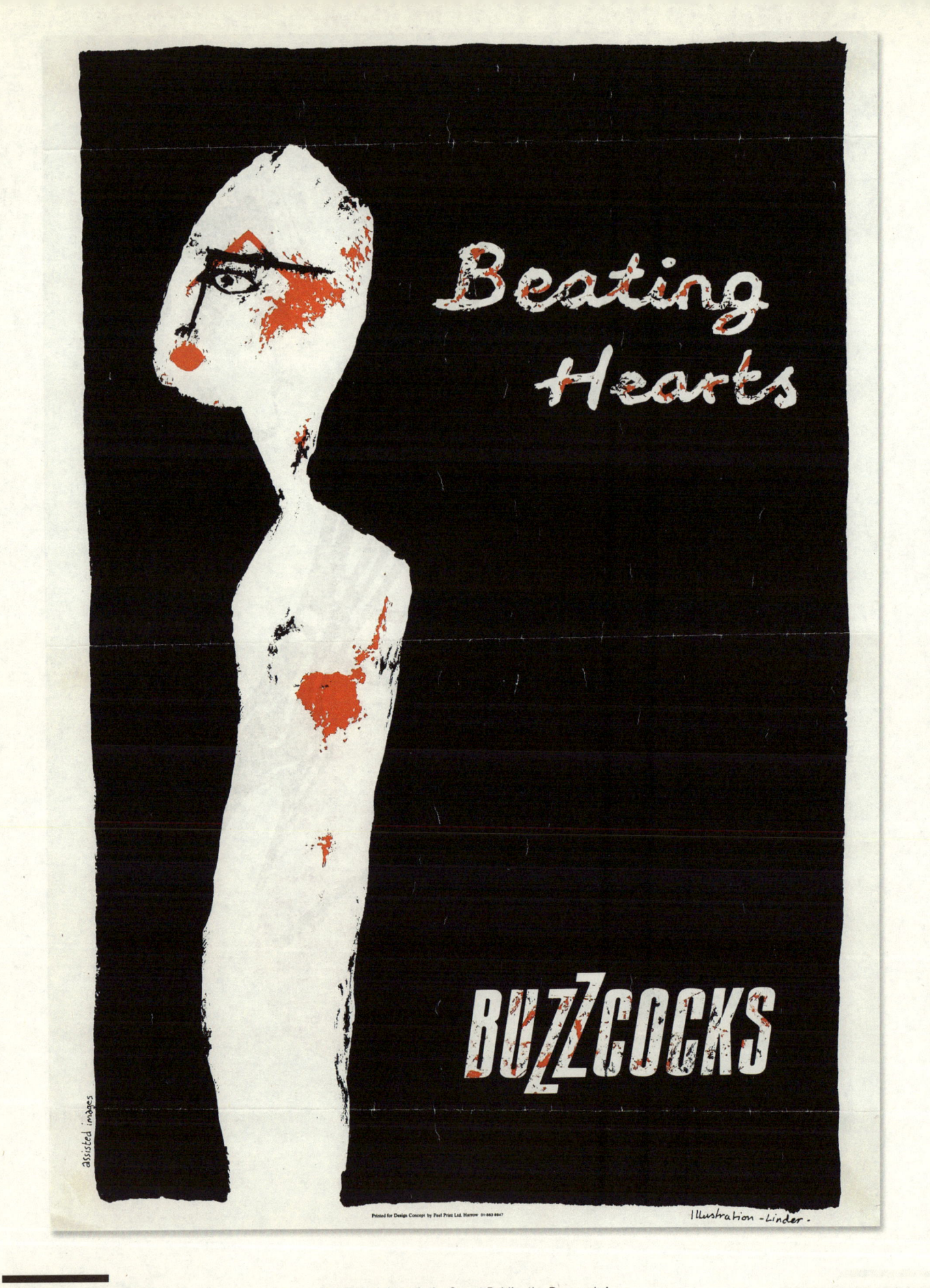

POSTER FOR BUZZCOCKS' ALBUM BEATING HEARTS
Linder Sterling
1979
70.4 x 48.8 cm, 27¾ x 19¼ in

Distributed through the Secret Public, the Buzzcocks' fanzine. Sterling's group Ludus also supported the band on part of its 'Beating Hearts' tour that year.

JOHN COOPER CLARKE
Barney Bubbles
1979
25.4 x 17.7 cm, 10 x 7 in

In this book by English performance poet John Cooper Clarke, 12 poems accompany photographs by Kevin Cummins, Tom Sheehan and Paul Slattery. Clarke opened for major punk and new wave acts, including the Sex Pistols, Joy Division, Siouxsie and the Banshees and Elvis Costello.

POSTER FOR ELVIS COSTELLO AND THE ATTRACTIONS' ALBUM ARMED FORCES
January 1979
75.5 x 50.1 cm, 29¾ x 19¾ in

FLYER FOR BLONDIE'S APPEARANCE ON THE MIDNIGHT SPECIAL
19 January 1979
22.8 x 30.4 cm, 9 x 12 in

Advertises Blondie's appearance on the US television show *The Midnight Special*, four months after the release of their third album, *Parallel Lines*.

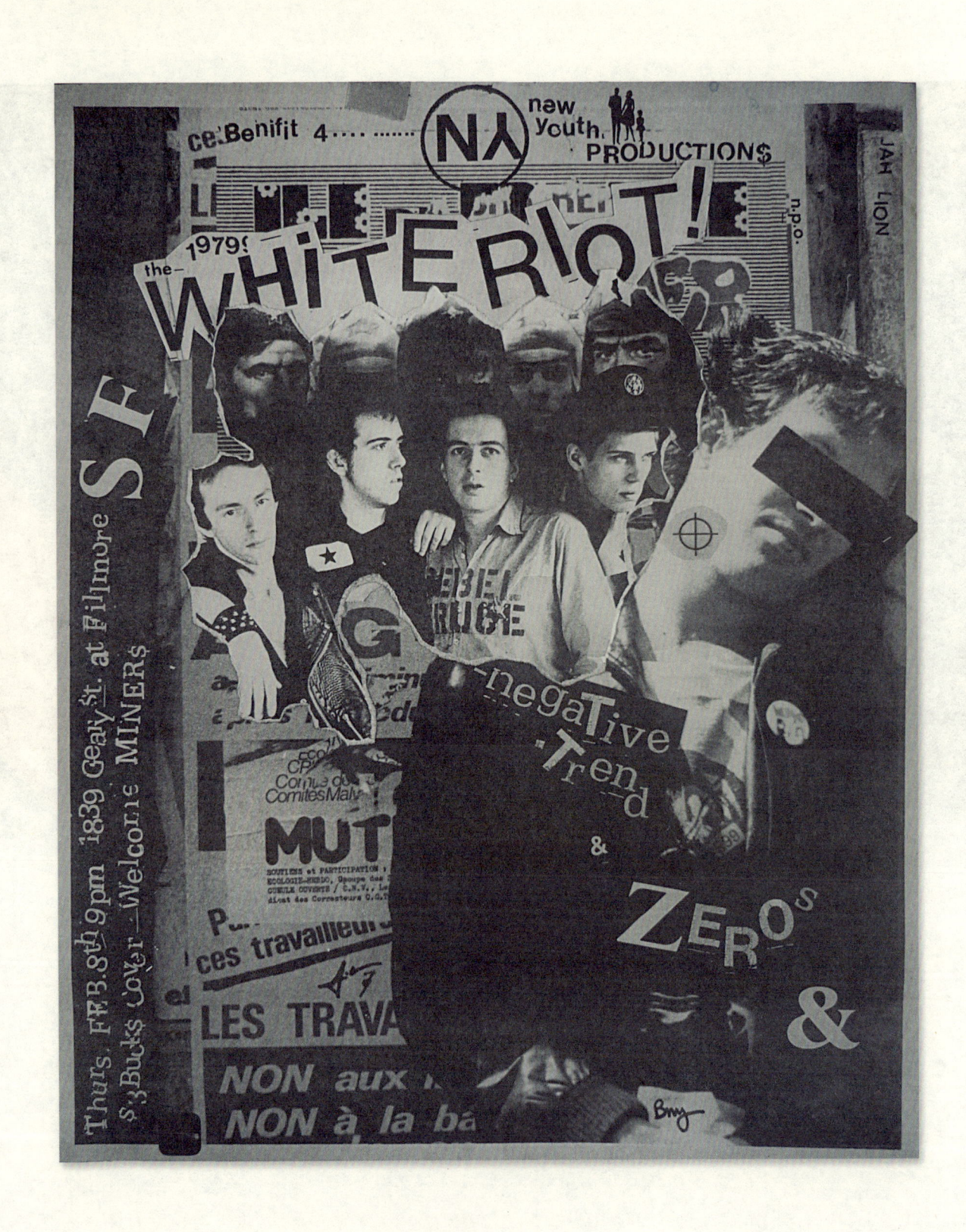

POSTER FOR THE CLASH'S US TOUR, SAN FRANCISCO GIG
8 February 1979
55.8 x 43.1 cm, 22 x 17 in

The Clash toured the US for the first time in 1979, with Bo Diddley as their opening act.

'FROM BEYOND THE GRAVE' POSTER FOR THE SEX PISTOLS' SINGLE 'SOMETHING ELSE'
Jamie Reid
9 February 1979
100.3 × 69.8 cm, 39½ × 27½ in

The campaign for 'Something Else' from *The Great Rock 'n' Roll Swindle* began just one week after the announcement of the death of Sid Vicious. 'Something Else' would be the band's best-selling single. Of his poster design, Reid said, 'The "From Beyond the Grave" poster was used as a comment on media and personality necrophilia. It was thought to be in very bad taste.'

FLYER FOR REMA REMA AND THE MONOCHROME SET AT ACKLAM HALL
22 February 1979
20.3 x 27.9 cm, 8 x 11 in

Some members of the Monochrome Set were briefly in the band the B-Sides with Stuart Goddard, prior to his transformation into Adam Ant. The group's best-known song is 'He's Frank'.

**INSERT FROM CRASS'S ALBUM
THE FEEDING OF THE FIVE THOUSAND**
February 1979
27.9 x 27.9 cm, 11 x 11 in

FLYERS FOR THE UK SUBS' TOUR
February 1979
29.2 x 20.9 cm, 11½ x 8¼ in

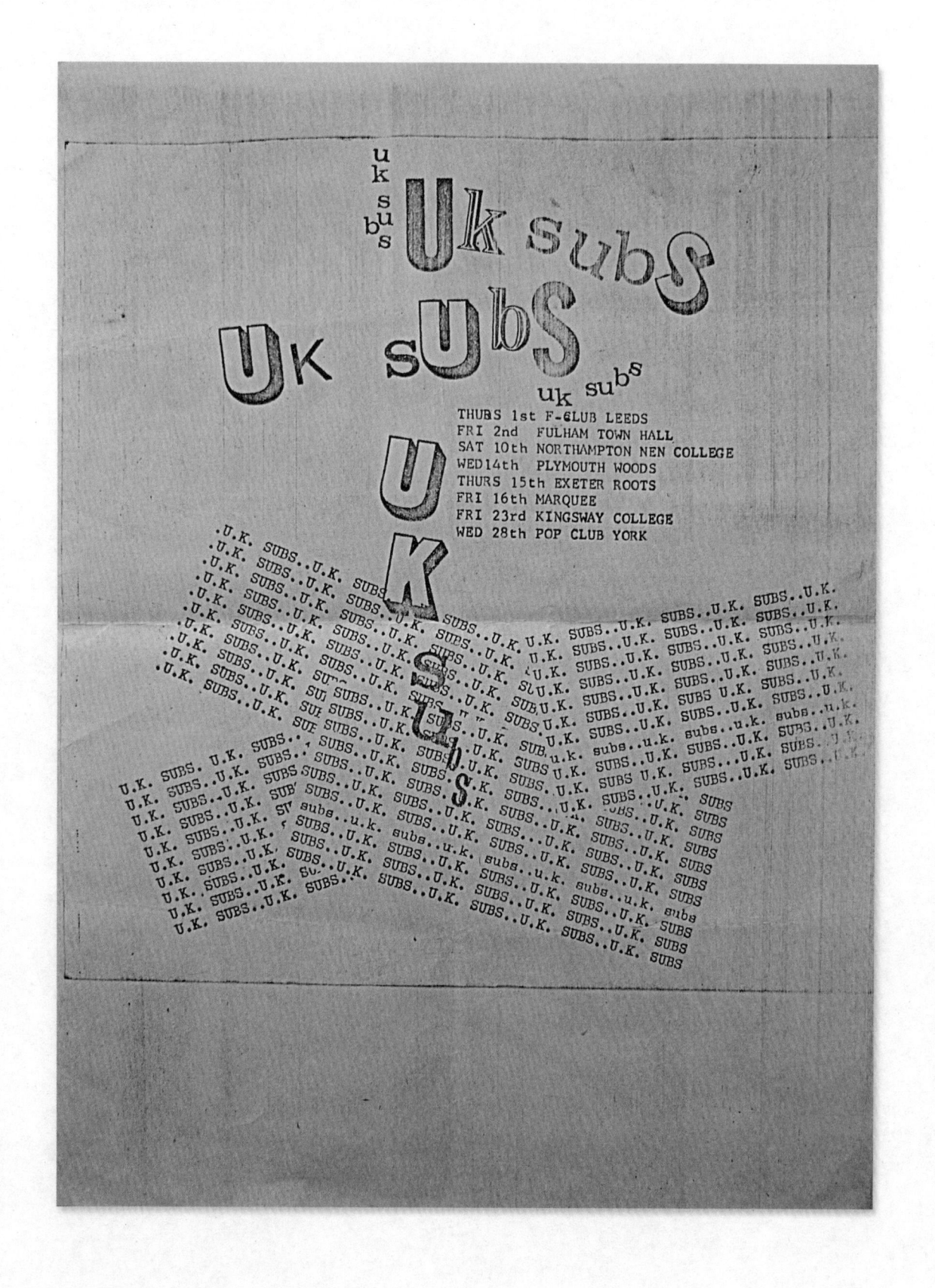

THURS 1st F-CLUB LEEDS
FRI 2nd FULHAM TOWN HALL
SAT 10th NORTHAMPTON NEN COLLEGE
WED 14th PLYMOUTH WOODS
THURS 15th EXETER ROOTS
FRI 16th MARQUEE
FRI 23rd KINGSWAY COLLEGE
WED 28th POP CLUB YORK

*PUNKS
OF LONDON

YOU SHOULD ALL KNOW BY NOW THAT THE BEAUFORT MARKET, KING'S ROAD, CHELSEA IS DUE TO CLOSE ON SATURDAY MARCH 31st.

WELL, WE ARE PLANNING TO HAVE A PARTY TO SHOW THE KING'S ROAD THAT THE PUNK SCENE IN LONDON WILL NOT TOLERATE SUCH A CLOSURE TO MAKE WAY FOR A McDONALD'S HAMBURGER STORE.

IF YOU'RE REALLY INTO PUNK — MAKE THE STAND WITH ME AT ONE O'CLOCK SATURDAY 31st MARCH. OUTSIDE BEAUFORT MARKET. BRING YOUR OWN BOOZE THAT WILL SAVE ME HAVING TO PAY FOR IT (know what I mean).

DON'T EXPECT ANYTHING, BUT DO EXPECT SOMETHING.

SEE JA

Jock

FLYERS FOR PROTEST WITH PERFORMANCE BY THE CLASH
Jock McDonald
31 March 1979
29.8 x 20.9 cm, 11¾ x 8¼ in

The Clash did a free gig to protest the closure of Beaufort Market, Kings Road, the cultural epicentre for punk and post-punk acolytes. Police denied the band permission to perform, but they played anyway. A riot ensued, and dozens were arrested. The event was organised by local stall owner and punk promoter Jock McDonald, who subsequently managed several bands, including the Bollock Brothers, the Sex Bristles and 4" Be 2".

Market Clash benefit?

THE CLASH, who turned up at Saturday's punk protest at the closure of London's Beaufort Market, but did not play, are considering playing a benefit show for the 100 or so protesters arrested during the demo.

Stallholder and demo organiser Jock McDonald said the band had verbally agreed to play a special benefit to help those charged with various offences from assaulting police to criminal damage — among those arrested were McDonald's two brothers.

The Clash were due to headline a series of bands playing at the Market, in Kings Road, but backed off in the face of a writ served by the police. Allan Jones at the demo — page 10.

KINGS ROAD RIOT

Punks clash

OVER 2000 punks clashed with police in London's Kings Road last Saturday after a protest over the closure of the Beaufort Market as a "punk centre."

The Clash were to have played a concert at the market but this was abandoned after the Metropolitan Police Special Patrol Group moved in to break up fighting between punks and the police.

75 people were arrested after what was described as a pitched battle in which three policemen were injured.

Mr McDonald, tireless in his campaign against injustice (and doubtless eager for publicity), was as equally determined that the punks should not surrender their bastion without a final display of disaffection. He therefore contrived a last stand on Saturday; the word went out that a clutch of bands, headlined by the Clash, would appear.

IF THE CLASH DON'T DO THE CONCERT FOR THE ONES ARRESTED I WILL FIND SOMEONE WHO WILL.

MORE DEMO'S ARE PLANNED FOR THE FUTURE

Don't let me down now WE ARE WINNING

:Jock:

McDonald's two brothers (one of whom was smashed over the head with a riot stick) were arrested in this fracas. They have both since been refused bail. There were, according to McDonald, over 100 arrests on charges ranging from obstruction to assaulting the police. — ALLAN JONES.

However, we understand another demo — against the closure of Beaufort Market — is being planned for Sunday outside Buckingham Palace.

Bearing in mind that total fines are likely to run into four figures, and that some of the arrested kids will be hard-pushed for bail, McDonald has stated that a benefit concert is in the pipeline, and that The Clash have tentatively agreed to take part.

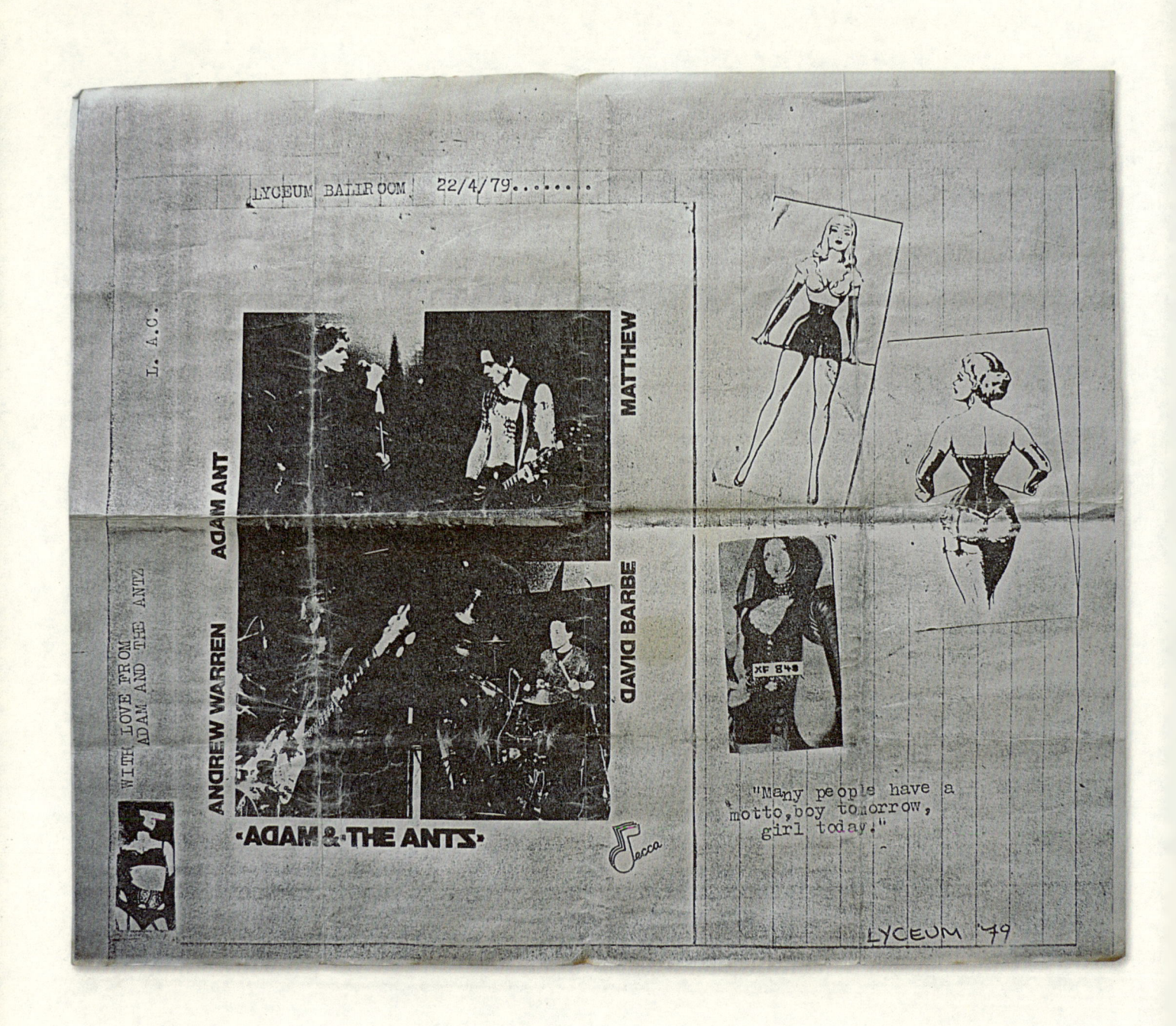

**FLYER FOR ADAM AND THE ANTS
AT THE LYCEUM BALLROOM, LONDON**
22 April 1979
21.5 x 25.4 cm, 8½ x 10 in

POSTER FOR PENETRATION AT MOUNTFORD HALL, LIVERPOOL
27 April 1979
75.5 × 50.8 cm, 29¾ × 20 in

During this concert in Liverpool, Penetration played its single 'Danger Signs', and lead singer Pauline Murray took a memorable fall from the stage after some enthusiastic dancing.

POSTER FOR BLONDIE'S SINGLE 'SUNDAY GIRL'
[May] 1979
49.5 x 49.5 cm, 19½ x 19½ in

Blondie released their 10th single, 'Sunday Girl', which became their second to reach No. 1 in the UK. The B-side was 'I Know But I Don't Know'. Both tracks appeared on Blondie's third album, *Parallel Lines*. The 12" also offered a French version of the non-LP track 'Sunday Girl'.

**FLYER FOR BRIAN JAMES WITH VERMILION
& THE ACES AND FASHION AT THE MUSIC
MACHINE, LONDON**
3 May 1979
33 x 21 cm, 13 x 8¼ in

> EVERYBODY
> AFTER WE BEAT ENGLAND AT WEMBLEY, WE ARE GOING TO THE SEASIDE (I DO LIKE TO BE BESIDE THE SEASIDE. DONT YOU?) ALL THE PUNKS, SKINS, FREAK'S, CRUMPET, FAG'S, POSER'S ARE INVITED.
> WHY?
> JUST TO PROVE THAT THE PUNK SCENE ETC. IS STILL THE BEST THING SINCE SLICED BREAD.
> MEET AT THE SEAFRONT ON MONDAY 28th MAY AT 2 O'CLOCK
> FUNFAIR / FOOTBALL / CRUMPET / BEER /
> ANY IMFORMATION CAN BE OBTAINED FROM 1) LAST RESORT (MICKY) (PETTICOAT Lane)
> 2) BLOOZ - BAB'S SHOP, (KEN-MARKET
> JOCK McDONALD

> **Will the punks rock Brighton?**
> SECRET plans are being drawn up this week for a punk bank holiday invasion of Brighton.
> Says organiser Jock MacDonald: "The idea is to hold a 1,000-a-side football match there next Monday and prove that the punk scene is still the biggest thing around London.
> "Thousands of Scottish punks are coming down at the weekend for the England-Scotland match at Wembley and they'll be staying on until Monday when we'll have our own version of the game at Brighton."
> After the match, several punk stars are planning to play in Brighton, including Johnny Rotten's brother, Jimmy Lydon, who will be debuting his band under the pier.
> But MacDonald emphasises it won't be like the mods-and-rockers clashes at the resort in the Sixties.
> "The punks won't be looking for trouble," he says. Nevertheless—I know where I won't be spending my bank holiday.

PUNK FLYER FOR DAY TRIP TO BRIGHTON
Jock McDonald
28 May 1979
29.2 x 20.9 cm, 11½ x 8¼ in

Inviting 'Everybody: The punks, skins, freaks, crumpet, fags, posers' to congregate at the Brighton seafront, to prove that 'the punk scene etc. is still the best thing since sliced bread'.

TEMPORARY HOARDING #9
1979
29.8 x 20.9 cm, 11¾ x 8¼ in

Features Ruts, Gang of Four, RAR news, reviews and more.

TOM ROBINSON BAND,
TRB NEWS SHEET BULLETIN #10
May 1978
29.8 x 20.9 cm, 11¾ x 8¼ in

FLYER FOR THE MO-DETTES AT ACKLAM HALL
31 May 1979
29.8 x 20.9 cm, 11¾ x 8¼ in

This all-girl punk band formed initially as a one-off to play at the popular post-punk venue Acklam Hall in support of the Vincent Units. However, the band lasted another three years and, in 1980, released their only album *The Story So Far*.

MARGARET THATCHER POSTER
Conservative Party
[May] 1979
[unknown dims]

Issued by the Conservative Central Office on the occasion of Margaret Thatcher's 1979 election victory.

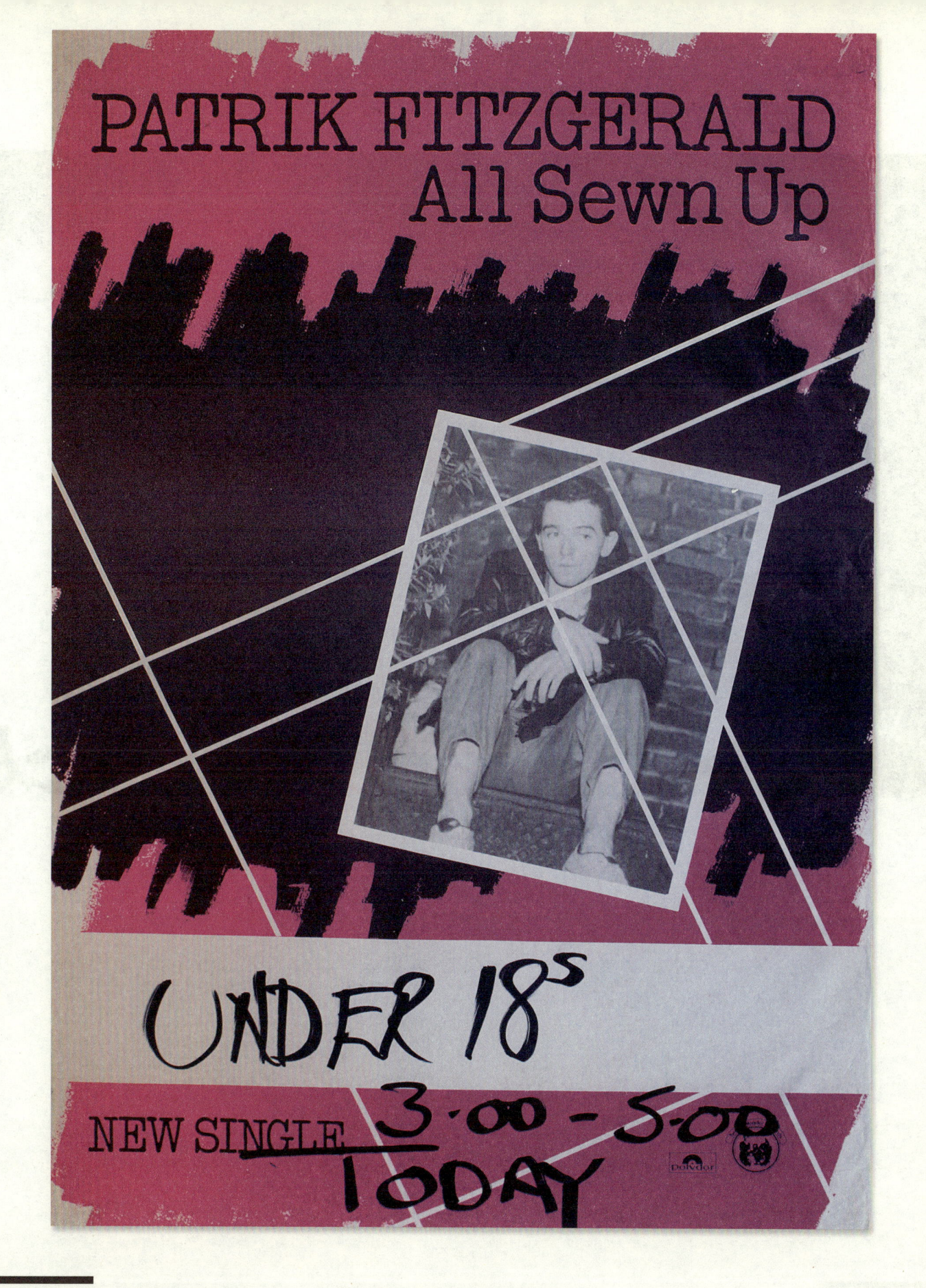

POSTER FOR PATRIK FITZGERALD'S SINGLE 'ALL SEWN UP'
2 June 1979
74.9 x 49.5 cm, 29½ x 19½ in

Known as a 'punk poet', Fitzgerald defied expectations of type, bringing a punk sensibility to more identifiably folk forms. Performing on acoustic guitar, often by himself, his shows also incorporated poems and storytelling.

**POSTER FOR PUBLIC IMAGE LTD'S SINGLE
'DEATH DISCO'**
June 1979
69.8 x 100.3 cm, 27½ x 39½ in

**FLYER FOR THE SINCERE AMERICANS, WITH
BAUHAUS, THE COILS, JOHN PEEL AND THE
DISCO ZOMBIES AT THE PADDOCK, HARPOLE**
16 June 1979
32.3 x 37.4 cm, 12¾ x 14¾ in

POSTER FOR CHELSEA'S ALBUM CHELSEA
June 1979
101.6 x 75.5 cm, 40 x 29¾ in

Chelsea's eponymous debut album appeared on Step Forward Records.

POSTER FOR THE SEX PISTOLS' SINGLE 'C'MON EVERYBODY'
22 June 1979
92.7 x 69.8 cm, 36½ x 27½ in

Advertises the fourth single released in connection with *The Great Rock 'n' Roll Swindle*, and the second Eddie Cochran cover sung by Sid Vicious. The B-side features an orchestral version of the Pistols' 'God Save the Queen'.

POSTER FOR ADAM AND THE ANTS' 'ZEROX' TOUR
July 1979
73.6 x 50.8 cm, 29 x 20 in

The silkscreened UK poster features an example of Futurist time-lapse photography.

INTERNATIONAL ANTHEM #2
Crass, Gee Vaucher
1979
[unknown dims]

Back from New York with material for the second, so-called 'Domestic Violence' issue, Gee Vaucher turned it into a Crass-centric publication, as reflected in the prominence of the band's logo and the incorporation of their idiosyncratic numbering system. Features Vaucher's paintings and photo-collages (including the cover of Crass's album *The Feeding of the Five Thousand*), the lyrics for 'Asylum' and 'Berketex Bribe', and a long, hallucinatory Penny Rimbaud text, 'Fray Bentos and Other Personnel'.

EMMA #80
1 September 1979
[unknown dims]

Publishing house D. C. Thomson put 'Top Popster' Elvis Costello on the cover of the penultimate issue of the girls' comic *Emma* in 1979.

**POSTER FOR BUZZCOCKS' US TOUR DEBUT
AT THE SANTA MONICA CIVIC CENTER**
12 September 1979
53.3 x 33 cm, 21 x 13 in

POSTER FOR THE SLITS' ALBUM CUT
September 1979
50.8 x 75.5 cm, 20 x 29¾ in

Photographer Pennie Smith shot the cover for the Slits' *Cut*, in which the three musicians are topless. Smith was working for *NME* magazine at the time.

**POSTER FOR ADAM AND THE ANTS' ALBUM
DIRK WEARS WHITE SOX**
October 1979
72.3 × 96.5 cm, 28½ × 38 in

'Dirk' refers to the English actor Dirk Bogarde. The album blends post-punk riffs and vestiges of glam rock with funk and soul in songs about fetishes, historical figures and art history. The album enjoyed a cult following but did not achieve wide commercial success. Seeking greater publicity, Adam hired Malcolm McLaren, manager of the Sex Pistols. In January of the next year, however, McLaren convinced the rest of the band – guitarist Matthew Ashman, bassist Leigh Gorman and drummer Dave Barbarossa – to leave the Ants and form Bow Wow Wow, fronted by Annabella Lwin.

TEMPORARY HOARDING #10
November/December 1979
42.5 x 30.4 cm, 16¾ x 12 in

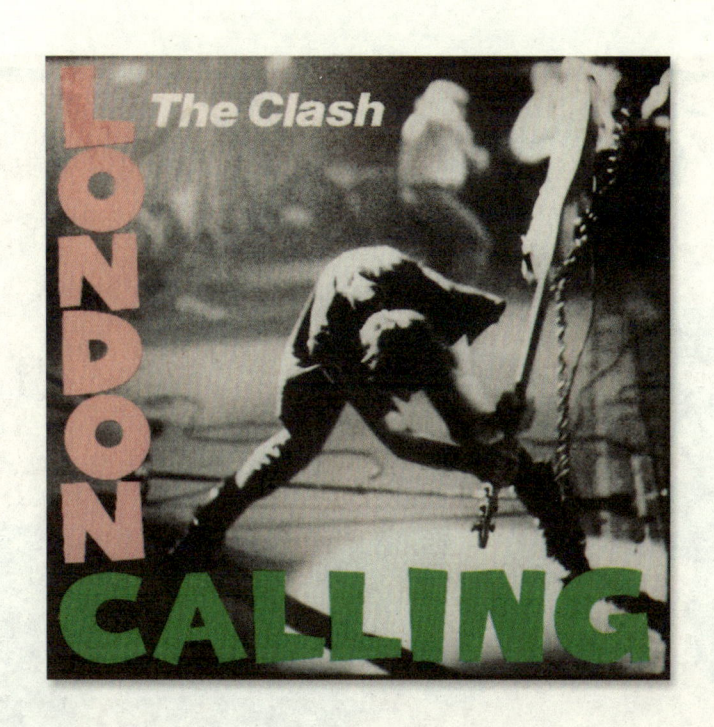

**STICKER FOR THE CLASH'S ALBUM
LONDON CALLING**
December 1979
8.2 x 7.6 cm, 3¼ x 3 in

The Clash seldom appeared on official posters, but this is an exception. Photographer Pennie Smith captured the iconic image of Paul Simonon smashing his bass guitar onstage during a 1979 concert in New York. The sticker is based on Ray Lowry's sleeve design for the band's third album, with its conscious echo of Elvis Presley's debut album. Includes the original Epic Records catalogue number printed in the bottom border.

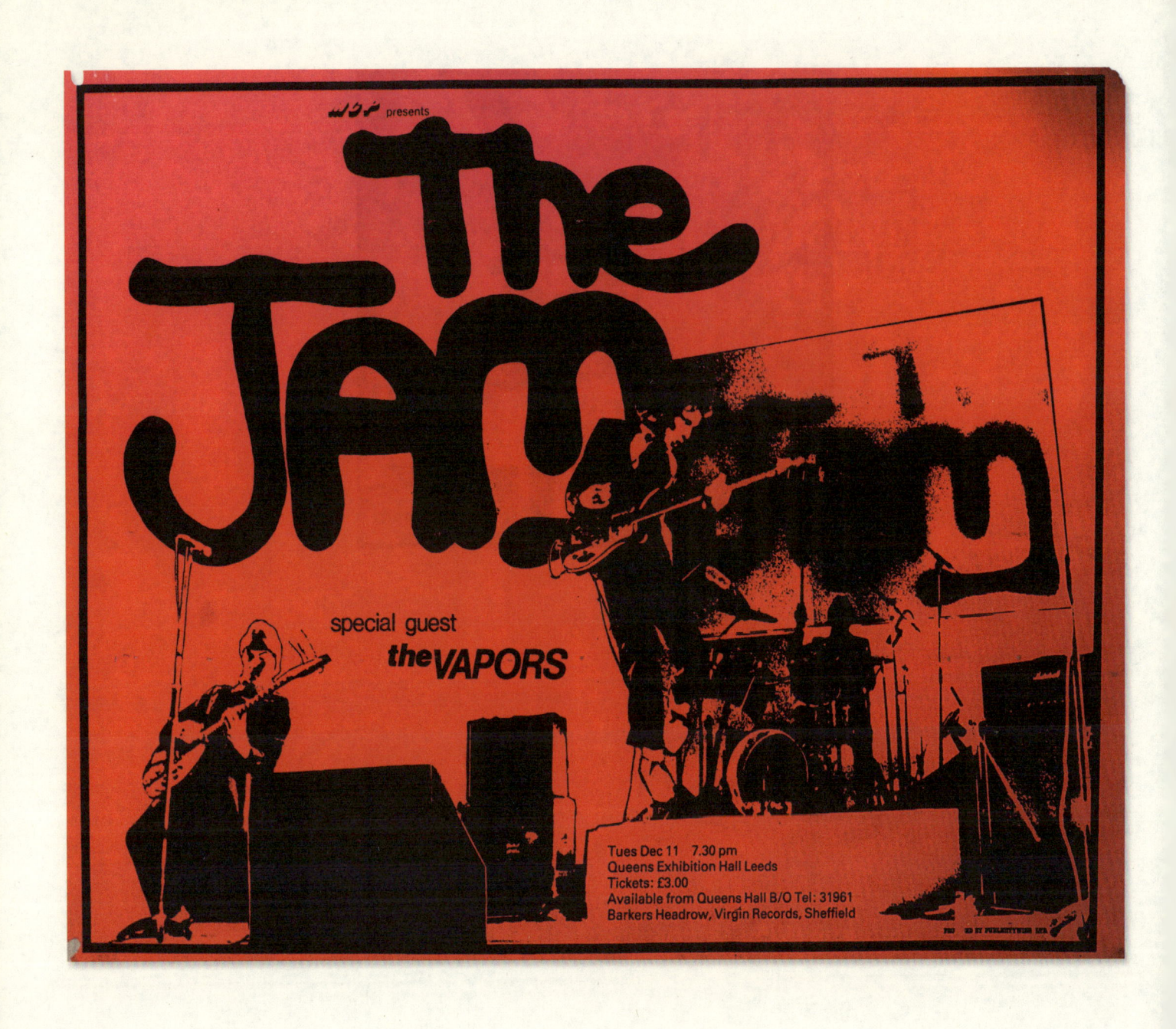

POSTER FOR THE JAM AT QUEENS HALL, LEEDS
11 December 1979
80.6 x 108.5 cm, 31¾ x 42¾ in

This poster for the Jam's 'Setting Sons' tour with the Vapors features designer Bill Smith's familiar graffiti-style logo, which he created for the band's 1977 album *In the City*.

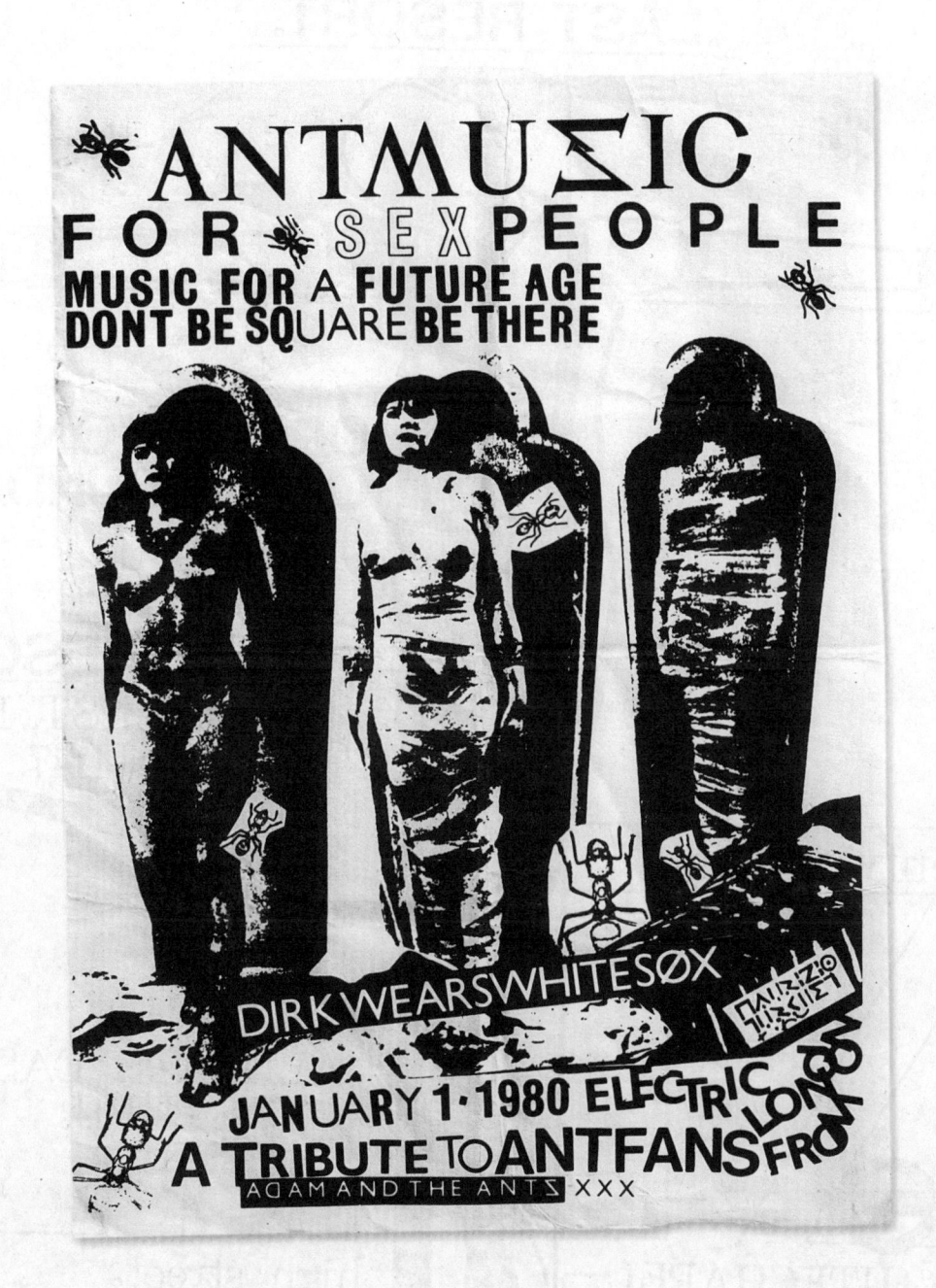

FLYER FOR ADAM AND THE ANTS' 'MUSIC FOR A FUTURE AGE' AT THE ELECTRIC BALLROOM
1 January 1980
20.9 × 14.6 cm, 8¼ × 5¾ in

This is the only show where Leigh Gorman played bass for the Ants.

FLYERS FOR THE LAST RESORT
1980
29.8 x 20.9 cm, 11¾ x 8¼ in
31.7 x 22.2 cm, 12½ x 8¾ in

The flyers advertised the skinhead shop in East London.

THE LAST RESORT

The LAST RESORT

PeTTiCOAt LAne EaSt EnD

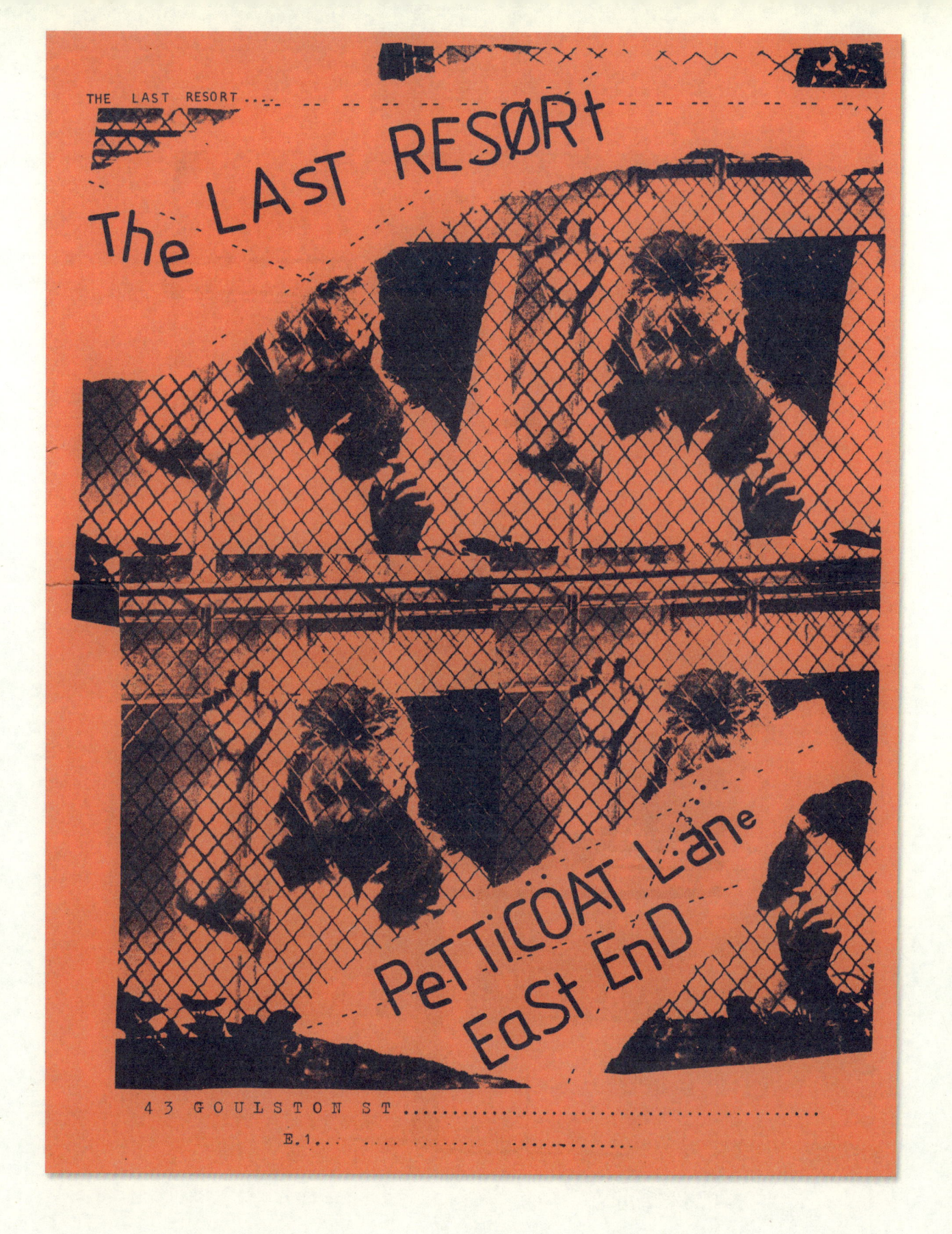

43 GOULSTON ST
E.1

POSTER OF JOE STRUMMER, THE CLASH AT CBGB, NEW YORK
1980
74.9 x 50.8 cm, 29½ x 20 in

Original photo by Jill Furmanovsky, printed in an edition of 1,000 by X3.

IN THE MONTH OF APRIL, 1977. MARK P. REVIEWED THE FIRST CLASH ALBUM IN
THE NINTH ISSUE OF SNIFFING GLUE......
the clash album is like a mirror. it shows us the truth. to me it is
the most important album ever released. its as if im looking at my life
in a film. a story of life in london. playing in and out of the flats.
a school that didn't even know what an o level was. a job that sat me
behind a desk and nicked my brain. all that shit is no longer in the
dark. the clash tells the truth..............
                                        MARK P.
i despise the clash, they were so important, it makes me want to cry
when i see them now, they let a lot of people down, how could they do
it after all they said, they make me sick. they can stuff their punk
credentials 'cos its them that takes the cash.......
                                        DAP 80...

PLASTIC LIVE's

MICHAEL WHITE presents

THE CLASH HEAVY METAL   punk is dead.

The eND

this is the first issue of what we hope will be a series of fanzines
which will be handed out at certain concerts.
we're not trying to preach to anyone, we just had to get certain things
off our chests. if you hated it and thought it was a load of bollocks,
please write and tell us why, the address is below. or if you want to
write articles for us to put into the following issues please write
its important that we work together because as a group we're a threat
to the scabs who run the system.
if you're in a group or know of a group playing or looking for concerts
please write and tell us 'cos we would like to know, thanks......

                                        DAVID&JULEY
                                        65, meadow close
VOLUME ONE   raynes pk.
                                        london. s.w.20.

A BIG THANKS TO CRASS FOR THE INSPIRATION AND FOR MAKING US FEEL LIKE
ITS 1977 all OVER AGAIN......

FLYER FOR VOLUME ONE
1980
29.2 x 20.9 cm, 11½ x 8¼ in

Discusses the Clash and asks for letters, reviews and contributions.

NN4 9PZ ISSUE #3
1980
29.8 x 20.9 cm, 11¾ x 8¼ in

Featuring the Ruts, Crass and Bauhaus.

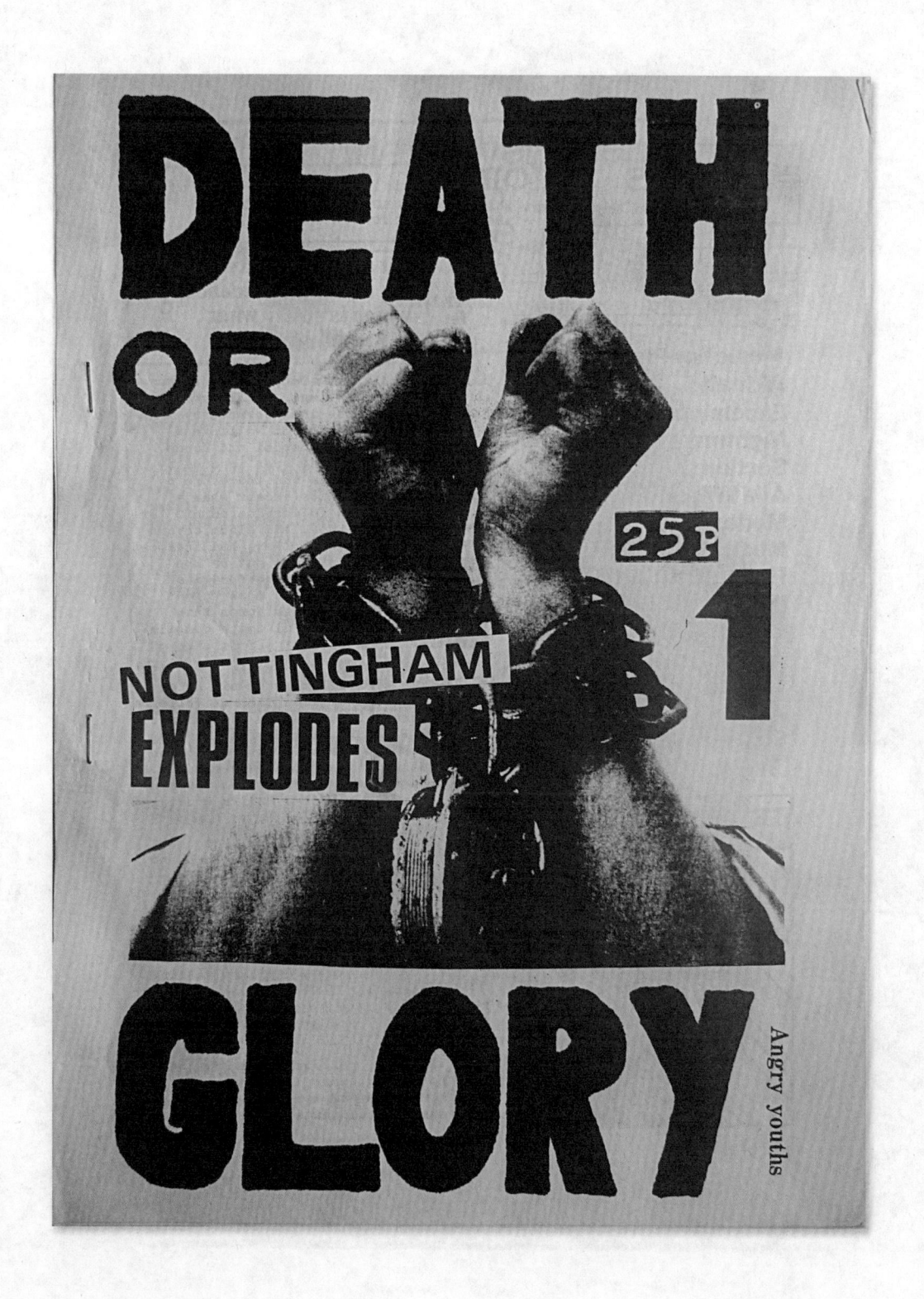

**DEATH OR GLORY #1,
'NOTTINGHAM EXPLODES'**
1980
[unknown dims]

**FLYER FOR THE SLITS, THE VINCENT UNITS
AND MOA AMBASSA AT UNIVERSITY OF LONDON**
18 January 1980
29.2 × 20.9 cm, 11½ × 8¼ in

POSTER FOR PUBLIC IMAGE LTD US TOUR
1980
55.8 × 35.5 cm, 22 × 14 in

During its first US tour, PiL appeared on *American Bandstand* on May 17. Lydon brought the audience on stage to dance, while the band pretended to play 'Poptones' and 'Careering'.

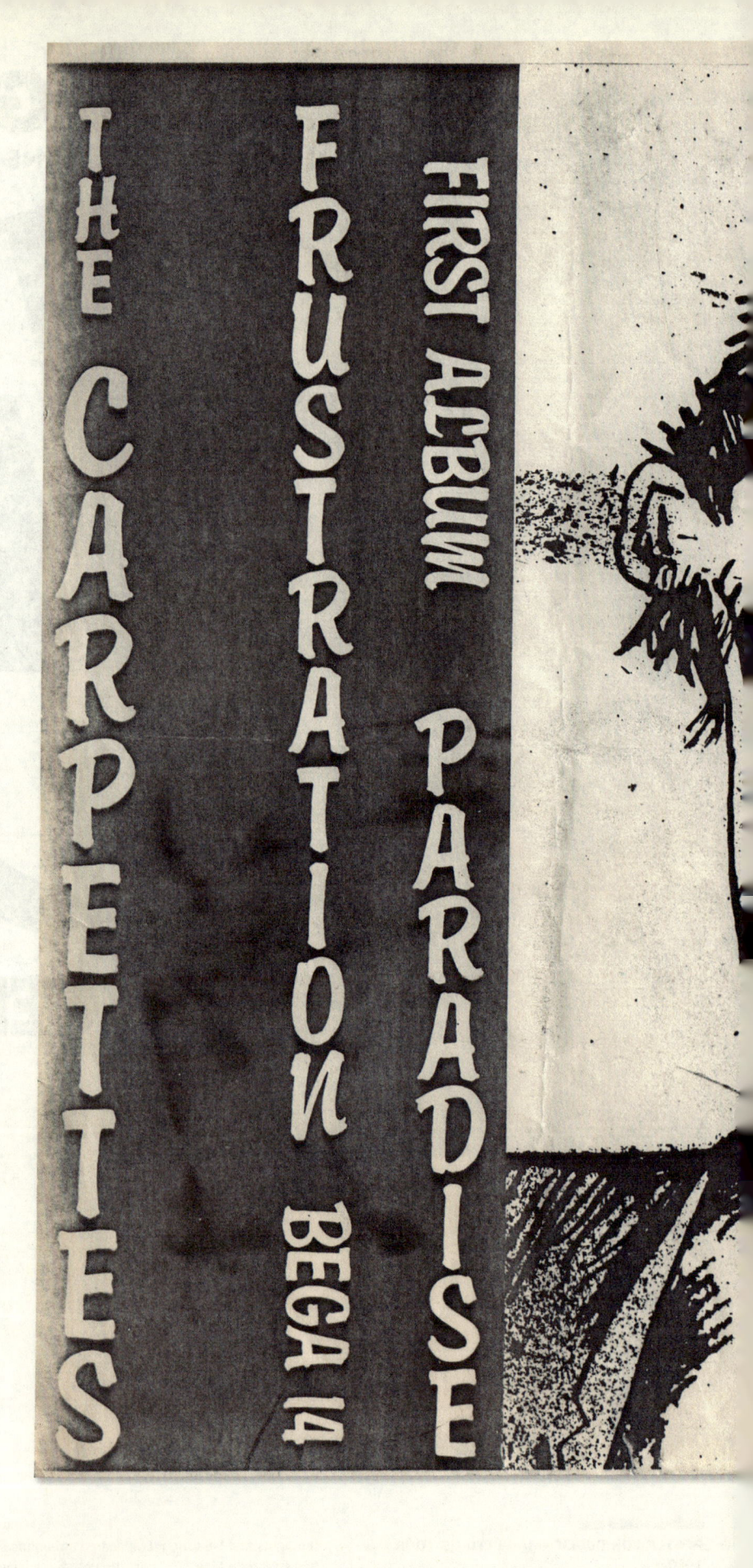

FLYER FOR THE CARPETTES AT THEATRE WORKSHOP, UNIVERSITY OF LONDON
12 February 1980
20.9 × 29.8 cm, 8¼ × 11¾ in

THE CARPETTES

TUES 12TH FEB.
RECORDING LIVE!
Theatre Workshop,
UNIVERSITY of LONDON

YOUNG COMMUNIST LEAGUE FLYER, 'SHORT SHARP SHOCK'
1980
20.9 x 14.6 cm, 8¼ x 5¾ in

This double-sided flyer protests 'the Tory answer to Youth Unemployment'.

THE GREAT ROCK 'N' ROLL SWINDLE NEWSPAPER
The Sex Pistols, Michael Moorcock
May 1980
36.1 x 29.8 cm, 14¼ x 11¾ in

The 'newspaper of the book of the novel of the film of the record of the Sex Pistols' claimed the cover. The publication is printed in the style of a broadsheet newspaper and contains numerous photos of the band.

A later edition differs in format and quantity of photos. The text, reportedly written by Michael Moorcock in only 10 days, was later republished under the title *Gold Diggers of 1977*.

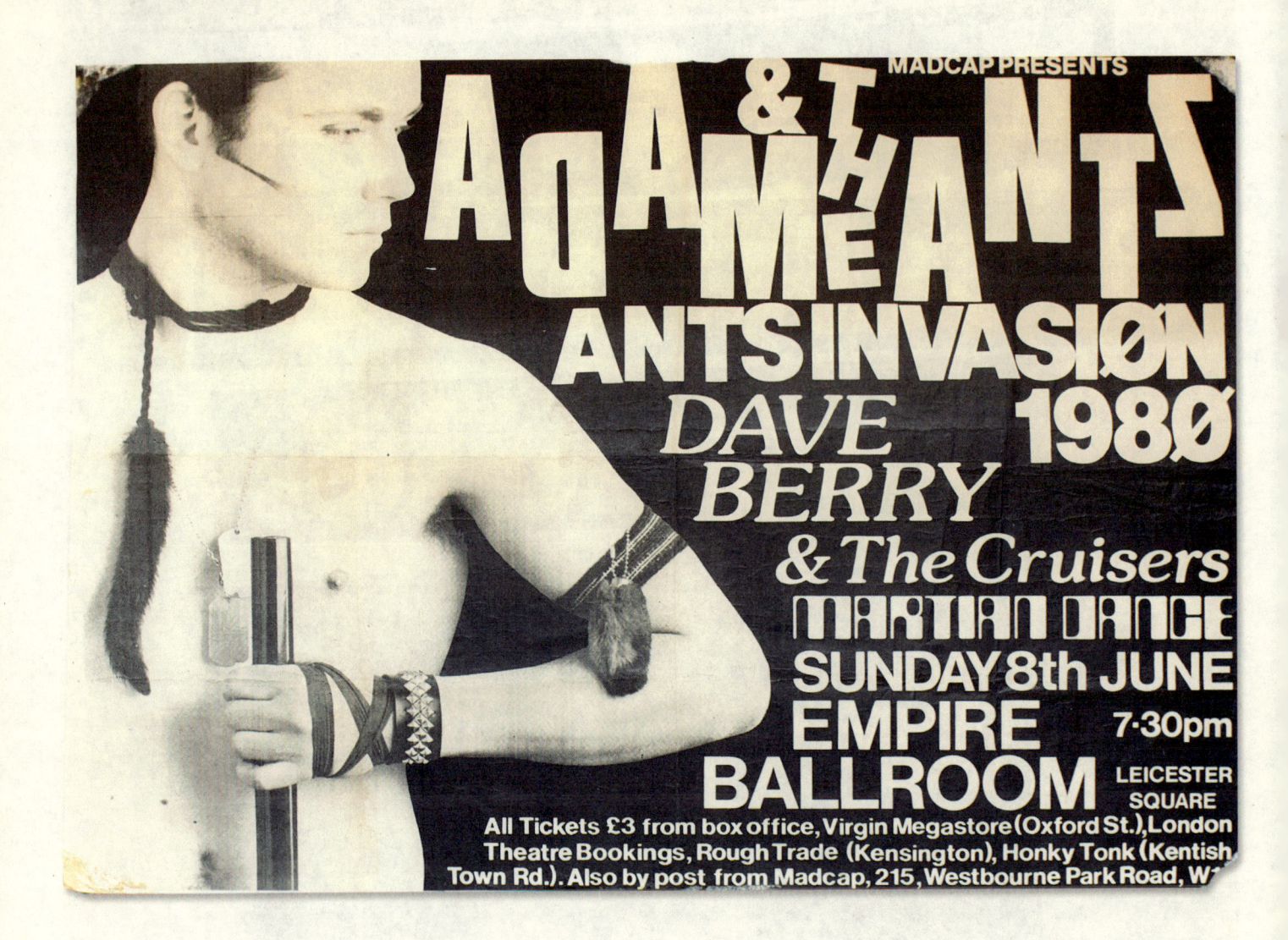

**POSTER FOR ADAM AND THE ANTS ET AL
AT THE EMPIRE BALLROOM, LONDON**
8 June 1980
75.5 × 102.8 cm, 29¾ × 40½ in

This Adam and the Ants gig at the Empire Ballroom on their 'Ants Invasion' tour was supported by Dave Berry and the Cruisers and Martian Dance.

FLYER FOR THE CLASH AT COLSTON HALL, BRISTOL
10–11 June 1980
14.6 x 20.9 cm, 5¾ x 8¼ in

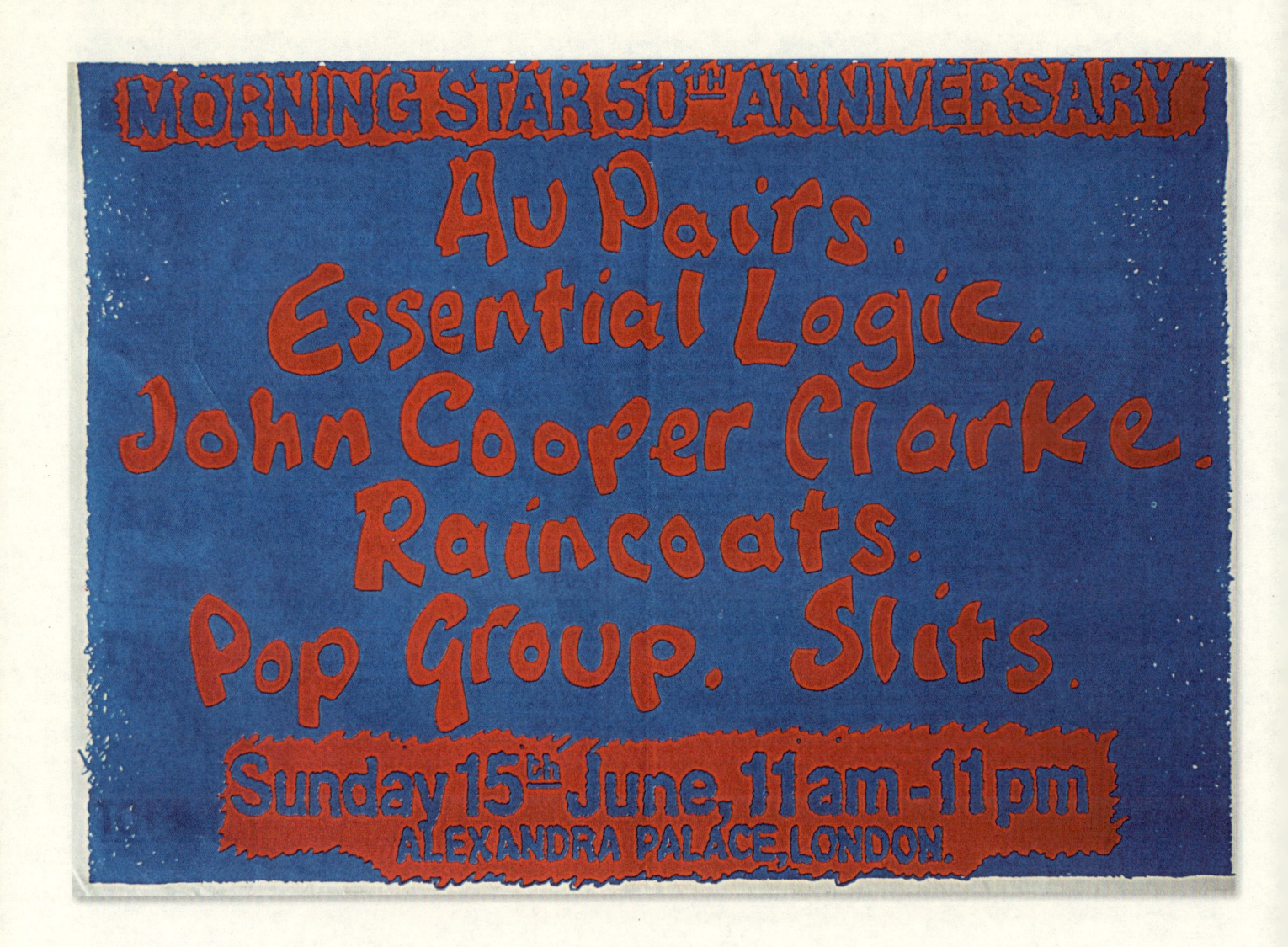

BEAT THE BLUES FESTIVAL WITH THE SLITS ET AL AT ALEXANDRA PALACE, LONDON
15 June 1980
14.6 x 20.9 cm, 5¾ x 8¼ in

The festival celebrating the 50th anniversary of the *Morning Star*, a left-wing newspaper, featured the Slits, the Pop Group, the Raincoats, Essential Logic, Au Pairs and Manchester post-punk poet John Cooper Clarke.

POSTER FOR CRASS AND THE POISON GIRLS AT THE ASHTON COURT FESTIVAL BENEFIT, TRINITY HALL, BRISTOL
18 June 1980
41.9 × 29.8 cm, 16½ × 11¾ in

FIGHT WAR - NOT WARS

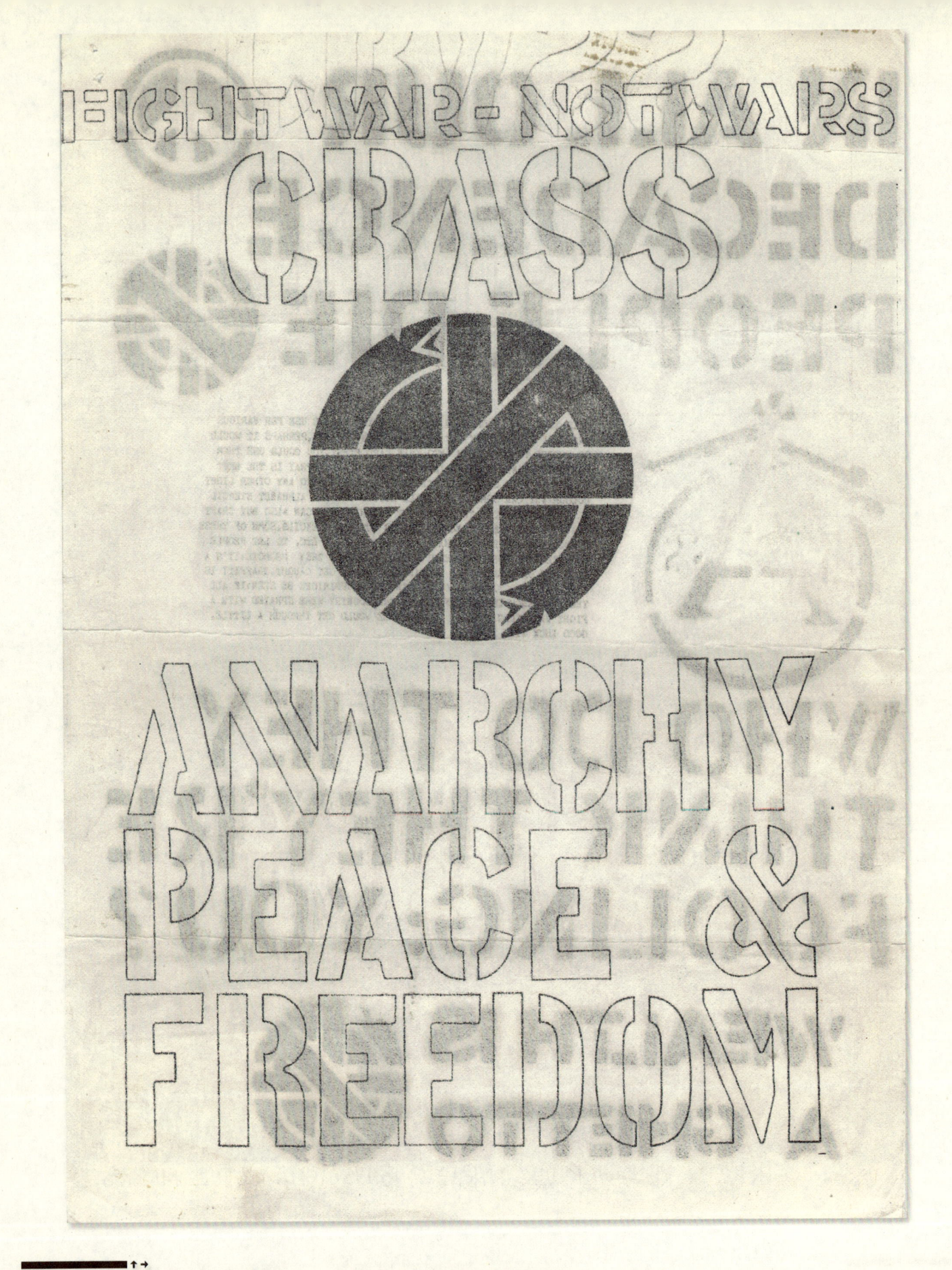

CRASS

ANARCHY
PEACE &
FREEDOM

CRASS, 'IN ALL OUR DECADENCE PEOPLE DIE'
GRAFFITI STENCILS
1980
29.8 × 22.2 cm, 11¾ × 8¾ in

The Crass logo is a composite of several icons of authority, including the Christian cross, the swastika and the Union Jack, combined with a two-headed snake consuming itself. The logo lent itself to reproduction as a stencil for fans.

IN ALL OUR DECADENCE PEOPLE DIE

THIS IS A SAMPLE OF SOME OF THE SPRAYS THAT WE USE FOR VARIOUS
GRAFFITI PROJECTS, IF YOU CUT THIS STENCILS OUT, PERHAPS IT WOULD
BE BETTER TO COPY THEM ONTO THIN CARD FIRST, YOU COULD USE THEM
FOR DECORATING CLOTHING, IN WHICH CASE SILVER SPRAY IS THE BEST
TO USE IF IT'S ONTO BLACK CLOTHES, OR IF ITS ONTO ANY OTHER LIGHT
COLOUR ANY CAR SPRAY PAINT WILL DO. YOU CAN BUY ALPHABET STENCIL
KITS IN MOST SHOPS THAT SELL ART MATERIAL, YOU CAN ALSO BUY CRAFT
KNIVES WHICH ARE THE BEST TYPE FOR CUTTING STENCILS. SOME OF THESE
STENCILS ARE THE ONES THAT WE USE ON POSTERS ETC. TO LET PEOPLE
KNOW THAT WE DON'T AGREE WITH THE SHIT THAT THEY PROMOTE. IT'S A
GOOD WAY OF SPENDING AN EVENING, BUT DON'T GET CAUGHT. GRAFFITI IS
A REALLY EFFECTIVE WAY OF LETTING YOUR OPPINIONS BE SEEN. IF ALL
THE ARMY RECRUITMENT OFFICES IN THE COUNTRY WERE SPRAYED WITH A
FIGHT WAR STENCIL MAYBE THE MESSAGE WOULD GET THROUGH A LITTLE.
GOOD LUCK WITH THEM.

WHO DO THEY THINK THEY'RE FOOLING: YOU?

WEALTH IS A GHETTO

IN THE CITY #15
Peter Gilbert, Francis Drake
July 1980
29.8 x 20.9 cm, 11¾ x 8¼ in

Features Poison Girls, the Gadgets, Crass, Suicide and the Method.

**FLYER FOR THE DAMNED AT THE NITE CLUB,
EDINBURGH**
19 July 1980
15.2 x 20.9 cm, 6 x 8¼ in

POSTER FOR 4" BE 2" SINGLE 'FRUSTRATION'
July 1980
48.8 x 74.2 cm, 19¼ x 29¼ in

Jimmy Lydon, brother of John Lydon (aka Johnny Rotten) founded the group with Jock McDonald. John produced the single.

POSTER FOR THE PLASMATICS AT HAMMERSMITH ODEON
8 August 1980
75.5 x 50.8 cm, 29¾ x 20 in

The Plasmatics were scheduled to make their UK debut at the Hammersmith Odeon. The band flew to London for a sold-out show, during which they planned to blow up a car onstage. Before the show, frontwoman Wendy O. Williams, dressed in a nurse's uniform, announced to reporters that she had come to give the British people a 'cultural enema'. The Greater London Council banned the performance, citing the band's 'anarchist' tendencies.

BREAKING GLASS BUTTON
1980
12 cm, 4¾ in diameter

The film *Breaking Glass*, written and directed by Brian Gibson, stars Phil Daniels and Jonathan Pryce, with Hazel O'Connor as Kate, a young new wave singer who struggles to succeed in show business, and is promoted and then exploited by the music industry. The film is often cited for its depiction of pre-Thatcherite Britain during the 'Winter of Discontent' in 1978–79, with public unrest, racial and class tensions and a rebellious teenage underclass.

SHOP FLYER FOR BREAKING GLASS
1980
36.8 x 26.6 cm, 14½ x 10½ in

NEW ROSE #2, THE DAMNED FANZINE
September 1980
[unknown dims]

Contains articles on Splodge and Malcolm Owen, singer of the Ruts, who had died in July. Signed by Captain Sensible.

**FLYER FOR ADAM AND THE ANTS
AT TOP RANK SUITE, BRIGHTON**
1 December 1980
14.6 x 20.9 cm, 5¾ x 8¼ in

The group had released its second album, *Kings of the Wild Frontier*, just a few weeks prior to this show. The album would reach No. 1 on the UK charts.

MENTAL CHILDREN #1
1980
29.8 x 20.9 cm, 11¾ x 8¼ in

The cover is influenced by the photograph on the Slits' first album.

MENTAL CHILDREN #2
1980
29.8 x 20.9 cm, 11¾ x 8¼ in

Features articles on Siouxsie and the Banshees, the Mo-dettes and the Clash movie, *Rude Boy*.

GRAFFITI PROJECTS. IF YOU CUT THIS STENCIL
BE BETTER TO COPY THEM ONTO THIN CARD FIR
FOR DECORATING CLOTHING, IN WHICH CASE SIL
TO USE IF IT'S ONTO BLACK CLOTHES, OR IF I
COLOUR ANY CAR SPRAY PAINT WILL DO. YOU CA
KITS IN MOST SHOPS THAT SELL ART MATERIAL
KNIVES WHICH ARE THE BEST TYPE FOR CUTTIN
STENCILS ARE THE ONES THAT WE USE ON POST
KNOW THAT WE DON'T AGREE WITH THE SHIT TH
GOOD WAY OF SPENDING AN EVENING, BUT DON'
A REALLY EFFECTIVE WAY OF LETTING YOUR OP
THE ARMY RECRUITMENT OFFICES IN THE COUNT
FIGHT WAR STENCIL MAYBE THE MESSAGE WOULD
GOOD LUCK WITH THEM.

WHO DO TH
THINK THE
FOOLING: Y
WEALTH IS
A GHETTO

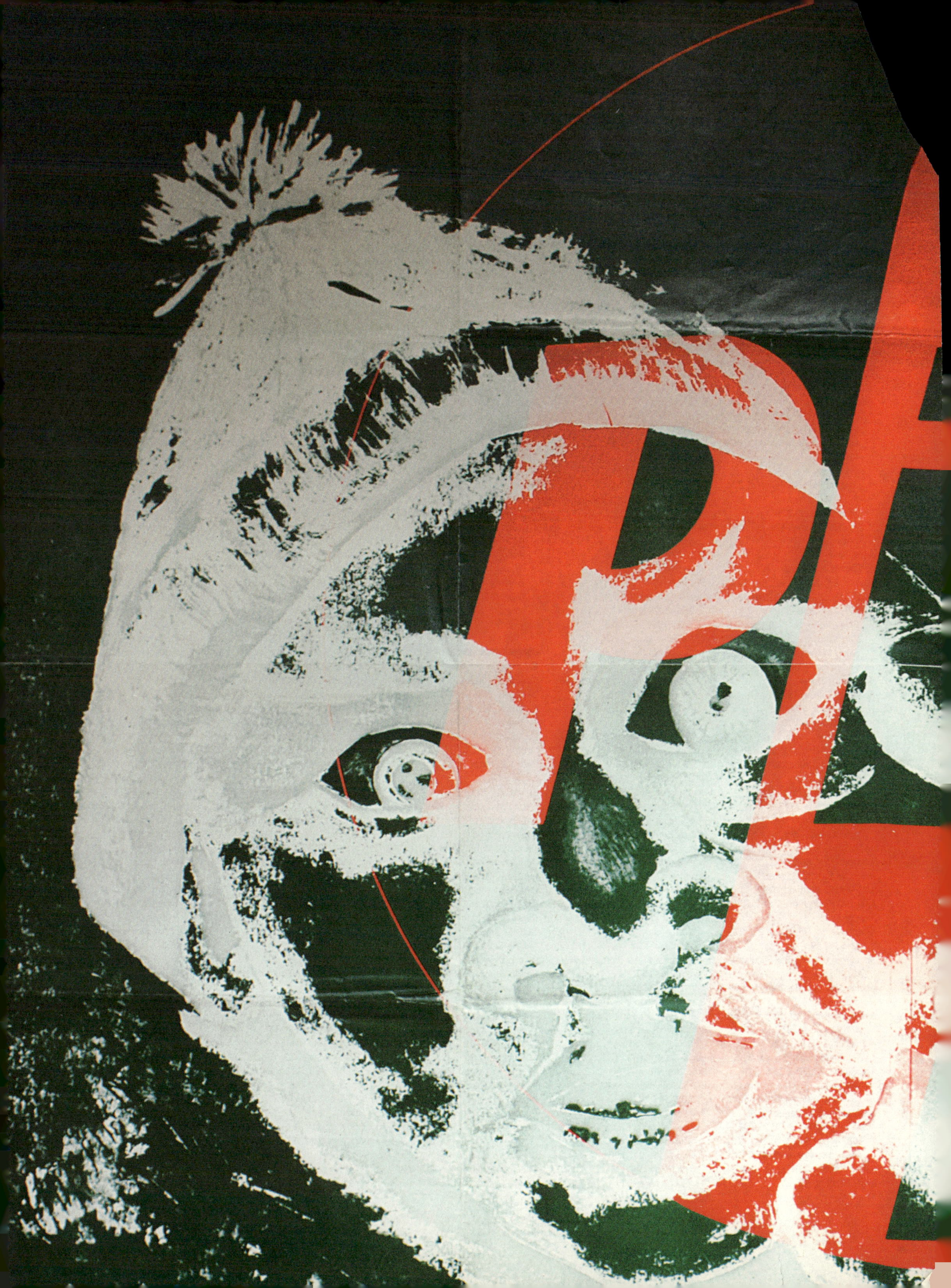

4AD 22
4" Be 2" 452, **498**
 'Fru*s*tration' **498**
48 Thrills 21, 22, 74, 80, 95, 110
100 Club 22, **28**, 29, 33, 37, **38**, **371**
100 Nights at the Roxy (Dempsey) **317**
400 Ballroom **340a**
999 (band) 17, 132, 189, 205, 228, 243, **243**, 438
 Nasty! Nasty!' 243
999 (zine) 415

A

Acklam Hall 186, **186**, 422, **422**, **423**, **448**, **461**
Acme Attractions 302
Adam and the Ants 17, 120, 255, 281, **288**, 369, 371, 372, 373, **373**, **374**, 375, 394, 426, 429, **436**, **437**, 454, 468, **473**, 477, **490**, **503**
 Dirk Wears White Sox **473**
 'Kings of the Wild Frontier' **374**
 'Physical (You're So)' 373
 'Press Darlings' **374**
 'Young Parisians' **426**
 'Zerox' **468**
Ades, Dawn 23
 Photomontage 23
Adverts 17, **70**, **79**, 80, 94, **122**, **152**, 155, 199, **199**, **209**, **221**, **251**, **276**, **338–339**, 404
 'Bored Teenagers' 199
 'Gary Gilmore's Eyes' 199
 'Safety in Numbers' **251**
'Ain't It Strange' (Smith) 71
Album, The (Eater) **258**
Alexandra Palace **492**
Alexandra Park **407**
'Alison' (Costello) **109**
Allan, Johnnie 343
'All Sewn Up' (Fitzgerald) **463**
Alternative TV 206, **207**, 220, **220**, **279**, **393**
 'How Much Longer' 279
 'Life After Life' **393**
 'Love Lies Limp' 206, **207**
 'You Bastard' **279**
A&M 128
Amazorblades 265
American Bandstand 485
AN1 (Plastic Bertrand) **397**
Anarchist Street Army (ASA) 17
Anarchy 435
Anarchy in the UK (Reid) 21, 22, **52–53**, 159
'Anarchy in the UK' (Sex Pistols) **48**, **49**, **50**, **51**
'Another Girl, Another Planet' (Only Ones) 370
Another Music in a Different Kitchen (Buzzcocks) **357**
Anscombe, Isabelle 315
 Not Another Punk! Book 315
Ant, Adam 22, **356**, **371**, 414, 448, 473
 See also Adam and the Ants
Anti-Apartheid Movement 385
Anti-Nazi League 17, 21, **166–168**, 310, **361**, 378, 385, **385**, **406**, 418, **418–419**, **420**
Apollo Theatre **290**
Arista Records 42

Armed Forces (Elvis Costello and the Attractions) **444**
Art Attacks 190, **190**, **205**
ASA See Anarchist Street Army (ASA)
Ashman, Matthew 473
Aswad 17, 102, 410, **418–419**
'Asylum' (Crass) **469**
Auntie Pus 255
Aurum Press 315
'Automatic Lover' (Vibrators) **341**
Automatics 223

B

'Baby Baby' (Vibrators) **108**
Barbarossa, Dave 473
Batchelor, Dave 117
Bauhaus **465**, **482**
Bayley, Roberta **290**
Bazooka Joe **239**
Beastly Cads 79
Beating Hearts (Buzzcocks) **442**
Beaufort Market 452
'Berketex Bribe' (Crass) **469**
Biggs, Ronald (Ronnie) **403**
'Bingo Master Breakout' (Fall) **414**
Birmingham Rag Market **181**
Black, Jet 64
Black Flag 17
Blade, Andy 40
 The Secret Life of a Teenage Punk Rocker 40
Blank Generation (Poe, Král) 45, **45**
Blitz **278**
Blitzkrieg Bop **391**
Blockheads 22
Blondie 45, **56**, 191, 266, **266–267**, **353**, **412**, **416**, **445**, **456**
 Blondie **56**
 'Contact in Red Square' **353**
 'Denis' **353**
 'I Know But I Don't Know' **456**
 'Kung Fu Girls' **353**
 Parallel Lines 412, 445, 456
 'Picture This' **412**
 'Rip Her to Shreds' **266–267**
 'Sunday Girl' **456**
Blondie (Blondie) **56**
Blue Öyster Cult **30**, **31**
Blunt Instrument 223
Bogarde, Dirk 473
Bolan, Marc 268
Bollock Brothers 452
Bomp! **272–273**
Bondage **58**
Boomtown Rats **60**, **198**, 202, **208**, 245
 Boomtown Rats **208**
Boomtown Rats (Boomtown Rats) **208**
Boot, Adrian 198
 Boomtown Rats (poster) **198**
Bored Stiff **157**
'Bored Teenagers' (Adverts) 199
'Born to Lose' (Johnny Thunders & the Heartbreakers) **134**
Boston, Virginia **316**
 Shockwave **316**
Bowie, David 103, 378
Bow Wow Wow 473
BOY clothing store 302, **303–305**
'Boy Looked at Johnny, The':
 The Obituary of Rock and Roll (Burchill, Parsons) 314
Boys 17, **79**, **91**, **196**
 The Boys **196**
 'I Don't Care' **91**

Boys, The (Boys) **196**
Breaking Glass (Gibson) 500, **500**, **501**
Bright, Bette 346
Brighton Polytechnic 115
Brilleaux, Lee 69
Bristol Archive Records 203
British Movement 17
British National Party 162
Broad, William See Idol, Billy
Brockwell Park 418
Brooklands College **76**
Browne, Jackson 68
B-Sides **448**
Bubbles, Barney 21, 22, **194–195**, 212, **212**, **213**, **292**, **441**, **443**
 Graham Parker (poster) **292**
 Ian Drury's Album New Boots and Panties!! (poster) **212**, **213**
 The Ian Drury Songbook **441**
 Ian Drury & the Blockheads (poster programme) **194–195**
Buccaneer **117**
Buckwell, Richard 378
Burchill, Julie 314
 'The Boy Looked at Johnny': The Obituary of Rock and Roll 314
Burk, Fred 117
Burn, Gordon 179
 'Good Clean Punk' 179
Buzzcocks 23, 27, **43**, **82**, **86**, **98**, 113, 133, **149**, 170, **172**, 228, 236, 274, **274**, **338–339**, **357**, **358**, **364**, **390**, **407**, 429, **442**, **471**
 Another Music in a Different Kitchen **357**
 Beating Hearts **442**
 'I Don't Mind' **390**
 'Orgasm Addict' 23, **274**

C

Cale, John 135
Callis, Jo 306
Campbell, Craig 130, **130**
 Trash-77 130, **130**
Campbell, Nell 369
Camp Times 142
Candybeat 504 **204**, **306**
Cane **278**
Cannibals 72
'Can't Stand Still' (Headache) **260**
Capital Radio 17
Captain Sensible 115, 408, **502**
'Career Opportunities' (Clash) **388**
Carnochan, Ian (Knox) 143
Carpettes **486–487**
Carrington, Susan 98
Catwoman, Soo 21, 22, **52**
CBGB **480**
CBS Records 374
Central Saint Martins 275
Chaos, Dave **298**
Charles II, King of England 141
Chelmsford Prison **34–35**
Chelmsford's Dead **90**
Chelsea (band) 17, **49**, **61**, **67**, **74**, **75**, **79**, 80, **135**, **144**, 155, **186**, **188**, **421**, **430**, **466**
 Chelsea **466**
 'Right to Work' **144**
Chelsea (Chelsea) **466**
Cherry Vanilla 82, 98, 236
Childers, Leee 96
'Chinese Rocks' (Johnny Thunders & the Heartbreakers) **134**
Chiswick Records 206
Christopherson, Peter 303, **303**
 The Strength of a Country Lies

in Its Youth (BOY poster) **303**
Chrysalis 56, 266
Cimarons **434**
Clapton, Eric 378
Clarke, John Cooper 102, **172**, **431**, 443, 492
 John Cooper Clarke 443
Clash 17, 22, 27, **37**, **43**, **46**, **54**, **61**, 66, **74**, **82**, **86**, **90**, 94, 95, **100**, 102, 103, **111**, **112**, **113**, **114**, **118–119**, **121**, **130**, **135**, 161, **171**, **181**, 192, **200–201**, 206, **226**, 232, **257**, **269**, **269**, 275, **275**, **329**, **344**, **345**, 378, 380, 388, 398, 402, **402**, 410, **428**, 429, 439, 446, **446**, 452, **452**, **453**, 475, **475**, 480, **491**, **505**
 'Career Opportunities' **388**
 'Clash City Rockers' **344**, **345**
 'Complete Control' **226**
 'Guns on the Roof' **402**
 London Calling **475**
 'London's Burning' **121**
 'Remote Control' **121**
 '(White Man) in Hammersmith Palais' **398**
 'White Riot' **94**
'Clash City Rockers' (Clash) **344**, **345**
Clash Songbook, The (Simonon, Jones) **329**
Clayson & the Argonauts 265
Clouds **283**
'C'mon Everybody' (Sex Pistols) **467**
Cochran, Eddie 467
Cock Sparrow **185**, **330**
 'We Love You' **185**
Coils **465**
Coliseum Cinema **86**
Collier, Pat 143
Collis, John 64
'Complete Control' (Clash) **226**
Conran, Sebastian 181, 269, **269**, 275, **275**
 Clash (promo card) **275**
 Clash and the Slits at the Birmingham Rag Market Festival (advertisement) **181**
 Clash's Out of Control Tour, with Richard Hell & the Voidoids (poster) **269**
Conservative Party 462
'Contact in Red Square' (Blondie) **353**
Copeland, Stewart 183
Corré, Joe 21
Cortinas 69, **79**, 80, **101**, **150**, 183, **183**, **186**, **188**, 203, **203**, 285, **285**, **286**, **288**
 'Defiant Pose' **285**, **286**
 'Fascist Dictator' **150**
Costello, Elvis 93, **109**, **184**, 204, **366**, 443, **470**
 'Alison' **109**
 My Aim Is True **184**
 'Welcome to the Working Week' 109
 See also Elvis Costello and the Attractions
County, Jayne 84, **84**
 See also County, Wayne
County, Wayne 82, 84, **84**, **217**, 232, 369, **413**, 429
 See also Wayne County & the Electric Chairs
Crabbe, Buster 72, 265
Crabs **250**
Crackers 172, **172**, 190, 205, **205**
 See also Vortex
Crass 17, **328**, **449**, 469,

469, 482, **492**, **493**, **494**, **494–495**, **496**
 'Asylum' 469
 'Berketex Bribe' 469
 The Feeding of the Five Thousand **449**, 469
Cripes 83
Cummins, Kevin 443
Cut (Slits) **472**
Czezowski, Andrew 98

D

Dada 23
Damned 36, 39, 44, 54, 60, **77**, **93**, **94**, 98, **101**, 115, **122**, **152**, 161, 170, **200–201**, 230, 280, 282, **282**, **283**, 299, 408, **440**, **497**, **502**
 Damned Damned Damned **93**, 122, **122**
 Damned's Disciples Song Book **299**
 'Neat Neat Neat' 122, **122**, **230**
 'New Rose' 44, **282**
Damned Damned Damned (Damned) **93**, 122
'Danger Signs' (Penetration) **455**
Daniels, Phil 500
Dansette (record player) 17
Darts 64
Dave Berry & the Cruisers 490
Davis, Julie 62
 Punk 62
'Day the World Turned Day-Glo, The' (X-Ray Spex) **368**
Dazed and Confused 318
Dead Boys **60**, 244, 280, **282**, **282**, **283**
 'Sonic Reducer' 280
 Young, Loud and Snotty **244**
Dead Fingers 262
Deaf School **346**, **347**
'Death Disco' (Public Image Ltd) **464**
Death or Glory **483**
Decca Records 222, 426
Deep Throats 348
'Defiant Pose' (Cortinas) **285**, **286**
Demoriane, Hermine 369
Dempsey, Michael 317
 100 Nights at the Roxy 317
'Denis' (Blondie) **353**
Depressions **239**, **354**
Deptford Fun City Records 279, 394
Desperate Bicycles 261
Devo 360
Devoto, Howard 274, 357
Diddley, Bo 446
Dingwalls **96**, 220
Dirk Wears White Sox (Adam and the Ants) **473**
Disciples Song Book (Damned) **299**
Disco Zombies **465**
Disease 74
Doctors of Madness 219
Donaldson, Ian Stuart 386
Drake, Francis 276, 277
Drayton, Tony 17, 22, **22**, **47**, 130, **180**, **192**, 220, **262**, **414**, **429**
 Ripped & Torn 17, 22, **22**, **47**, 130, **180**, **192**, 220, **262**, **414**, **429**
Dr Feelgood 41, 69, 216
Dr Martens 17
Drones **79**
Drury, Ian 99, 212, **212**, **213**
 See also Ian Drury & the Blockheads

E

Eagles 68, **68**
   Hotel California 68
Eater 58, 64, **78**, **79**, **85**, 96, **98**, 232, **258**, **391**
   The Album **258**
   'Outside View' **85**
Eckford and Stimpson 21
Eddie 143
Eddie and the Hot Rods 32, **49**, 64, 69, 191
Edwards, Alan 99, **99**, **132**, **216**
   Strangled 99, **99**, **132**, **216**
Edwards, Alison **293**
   Punk Rock Rules OK? **293**
Edwards, John *See* Eddie
Electric Ballroom 17, 413, **434**, **477**
Electric Chairs *See* Wayne County & the Electric Chairs
Electric Circus 54
Elizabeth I, Queen of England 369
Elizabeth II, Queen of England 124, **125–130**, 138, **139–142**, 141, 147, 180
   Silver Jubilee 21, 138, **139–142**, 147
Ellis, John 143
Elvis Costello and the Attractions **418–419**, **444**
   Armed Forces **444**
Emma **470**
Empire Ballroom **490**
England's Dreaming (Savage) 88
'England's Screaming' (Hughes, Shaw) 272, **273**
Eno, Brian 369
Epic Records 143, 475
Eraserhead **429**
Eric's **116**, 360, **360**, **440**
Essential Logic **492**
Essex New Wave **348**
Exodus 422

F

Fab Gear **301**
Fall 149, **172**, 414, **421**
   'Bingo Master Breakout' 414
'Fascist Dictator' (Cortinas) **150**
Fashion **457**
Feeding of the Five Thousand, The (Crass) **449**, 469
Fielding, Nigel 174
   The National Front 174
Fife, Fay 306
Fillmore, San Francisco **446**
Films and Filming **356**
Findlay, Bruce 83
   Cripes **83**
'Firing Squad' (Penetration) **392**
Fitzgerald, Patrik **278**, **354**, 380, 394, 463, **463**
   'All Sewn Up' **463**
F. J. Warren Ltd **140**
Flamin' Groovies **32**, **60**
Flies **205**
Fowley, Kim 81
Foxx, John 350
Freedom bookshop 17
French, Michael 386
'Frustration' (4" Be 2") **498**
Furmanovsky, Jill **183**, **206**, **480**

G

Gadgets **496**
Gang of Four **459**
Garrett, Malcolm 21, 22, 23, **274**
   Buzzcocks' Single 'Orgasm

Addict' (poster) **274**
   'Orgasm Addict' 23
   'Gary Gilmore's Eyes' (Adverts) **199**
Gay Switchboard 224
GBH **78**
Generation X 59, 64, 67, **67**, **74**, **88**, **110**, 137, 155, **177**, 190, **190**, 193, **197**, 206, **214**, **215**, **218**, 240, 268, **268**, 276, **296**, **338–339**, **348**, **355**, **363**
   'Perfect Hits' **296**
   'Ready Steady Go' **348**, **355**
   'Your Generation' **214**, **215**, 268
Gibbs, Derek 60
Gibson, Brian 500, **500**, **501**
   Breaking Glass 500, **500**, **501**
Glitterbest 52, 247
Goats 223
Goddard, Martyn 123
Goddard, Stuart *See* Ant, Adam
'God Save the Queen' (Sex Pistols) **125**, **126–127**, 130, 145, 147, 180, **467**
'God Save the Queen' artwork 124, **125–130**
Go-Go's 59
Gold Diggers of 1977 (Moorcock) **489**
Goldsmith, Lynn 42
'Good Clean Punk' (Burn) **179**
Goodman, Dave 85
Gorillas **70**
Gorman, Leigh 473
Goulden, Eric *See* Wreckless Eric
Grand Hotel 265
Gravelle, Peter 93, **93**
Gray, Christopher 248
   Leaving the 20th Century 248
Greater London Council 499
Great Rock 'n' Roll Swindle (newspaper) **489**
Great Rock 'n' Roll Swindle, The (Temple) [film] 17, 414, **445**, 447, **467**
Gremlins 348
Greyhound 17, **338–339**
Grimes, Carol 102
Grugeon, Peter 124, **125**
Guardian 412
'Guns on the Roof' (Clash) 402

H

Ha! Ha! Ha! (Ultravox) **235**
Halpin, Geoff **208**
   Boomtown Rats' Debut Album (poster) **208**
Hammer Films 257
Hammersmith Odeon **264**, **432–433**, 499, **499**
Hareward, John 303
Harper's Bazaar 93
Harry, Debbie **56**, 191, **266**, **353**, 412, **412**, **416**, **456**
Harry, Warren 265
Headache **260**
   'Can't Stand Still' **260**
Headon, Topper 402
Heartbreakers *See* Johnny Thunders & the Heartbreakers
Hector, Jessica **70**
Hell, Richard *See* Richard Hell & the Voidoids
Hennessy, Val 313
   In the Gutter 313
HMV 17
Hogg, Brian 83
   Cripes **83**
'Holidays in the Sun' (Sex Pistols) 247, **248–249**
Holland, Glynis **293**

Punk Rock Rules OK? **293**
Holly, Buddy 184
'Hong Kong Garden' (Siouxsie and the Banshees) **411**
Hope & Anchor **284**
   Hope & Anchor Front Row Festival (album) **284**
Horne, Nicky 17
Hornsey College of Art 371
Hot as the Rods **72**
Hotel California (Eagles) 68
'How Much Longer' (Alternative TV) **279**
Huddle, Roger 102, 378
Hughes, Don 272
'England's Screaming' 272, **273**
Human League **437**
Hutt, Geoff 27
Hynde, Chrissie 115

I

Ian Drury Songbook, The **441**
Ian Drury & the Blockheads 194, **194–195**, 212, **212**, **213**, **259**
   New Boots and Panties!! **212**, **213**, 259
   'Sex and Drugs and Rock 'n' Roll' 194
   'Sweet Gene Vincent' **259**
   'You're More than Fair' 259
ICA Theatre 46
Idiot, The (Pop) 94
Idol, Billy 67, 93, 193, 218, 232
'I Don't Care' (Boys) **91**
'I Don't Mind' (Buzzcocks) **390**
'I Know But I Don't Know' (Blondie) **456**
Ince, George 224
Ingham, Jonh 59, **59**
   London's Burning 59
Institute of Contemporary Arts Cinema Club **232**
International Anthem **469**
International Socialists *See* Socialist Workers Party
In the City (Jam) **123**, **476**
In the City (zine) 276, **277**, **496**
'In the City' (Jam) **123**
In the Gutter (Hennessey) 313
Introduction to the National Front, An (National Front) **163**
Invaders **432–433**
Island Records 297

J

Jackson, Timothy **289**
   Suicide's Debut Album Suicide (poster) **289**
Jah Wobble 427
Jah Woosh 250
Jam 58, **72**, **74**, **79**, **82**, **99**, **110**, 113, **114**, **123**, 137, **148**, **157**, **200–201**, **476**
   In the City **123**, **476**
   'In the City' **123**
James, Brian 44, **457**
James, Tony 193
Jarman, Derek 356, 369, **369**
   Jubilee 356, 369, **369**
Jett, Joan 40
John Cooper Clarke (Clarke) **443**
Johnny Moped **79**, **98**, **115**, **117**, **135**, **408**
Johnny Thunders & the Heartbreakers 32, **45**, **54**, **82**, 96, **118–119**, **134**, **170**, **172**, **200**, **242**
   'Born to Lose' **134**

'Chinese Rocks' **134**
   LAMF **134**, **242**
Johnson, John 60
Jolt **187**, 219, 245
Jonathan Richman and the Modern Lovers **32**, 161
Jones, Allen 371
Jones, Barry **87**, **98**, **98**
   Siouxsie and the Banshees and the Slits at the Roxy, London (flyer) **87**
Jones, Mick **329**, **388**
   The Clash Songbook **329**
Jones, Steve 252, 402
Jones, Terry **315**, 417, **417**
   Not Another Punk! Book **315**
   Public Image Ltd's Single 'Public Image' (poster) **417**
Jouret, Roger **397**, **397**
Joy Division 443
Jubilee (Jarman) 356, 369, **369**
Jubilee Day 138, 141
Just Another Country **58**

K

Kaye, Gordon 178
Kaye, Lenny 81
Killjoys **250**, **278**
King, David **380**, 385, **385**, **407**
   Anti-Nazi League, Stop the Nazi National Front **385**
   Buzzcocks and Steel Pulse, Northern Carnival at Alexandra Park, Manchester (poster) **407**
   Rock Against Racism Carnival, Victoria Park (poster) **380**
King's College 268, **268**
King's Hall **359**
'Kings of the Wild Frontier' (Adam and the Ants) 374
Kodick, Peter Gravelle *See* Gravelle, Peter
Král, Ivan 45, **45**
   Blank Generation 45, **45**
Krivine, John 302, 303
   BOY clothing store 302, **303–305**
Kubie & the Rats **79**
'Kung Fu Girls' (Blondie) **353**

L

Label Records 258
Lafayette Club **146**
LAMF (Johnny Thunders & the Heartbreakers) 134, **242**
Lancaster University **431**
Last Resort **386**, **478**, **479**
League of Empire Loyalists 162
Leaving the 20th Century (Gray) 248
Lee, C P 178, **178**
   Sleak 178, **178**
Leeds Polytechnic 118–119, **134**, **153**, **183**, **230**
Lennon, John 178
'Let's Submerge' (X-Ray Spex) **284**
Letts, Don **70**, 232, **232**, **233**, 302
   The Punk Rock Movie **232**, **233**
Leveller **396**
Levene, Keith 427
Levi & the Rockats **334**, **335**
Lewis, Lew **39**, 64
'Life After Life' (Alternative TV) **393**
Little Bob Story 60
Live Wire **155**
Locarno **359**, **363**
London (band) **229**, **229**

'No Time' **229**
London Calling (Clash) **475**
'London Girls' (Vibrators) **151**
London's Burning 59
'London's Burning' (Clash) **121**
London SS 282
Look at the [Fucking] Time **137**
Loughborough University **346**, **347**
'Love Lies Limp' (Alternative TV) **206**, **207**
'Lovers of Today' (Only Ones) **131**
Lowe, Nick **39**
Lowry, Ray 475
Ludus **442**
Lurkers **79**, 137, **180**, **186**, **187**, 190, **190**, 216, 276
Lwin, Annabella 473
Lyceum Ballroom **454**
Lydon, Jimmy **498**
Lydon, John **417**, **417**, **427**, **485**, **498**
   See also Rotten, Johnny

M

Macauley, Roco **269**
MacGowan, Shane **58**, **58**
   Bondage **58**
MacManus, Declan Patrick *See* Costello, Elvis
Madness 346
Man in the Moon **120**, **120**
Maniqui **187**
Marc **268**
March Artists 190
Marley, Bob 417
Marquee Club **88**, 137, **203**, **203**, **236–237**, **285**, **288**, 351, **404–405**, **408**
Marshal, Steve **331**
Martian Dance **490**
Matt Vinyl & the Decorators **283**
Mayhew, Robin 143
MC5 191
MCA **229**
McDonald, Jock 17, **352**, **436**, **436**, **437**, **452**, **452**, **453**, **458**, **498**
   Day Trip to Brighton (flyer) **458**
   Jock McDonald Presents Adam & the Ants, UK Subs and the Pack at the Rainbow Theatre (flyer) **436**
   Jock McDonald Presents Adam & the Ants at the Rainbow Theatre (flyer) **437**
   Protest with Performance by the Clash (flyer) **452**, **453**
McLaren, Malcolm 21, 26, 52, 302, 473
'Me and My Desire' (999) **438**
Meat **219**, **219**
Melody Maker **173**, **271**
Members **437**
Menace 17, **354**
Mental Children **504**, **505**
Mercer, Mick **281**, **281**
   Panache **281**
Métal Urbain **223**, **270**
Method **496**
Midnight Special **445**
Miller, John 190
Mirrors **278**, **354**
Mistakes **278**
Misty **418–419**
Moa Ambassa **484**
Models **101**, **245**, **276**
Mo-Dettes **461**, **461**, **505**
   The Story So Far **461**
Monochrome Set 422, **448**, **448**
Moon, Tony **64–65**, **64–65**, **69**,

509

[...] 216
[...]65, 64–65, 69,
[...], 132, 216
[...]el 489, **489**
[...]rs of 1977 489
[...]nny 404
[...] See Johnny Moped
[...] On 55, 97
Morning Star 492
Morris, Dennis 417, **417**
 Public Image Ltd's Single 'Public Image' (poster) **417**
Mortimer, Sir John 252
Motorhead 338-339
Motors 236, **288**
Mott, Toby 15–17, 21, 22, 23
Mountford Hall 282, **455**
Murray, Pauline 157, **455**
Music Machine 17, **421**, **457**
Music Week 145
My Aim Is True (Costello) 184
'My Way' (Sex Pistols, Vicious) **399**, **400–401**

N

Napier-Bell, Simon 229
Nashville 17, **26**, 27
'Nasty! Nasty!' (999) 243
National Abortion Campaign 224
National Committee Against Fascism **169**
National Front (NF) 17, 21, 137, 162, **163–165**, 168, 169, 174, 307, **308**, **336**, 377, 378, 385, **387**, 418
 An Introduction to the National Front 163
 Hang IRA Murderers (poster) **164**
 National Front News (poster) **336**
 Work Not Dole Now (poster) **165**
National Front, The (Fielding) 174
'Neat Neat Neat' (Damned) 122, **122**, 230
Needs, Kris 68, **68**
 'Over the Top' **68**
Negative Reaction **424**
Never Mind the Bans (Reid) 22
Never Mind the Bollocks, Here's the Sex Pistols (Sex Pistols) 124, **252–253**, **254**, **256**, 271
New Boots and Panties!! (Ian Drury & the Blockheads) 212, **213**, 259
New Hearts 219
New Musical Express (NME) 17, 27, **41**, **100**, **147**, **181**, 183, 194, 272, 314, **472**
New Rose, the Damned Fanzine **502**
'New Rose' (Damned) **44**, 283
New Wave Compilation Album (Vertigo) [poster] **60**
New Wave Magazine 22, 89, 94, 114, 136, 170, **193**, 240, 261
New Wave News 202
New York Dolls 60, **192**
NF See National Front (NF)
Nite Club **497**
NME See *New Musical Express* (NME)
NN4 9PZ **482**
'No More Heroes' (Stranglers) 231
'No One Is Innocent' (Sex Pistols) **403**
Not Another Punk Book! (Jones, Anscombe) 315
'No Time' (London) 229

Now **205**
Now 4 Idiot 6 **228**
'Now I Wanna Sniff Some Glue' (Ramones) 30

O

O'Connor, Hazel 500
'Oh Bondage, Up Yours!' (X-Ray Spex) **241**, 284
Oh Boy! 22, **112**
Oi! 386
Only Ones 131, 236, **239**, 370
 'Another Girl, Another Planet' **370**
 'Lovers of Today' 131
'Orgasm Addict' (Buzzcocks) 23, **274**
'Orgasm Addict' (Garrett) 23
Otway, John 68, 228, 240
Our Price 17
Outlook **148**
Outsiders 223, 245
'Outside View' (Eater) **85**
Oval Records 343
'Over the Top' (Needs) 68
Owen, Malcolm 502

P

Pack **436**, **437**
 See also Theatre of Hate
Paddock **465**
Panache 281
Paolozzi, Eduardo 371
Parallel Lines (Blondie) 412, 445, 456
Parker, Graham 68, 292
Parsons, Dave 76
Parsons, Tony 314
 The Boy Looked at Johnny': The Obituary of Rock and Roll 314
Patti Smith Group 42, 43, 45
 See also Smith, Patti
Pavilion 358
Peel, John **465**
Penetration (band) 219, 392, **439**, 455, **455**
 'Danger Signs' **455**
 'Firing Squad' 392
Penetration (zine) 133, 157
Pepperwell Ltd. **182**
'Perfect Hits' (Generation X) **296**
Perry, Mark 30, **31–32**, 36, 38, 43, 49, 57, 66, 70, 82, 101, 102, 135, 161, 206–207, 272
 Sniffin' Glue 17, 22, 30, **31–32**, 36, 38, 43, 49, 57, 66, 70, 82, 101, 135, 161, 206–207, 272
Photomontage (Ades) 23
'Physical (You're So)' (Adam and the Ants) 373
'Picture This' (Blondie) 412
Pigs **285**
PiL See Public Image Ltd
Pink Fairies 39
Plasmatics **499**, **499**
Plastic Bertrand **397**, **397**
 AN1 **397**
Playhouse Theatre 113
Poe, Amos 45, **45**
 Blank Generation 45, **45**
'Pogo Dancing' (Vibrators) 338
Pogo Records 146
Pogues 58
Point-Blank 159
Poison Girls **492**, **493**, **496**
Police 98, 183, **183**
Polydor 17
Poly Styrene 102, 240, **241**

Polytantric Press 63
Pop, Iggy 21, **36**, **89**, 94, 133, 143
 The Idiot 94
Pop Art 23
Pop Group **203**, 492
Powell, Enoch 378
Power in the Darkness (Tom Robinson Band) 406
Poynor, Rick 19–23
Prefects 90
Presley, Elvis 209, 475
'Press Darlings' (Adam and the Ants) **374**
Pretenders 115
'Pretty Vacant' (Sex Pistols) **158**, **159**, **160**, **176**
Private Stock Records 56, 266
Project of Living Artists 289
Pros 336
Pryce, Jonathan 500
Psychedelic Furs 422
'Public Image' (Public Image Ltd) **417**, **427**
Public Image Ltd **417**, **427**, **427**, 429, **464**, 485, **485**
 'Death Disco' **464**
 'Public Image' **417**, **427**
Punk 22, **200–201**
Punk (Davis) 62
Punk, The (Sams) 63
Punk Rock Movie, The (Letts) **232**, **233**
Punk Rock Rules OK? 22, **293**
Punkture 171, **189**
Pure Mania (Vibrators) 21, **143**, 153
Pursey, Jimmy 76, 245, 246, 394

Q

Q 30
Queens Hall **476**
'Questions' (Suburban Studs) **154**

R

Racial Preservation Society 162
Radiators 245
Radio Ethiopia (Smith) **42**, 43
Radio & Record News 176
Rainbow Theatre **436**, **436**, **437**
Raincoats 422, 492
Ramones 21, 30, **31**, 45, 60, 71, **118–119**, 136, 180, 290, 439
 'Now I Wanna Sniff Some Glue' 30
Raped **270**
RAR See Rock Against Racism (RAR)
Rat Club 220
Rattus Norvegicus (Stranglers) 99
Raw Power **331**
Raynor, Stephane 302
 BOY clothing store 302, **303–305**
Razor Blades and Long Shot See *Sleak* (Lee)
'Ready Steady Go' (Generation X) **348**, **355**
'Reconnez Cherie' (Wreckless Eric) 343
Record Mirror 186, 205, **209**, **376**, **416**
Recordsville 17
Red Star Records 289
Reed, Lou 71, 114
Rehearsals 402
Reid, Jamie 17, 21, **21**, 22, **48**, **52–53**, **54**, 124, **125**,

126–129, 158, 159, 160, **247**, **248–249**, 256, 278, **287**, **399**, 447
 Anarchy in the UK 21, 22, **52–53**, 159
 From Beyond the Grave poster for Sex Pistols' Single 'Something Else' (poster) **447**
 Never Mind the Bans 22
 Sex Pistols (sticker) **126**
 Sex Pistols' Album Never Mind the Bollocks, Here's the Sex Pistols (poster) **256**
 Sex Pistols' 'Anarchy in the UK' Tour at the Electric Circus, Manchester (flyer) **54**
 Sex Pistols at the 100 Club, London (flyer) **33**
 Sex Pistols' Never Mind the Bans UK Tour (promo) **287**
 Sex Pistols / Sid Vicious Single 'My Way' (poster) **399**
 Sex Pistols' Single 'Anarchy in the UK' (poster) **48**
 Sex Pistols' Single 'God Save the Queen' (French postcard) **129**
 Sex Pistols' Single 'God Save the Queen' (poster) **125**, **128**
 Sex Pistols' Single 'God Save the Queen' (sticker) **127**
 Sex Pistols' Single 'Holidays in the Sun' (poster) **247**, **248–249**
 Sex Pistols' Single 'Pretty Vacant' (banner) **160**
 Sex Pistols' Single 'Pretty Vacant' (poster) **158**, **159**
Release 224
Rema Rema **448**
'Remote Control' (Clash) 121
'Retro' (Ultravox) **350**
Revolution 388, **389**
Rezillos 83, **171**, 288, **290**, 306
Rhodes, Bernie 17
Richard Hell & the Voidoids 21, **39**, 45, **60**, **257**, 269
Richmond, Sophie 52
Ridgers, Derek **316**
 Shockwave **316**
'Right to Work' (Chelsea) 144
Right to Work Campaign 149, **149**
Rimbaud, Penny 469
'Rip Her to Shreds' (Blondie) **266–267**
Ripped & Torn 17, 22, **22**, 47, 130, **180**, **192**, 220, **262**, **414**, **429**
Riviera, Jake 184
Robertson, Sandy 22, **22**, 71, **71**, 81, **156**, **234**, **291**
 White Stuff 22, **22**, 71, 81, **156**, **234**, **291**
Rock Against Racism (RAR) 21, 102, 103, **104–107**, 149, **149**, 224, 378, **379–384**, **418–419**, **420**, **431**, 459
 Right to Work Campaign with Buzzcocks and the Verbals (poster) **149**
 Temporary Hoarding 102, **103**, **104–107**
Rocket from the Tombs 282
Rogers, Wayne See County, Wayne
Romney, John **424**
 Negative Reaction **424**
Roogalator 39
Rosselson, Leon 310
Rotten, Johnny 102, 161, 173, 180, 252, **262**, **294**, **304**
Rotten to the Core **298**
Rough Trade 17, 47, 59, **150**
Roundhouse 30
Roxy Theatre 51, **67**, **75**, **78**, **79**,

84, 87, 92, 98, **98**, 115, 120, 137, 155, 199, 203, **223**, 232, 241, 268, 352, **352**, **430**
Ruff Edges **197**
Runaways 40, 41, **60**, 81
Rushent, Martin 231
Rushton **410**
 Carnival Against the Nazis Event, Edinburgh (poster) **410**
Russell Club **409**
Ruts **422**, **459**, **482**, 502

S

'Safety in Numbers' (Adverts) **251**
Saints 43, **200–201**
Sams, Gideon 63
 The Punk 63
Santa Monica Civic Center **471**
Santana 68
Satellites **60**, 422
Saunders, Red 378
Savage, Jon 23, **23**, 88, **88**, 296, **318–327**
 England's Dreaming 88
 Generation X at the Marquee (flyer) **88**
 Generation X's Single 'Perfect Hits' (poster) **296**
 The Secret Public 23, **23**, **318–327**, 442
Saville, Peter 17
Screen on Islington Green 27, **27**, 43, **158**
Search & Destroy 244
Searchlight 377
Secret Life of a Teenage Punk Rocker, The (Blade) 40
Secret Public, The 23, **23**, **318–327**, 442, **442**
Seditionaries 17, 302
Sex (boutique) 301
'Sex and Drugs and Rock 'n' Roll' (Ian Drury & the Blockheads) 194
Sex Bristles **452**
Sex Pistols 21, **21**, 22, 26, **26**, 27, **27**, **28**, **29**, 33, **34–35**, 36, **37**, **41**, 48, 49, **50**, **51**, **52**, **54**, **58**, 59, 64, 71, 88, 93, 110, 124, **125**, **126**, **126–129**, 130, 143, 145, **147**, 155, **157**, **158**, 159, **159**, **160**, 173, **173**, **176**, 180, 182, **182**, 189, 192, **192**, **200–201**, 232, 247, **247**, **248–249**, 252, **252–253**, **254**, **256**, 262, 263, 271, 272, 282, 287, **287**, **298**, 312, 332, 376, **399**, **400–401**, 402, 403, 414, 417, 427, 439, 443, 445, 447, **447**, 467, **467**, 473, 489, **489**
 'Anarchy in the UK' **48**, 49, 50, **51**
 'C'mon Everybody' **467**
 'God Save the Queen' **125**, **126–129**, 130, 145, 147, 180, **467**
 'Holidays in the Sun' **247**, **248–249**
 'My Way' **399**, **400–401**
 Never Mind the Bollocks, Here's the Sex Pistols 124, **252–253**, **254**, **256**, 271
 'No One Is Innocent' **403**
 'Pretty Vacant' **158**, **159**, **160**, **176**
 'Something Else' **447**
Shades **429**
Shakin' Street 79
Sham 69 **76**, **79**, 92, **186**, 202, 204, 219, 236, **239**, 245, 246, **246**, 263, 342, 359, 363,

418–419, 425, 429, 434
'Song of the Streets (What 'ave We Got)' 246
Tell Us the Truth 342
That's Life 425
Sharn, Hannah 208
Shaw, Greg 272
 'England's Screaming' 272, **273**
Sheehan, Tom 443
Shelley, Pete 274, 357
Shockwave (Boston, Ridgers) 316
Shoplifters 223
Shosubi, Sarah **97**
 More-On **97**
Sideburns 64–65, **64–65**, 69, 73, 99
 See also Strangled
Silver Jubilee 21, 138, **139–142**, 147, 369
Simon, Kate 113, **113**
Simonon, Paul 329, 402, **475**
 The Clash Songbook 329
Sinatra, Frank 400
Sincere Americans 465
Siouxsie and the Banshees 37, 79, 87, 98, **116**, 204, 217, 232, 255, **338–339**, 369, 409, 411, 443, **505**
 'Hong Kong Garden' 411
Sire Records 257
Situation 300
Situationists 124, 159
SKAN *See* Skools Against Nazis (SKAN)
Skools Against Nazis (SKAN) 310
 SKAN Magazine 310, **311**
Skrewdriver 386
Skyhooks **60**
Slam (Suburban Studs) 146
Slattery, Paul 439, **439**, 443
Slaughter & the Dogs 79, 134, 222, **222**, 232, **270**, 391
 'Where Have All the Boot Boys Gone?' **222**
Sleak (Lee) 178, **178**
Slimey Toad 117
Slits 86, 90, 113, 153, 181, 191, 202, 232, 302, **364**, 369, 422, **422**, 423, 472, 484, 492, 504
 Cut 472
Smith, Bill **123**, 476
Smith, Mark E. 102
Smith, Patti 21, **42**, **43**, **60**, 68, 71, **71**, 81, **156**, 234, 291, **475**
 'Ain't It Strange' 71
 Radio Ethiopia **42**, 43
Smith, Pennie 472
Snatch 46
Sniffin' Glue 17, 22, 30, **31–32**, 36, 38, 43, 49, 57, 66, 70, 82, 101, 135, 161, **206–207**, 272
Snivelling Shits **421**
Snow, George 243, **243**
Socialist Workers Party (SWP) 17, 21, 174, **174**, 309
 Demonstration Against Racism (poster) **174**
Soho Records 17
Solid Waste 239
'Something Else' (Sex Pistols) **447**
'Song of the Streets (What 'ave We Got)' (Sham 69) 246
'Sonic Reducer' (Dead Boys) 280
Sore Throat **432–433**
Sounds 59, 71, 120, 147, **147**
Spare Rib 224
Specials 402
Speedometers 354
Spiers, Kenneth *See* Spizz
Spitfire Boys **250**
Spizz 409

Spizz 77 **270**
Spizzenergi 409
 'Where's Captain Kirk?' 409
Spizzoil 409
Splodge 502
Spungen, Nancy 376
Squeeze 99, 132, **197**
Star Monthly 366
Steel Pulse 17, 190, **190**, 310, 378, **380**, 407
Step Forward Records 17, **144**, 285, **286**, 466
Sterling, Linder 17, 23, 274, **274**, **318–327**, 442
 Buzzcocks' Album Beating Hearts (poster) **442**
 Buzzcocks' Single 'Orgasm Addict' (poster) 274
 The Secret Public **318–327**
Stevenson, Nils 26, **26**
 Sex Pistols at the 100 Club, London (flyer) **29**
 Sex Pistols at the Nashville, London (flyer) **26**
Stevenson, Ray 22, **48**
Stiff Little Fingers **422**
 'Stiff Little Fingers' (Vibrators) 151
Stiff Records 17, **39**, 44, 77, 109, **109**, 184, 343
 Disciples Song Book 299
Sting 183
Stiv **244**
Story So Far, The (Mo-Dettes) 461
Strangled 99, **99**, 132, **216**
Stranglers 64, **79**, 89, 99, 114, 143, **170**, 189, **200–201**, 202, **231**, 243
 No More Heroes 231
 Rattus Norvegicus 99
Straps **436**
Strife 133
Strummer, Joe 22, **130**, 269, **480**
Subscription Room 349
Suburban Press 22, 52, 124, 159
Suburban Studs 40, 146, 154, **349**
 'Questions' **154**
 Slam 146
Subway Sect 46, 49, 86, 90, 113, **363**
Sucks, Jane 205
Suggs 346
Suicide 21, **289**, 402, 404, 414, **496**
 Suicide **289**
 Suicide (Suicide) **289**
Summers, Andy 183
'Sunday Girl' (Blondie) **456**
Sunday Mirra 263, **333**, 369
Sunday Times 243
Sunday Times Magazine 179, 385
Swan, Daniel 203, 285
'Sweet Gene Vincent' (Ian Drury & the Blockheads) 259
SWP *See* Socialist Workers Party (SWP)

T
T. Rex 268
Talking Heads 45, **60**
TAN *See* Teachers Against the Nazis (TAN)
Tarts 223
Teachers Against the Nazis (TAN) 307, **307**, 310
 TANkit **307**
Teachers Club 307
Teddy Boys 17, 334, 335
Tell Us the Truth (Sham 69) 342
Temple, Julien
 The Great Rock 'n' Roll Swindle

17, 414, 445, 447, 467
Temporary Hoarding 102, **103**, **104–107**, 394–395, 459, 474
 Rock Against Racism Carnival Issue 382–383
Thatcher, Margaret **462**, 500
That's Life (Sham 69) 425
Thin White Duke *See* Bowie, David
Third World 431
Thomson, D. C. 470
Thrills, Adrian 21, 22, 74, 80, 95, 110
 48 Thrills 21, 22, 74, 80, 95, 110
Throbbing Gristle 161
Thunders, Johnny **200–201**, 232
 See also Johnny Thunders & the Heartbreakers
Tiberi, John 399
 Sex Pistols / Sid Vicious Single 'My Way' (poster) 399
Tickets 223, **278**
Tom Robinson Band 24, 102, 103, **224–225**, 238, 365, 378, **380**, 406, 460
 Power in the Darkness 406
 'The Winter of '79' 103
Tony D *See* Drayton, Tony
Top Rank Suite **503**
Tosh, Peter 394, **395**
Total Punk **294–295**
Tower Records 17
Transmitters 137
Trash-77 130
Trinity Hall **493**
Tubes 264, **264**
 'White Punks on Dope' 264
Tyla Gang **39**
Tyneside Free Press 157
 Bored Stiff 157

U
UK Subs **436**, 437, 450, 451
Ultravox 227, **227**, 229, 235, **276**, 297, 350, **350**
 Ha! Ha! Ha! 235
 'Retro' 350
 Ultravox! **297**
Ultravox! (Ultravox) **297**
United Artists 274
United Troops Out Movement 362
 Repeal the Terror Act 362
University of Lancaster 152
University of London 484, 486–487
Unwanted 219, 278
Up 'n' Coming 72, **265**

V
V2 (Vibrators) 341
Vapors **476**
Varian, Dave 94
Vaucher, Gee 328, 469, **469**
 Crass Autopsy Film Project & Soundtrack (poster) 328
Vega, Alan 289, **289**
 Suicide's Debut Album Suicide (poster) 289
Verbals 149
Vermilion & the Aces **457**
Vermorel, Fred 312
 The Sex Pistols 312
Vermorel, Judy 312
 The Sex Pistols 312
Vertigo **60**
Vibrators 21, 69, **73**, 108, 114, 143, **143**, 151, 153, 171, **200–201**, **210–211**, 338, **338–339**, 340, 341

'Automatic Lover' 341
'Baby Baby' **108**
'London Girls' **151**
'Pogo Dancing' 338
Pure Mania 21, **143**, 153
'Stiff Little Fingers' **151**
V2 341
Vicious, Sid 158, **192**, 376, 399, 400, **400–401**, 447, 467
 'My Way' 399, **400–401**
Victoria Hall 364
Victoria Park 380, 382
Viletones 429
Vincent, Gene 259
Vincent Units 461, **484**
Virgin Records 17, **160**, 252, 276, 417
Vogue 93, 243
Void 255
Volume One 481
Vortex (club) 172, **172**, 190, 205, 206, **217**, 219, 239, 246, 250, 255, **270**, 278, 354
Vortex (zine) 245

W
Walters, Julie 178
Ware, Veronica 377
 Women and the National Front 377
Warner Bros. 254
Wasps 223
Wayne County & the Electric Chairs 180, **217**, 334, **335**, 413
WEA 146
Weirdos 262
'Welcome to the Working Week' (Costello) 109
Wellington-Lloyd, Helen 26, **26**
 Sex Pistols at the 100 Club, London (flyer) **29**
 Sex Pistols at the Nashville, London (flyer) **26**
'We Love You' (Cock Sparrer) **185**
Westwood, Chris 186
Westwood, Vivienne 21, 52, 301, 302
 Sex (boutique) 301
Wham! 229
'Where Have All the Boot Boys Gone?' (Slaughter & the Dogs) **222**
'Where's Captain Kirk?' (Spizzenergi) 409
'White Man in Hammersmith Palais' (Clash) **398**
'White Punks on Dope' (Tubes) 264
'White Riot' (Clash) **94**
White Stuff 22, **22**, **71**, **81**, **156**, **234**, **291**
Who 216
WH Smith's 17
Widgery, David 103
Willcox, Toyah 369
Williams, Wendy O. 499, **499**
Wilson, Tony 102
Windmill Club 218, 221, 227, **227**
'Winter of '79, The' (Tom Robinson Band) 103
Wire **98**, 204, **239**, 263
Wolff, Michael 269
Wolff Olins 269
Wonderful World of Wreckless Eric, The (Wreckless Eric) 424
Woods, Dave 190
Woolworths 17
Worst 228
Wreckless Eric 343, **424**
 'Reconnez Cherie' 343
 The Wonderful World of Wreckless Eric 424

X
X-Ray Spex 79, 98, 120, 170, 204, 236, 241, 284, 368, 37[?], **380**, 414, 432–433, [?]
 'Let's Submerge' 284
 'Oh Bondage, Up Yours!' **241**, 284
 'The Day the World Turned Day Glo' 368

Y
YCL *See* Young Communist League
'You Bastard' (Alternative TV) 27[?]
Young, Loud and Snotty (Dead Boys) 244
Young Communist League 175, **488**
'Young Parisians' (Adam and the Ants) 426
'You're More than Fair' (Ian Drury [?] the Blockheads) 259
'Your Generation' (Generation X) **214**, **215**, 268

Z
'Zerox' (Adam and the Ants) 4[?]
Zigzag **68**, 191
Zips 79

Phaidon Press Limited
Regent's Wharf
All Saints Street
London N1 9PA

Phaidon Press Inc.
65 Bleecker Street
New York, NY 10012

phaidon.com

First published 2016
© 2016 Phaidon Press Limited

ISBN 978 0 7148 7275 9

A CIP catalogue record for this book is available from the British Library and the Library of Congress.

All rights reserved. No part of this publication may be reproduced, stored in a retrieval system or transmitted, in any form or by any means, electronic, mechanical, photocopying, recording or otherwise, without the written permission of Phaidon Press Limited.

All images in this publication were selected from The Mott Collection.

Punk in Print: The Complete Mott Collection, 1976–1980, a three-volume limited edition set of thirty copies, was originally published by Andrew Roth and PPP Editions, 2015.

Artwork by Jamie Reid courtesy John Marchant Gallery. Copyright Sex Pistols Residuals.

Commissioning Editor: Deborah Aaronson
Project Editor: Sara Bader
Production Controllers: Nerissa Vales and Sue Medlicott
Design: João Mota
Cover Art: Garrick Gott

Printed in the UK